Edward A. Valentine

Jesus and the New Age

Edward A. Valentine

Jesus and the New Age

ACCORDING TO ST. LUKE

A COMMENTARY ON THE THIRD GOSPEL

Frederick W. Danker

'ON PUBLISHING HOUSE
   Box 9258
ouis, Missouri 63117

First Published in 1972
Second Printing, 1974
Third Printing, 1976
Fourth Printing, 1979

Library of Congress Number: 72-83650

ISBN: 0-915644-00-2

CONTENTS

FOREWORD

Dr. William Danker, professor of missions at Concordia Seminary, has characterized his brother Fred to me as a man of "irrepressible good cheer." Such, indeed, he is, and his daily welcome to me as I pass his adjacent office has brightened many a morning. Fred Danker is also a man of mature scholarly competence and of Christian conviction. This publication gives joyful testimony to the author's confidence in his own product. He has tested it with many classes of students and now sends it forth to help others become more intimately acquainted with Luke and with Luke's Lord.

When I asked Fred Danker to contribute a commentary on Luke for a projected commentary series, I knew that the manuscript would be delivered promptly and that it would be both scholarly and pointedly relevant. I could not then anticipate that it would prove to be such a scandal of relevance that it would help precipitate the scuttling of the entire project. Salvaged from the wreckage, this volume will serve well the purposes for which it was intended. It will lead the concerned reader to an intelligent understanding of the ancient text in its original intention. But it will also help that text come to life in the reader's modern context.

Luke is easily the most human and congenial of the synoptic evangelists. Fred Danker is easily one of the most human of scholars. He gives the lie to every caricature of the learned pedant in an ivory tower. I wish him and the child of his genial and original scholarship godspeed.

Walter J. Bartling
Saint Louis, Missouri
Jubilate Sunday, 1972

PREFACE AND INTRODUCTION

The Gospel According to St. Luke is part of a twin-work that includes also the Book of Acts. In most translations these two parts are separated by the Gospel According to St. John, and many readers fail to appreciate the continuity of thought expressed by the writer. The reader of this commentary may therefore wish to read first all of Luke's work and then to use both this commentary on the Gospel and a commentary on Acts as aids to understanding. One of the most recent and illuminating for the Greekless reader is Robert H. Smith, *Acts* ('Concordia Commentary'), St. Louis, 1970. The commentary on Luke is so designed that it can be read also as a self-sustained narrative in several sittings, with a gain in appreciation of the dramatic impact of Luke's style of writing.

THE AUTHOR

A Christian named Luke is mentioned three times in the New Testament. Colossians 4:14 identifies him as a physician especially dear to Paul. Philemon 24 says that he was a colleague of the apostle. 2 Timothy 4:11 indicates that he was a man of loyal dependability, not hesitating to run the risk of association during Paul's imprisonment. From distinctions made in Colossians 4:10-14 it is possible to infer that this Luke was a Gentile. Acts 13:1 and Romans 16:21 mention a 'Lucius,' but since Paul calls him a 'kinsman,' that is, a Jew, identification with the physician is questionable. Moreover, Lucius was a common Roman name.

Whether Luke the physician and companion of Paul actually wrote the Third Gospel is heavily debated. In view of the tendency on the part of early tradition to ascribe New Testament writings to apostles, association of the Third Gospel with one who was not an apostle in the narrow definition of the term is not to be lightly dismissed. Once it was thought that its language clearly pointed to a physician as the writer. At best, such a demonstration would merely indicate that the tradition is not to be slighted in the absence of other evidence to the contrary. However, ancient medical terminology was not nearly so technical as in our day, and numerous writers outside the medical profession used expressions similar to those found in the Third Gospel. The fact that the author (Luke 8:43) revises what appears to be a harsh indictment of physicians in Mark 5:26 is no certain indication that he here defends the medical profession, for he often abbreviates Mark and softens some of his judgments. In this particular case he aims to emphasize the woman's desperate situation. No one was able to heal her.

Since the gospel and the Book of Acts are two parts of a single work
(see the prefaces, Luke 1:1-4 and Acts 1:1-2), exploration of the problem
of authorship requires skill in linguistic analysis and comparison of the
data in Acts with those in the Pauline epistles. Technicalities of such
inquiry preclude discussion in a brief introduction, and the reader is referred to more detailed information available, for example, in *The Inter-
preter's Dictionary of the Bible*, under the articles: "Luke, Gospel of"
and "Acts of the Apostles." Since tradition is not an infallible source
of historical veracity, and since the identification of the author with
Paul's 'beloved physician' rests on a number of inferences, the anonymity
of the twin-work must be respected. For easy reference, however, the name
Luke will be used throughout this commentary.

If the author's professional identity is in a kind of twilight zone,
the same may not be said of his literary credentials. He does not take
second rank among Hellenistic writers. His linguistic versatility and
compositional technique combine with an extraordinary perception of the
substantive issues of history so as to produce a theological work permea-
ted with dramatic sensitivity. Especially elegant is his employment of
double entente, that is, the use of diction that in certain contexts admits of two interpretations.

PURPOSE

A writer's purpose can be determined either from his own explicit
statement of purpose or from a literary analysis of his entire work. From
his preface in Luke 1:1-4 one might conclude that it was the writer's aim
to provide Theophilus with more exact information concerning events and
circumstances of vital interest to early Christian communities. A thorough
study of the twin-work suggests, however, a broader circle of readers, who
are to receive further instruction and resources for evaluating especially
theological issues.

If Theophilus was a Roman official (see the commentary on 1:1-4), Luke
may well have written his work with two fronts in mind. While addressing
himself primarily to the Christian community, he could draw up his material
in such a way that the Roman officer would be compelled to revise certain
misunderstandings provoked by members of the Church or by earlier writers
or traditions. The outline at the end of this introduction calls attention
to the large space accorded by Luke to such misunderstanding.

Fundamental to the Christian message was the belief that Jesus was a
king. But the community was far from unified in its definition, and the
precise relation between Jesus and messianic expectation among Jews was a
subject of constant debate. Luke does not hesitate to affirm that Jesus
is a king, but through his clarification of Jesus' identity as Messiah, or
Christ, he is able at the same time to inform Theophilus that Jesus is no
competitor to Caesar's throne.

One of the chief areas of disagreement in the early community was the
subject of *apocalyptic*, a term derived from a Greek word meaning 'disclosure,'

and specifically used with reference to the unveiling of events at the end of history. Examples of this type of writing in the canonical Old Testament include Isaiah 24-27; Ezekiel 37, Daniel, Joel, Zechariah 12-14. A number of writings not included in the canon of Sacred Scripture are also devoted to this theme. Especially significant are the books ascribed to Enoch, The Assumption of Moses, and IV Ezra. Their themes and descriptions fired popular imagination and anticipation of spectacular developments on earth and in the heavens.

Basically, apocalyptic thought, kaleidoscopic in its variety as well as in its verbalized descriptions, sees the world as a battle-ground between God and the forces of evil. At some time God would crush the opposition, either by setting up a new reign on earth, or by destroying the old order and ushering in a new creation. Resurrection of the righteous would, of course, be a central feature of such hope. In either case those on the side of God would be privileged participants in the new regime.

In the face of such expectation a writer who attempted to vindicate the Christian claim could not evade resolution of several pressing problems: 1. If Jesus is the deliverer at the end-time, the power of Satan ought to be destroyed. Yet Jesus himself died an ignominious death and demonic forces still appear to be in control. 2. If Jesus is the deliverer, the wind-up of history ought to be taking place and one should be able to point to clear signs that the end is in fact near. Evidently false prophets would find the church easy pickings. 3. If Jesus is the deliverer, certainly his own nation ought to respond to his coming. Yet his own religious and theological establishment rejected him.

The Problem of Demonic Power

In answer to the first question, Luke shows that Jesus not only overcame the temptations of Satan but made a frontal attack on demonic forces by curing the demon-possessed. His death came about through alliance of established religious forces and demonic powers. Making use of a dominant motif in wisdom literature (such as Proverbs, Wisdom of Solomon and Sirach) that the wise man is ultimately triumphant, Luke shows that Jesus is vindicated by God himself through the resurrection. Suffering and death are necessary factors in Jesus' ascent to glory. Demonic forces still attempt to reclaim their power, but Jesus' victory over demons, demonstrated both in his healings and in his faithful surrender to God's purpose climaxing in the crucifixion, assures the Christian community that they will not fall victim to demonic devices. The Book of Acts therefore presents a number of recitals of apostolic success over the forces of evil.

The Problem of Signs of the End-Time

Complicating the problem of the end-time was misunderstanding concerning the coming of the Son of man. Was Jesus one in a series of end-time figures, or is he to be identified with the Son of man spoken of in Enoch

and in Daniel? Luke's basic answer is formulated in a two-stage doctrine. Jesus is the Son of man, and he does come to usher in the Kingdom. He is the Son of man both in a very human sense and in a supra-
human dimension. The Kingdom comes to expression at the Cross. Death
is the entry to enthronement. No spectacular apocalyptic demonstrations
are therefore necessary to *validate* that Kingship. The end-time has in
fact begun, and the church lives in the entire period of the end-time.
At what is usually termed judgment day, but in Lukan thought the <u>end of
the end-time</u>, Jesus will reappear and thus fulfill expectations concerning the Son of man. Between these two stages the church carries out
her missionary task.

Associated with the question about the Son of man was the expectation of a reappearance of Elijah (see Malachi 4:5). His coming would
signal the end-time and the wind-up of history. Some Christians viewed
John the Baptist as fulfillment of this expectation, but were distressed
that the end of the end-time was not actually taking place. Since according to some popular notions the Messiah was to make a glorious appearance
when Elijah returned, the question was naturally asked: Is Jesus really
the Messiah? Conversely, since Jesus, although acknowledged as Messiah,
did not in fact usher in the apocalyptic era as popularly conceived, was
it not perhaps a mistake to identify John as Elijah? Luke answers: John
is not Elijah, but he did function as a prophet calling the nation to
repentance. Jesus himself is in some ways an Elijah-figure and therefore
needs no Elijah-forerunner to verify his credentials as authentic deliverer of the wind-up announced in Malachi 3. Absence of apocalyptic 'signs'
is therefore due to the fact that the Kingdom comes in the two stages defined by Luke.

For the benefit of those who anticipated a prophet like Moses, Luke
shows that Jesus is more than Moses and replaces Moses as the official
teacher in the Israel of the end-time. A new Exodus takes place under
him, and the twelve apostles form the core of a fresh Israel that is in
continuity with Israel of time past.

Once Luke's basic orientation on apocalyptic is grasped, the reader
will not be surprised at the evangelist's frequent use of apocalyptic
terminology described by someone as evidence of an 'apocalyptic jag.' Luke
is not opposed to apocalyptic language or apocalyptic hope as such but
to the mistaken notion that God's fulfillment must match the specific
description. Traditional apocalyptic is not to be read as a literal
blueprint for God's action. Rather, Jesus is the blueprint for understanding apocalyptic hope. What happens in the life and time of Jesus is
not to be matched against traditional apocalyptic description, in such a
way that the apocalyptic description determines whether Jesus' credentials
are in order. Jesus in his person *is* the revelation, *the apocalypse*.
Therefore such normal ingredients of apocalyptic writing as angels and
references to responses of fear or astonishment, and even the recital of
the Transfiguration of Jesus are included to let the reader know that
he must shift his thinking away from the end of history and associate
apocalyptic hope especially with God's present communication focused in
Jesus as the center of the New Age. Stated formally, Luke christologizes

and historicizes apocalyptic. In the process of making his point Luke experiences no difficulty with his readers because of his retention of traditional apocalyptic description for the final wind-up of history, for such expectation he shares with his contemporaries. But his contribution is the demonstration of continuity in terms of divine revelation between the time of Jesus' appearance and the end of history as we know it. In brief, Luke's use of apocalyptic terminology in connection with events that would not be considered apocalyptic from the standpoint of his opposition is one of the many strokes of literary genius that permeate his work. But the literary genius is at one with the theological perspective. Such a shift in apocalyptic thinking requires faith. By eliminating the weird and the bizarre as a rallying point for Christian identity Luke disencumbered the church of the necessity of determining Jesus' messianic credentials through proofs supplied by 'signs.' Thus he paved the way for a truly ecumenical awareness and prepared the church for a functional existence in history.

The Problem of a Nation's Rejection

Not only did the repudiation of Jesus by the religious leadership bear on the question of Jesus' messianic credentials, but it raised the further question of the church's validity as legitimate participants in the promises to which Israel claimed to be heir. Luke therefore stresses the criteria of the New Age. The high and mighty, including especially those who might be classified as the religious establishment, have no assured automatic claim to the Kingdom. God reaches out to the lowly, the outcasts, women, 'tax collectors and sinners.' These form a large percentage out of which God fashions the end-time social register. Jesus is an obedient Israelite, the Son of God par excellence. Those who rely on traditional associations are warned not even to begin to say, 'We have Abraham as Father' (Luke 3:8).

Instead of discussing theories of redemption or atonement Luke lays emphasis on the Kingdom, its moral expectations and the status of its candidates. In certain respects, therefore, his Christology is closer to that of the earliest community and his doctrine of redemption less complicated than that of Paul. God's revelation in Jesus discloses his willingness to receive sinners into his presence. Not conformity to traditional ritual patterns, but dissatisfaction with past performance and acceptance of the Lordship of Jesus Christ determine a valid association with God. Undivided allegiance, marked especially by renunciation of worldly criteria of success, including money and social status, is the chief characteristic of the follower of Jesus. Thus the love of a sinful woman (chapter 7) is credited to her recognition of forgiveness mediated through the presence of Jesus. Zacchaeus is declared a son of Abraham (Luke 19:9), for he responded to the love of Jesus with a promise to give half his goods to the poor and a fourfold restoration to his victims.

Salvation is freedom for access to God, release from stifling religious tyranny and liberation from commonly accepted standards of behavior that do not meet the requirements of a claim to be interested in God. Such

ncompromising rejection of the *status quo* naturally would invite the
criticism that Luke flippantly and satirically engages in the popular
game of assaulting 'the establishment,' thereby negating the value of
is stress on *love*. But Luke, following his Master, plays no games.
ove and truthful confrontation are not mutually exclusive. The fact
s that Jesus' and the early community's constant battle was with
orces of reaction, exploitative interests and powers allergic to any
roposal from the future, and no responsible commentator can white-wash
istory. Therefore, if the word 'system' or 'establishment' occurs quite
ften in the commentary, this is not to be construed as a reading of the
resent into the past, but as a means to convey Luke's appreciation of
he issues that surface in his gospel. Luke's gospel contains a broad
ange of sandal sizes to fit any foot. The reason he sounds so contem-
orary is due to his broad grasp of humanity in its universal aspects.

OURCES

Luke was not the first to write a gospel. His preface clearly indi-
ates that he has a knowledge of other documents. A comparison of his
ccount with those composed by Mark and Matthew reveals that he was in
arge debt to Mark, either as we have it in its present form or in a
ecital so similar that for all practical purposes we may assume use
f Mark substantially as we know it. The manuscript support for Jose
'Callaghan's view of very early origins of Mark's Gospel (see *Biblica*
3, 1972, 91-100) awaits further assessment, but from what has been
ublished it does not appear that generally accepted views of the rela-
ionship between Luke and Mark will be seriously affected. What has
een found at Qumran may be representative of material on which Mark or
ke or both may have drawn.

Luke used another source also employed by Matthew. This source is
rdinarily designated 'Q,' an abbreviation of the German word *Quelle*,
eaning source. Whether Q was a written account or an oral tradition
ith variations cannot be decided with certainty, but I share the view
hat the evidence points to written sources. The designation, in any case,
s useful as a means of reference to identify the material common to
atthew and Luke, but not found in Mark. This is a general rule of thumb,
ut some allowance must be made for overlapping in the sources. That is,
ome Q material may also have contained recitals that are now found in
ark and some Markan material may have had parallels in Q. If construed
s a document, Q included most or all of the following material in Luke's
ospel: 3:7-9, 16-22; 4:1-13; most of 6:20-49; some of 7:1-10 and most
f 18-35; 9:57-60; 10:2-16, 21-24; perhaps 11:2-4 and most of 9-51; 12:
-12 and most of 22-34, 39-46, 51-59; 13:18-29, 34-35; 14:11, 15-24, 26-
7, 34-35; 16:13, 16-18; 17:1-6, 23-24, 26-27, 33-35, 37. From the paral-
el passages listed under each reference in the commentary the reader will
e able to determine the extent and identity of the probable Markan and Q
urces utilized by Luke. If only Matthaean parallels are cited, the
eader may assume that at that point in the narrative Luke draws on Q ma-
erial, for by the rule of thumb Q is material common to Matthew and Luke
t not found in Mark.

In a number of places the reader will note that no parallels from Mark or Matthew are listed. Such passages suggest that Luke drew on a special source, usually labeled by scholars with the letter 'L.' Much of this source is represented in 9:51-18:15. The Infancy narratives (chapters 1-2) are drawn perhaps from still another source. As indicated above, Luke does not appear to have had access to Matthew's gospel, but he does display acquaintance with Wisdom literary tradition, including Sirach and Wisdom (of Solomon). Luke ranges freely in the Old Testament, with special interest in the prophet Isaiah. This heavy dependence of Luke on the Old Testament poses a special problem, for inclusion of the supporting biblical data runs the hazard of marring the continuity and disrupting the train of thought. However, the student who desires to explore in greater depth the history of Luke's form of the text would be unnecessarily frustrated through omission of the citations and he might also find some of the conclusions, apart from the supporting evidence, inexplicable or arbitrary. Therefore, instead of abbreviating, excising, or relegating evidence to footnotes, I have made liberal use of parentheses. The speed-reader who wishes merely to follow a story that is good in its own right and is willing to postpone his exploration of the details will quickly learn to skip over the parentheses and stay on the main line. Leaders of study groups may welcome the bountiful supply of resource material for further study.

The first three gospels, when compared with the Gospel according to John, suggest a mutuality of composition that can best be described as 'synoptic,' that is, 'seeing together.' This is due to the fact that Matthew and Luke independently draw on Mark and Q. Yet neither Matthew nor Luke is a slave to the sources, nor do they engage in mechanistic compilation of materials. Luke's theological and apologetic interests prompt him to modify and rearrange in accordance with his statement of purpose, to present an 'orderly' account (1:4). The reader is therefore not to be dismayed by variations in the recitals when compared with those in the other gospels. Words of Jesus and stories about him were used in sermons and other types of instruction. Their meaning was constantly subject to fresh inquiry and application, and the form in which they are cast is the result of much lively usage. The process of application continues in the use to which they were put in development of the presentations made in the individual gospels. Thus the gospel writers are not only compilers but editors. The process is similar to that employed by preachers who expand on a text of Scripture.

As Lord of the Church, Jesus speaks to each succeeding generation. Therefore it is impossible to recover without argument the very words of Jesus spoken on a given historical occasion. The church possessed a lively awareness of the power of the Spirit in its midst, and this Spirit prompted Christians to ponder the significance of Jesus and his words and actions for their time. Even fresh sayings would be uttered, for the Lord had not ceased to speak. Hence the gospels are not less authoritative or less 'true' than would be a biographical record. The evangelists are not interested in writing biography for biography's sake. Indeed, a biography in the strict sense of the word would be no gospel, and one of the harmful effects of red-letter editions of the New Testament has been to suggest that Jesus' words are somewhat more authoritative than other words in the New Testament. The result is a canon within a canon and a credibility gap in the Church's affirmation of inspiration: 'All scripture is inspired by God' (2 Timothy 3:16). Unfortunately St. Paul's stature as a theologian has in the course of the history of theology so overshadowed the evangelists that they are popularly thought of as story-tellers without theological brains. Positivistic-philosophical presuppositions which tend to read contemporary interest in scientific exactitude into the Scriptures have, under the guise of harmonistic intention, made a large contribution to such negative assessment. But once the reader of the gospels avoids the pitfall of attempting to harmonize the gospels in terms of his twentieth century mind-set he will appreciate the rich and varied pattern of proclamation of the Kingdom of God and will endeavor to hear out each gospel writer on the Spirit's own terms. Each gospel has its own distinctive message. Yet there is only one Gospel. Hence the gospels are each entitled: *The Gospel* according to ....

DATE

Luke appears to write after the destruction of Jerusalem (A.D. 70). It has been argued that the absence of any specific reference to the fall of the city and the fact that Luke concludes the twin-work without any reference to Paul's death prove that the two books were completed in the decade preceding the destruction. The argument relating to Paul's death rests on the assumption that an historian would necessarily include events that transpired up to the time when he put his data into final literary form. The fact is that Luke has achieved his purpose with the present ending of Acts. He has demonstrated that the religious leadership is consistent in its rejection of Jesus and he has explained how it happened that the apostles made their outreach to the Gentiles. Acts 28, therefore, concludes with a summary statement of one of Luke's dominant themes: Jesus' credentials are not invalidated by the rejection of his claims through the religious leadership. Neither is a specific reference to the destruction of Jerusalem required, for the horrible catastrophe was well known. Instead, Luke assumes knowledge of the event and interprets numerous sayings and actions of Jesus in the light of that catastrophe. His use of Mark, written either shortly before or after the destruction of Jerusalem, points to a date some time in the late 70's or early 80's of the first century.

TEXT

This exposition of Luke's Gospel uses as basic point of reference for the Greekless reader the *Revised Standard Version: New Testament* (Thomas Nelson & Sons: New York, copyright 1946). References to other parts of the canon are also cited according to this version. The reader will find pertinent Lukan text from the RSV either underlined or in double quotation marks for quick reference. Single quotation marks, except in the case of quotation of phrases or passages from the RSV found *outside* the immediate context indicate my own translation or paraphrase of the original text. The reader can in such cases easily infer the word or phrase in the RSV, or in any other translation he may care to use, that corresponds to the interpretation given in the commentary. Thus the Greekless reader can know what the original, in my judgment, expresses, and the student with Greek can readily check against the original and other discussions of the text. Also quotations from other parts of the Bible outside the immediate text or from secular writers are enclosed in single quotes but the sources except in a few cases of common debt, are clearly identified. Translations of Latin and Greek authors are my own unless otherwise specified. Technical and street-terms are likewise to be found in single quotes, but the reader should have no trouble identifying them or their meaning.

A word of explanation for the choice of RSV is necessary in view of the peculiar history of the commentary. First, the RSV is the version most generally found in parishes and it is especially useful for use in a commentary because the sequence of the words and phrases is quite close to that of the original. Second, the RSV was to be printed in a series published under the auspices of The Lutheran Church - Missouri Synod. However, generally accepted scholarly approaches used in this commentary proved an obstacle to endorsement. Reference to Luke's use of Mark and Q was considered 'highly subjective' and 'tenuous,' as was almost any suggestion of editorial work by Luke, especially in relation to Mark. It was also suggested that references to the Old Testament and other Jewish writings were in too great abundance. Especially under attack were my interpretation of Lukan apocalyptic as well as points of practical application and engagement with the contemporary scene. Termination of the joint editorship of colleagues Walter Bartling and Albert Glock, who struggled valiantly for honest scholarship, followed shortly after withdrawal of the commentary. To prepare the work for publication through other recognized channels would have required an entirely new format, and would also have involved another long period of delay. The present medium was therefore chosen as the best vehicle immediately available for sharing the product of a long-term investment of time and scholarship. Those familiar with specialized studies of the gospels will readily recognize results that are the distinctive contributions of other scholars as well as those that are the necessary and universal product of application of generally accepted methodology. To burden this commentary with references to the innumerable articles that have appeared in specialized journals in the past few decades would therefore merely duplicate for a few what is already accessible, to cite but four, in J. M. Creed, *The Gospel According to St. Luke* (London, 1953), Walter Grundmann, *Das Evangelium Nach Lukas*, 3d ed. (Berlin, 1964), Hans Conzelmann, who gave fresh impetus to Lukan study with *Die Mitte der Zeit: Studien Zur Theologie des Lukas*, in *Beiträge zur historischen Theologie* 17 (Tübingen, 1954; 5th ed. 1964), translated by Geoffrey Buswell, *The Theology of St. Luke* (London and New York, 1960); and especially Heinz Schürmann, *Das Lukasevangelium*, the first installment of which was published, with an extensive bibliography, by Herder in late 1969. My own draft had been already completed early in 1969 for publication in the 'Concordia Commentary' series but delay in production has made it possible to explore Schürmann's excellent contribution to Lukan study. Those who charged me with excessive emphasis on apocalyptic terminology and thematic

ι Luke must now encounter the independent witness of Schürman, for I
ιs compelled by his display of the evidence to use the term 'apocalyptic'
ven more frequently than in my earlier draft.

The translation of the Revised Standard Version is based on a recon-
ιructed text, derived from consideration of the best evidence available
ι the revisers. Such a text is called *eclectic*, and has no corresponding
ιistence in any single manuscript. Scholarly judgment differs on proba-
ιe originality of certain readings. My reasons for preferring an alter-
ιte text in certain instances are given at the appropriate place in the
ιmmentary.

A translator's task differs from that of the commentator. The former
ι obligated to render the original, within as brief a compass as possible,
ιto understandable contemporary idiom. Since resources in languages are
ιt always parallel, a single word used to convey a number of ideas in
ιe original language may be variously rendered in a translation. A com-
ιntator, however, is under obligation to display as much as possible the
ιrbal phenomena of the original, so that especially the Greekless reader
ιy capture some of the nuances of argument necessarily lost in a transla-
ιon. A translator may also omit, for example, particles used by the orig-
ιal writer. One of Luke's favorite introductory phrases is: 'And be-
ιld!' Frequently the revisers paraphrase or simply ignore this expression,
ιt awareness of its existence may contribute to the reader's understanding
ι Luke's methods of argumentation. This must be said, lest the reader
ιsume that the RSV is unreliable! That would be a false assessment. In
ιme cases, however, revisers may entirely miss the point of the original.
ιrough the exercise of critical scholarship renewed appreciation of the
ιiter's intention may be gained.

ιKNOWLEDGEMENTS

Although the commentary, as noted earlier, can be read as a self-con-
ιined unit, it will in many cases undoubtedly serve as a reference tool.
ιholars will also find fresh interpretations advanced, that will, I hope,
ιntribute to solution of other Lukan 'problems.' Since this work is de-
ιgned to help the non-professional student of the Bible share in the re-
ιlts of scholarly research, technical jargon is held to a minimum. Fre-
ιent recapitulations will assist the student in following Luke's argument,
ιd the cross-references to earlier and later parts of his work will alert
ιm to the basic conceptual unity that pervades Luke's work. For illus-
ιation of the thought world in which Luke moves I have relied mainly on
ιeek and Roman and Jewish documents. The line between literary criticism
ιd homiletical application may not always appear clearly demarked, but
ιgagement with contemporary problems often turns the key to understanding
ι the ancient political, theological, social and moral issues. Such ex-
ιsure, of course, brings the ministry of Jesus and the message of the
ιrly church threateningly close to cherished idols and to the point at
ιich hostility may be involved. But a commentator who takes seriously
ιke's emphasis on the presence of the future cannot opt for the safe arch-
ιlogical haven. For such 'practical' encounter, then, I do not apologize.

Luke himself has set the pattern, and his gospel may yet prove to be one of the most vital theological forces in contributing to the resolution of some of the tensions of our time.

Thanks are due especially to Mr. Dan Demmas of Bardgett Printing and Publishing Company. He has been most generous with technical assistance. To my students especially, former and present, I shall be profoundly grateful for any criticisms or corrections they may supply.

HE IS RISEN!   April 2, 1972

d Testament Books	Apocrypha The following are cited in the commentary:	New Testament Books
nesis		Matthew
odus		Mark
viticus	Baruch	Luke
mbers	III Ezra (Esdras)	John
uteronomy	Judith	Acts
shua	1 Maccabees	Romans
dges	2 Maccabees	1 Corinthians
th	3 Maccabees	2 Corinthians
Samuel	Sirach (Ecclesiasticus)	Galatians
Samuel	Tobit	Ephesians
Kings	Wisdom (of Solomon)	Philippians
Kings		Colossians
Chronicles		1 Thessalonians
Chronicles	Pseudepigrapha	2 Thessalonians
ra		1 Timothy
hemiah	Assumption of Moses	2 Timothy
ther	Enoch (I Enoch)	Titus
b	IV Ezra (Esdras)	Philemon
alm(s)	4 Maccabees	Hebrews
overbs	Martyrdom of Isaiah	James
clesiastes	Psalms of Solomon	1 Peter
ng of Songs	Testaments of the	2 Peter
aiah	Twelve Patriarchs:	1 John
remiah	Reuben	2 John
mentations	Simeon	3 John
ekiel	Levi	Jude
niel	Judah	Revelation
sea	Issachar	
el	Zebulun	In addition to the Cairo
os	Naphtali	Geniza Damascus Document
adiah	Dan	(CD) the following scrolls
nah	Gad	from Qumran are cited:
cah	Asher	1QH Hodayot, The Psalms of
hum	Joseph	Thanksgiving
bakkuk	Benjamin	1QM The War of the Children
phaniah		of Light Against the
ggai		Children of Darkness
chariah		4Q Nahum Commentary on Nahum
lachi		1QS The Rule of the Community

hers:
rack-Billerbeck = Hermann L. Strack and Paul Billerbeck, *Kommentar zum Neuen stament aus Talmud und Midrasch*, 5 vols. (Munich, 1922-28; 2d ed. 4 vols. 5, 1954-61).
X = The Septuagint, the ancient Greek version of the Old Testament.
e Apocrypha and Pseudepigrapha are available in English in R. H. Charles, *e Apocrypha and Pseudepigrapha of the Old Testament in English.* (Oxford,1913).
e Frederick W. Danker, *Multipurpose Tools for Bible Study*, 3d rev. (St. Louis, 70), pp. 63-79 on the Septuagint; 204-208, on the apocrypha and pseudepigrapha.

JESUS AND THE NEW AGE

1-2. In his preface Luke follows literary convention of his time
and apologizes for adding yet another work to a long list of publica-
tions on the same subject. Scholars are almost unanimous in their
agreement that Mark and some form of a document consisting especially
of sayings, known as Q, were among the sources used by Luke in the composition of his gospel. The subject is more narrowly defined as things
which have been accomplished among us. These things would include
events in the life of Jesus, and his resurrection. It is by no means
certain that this preface has in mind the sequel known as the Book of
Acts (see Acts 1:1), but if Luke already had the latter in mind, then
the "things" include development of the Church's outreach in mission.
The words among us emphasize the writer's conviction that his community
is the center for the understanding of these events.

Many historians of antiquity failed to encourage confidence in
the citation of their data. So frequent was the gap between truth and
fiction that Lucian introduced his tongue-in-cheek *True History* with
the reminder: 'My lying is far more honest than theirs (other historians); for though I tell the truth in nothing else, I shall at least be
truthful in saying that I am a liar.' Luke refrains from such harsh
negative judgment. Others have undertaken (that is, they had as their
objective) to report what eyewitness and ministers (literally, helpers)
of the word delivered to the community. That they were not completely
successful is apparent from Luke's own decision to take pen in hand.
Some of them may even have been heretics (cf. Acts 20:29-30) who used
traditional material in the interests of their own perverse propaganda.
A form of the word delivered is elsewhere rendered 'tradition' (1 Corinthians 11:2). The word refers to the story of the events spoken of
in vs. 1. It is the normal term in historical writings for 'history'
and is so used in Acts 1:1. Even in the more common rendering 'word
of God' (as in Acts 6:4,7) the connotation 'story' is still dominant,
for the content of the "word" is the major events in the life of Jesus
(see Acts 10:37-44). The singular form (see Acts 10:44) is used to
comprise the various events recorded by various writers. The eyewitnesses were active also as participants (ministers) in the promotion
of the story (see Acts 26:16; 6:4). They had observed things from the
beginning, that is, from the time that Jesus began to carry out his
mission and to teach (see Acts 1:1-2; 10:37).

3-4. Luke contrasts his own work with those of the "many" and
submits his own qualifications. He has followed all things closely for

some time past. Since Luke includes infancy narratives and numerous
events in which he was not personally involved, the word followed must
refer to his investigation of, not merely involvement in, these events.
Everything refers to the matters discussed by his predecessors as well
as items that came to his attention independently of their inquiry.
Thus the scope of his work ought to commend it to his reader(s). Closely
emphasizes the care that has gone into his research. For some time past
is better rendered 'from the beginning.' Luke has made every effort to
trace events to their origins. Hence he includes infancy narratives.
Possessed of all these qualifications he aims to write an orderly account for Theophilus. Orderly does not here primarily mean chronological sequence but arrangement of material, so as to leave the reader
with clear impressions. His purpose is spelled out in the concluding
verse: that you may know the truth concerning the things of which you
have been informed. Not an annalistic type of recital, consisting of
memoirs or collections of sayings, but a persuasive presentation is
Luke's objective. Similarly the Roman poet Ovid assured his readers
that he would not ramble, but present things in their order (Metamorphoses 7,520).

The word for things is the plural of the term rendered "word" at
vs. 2. There is one story, but many accounts of that story. Since
some of these accounts have come to the attention of Theophilus and may
have caused him some confusion, Luke wants him to have one systematic
presentation that will give him a broader understanding and appreciation and the opportunity to form a more proper judgment. Actions or
sayings taken out of context, even though compilers claim that they are
guaranteed by eyewitnesses, may at a later time convey a false impression. Thus in his second volume (Acts 21:34) Luke relates how a Roman
officer heard some in a crowd shouting 'one thing, some another.'
Since he could not learn the 'facts' (a form of the word rendered truth
in Luke 1:4), he ordered Paul back to the barracks, evidently for further examination. Again, in Acts 25:26 Festus says that he has nothing
(definite) to write to Caesar about Paul. Luke hopes that his story
will clarify much for Theophilus and his own community. Theophilus,
to judge from the honorific most excellent, appears to be a Roman official who might do much to clear the Christians of charges of anti-Roman
activity. We do not know whether he was himself a Christian. Through
him as patron Luke's work goes out to the Church for her instruction
and admonition. Hence much that Theophilus might not grasp would nevertheless communicate to knowledgeable Christians.

Luke's preface helps us understand the frequent departures he makes
from the Markan gospel and the portions in Matthew known as Q. A modern historian would cite the data and then evaluate it. Luke is sparing in overt interpretive comment, relying in the main on arrangement
of traditional material, with modification of phrasing, paraphrases,
or deletion of matter that is irrelevant to his purpose. Thus his
work is not to be judged by the canons of modern scientific historical
writing. He does not write a 'Life of Jesus,' but 'The Things Fulfilled
Among Us.' Here we have history theologically interpreted. The archives
of Caesar's official library or Pilate's personal memoirs would, even if

they were to be discovered, contribute little or nothing to Luke's main theme. Luke is a disciple, and for this he makes no apology. Thomas Dekker once wrote:

> The best of men
> That e'er wore earth about him was a sufferer;
> A soft, meek, patient, humble, tranquil spirit,
> The first true gentleman that ever breathed.

From the manner in which Luke writes his story the reader can judge for himself who was a close second.

After his carefully worded preface, written in the finest Greek,
Luke begins his account. In a style reminiscent of the Septuagint
he drowns much of his literary skill and adapts himself to the language of his sources. The effect is something like that of a contemporary sermon delivered in the style of the King James Version. The
result is a recital that bears the marks of continuity with God's
action as recorded in the Old Testament.

ANNOUNCEMENT OF THE CONCEPTION OF JOHN   LUKE 1:5-25

5. The RSV omits the initial word "It came to pass." This word
is used in a related formal structure at 2:1. Two sets of data are
to be distinguished. Chapter 1 introduces John and Jesus to the
reader. Chapter 2 focuses attention on the person and mission of
Jesus, apart from any reference to John. Chapter 3 again introduces
John and Jesus, this time as grown men, but John disappears from the
scene completely, except for allusions to his previous activity.
The recital in chapter 1 begins with a reference to Herod the Great
who reigned over Palestine 37 to 4 B.C. Chapter 2 introduces the
Gentile ruler, Caesar Augustus.

Zechariah, a common name in the Old Testament, means 'The Lord
Remembers.' He was of the division of Abijah. David had organized
the Levites into divisions or courses (1 Chronicles 23:6). Each
division contributed in sequence a week's service at the temple.
Thus each division would serve twice a year. The division of Abijah was the eighth (1 Chronicles 24:10). Elizabeth was of the tribe
of Aaron and therefore shared the priestly ancestry of Zechariah,
as well as the name of Aaron's wife (Elisheba, Exodus 6:23). Elizabeth means 'God my oath.' Some Rabbis expressed the thought that
God's presence would rest only on pedigreed families in Israel (see
G.F.Moore, *Judaism*, 1954, II, 359). Zechariah and Elizabeth qualify
genealogically for the parentage of John the Baptist who is to stand
before Israel as a high priest.

6. They also qualify morally. According to rabbinic tradition
the division of Abijah had been under a cloud of suspicion for un-
chastity and idolatry (Strack-Billerbeck II, 68). If any suspicion
attached to this couple, Luke removes it by pointing out that both

were impeccable in their behavior (note the contrasting charge against
Samuel's sons, 1 Samuel 8:3). Their childlessness could not therefore
be charged to God's displeasure.

7. Luke expressly notes that Elizabeth was barren (literally, ster-
ile) and adds the comment about their advanced years in order to emphasize that hope for a child had long faded away. Thus this pair resembles
Abraham and Sarah (Genesis 17-18); Manoah and his wife, the parents of
Samson (Judges 13); and Elkanah and Hannah, parents of Samuel (1 Samuel 1).

8-10. Since there were large numbers of Levites (estimates run as
high as 18,000 priests and Levites in Palestine at the time of Jesus),
lots were cast to determine who would have the opportunity to serve
at a particular time. To burn incense in the holy place (emblematic of
prayers ascending to God; see Revelation 5:8; Psalm 141: 2) was a great
privilege, for God drew near to his people (cf. Exodus 30:1-9), who here
crowd outside in great numbers (cf. Luke 6:17; 23:27). According to rabbinic tradition they said: 'May the God of all mercy come to his temple
and may he graciously accept the offering of his people.' (Strack-Billerbeck II, 79) Luke frequently associates prayer with special moments in
his narrative (see 5:16; 6:12; 9:18, 28; 22:41). The reader is never
to forget the divine dimension. Like Daniel (see Daniel 9:20ff.), Zechariah finds himself at the center of apocalyptic action.

11-13. In the Old Testament it was customary to call attention to
God's presence by describing the reaction of the human participants. To
be troubled and filled with fear is a characteristic response to divine
manifestation or apocalyptic moment (cf. Daniel 7:28). The right side
of the altar signifies divine authority (cf. Luke 22:69). Do not be
afraid is a recurring phrase in the gospel (see 1:30; 2:10; 5:10; 8:50;
12:32) and echoes Old Testament phraseology (Genesis 15:1; Isaiah 7:4;
35:4; Daniel 10:12). Its usage here signals the fact that the time of
God's intervention for his people has arrived. God comes not to destroy
but to help. Zechariah has prayed for a son, and his petition is now to
be granted. The promise addressed to Zechariah is similar to the words
spoken to Abraham: 'Sarah your wife shall bear you a son, and you shall
call his name Isaac.' (Genesis 17:19) The name John ('God is gracious')
is explicitly mentioned in order to emphasize that God himself distinguished the mission of this son from that of the son of Mary. John is
not the Messiah (cf. Luke 3:15).

14. Joy is the keynote of the New Age (see 2:10; 15:6-10; 24:52;
Acts 8:8; 13:52), marked by gladness, that is, exultant shrieking, like
that of jubilant contestants. Such joy will not be confined to Zechariah,
but to many in Israel. "Many" is probably a semitic expression for the
totality of the people. There is no discriminatory clause in the invitation to God's banquet. In harmony with this pronouncement Luke later
says that John proclaimed good news to the people (3:18).

15. To be great before the Lord means that God will use John for
his own good purpose (cf. 7:26-28). He is to drink no wine nor strong
drink. This prohibition was imposed on priests before entry into the

tabernacle (Leviticus 10:9). John, who is to call the nation to repentance, is a priestly figure, the son of a priestly family. Special vows for a longer period, or for an entire life, were taken by Nazirites. Details, including abstinence from wine and strong drink, are given in Numbers 6. Samson, like John, was declared a Nazirite from his mother's womb (Judges 13), a semitic expression for 'before he is even born.' Instead of being under the influence of strong drink, he will be 'intoxicated' with the Holy Spirit (cf. Acts 2:13-21). To be filled with the Holy Spirit means to have one's life totally under the direction of God. Men like that are marked for death. 16. John's task will be to turn many of... Israel to the Lord their God. As a high-priest he will effect a reconciliation between God and his people by calling the nation to repentance.

17. This verse associates John with Elijah, but nowhere does Luke identify John as a second Elijah, as Matthew (11:14) and Mark (9:13) had done. According to John 1:21 the son of Zechariah denies that he is Elijah. Luke shares the viewpoint of the writer of the Fourth Gospel and in fact shows that Jesus, not John, is a kind of second Elijah. The credentials of Jesus are not to be determined by a spectacular apocalyptic sign, such as the reappearance of Elijah in the role of a predecessor. Hence Luke omits in his third chapter Mark's description of John, who appears there in the same type of garb worn by the Tishbite (Mark 1:6; cf. 2 Kings 1:8). Mark 1:2 interprets Malachi 3:1 as a prophecy about John making his appearance as the promised latter-day Elijah. Luke omits this portion of the quotation at Luke 3:4 and confines his citation of the Old Testament to Isaiah 40:3-5. At Luke 7:27 he introduces a composite quotation from Exodus 23:20 and Malachi 3:1, but indicates that the messenger goes before the face of *Israel* to prepare her way, which is to be one of obedience (cf. Exodus 23:21). Here at 1:17 Luke says that John will go before him. Him could refer to Jesus as Messiah (cf. 2:11), but the phrase is more probably to be understood in reference to "Lord God" of the previous verse. When God's way is prepared, through repentance, his rescuing action in Jesus, the Lord of the community, will be readily appreciated. Thus there is no inconsistency between this statement and that of 7:27, for the preparation of Israel's way is equivalent to preparing the way for the Lord.

John does not do his work as a second Elijah, but in the spirit and power of Elijah. Elijah was zealous for the right of the Lord. This also will be John's mission. His task will be to turn the hearts of the fathers to the children. These words are very similar to the phrasing in Sirach 48:10 (cf. Malachi 4:6) and mean that the fathers would recognize their children as God's righteous people and would rejoice that they were following in the ways of the Lord. A cultured Greek might well have recalled the lament of the Greek poet Hesiod about the Age of Iron, that father was unlike children and children unlike parent (*Works and Days* 182). The second phrase, and the disobedient to the wisdom of the just, in typical semitic fashion restates the previous thought with emphasis on moral change (cf. Daniel 12:3). In this way the people of Israel would be made ready and prepared for the Lord (cf. 1:76; 3:4; 7:27). Thus John is not an apocalyptic judge but a priestly prophetic figure who is to prepare the people for God's rescuing action.

18. How shall I know this, asks Zechariah. The RSV blurs the distinction between his question and Mary's query (vs. 34). Zechariah asks: 'On what basis shall I be sure of this?' Abraham made a similar inquiry (Genesis 15:8; cf. Judges 6:36-40). To Luke, who abhors demands for signs, Zechariah's request was reprehensible. Sign-seekers are typical of the unbelieving response to the ministry of Jesus (cf. 11:16, 29-30; Matthew 16:1; Mark 8:11; John 4:48; 1 Corinthians 1:22). Thus Zechariah, despite his righteousness, stands at the beginning of this gospel as a kind of ominous forecast. Yet his very appeal to physical impossibilities brings the divine deed into sharper prominence.

19. The angel now announces his name. I am Gabriel (cf. Tobit 12:15, 'I am Raphael'). He is one out of the select groups that stand in the presence of God. According to Enoch 40:9, Gabriel (perhaps meaning 'Man of God') is one of the four angels who are under special orders in the presence of God. Since he is an important figure in apocalyptic literature (see Daniel 8:16; 9:21), his presence is appropriate in this narrative, which describes the beginning of the end-time fulfillment. Zechariah, therefore, is in double jeopardy. Not only does he encounter one of God's highest officers, but Gabriel speaks for God himself and has brought him this good news (in the original a verb, 'evangelize'). This refers not only to the promise of a son, but to all that the son will do. To ignore the knell of judgment would be bad enough, but to disbelieve the good news, as Zechariah does, is to invite the tolling of the bell.

20. And behold, you will be silent and unable to speak. Zechariah is fortunate that a worse fate than dumbness does not befall him. This is itself a sign of the mercy of God. But his dumbness was also a prophetic sign, associated with rebellion (cf. Ezekiel 3:26-27). Here Zechariah, not the people, is the rebellious one, as the phrase because you did not believe my words clearly attests. But these words are of a sort that will find fulfillment in their time. Time here is not simply a moment of time, but the 'proper time,' or 'the time determined by God' (cf. 19:44). The phrase these things does not refer to everything in vs. 17 but is a general statement referring mainly to John's birth (see 21:31 for similar usage).

21. Since Zechariah lingered longer than was customary, the people wondered. Had God found some impurity in him and punished him? Because he was unable to speak, the people concluded he had seen a vision, for dumbness is an aftermath of apocalyptic experience (cf. Daniel 10:15-17). Thus the reaction of the people contributes a second dimension to the reader's understanding of the choice of sign in this narrative. According to Lukan doctrine, popular apocalyptic expectations lead to a distortion of the messianic hope. God, says the evangelist, does not mark the advent of the Messianic Age with spectacular signs, such as cosmic disturbances, but with the announcement of Good News. This good news *is* the apocalypse or revelation. Hence Luke uses what apocalyptic terminology he does incorporate in order to impress on his readers that the absence of traditional apocalyptic signs in the ministry of Jesus is no proof that Jesus is deficient in messianic credentials. In brief, experience of God's delivering hand, the basic theme of apocalyptic, is to be had in the least expected places and at the most unexpected times. Luke will expand on this thought through repeated reminders to watchfulness (see especially 21:34-36).

22-23. Not being able to speak, Zechariah contented himself with signing the anticipated benediction (see Numbers 6:24-26). Nor does he recover his speech within a few moments. Luke's form of the verb remained indicates that he is not to be cured for some time, about nine months in fact. After completing his period of service in the temple, the priest went to his home.

24. The identification of Elizabeth as Zechariah's wife is not superfluous. Gabriel had specifically said that *she* would bear Zechariah a son (vs. 13). Once Abraham had tried to circumvent the Lord's promise by accepting Sarai's offer of Hagar (Genesis 16). Zechariah, however, keeps faith with the angel's word. After the conception Elizabeth hid herself for five months. Thus Luke prepares the way for his subsequent recital of the encounter between Mary and Elizabeth. There was, he hints, no prior conversation between the two.

25. Elizabeth's explanation for her seclusion may suggest a motif of judgment (cf.Isaiah 26:20). In the face of the extraordinary circumstances surrounding her conception, she does not wish to incur further divine displeasure, such as was signalled by her husband's dumbness. In effect she is presented as saying: 'The Lord has intervened to take away from me the stigma of childlessness (cf. Genesis 30:23; Isaiah 4:1), but the way he has chosen to do it is indeed most frightening! What has he done to me?' First when Mary comes will she receive enlightenment through the Holy Spirit (vs. 41).

ANNOUNCEMENT OF THE CONCEPTION OF JESUS   LUKE 1:26-38

26. The first hint of a contrast between Jerusalem and Galilee is given at vs. 26. Events begin and end at Jerusalem, but Galilee is the major scene of Jesus' ministry and the place where witnesses will be gathered (cf. 23:5; Acts 10:37; 13:31). Nazareth was a little village, despised among the Jews (cf. John 1:46).

27. Since the parental home of Jesus was messianically unprepossessing, Luke emphasizes that Joseph (meaning, 'May [God] add [posterity]'), the legal father, was of Davidic ancestry. Mary, or Miriam (the meaning of the name is uncertain), was a virgin at the time of Gabriel's visit, and Luke wants it clearly understood that she has had no intimate relations with a man (cf. vss. 34-35; 2:7). She was betrothed to Joseph. To all intents and purposes she was his wife, awaiting only the climactic wedding ceremony and the consummation of their vows. In the East girls were ordinarily married between the ages of 13 and 18. There is no reliable evidence to suggest that Joseph was much older than Mary. At the time of the death of Jesus both of them would be considered old according to ancient calculation. John 19:26-27, which may suggest that

Mary was then a widow, tells us nothing about the age of Joseph. That
Gabriel, one of the highest members of the heavenly council, should
come to the insignificant village of Nazareth and present himself before this girl -- this is a miracle of the New Age and presages the
announcement of the Magnificat, that the mighty are brought low and the
humble exalted (vs. 52).

28. Gabriel's greeting is unusual, for women were ordinarily not
addressed in this way, and not even Zechariah heard words such as these.
Hail is equivalent to 'Greetings!' but conveys the sense of 'Rejoice!'
In similar fashion the prophet Zephaniah addressed the women of Jerusalem (Zephaniah 3:14; see also Zechariah 9:9; Joel 2:21; Lamentations 4:21;
and, by contrast, Hosea 9:1). In keeping with his eschatological doctrine
Luke suggests that the Messiah does not come in a spectacular demonstration of force in behalf of Israel but begins his reign among her in most
unprepossessing fashion. Mary, like the shepherds (Luke 2:8), is typical
of candidates for the kingdom in the New Age about to dawn.

O favored one in the original is a single word related to the noun
'grace' and rhymes in part with the word for "Hail." It means: 'You,
the recipient of a gift' or 'privileged one.' The angel explains this
with the additional phrase: the Lord is with you. Precisely the same
words were once spoken to Gideon (Judges 6:12; cf. Zephaniah 3:17) and
mean that God is about to intervene with a remarkable demonstration of
his power (cf. Luke 1:25, 49).

29. She is agitated (greatly troubled) even more so than was Zechariah (vs. 12). The diction is that of apocalyptic narrative. But in
her case it is not the vision but the saying that disturbs her. She
asked herself what sort of greeting this might be, that is, what the
salutation might mean.

30. As did Zechariah, Mary hears the consoling word: Do not be
afraid (a related expression appears in Zephaniah 3:16 LXX). The pronouncement of her name (cf. vs. 13) emphasizes the personal concern of
the Lord, before whom the humblest has identity. You have found favor
with God is a Semitic expression used also of Noah at Genesis 6:8. This
phrase includes the word resembling the one used in the angel's greeting
(vs. 28). The meaning again is that God is about to shower on her a
special benefit, not, however, in answer to a prayer as was the case
with Zechariah (vs. 13).

31. And behold introduces the extraordinary gift God brings her
(cf. Genesis 16:11; Judges 13:5). She is to have a son, whom she must
call Jesus. The form of statement closely resembles that of vs. 13.
Luke attaches great significance to the name (cf. 2:21; 3:23). Mary
will have other children (cf. 8:20), but her first-born (2:7) has his
destiny determined by God. "Jesus" is another form of the name of
Joshua, which means 'God Saves' (cf. 2:11). The name is reminiscent of
the promise in Zephaniah 3:17 (LXX).

32. Like John (see vs. 15), he is to be great, but there the similarity ends, for Jesus will be called the Son of the Most High. To be called means not only to have a name attached, but to be what the term signifies. Most High (cf. vss. 35, 76; 8:22; Acts 7:48; 16:17) is used often of God in the Old Testament. Jesus promised his disciples that they would be recognized as 'Sons of the Highest' (6:35). But Jesus, as the angel's succeeding words attest, enjoys a special status. However, the expression Son of the Most High does not here connote what later creedal statements mean by "Son of God." Rather it is a firm messianic statement in continuity with 2 Samuel 7:13-16; Psalm 89:26-29. These passages speak of the messianic deliverer who is to come from David's line.

33. Through Jesus God will in effect reign over Israel (cf. Zephaniah 3:15; Micah 4:7; 5:2). And there will be no end to his reign (cf. 2 Samuel 7:13 and see Psalm 2). Luke appears to be citing from Micah 4:7 (LXX), but omits the prophet's reference to 'Mount Sion' and instead of the words 'over them' has "over the house of Jacob" (cf. Isaiah 9:7). Jerusalem will give up its birthright, and the expression "house of Jacob" anticipates Acts 7:46. Nothing is said about abstinence from strong drink (cf. vs. 15), for Jesus will in fact attend many parties and drink the wine that is offered. But he will be unjustly charged with being a drunkard (7:34).

Through this description of Jesus' messianic credentials Luke affirms that he qualifies in every way for Israel's highest office. His crucifixion at the instigation of his own nation will not discredit him. The tragedy will be that Israel did not know the things that made for her peace (19:41-44). Thus Luke's work aims to give the lie to those who claim that Jesus could not be the Christ, or Messiah, since he failed to restore the ancient fortunes of Israel. If Israel as a nation fails, Jesus will nevertheless be successful in gathering a fresh Israel. The cross will be the place of his coronation (23:37-43) and his chosen disciples will sit on thrones judging the twelve tribes of Israel (22:30). Subsequent recitals in Luke's gospel, together with the culminating question in Acts 1:6, offer necessary corrective to the misunderstanding that some readers might have found in Luke 1:32-33.

34. Primarily the question asked by Mary gives Luke an opportunity to relate the singular circumstances surrounding the conception of Jesus. Secondarily, Luke displays a contrast between Mary and Zechariah. The latter had asked for a sign; Mary merely asks for further information. Thus she is a model of the 'poor' who are proper candidates for the kingdom promised in the words of vss. 32-33 (cf. 6:20). The rendering since I have no husband is delicate but obscures a Semitic idiom meaning, 'I know no man intimately' (cf. Genesis 19:8; Judges 11:39). Strictly speaking, the question would have been irrelevant, for Mary was betrothed and could look forward to a normal marriage. Luke evidently does not lay stress on the biological aspects of the query and does not anticipate that his readers should, while missing the main point of his narrative, ask overly-curious questions.

35. Holy Spirit and power of the Most High are parallel expressions
(for similar association of spirit with power, see vs. 17; 4:14; Acts
1:8; 10:38; Ephesians 3:16), as are also the verbs "come upon" and
"overshadow." Come upon is frequently used by Luke of God's intervention in man's affairs (cf. Luke 21:26; Acts 1:8; 8:24; 13:40). Overshadow is used elsewhere in the gospels only of the cloud at the Transfiguration (Luke 9:34; Mark 9:7; Matthew 17:5). The single other occurrence is Acts 5:15. The expression indicates the presence of God's
mighty power (cf. Exodus 40:35). John was to be filled with the Holy
Spirit after Elizabeth's conception (vs. 15), but Jesus is the product
of a unique demonstration of God's power. Thus the evangelist here
emphasizes *virginal conception*, not 'virgin-birth.' Some overly-curious
theologians have suggested, in contradiction of Luke 2:23, that Jesus
was born with a 'closed womb.' But Luke's principal aim is to prepare
the reader for the emphasis made in 3:23-38, that Jesus is to be identified with all humanity (strongly affirmed in Galatians 4:4), yet as
unique son of God.

Because of such action of the Holy Spirit this particular child
shall be called holy, and this in the face of the misunderstanding that
he must endure because of the popular uncertainty concerning his pater-
nity (cf. 7:34; John 8:41). Holy means 'set apart for God's service.'
Every first-born in Israel theoretically belonged to the priesthood,
but after the establishment of the Levitical priesthood a mother could
release her child from such service by paying five shekels (Numbers
18:15-16; cf. Exodus 13:12; Luke 2:23). Jesus will be "holy" in a
special sense. He will indeed be Mary's first-born (2:7), but first of
all he will be the Son of God. Similar terms are used to describe God's
people (cf. Exodus 4:22; Jeremiah 31:9) or the king of Israel (Psalm
2:7), but the evangelist, as is clear from vss. 36-37, uses the expression here in a unique sense. The Holy Spirit is to be the Father of
Jesus. A demon will attest the link between holiness and an intimate
relationship to God in the phrase: 'I know who you are, the Holy One
of God.' (4:34) The Sanhedrin will condemn Jesus for presumption
(22:70-71).

36. Like Miriam and Elisheba (Exodus 6:23; 15:20), Mary and Elizabeth are relatives of a sort. Although Mary requested no sign, the
angel encourages her faith with the example of Elizabeth's experience.
Not only has Elizabeth conceived, she is now in her sixth month.

37-38. Since Elizabeth is to some extent a second Sarah, the evangelist includes a paraphrase of Genesis 18:14: For with God nothing
will be impossible. In contrast to Zechariah (vs. 20), Mary believes
the word of the angel and identifies herself as a slave-girl (handmaid)
of the Lord (the term for 'master'). According to Isaiah 65:8, 13-15,
Israelites are slaves of God. Malachi 3:18 states that in the end-time
men will be able to distinguish between those who slave (RSV: 'serve')
for God and those who do not. Mary is thus a model of what Israel ought
to be, and her self-description is a mark of identity for the new community (Acts 2:18; 4:29; 1 Corinthians 7:22; 1 Peter 2:16).

PROPHETIC WORDS OF ELIZABETH   LUKE 1:39-55

   Encounter with Mary   LUKE 1:39-45

   39. A divine sign is not to be taken for granted, and Mary hastens
to see her relative (cf. 2:15). 40-41. In response to Mary's words of
greeting, the embryo in Elizabeth's womb makes a quick movement. Another
woman, barren for a long time, namely Rebekah, wife of Isaac, had a similar experience (Genesis 25:22; on suggestion of joy, cf. Psalm 114:4
'skipped'; Malachi 4:2 'leaping'; Psalm of Solomon 28:3!). Elizabeth is
filled with the Holy Spirit. Her son has already displayed the truth
of Gabriel's words (vs. 15), and she now speaks as a prophetess. A prophet was able to deduce from ordinary circumstances what was the mind
and intention of God (cf. Isaiah 7:14-17). Women frequently were gifted
with prophetic powers (Deborah, Judges 4:4; four daughters of Philip,
Acts 21:9; women in general, 1 Corinthians 11:5).

   42. In diction reminiscent of Judith 13:18-19 Elizabeth cries
out her response to God's activity in connection with Mary and pronounces
Mary a unique object of praise. No woman is as privileged as she. The
main focus, however, is not on Mary. It is customary in the East to
praise remarkable offspring by praising the parents (cf. 11:27-28). Luke
makes this clear through the parallel phrase: Blessed is the fruit of
your womb (cf. Genesis 30:1). Blessed here means that Mary's child is
to be the recipient of such honors and favors from God that people will
adore and praise God for the lavish display (cf. Luke 19:38).

   43. The Semitic form of this question parallels the query in
2 Samuel 24:21. Elizabeth recognizes Mary's child as her Lord, the title
applied to Jesus by the Christian community. The term was used variously
of God, kings, distinguished persons, or owners of slaves. In this
passage Elizabeth recognizes Mary's child as her Master. Before him she
is like a slave, unworthy to receive so distinguished a person as Mary.
Her words are important, for they set before the reader a clear distinction between John and Jesus (cf. Luke 3:15-16). 44. Even Elizabeth,
John's own mother, recognized the superiority of Jesus, and she was
merely echoing John's own understanding while he was yet unborn. At
Mary's greeting he jumped in ecstatic joy.

   45. A final verdict is pronounced on Mary, who serves as a model
of faith for Israel. The word for blessed is here different from the
term at vs. 42 and does not reappear until 6:20. It means 'fortunate'
or 'happy,' in the sense of being in good grace with God, often despite
appearances. Mary can count herself fortunate that in contrast to
Zechariah, she responded in faith, and she will not be disappointed, for
what the Lord God has said through Gabriel will come to pass. The verse
should be translated: 'And fortunate is she who believed, for she will
find the Lord's words fulfilled.'

The Magnificat

Elizabeth now summarizes in prophetic utterance the meaning of the
New Age that is dawning. Greek manuscripts favor Mary as the subject,
but the witness of Old Latin texts may take us closer to the original
text. In favor of Elizabeth as the speaker of the psalms are: a. The
pronoun in the phrase "Mary remained with her" (vs. 56) suggests that
Elizabeth is the speaker. If Mary had been the speaker we would expect
to read 'She remained with Elizabeth.' b. Expressions such as "low
estate" (vs. 48) and "mercy" (vs. 50) more naturally describe Elizabeth's
situation. Her childlessness brought her into reproach (vs. 25) and her
neighbors remark that the Lord had shown mercy to her (vs. 58). c. The
song is partly modelled after the song of Hannah (1 Samuel 2:1-10), a
childless woman who became the mother of Samuel. In an earlier description of herself (1 Samuel 1:11) Hannah uses precisely the words cited
at Luke 1:48a. d. A two-fold attestation from the aged parents of John
(the Magnificat by Elizabeth and the Benedictus by Zechariah, vss. 68-79)
would be in harmony with Luke's doctrine of the superior position enjoyed
by Jesus. Both of John's parents praise the Lord for the arrival of salvation that centers in Jesus. e. Elizabeth is described as "filled with
the Holy Spirit" (vs. 41). A prophetic message like the Magnificat is
therefore appropriately associated with her name. Since vs. 25 expresses Elizabeth's desire for seclusion, the psalm would have been inappropriate at that point. [Note: The view that Mary is the speaker enjoys very substantial scholarly support.]

The psalm is a literary mosaic, drawn from various parts of the Old
Testament, with frequent dependence on the Greek text known as the Septuagint (abbreviated LXX), and falls into two major divisions. Verses 46-50
express Elizabeth's personal experience and vss. 51-55 describe God as
Savior of Israel. Verses 46-47 lead naturally to the affirmation of vs.
48. Verse 49 finds parallel expression in vs. 50. Verses 51-53 present
three pairs of contrasts. Verses 54-55 summarize God's total activity in
behalf of Israel.

46-50. Verses 46-47 contain several phrases that echo verbatim the
Greek text of 1 Samuel 2:1. My soul magnifies the Lord! In most instances where RSV renders "soul" the reader can mentally substitute 'self'
or 'I.' The Hebrew word underlying the term means the totality of one's
being. 47. The word spirit refers to that which enlivens the individual.
When a person dies, not his 'soul,' in the Platonic sense of the term,
but his breath or life leaves him (cf. 23:46). Magnifies means that
Elizabeth recognizes the greatness of the Lord God and praises him for
his mighty deeds. Verse 47 is almost totally a reproduction of Habakkuk
3:18. For the description of God as Savior, see also Psalm 24:5; Sirach
51:1; Psalm of Solomon 3:6; 17:3).

48. This verse reproduces Hannah's words (1 Samuel 1:11). God
shows his saving action by helping those who are either the victims of
oppression or are scoffed at by their enemies. Low estate (better, 'humiliation') applies most naturally to Elizabeth, who has spoken of her

reproach (vs. 25; cf. Genesis 29:32, spoken by Leah who was loved less than Rachel; Psalm 31, especially vss. 7-11). The echo of Genesis 30:13 at Luke 1:48b points further to the association of humiliation with infertility. If the psalm is to be attributed to Mary, then the term connotes inferiority of social position.

49. Psalm 111:2,9 may have stimulated much of the wording of this verse. However, Deuteronomy 10:21 parallels closely the first line. Verse 50 is an amplification of the thought in vs. 49. God's mercy (expressed in his rescuing action) corresponds to the "great things," and those who fear him (Psalm 103:11, 13, 17) are those who recognize that his name is "holy". In brief, one does not take lightly a God who can perform such wonders. Pride and arrogance are typical of those who do not recognize the holiness of God, and to these the prophetess now turns her attention.

51-53. Typical of prophetic language is the use of the past tense to describe the certainty of God's fulfillment of his promises. Verse 51 combines expressions from Psalm 118:15 and 89:10. The thought is: 'God displays His power and nullifies the plans of those who are arrogant in thought and mind.'

52. 1 Samuel 2:7 underlies the thought expressed in vs. 52, but the language is closer to that of Sirach 10:14 and Ezekiel 21:26. The mighty contrast with those in the despised lower classes, who were also frequently victims of oppression.

53. 1 Samuel 2:5 is the text for vs. 53, but the language is derived from various sources, including Psalm 107:9 and 146:7. Taken together, vss. 51-53 express the revolutionary character of the New Age. These lines could be understood in an anti-Roman sense, and to some it would appear that Jesus had failed to meet the specifications spelled out in this song, so expressive of the traditional hope. However, Luke does not here refute popular expectation but shows in his subsequent record of the activity of Jesus that traditional hope must undergo modification if the Messianic mission of Jesus is to be understood. At Nazareth (4:18-19) and later near a mountain (6:20-26) these words of the Magnificat will find fulfillment (see also 16:19-31).

54-55. Verse 54 echoes Isaiah 41:8-9 and Psalm 98:3. God does not forget Israel, his servant. By sending the Messiah into her midst, God shows that he has not forgotten how to display his love for his chosen people. 55. Most appropriately Elizabeth concludes with a reference to Abraham, to whom Isaac was given in his old age, born of a woman who had long been barren. The language of vs. 55 is closely akin to that of Micah 7:20 and Genesis 17:7-8.

RETURN OF MARY

Mary remained with Elizabeth for <u>about three months</u>. This would approximate the time of Elizabeth's parturition. However, the fact that Luke does not have Mary take part in the next developments is not at all strange. The lives of John and Jesus are to some extent parallel, but Luke is at pains to keep the two separated, with the exception of the encounter described in vss. 41-44 (but this is prior to the birth of either one) and at 3:31 (and here Luke does not explicitly mention John). Jesus is the Christ, not John. And the credentials of Jesus are not validated by John, but by God himself.

THE BIRTH OF JOHN

Birth and Circumcision

<u>57-58</u>. Elizabeth evidently remained in retirement (cf. vs. 24) until the time she was to give birth, for her neighbors and relatives now hear the news. What they hear corresponds in phrasing to vss. 46 and 50. Elizabeth had 'magnified' the Lord, and now the Lord 'magnifies' (<u>shown great</u>; cf. Genesis 19:19) his mercy to Elizabeth. The joint rejoicing of the women is a proper response to God's action (cf. 15:6,9).

<u>59</u>. According to instructions cited at Genesis 17:9-14, the child is circumcised on the eighth day. Jewish children were ordinarily given a name at the time of birth. Association of the naming with the rite of circumcision, is exceptional (see also 2:21) and may reflect influence of hellenistic practice. In Old Testament times it was customary for the mother to name her child (cf. Genesis 29:32-35; Tobit 1:9 cites an exception). Often a child would be named after a grandfather, but in view of the extraordinary circumstances attention is here focused on the father.

<u>60-61</u>. In response to the clamor for the paternal name (Luke's grammar suggests that they were already referring to the infant by the name Zechariah) Elizabeth insists that he is to be called <u>John</u>.

<u>62</u>. Although there is no suggestion in vs. 22 that Zechariah had also been afflicted with deafness, in the popular mind dumbness and deafness would be inseparably connected. Therefore the story observes that the relatives made signs to the father, and the miracle of restoration of speech is all the more apparent.

<u>63</u>. With the aid of a <u>writing tablet</u> (wood coated with wax) he informs them emphatically: "John *is* his name." Elizabeth used the future tense. Zechariah's statement in the present tense takes the reader back to the pronouncement at vs. 13. The name has already been fixed by divine decree. <u>And they all marvelled</u>. These words suggest that Luke wants his readers to understand that Elizabeth's insistence on the name John was the result of her prophetic inspiration (vs. 41) and found a remarkable endorsement in Zechariah's verdict. It is contrary to the formal

requirements of such narrative to inquire whether Zechariah had or
had not earlier communicated this detail to his wife.

64. Gabriel had spoken of "the day that these things come to pass"
(vs. 20). The moment has arrived. Zechariah had been struck with dumbness for his unbelief. Now he displays faith in God's purpose, and the
sign is removed. He then proceeded to praise God. The content of that
praise is given in vss. 68-79, but first the evangelist records the reaction of the people.

65. Fear had fallen on Zechariah at the announcement of John's
birth (vs. 12); now fear comes over all the neighbors. There is an apocalyptic tone in the narrative, and all who hear the wonderful things
that were being recited laid them up in their hearts (cf. 1 Samuel 21:12;
Daniel 7:28; Luke 2:19). 66. Comments followed two lines of expression.
Some said, "What then will this child be?" Others said, 'The hand of the
Lord is with him,' that is, he will be a mighty instrument of the Lord
(cf. Isaiah 41:20). (RSV, following other manuscript tradition, reads
the last part of vs. 66 as an explanation by the evangelist.)

The Benedictus

Zechariah, filled with the Holy Spirit (cf. vs. 41), now interprets
the will of God for his child. As Elizabeth had done (vss. 46-55),
Zechariah gives expression to Luke's main theme, salvation. Elizabeth
began with personal references (vss. 46-50); Zechariah begins with the
people of God (vss. 68-75). The verbs are again, for the most part, in
the past tense, for God's salvation will most certainly come to pass.

68-75. The first part of vs. 68 reproduces words found at Psalm
41:13; 72:18. Visited means that God has intervened when the fortunes
of his people were at low ebb. Luke will make a point of this at 19:44,
for Israel failed to realize that God's visitation was indeed taking
place. The alternative is a visitation of Judgment. In harmony with
the theme of visitation Luke displays Jesus as a guest in various places
(cf. 7:36-50; 10:38-42; 19:1-10). The phrasing redeemed his people is
similar to that of Psalm 111:9. The Messiah was to release God's people
from the yoke of their oppressors (cf. Luke 2:38; 21:28; 24:21).

69. Psalm 132, especially vs. 17, is the most probable Old Testament source for vs. 69. A horn is an emblem of power. God's power is
to display itself in an offshoot from David. Zechariah gives expression
to the conviction that the Messianic era dawns with the arrival of John,
but John is subordinate to the Davidic Messiah. Thus Zechariah's statement parallels that of Elizabeth at vs. 43 and echoes the fifteenth benediction of the Jewish prayer Shemoneh Esre (Strack-Billerbeck IV, 213).

70. This verse is similar in form to vs. 55. Zechariah, himself a
prophet, brings to summation what the ancient prophets declared and promised. Verse 71 continues the theme of salvation taken up at vs. 69,
only this time in language reminiscent of the Exodus (cf. Psalm 106:10

and see Psalm 18:17; Zephaniah 3:15). Zechariah's words here are not to be taken in a strictly spiritual sense. He gives expression to traditional national hope. Luke's task will be to explain how Jesus can be the Messiah despite the fact that this hope never came to fulfillment (note the disappointment expressed at 24:21).

Verses 72-73 share much in common with Psalm 105:8-9 and Micah 7:20 and emphasize that God keeps faith with Israel's ancestors, especially Abraham (cf. Genesis 22:16-18). A covenant is an agreement initiated by God himself. As sovereign, God promises to protect those who come under the jurisdiction of his covenant. Hence the history of Israel is a continuing story of rescue out of disaster (see Exodus 2:24). God keeps covenant even though his people fail to fulfill their responsibilities.

74. Deliverance from the hands of the enemy means that one can live without fear. 75. The aim of such deliverance is that Israel carry out her function as a nation of priests (cf. Exodus 19:6; 1 Peter 2:9) and "serve" God in conformity with his will and purpose (cf. Jeremiah 30:8-9). At this point the Messianic hope takes on a more spiritual cast in the direction of Luke's stress on personal morality. Holiness describes the proper attitude in respect to God; righteousness is conformity with God's precepts, especially as they involve one in relation to others (cf. Wisdom 9:3).

76-79. Zechariah now addresses his own child. The phrase prophet of the Most High appears as a Messianic title in Testament of Levi 8:15. The question will be asked of John whether he is the Messiah (Luke 3:15). Since the messianic hope took various directions during the lifetime of John and Jesus, Luke does not hesitate to permit messianic notions associated with John to stand at this point. But he has given priority to the "horn" of salvation in the house of David (vs. 69), and through the recital at 2:1-14 (note especially vs. 11) will correct any erroneous deductions that might have been prompted by traditional messianic expectations. At the same time this personal address to the child modifies materialistic messianic hopes by making forgiveness of sins the dominant feature (cf. 7:47).

As a prophet, John is to go before the Lord to prepare his ways. These words appear to be a combination of thoughts expressed in Malachi 3:1 and Isaiah 40:3. In both these Old Testament passages the way is prepared before God (cf. Luke 1:17). The words in Luke are not strictly parallel to Mark 1:2, where the initial phrasing is taken from Exodus 23:20. In other words, Zechariah does not say that John in his person as an apocalyptic figure validates the credentials of the messiah, a role never performed by John in Luke's narrative. Thus Luke prepares the way for a correct understanding of John's function as one whose proclamation does not usher in the end of the end-time but sounds the note of repentance (see on 1:17 and cf. Acts 13:23-24), without which God's salvation, present in Jesus' person, will be lost in misunderstanding.

In order to dissipate such misunderstanding based on traditional

apocalyptic expectations and to discourage what he considers crass interpretations of Malachi, Luke presents the origins of Jesus and John in
parallel accounts. John has no relative temporal advantage over Jesus.
His ministry ends almost as soon as it begins (cf. 3:18-19) and Jesus
comes on the scene to announce Good News to the people. Thus John is the
one anticipated by Malachi, but his message, not his person, prepares the
way of the Lord spelled out in Jesus the Messiah.

77. John will prepare the way of the Lord God by announcing salvation. In contrast to the national-political rescue announced in vs. 71,
this salvation comprises forgiveness of their sins.

78. Forgiveness is the result of God's mercy. Luke nowhere spells
out an intricate process whereby God removes sin. God simply displays
his willingness to share himself and his gifts with men (cf. Jeremiah
31:34). He demonstrates his good pleasure (2:14) by sending his Messiah.
After his gift of Jesus is rejected, he gives Israel a fresh opportunity
to enjoy his fellowship (cf. 24:47; Acts 5:31). Not even the crucifixion
can nullify God's profound love. In brief, Jesus in his person as God's
gift to the world, as one who associates also with the lowly, the outcasts,
the publicans and sinners, is the living demonstration of God's forgiving
intent. John will parallel this activity of Jesus by his proclamation of
a 'baptism of repentance for the forgiveness of sins' (3:3).

The second line of vs. 78 may be translated: 'in which the light-
filled branch from on high shall visit us.' God's mercy ("in which";
cf. Testament of Levi 4:4) is the point of origin or the source for the
visitation (the word for "visit" echoes the word in vs. 68). God's visitation takes place in forgiveness. The word rendered *dayspring* in the
margin of RSV is used in Jeremiah 23:5 LXX in the sense of 'shoot' or
'branch' (cf. Jeremiah 33:15; Zechariah 3:8; 6:12). This association may
have combined in the tradition with the thought of Isaiah 9:1 and 42:7
(cf. Numbers 24:17 and Luke 1:79) and prompted the use of a term that ordinarily refers to the rising of heavenly bodies. In any event, "dayspring" may be a case of double entente, but the expression clearly refers to the Messiah (cf. Matthew 2:2). From on High does not specify
pre-existence, but the fact that God is the Giver of the Messiah (cf.
Strack-Billerbeck II, 113).

79. Isaiah 9:1 and 42:7 (cf. Psalm 107:10) are the probable sources
for the first part of this verse. Darkness and death were frequently
associated in lamentations about the hazards and brevity of life. The
grave would offer no further opportunity for the fellowship with God
once enjoyed on earth (cf. Psalm 6:5). The New Age will be marked by
the dispelling of darkness, symbolized especially by blindness (cf.
Isaiah 59:10). Fear of death, marked by frantic love for gain will dis-
solve in the presence of One who will point his disciples to the true
riches (cf. Luke 9:24; 12:4-7, 32-34). Thus the light aims to guide
those who are sitting in darkness but dare not move because they will
stumble (cf. Isaiah 59:10; Micah 7:8). The way of peace, according to
Isaiah 59:10, is associated with justice. When justice is perverted
and the rights of the neighbor violated, there is no peace and man's sin

cries out against him (Isaiah 59:12-15). Only those who turn from transgression will experience God as a Redeemer (Isaiah 59:20; cf. Luke 1:74).
Israel will fail to recognize the things that make for her peace (19:42).
Instead of being rescued out of the hands of the enemy (1:74), Jerusalem's
enemies will destroy her utterly (19:43-44). Thus Luke conditions fulfillment of the material hope of Israel (1:68-74) on acceptance of the
guidance given by the Messiah to God's people. Messianic credentials are
therefore independent of the fate of Israel as a nation. Not apocalyptic
speculation nationally oriented, but searching of the deepest motive for
living is to mark the congregation of the end-time. Such is the dialetic
that comes to expression in Luke's masterful juxtaposition of apparently
divergent traditions.

John's Retirement to the Wilderness   LUKE 1:80

This verse concludes the first of Luke's two major recitals dealing
with the infancies of John and Jesus. It is parallel in form to 2:40,
which concludes the second installment. Like Samson (Judges 13:24-25),
John grows physically and spiritually. To become strong in spirit means
to develop inner resources for the understanding and performance of God's
will (cf. Ephesians 3:16-19).

It has been suggested that John the Baptist was associated with
communities that settled near the Dead Sea. There are, however, a number of differences between John and the Essenes and members of the community at Qumran. For example, his proclamation does not consist of
legal prescriptions and it is addressed to all who come and not merely
to a closed fellowship. Hence the phrase in the wilderness is not to be
taken as evidence for indoctrination of John in one or the other of these
communities. Rather Luke emphasizes that John and Jesus are to be kept
separate. Of Jesus Luke says that he was brought up in Nazareth (2:50;
4:16). The day of his manifestation refers to the beginning of John's
public ministry. In Luke only Jesus (10:1) or God (Acts 1:24) is the
agent of such demonstration. Hence John does not appear until the word
of the Lord comes to him (3:2).

Through his recital of the content of chapter 1 Luke achieves the
following:

1. The Messianic Era dawns with the anouncement of the births of
    John and Jesus.

2. John shares in the power and spirit of Elijah, but Jesus is the
    heir to David's throne. Thus John is subordinate to Jesus and
    his ministry does not validate that of Jesus.

3. The Messianic Era is not to be accompanied by spectacular apo-
    calyptic developments, but by a preparation of the people for
    the performance of God's will.

4. Faith is the criterion of a people prepared for the Lord.

Zechariah's sign-seeking is repudiated. Mary anticipates the disciple who will hear the word of God and keep it.

5. The New Age is a time of revolution, but not in a political sense. God raises the lowly and depresses the mighty.

6. The national hope of Israel is dependent on her recognition of the things that pertain to her peace. Moral earnestness is the primary mark of the New Age, and a fresh understanding of redemption and salvation, independent of the national fortunes of Israel, is now possible.

7. The New Age is in continuity with the promises made to Abraham and the Fathers.

8. The Holy Spirit is the documentation for God's action in the New Age.

LUKE 2:1-2

BIRTH AND CHILDHOOD OF JESUS   LUKE 2:1-52

In chapter 1 Luke described a number of features of the Messianic
Age. John and Jesus were introduced in parallel recitals, but the
superiority of Jesus was clearly indicated. Now Luke proceeds to show
that in Jesus the main outlines of the New Age begin to take shape. Many
of the themes accented in chapter 1 are repeated in chapter 2, itself
a masterpiece of literary economy.

   Birth of Jesus   LUKE 2:1-7

   1. Those days is sufficiently vague to make allowance for the decree
issued by Caesar Augustus. Augustus made a number of administrative re-
forms during his reign (27 B.C. to A.D. 14), and military and fiscal concerns encouraged the taking of various types of census in the course of
his control of the empire that numbered from 70-100 million inhabitants.
There is no evidence of one edict covering all of the empire, to be im-
plemented in one comprehensive operation, and Luke's phrasing does not
demand such an interpretation. Augustus came from the ranks of the people and mastered well the art of gradualism. The local census held in
Palestine at the time of the birth of Jesus is presented as part of a
developing imperial program, and Luke refers to the decree in terms of
policy rather than express provision.

   2. Greater difficulty attaches to the date of the Palestinian census. Since Herod died in 4 B.C., and since the announcement to Zechariah
took place in the days of Herod, the birth of Jesus must have occurred
either very close to that date or at the most two to three years earlier.
Luke knows of a census that took place in A.D. 6-7 (Acts 5:37). Josephus
alludes to it in his *Antiquities of the Jews* (17,13,5; 18,1,1). But
there is no evidence for a census in Palestine for the years immediately
preceding the death of Herod. However, it must be recognized that Josephus speaks of a collection of taxes in connection with the imperial
operation of A.D.6. Luke may well be describing the first stage, the
enrollment of inhabitants for the purpose of determining tax liability.
The collection of taxes would take place later. Again, the reader must
be on guard against reading into the past modern methods of gathering
statistical detail. In the Roman Empire this would be a long-drawn out
process.

   More problematic is the reference to Quirinius. Tertullian, an
ancient church father, did not hesitate to correct Luke and offers in
place of Quirinius the name of Saturninus (*Against Marcion*, 4:19). But
this view is also attended with difficulties. Quirinius was well known
for his extraordinary administrative capacity (cf. Josephus, *Antiquities*
18,1,1), and served, with brief interruptions, as a kind of commander-in-
chief in the East from 12 B.C. to A.D. 16. That he was engaged in some
official capacity at the time of the birth of Jesus, which certainly
falls in the general period of his activity, is very probable. As to
his exact title or particular duties during the range of time assigned

23

to the events recorded in 2:1-7, history has left us in ignorance. If Luke is less explicit than we might wish, it is nevertheless improbable that on the matter of the census he would have put himself in patent contradiction to his later statement at Acts 5:37. Confusion about Quirinius would be forgivable (how many Roman officials could even have called the roll of Rome's consuls?) but Theophilus might have his doubts about an historian who was ill-informed about Rome's first major census.

3. It is easy, however, to lose the thread of Luke's argument in debate on archaeological detail. His chief interest is to sketch the birth of Jesus against the background of imperial policy and show how Jesus happened to be born at Bethlehem. On the assumption that the practice, for which there is support in papyri from Egypt, also applied to Palestine, Luke relates that each went to his own city.

4. The name Augustus would have reminded some readers of the glorious expectations associated with that emperor's reign. In 27 B.C. the Senate urged him to head the State and voted him the title 'Augustus,' meaning 'One who is worthy of great honor,' approved by gods and men. An inscription found at Priene, celebrating his birthday in 9 B.C., commemorates the birth of Augustus as the 'beginning of the good news (gospel)'. The inscription reads in part:

> Providence, that orders everything in our lives, has
> displayed extraordinary concern and compassion and
> crowned our life with perfection itself. It has brought
> into the world Augustus and filled him with a hero's
> soul for the benefit of mankind. A Savior for us and
> our descendants, he will make wars to cease and order all
> things well. The Epiphany of Caesar has brought into ful-
> fillment past hopes and dreams. Not only will he put into
> the shade the benefactors who have gone before him, but he
> will leave for posterity no hope of surpassing him. The
> birthday of this God is for the world the beginning of the
> Gospel-festivals celebrated in his honor.

About the time this inscription was made, Jesus was born at Bethlehem. The contrast between two emperors has never been more eloquently expressed. What Luke does not say about Augustus gives profounder meaning first to what he has said earlier in chapter 1 about the messianic age and secondly to the restrained recital he is about to make of the birth of Israel's King. The Davidic credentials of Joseph were spelled out also at 1:27; of the Messiah, at 1:32-33, 69. Jesus is to be born, not in Galilee, but in Judea, for neither the Messiah nor even any prophet of note comes from Galilee (cf. John 7:41,52). Bethlehem is David's town (1 Samuel 16:1; cf. Micah 5:2).

5-6. The phrase his betrothed reminds the reader that Mary stands in the same relation to Joseph as was stated earlier at 1:27. Ordinarily a betrothed couple would not travel together like this, therefore Luke undoubtedly invites his readers to understand that Joseph and Mary are legally married. The reference to her pregnancy accounts for the fact that while they were in Bethlehem she gave birth (cf. 1:57).

7. The term first-born emphasizes that this son has the right of inheritance to the throne of David. Jesus is here distinguished from other children of Mary and Joseph who might lay claim to special privilege (cf. 8:19-21). Had Luke wished to state that Jesus was her only son he would probably have written, 'only son' (cf. 7:12; 8:42; 9:38). Like any infant, this baby requires normal attention, and is wrapped in cloths, and laid in a manger, that is, a feeding trough (not, however, a wooden crate on legs). Others, because of him, will recline in the Kingdom of God (13:29), but his head rests where the cattle have fed, in extraordinary contrast to expectations raised by 1:32-33. Luke explains the strange phenomenon with his observation that there was no place for them in the inn.

The rendering "inn" is scarcely correct. Luke would know that inns of that time were the haunts of ill-bred people and often poorly kept. But despite his emphasis on Jesus' association with publicans and sinners, it is doubtful that he would go to this length to make a point. In 10:34 he uses another term for 'inn,' but at 22:11 he uses the same term that is found here at 2:7, and there is no question that in this later passage a room in a house is meant (cf. 22:12). Luke evidently concludes that Bethlehem would have a number of visitors, and a crowded room would be no place for a couple in these straits. Animals were often quartered, as they are to this day even in some European villages, near the family quarters. But pictures that have cows and asses looking into the crib are patent invention. The inference that the birth took place in a cave can be traced to local legend associated with pagan cult. Caves were favored haunts for divine activity. Suggestions of a gruff and inhospitable innkeeper are, of course, part of later legend, and like most of the post-canonical imaginary additions of folk piety are out of harmony with the integrity and sobriety of the narrative, which is as far from sentimentality as it is sublime in simplicity. What Luke does aim to say in all this is: Jesus does not come with expected apocalyptic splendor. To associate oneself with the fortunes of a Messiah who lacks all recognized status will call for a counting of the cost (14:25-35). For the 'Son of man has nowhere to lay his head.' (9:58) George MacDonald summed it well:

> They all were looking for a king
> To slay their foes and lift them high:
> Thou cam'st, a little baby thing
> That made a woman cry.

The Shepherds

8. The Magnificat announced the revolutionary character of the
New Age (1:51-53). Luke now shows how those words are to be understood.
He introduces his readers to shepherds, who are the first to receive the
announcement of the birth. Bethlehem, as a locale of shepherds, is
mentioned at Genesis 35:19-21; 1 Samuel 17:12; Micah 5:2-4. Servius, a
commentator on the Roman poet Virgil (*Eclogues* 10,26), notes that 'divin-
ities are especially in the habit of revealing themselves to rural
people.' Rabbis thought otherwise. According to one evaluation, 'the
testimony of robbers, shepherds, violent men, and in fact all who are
under suspicion when it comes to money, is invalid.' (Strack-Billerbeck
II, 114). But these shepherds share a profession with the most blue-
blooded in Israel; Abraham, Moses, and David, and they are emblematic
of those who will share the Kingdom with the patriarchs (cf. Luke 13:
28-29).

Keeping watch over their flock by night is equivalent to 'keeping
night-watch over their flock.' The point is not that they received the
news during the night, but that they were ready for it when it came,
apparently at daybreak. Thus is anticipated the thematic note expressed
in 12:16-21; 35-40; 17:26-37; 21:34-36; 22:39-46. Since the apocalyptic
wind-up cannot be determined by the usual signs, readiness at all times
is required lest the revelation of God go unnoticed, as it did for almost
everyone but the shepherds on the day that God brought his Son to birth.

9. An angel of the Lord appeared. Jakob Wetstein, that indefatigable
collector, in the eighteenth century, of Rabbinic and classical parallels
to the New Testament, calls attention to a number of instances in Greek
literature in which the word appeared is used of communication between
gods and men with the help of dreams and visions. Also elsewhere Luke
uses this term of heavenly visitation (21:34; 24:4; Acts 12:7; 23:11).
The glory of the Lord (cf. Isaiah 40:5; 60:1-2; Ezekiel 8:4; 9:3; 10:19)
is the brilliant effulgence marking the presence of God. "Glory" also
means true worth or dignity. A king, for example, may be despised by
his enemies, but in victory he will be seen for what he really is, a powerful potentate who gives orders to his new slaves. Glory stands in
contrast to the night, for this is the time of the 'dayspring' (1:78).
Glory is mentioned here and omitted at 3:5, for the glory is not seen by
all flesh, whereas God's salvation is to be made known to all the nations.
In Isaiah 40:5 (LXX) glory and salvation are brought into close association. God's profoundest demonstration of his being is in an act of rescue.
The announcement that a 'Savior' (Luke 2:11) has been born therefore accords well with the "glory of the Lord." Such glory is not to be seen
again until the Transfiguration (9:31), and it anticipates the final success of Jesus (24:26).

10. The reaction of the shepherds is similar to that recorded at
1:12. Instead of being filled with fear they are to recognize the presence of good news (cf. 1:19), a theme that Luke will never let go (cf.
3:18; 4:18 etc.) Like Zechariah they are sharers in joy (1:14), here

described as <u>great</u>, and of a sort that applies to <u>all the people</u>, that is, to the entire nation of *Israel* (cf. 1:16-17, 68, 77; 2:32b), which in turn is to be a source of blessing to all the world (2:32a; cf. Genesis 12:3). All ceremonial requirement is shattered with this one piece of good news, for even 'unclean' shepherds are welcome in God's presence.

11. <u>For to you is born this day in the city of David a Savior, who is Christ the Lord.</u> The word <u>for</u> is important. It introduces a phrase that explains why the joy is great for all the people. <u>To you</u>, namely the shepherds, a Savior has been born. No good news was ever more personalized. Mangy, stinking, bathless shepherds are in their ritual uncleanness an encouragement for all who lack religious status. All chief seats are melted down in the white heat of this glory. <u>Today</u> is one of Luke's favorite words (cf. 3:22; 4:21; 5:26; 13:32-33; 19:5,9; 23:43). Not in some future apocalyptic hour, but at that very moment, a Savior makes his appearance. The popular conception that the birth took place at night is Christmas legend, perhaps traceable to Wisdom 18:14-15. <u>Savior</u> echoes the double theme of the Benedictus. Jesus is to spell fresh hope for the nation as a whole (Luke 1:69, 71) and for the individual in particular (1:77; 19:9). God carries on his work of salvation (cf. 1:47) through Jesus (cf. Acts 4:12; Luke 7:50; 8:48; 9:24; 13:23; 17:19; 18:42; 19:9-10). The hellenistic world had many gods and rulers called "Savior" (see the comment on Augustus, Luke 2:4). It must have seemed ludicrous to some that this child born at Bethlehem could qualify as a savior. Luke does not apologize. This is part of the revolutionary character of the New Age -- the unexpected becomes an invitation to faith. William Cowper expressed it this way:

> O! how unlike the complex works of man
> Heaven's easy, artless, unencumbered plan!

This Savior is both <u>Christ</u> and <u>Lord</u> (cf. Acts 2:36 and see Luke 1:43). Thus the term "Lord" interprets "Christ" for the Greek world. <u>In the city of David</u> specifies again that Jesus the Messiah is of Davidic descent (cf. Luke 1:69).

12. The shepherds do not ask for a sign, but the angel nevertheless gives them one. It almost sounds like a joke: <u>you will find a babe wrapped in swaddling cloths and lying in a manger.</u> Yet it is a sign. The shepherds are not to be disappointed after their vision. The very humble circumstances of this Savior's birth (cf. vs. 7) are his choicest credentials. He identified with peasant people at his birth. At his crucifixion he will identify with a robber (23:43). Such identification will exact a price from him who would understand God's work in and through him -- that price is faith! (cf. 7:9) To Solomon, the personification of wisdom, was attributed the confession that like all others he was nursed in <u>swaddling cloths</u> (Wisdom 7:4). A greater than Solomon is here (11:31) but in addition to wearing swaddling cloths he must lie in a manger. Like wisdom itself, he is a stranger to the world (cf. Enoch 42:1-2); and the Son of Man has no place to lay his head (Luke 9:58). Isaiah 1:3 complains: 'The ox knows its owner, and the ass

its master's crib; but Israel does not know, my people does not understand.' This passage may well have been a stimulant in the recitation
of the tradition from which Luke drew. If so, the sign is indeed prophetic.

   13. The word suddenly marks either an end-time (eschatological) or
a supernatural occurrence (cf. 9:39; Acts 9:3; 22:6; see also Acts 2:2;
16:26; 28:6, where a related term is used). Luke surrounds the announcement of the humble birth with two declarations of glory, themselves a
cradle of consummate literary artistry. The second of these speaks of
a multitude of the heavenly host. Daniel 7:10 indicates what is meant
by multitudes. (See also Psalm 68:17; Enoch 40:1; 71, 7-11). The
phrase heavenly host (cf. Acts 7:42) is used in the Old Testament of
heavenly bodies (cf. Jeremiah 19:13) and in intertestamental times of
angels associated with these stars (cf. Enoch 43). Some of the angels
disobeyed God's orders and raised up a race of giants (cf. Enoch 10;
Jude 6-7 and see Genesis 6:2). They are called 'wandering' (that is,
erring) 'stars' at Jude 13, in a metaphor describing false teachers.

   14. Psalms 147-150 are the best commentary on vs. 14, which is
composed of two separate statements, connected by the conjunction and
(RSV interprets this conjunction as a part of the pronouncement):

               "Glory to God in the highest"
                          and
        "On earth peace among men with whom he is pleased."

Glory refers to the recognition taken of God's mighty action in man's
behalf. Jesus is the instrument of that action. Thus this passage anticipates the amplification of the theme of glory and glorification expressed in 4:15; 5:25-26; 7:16; 13:13; 17:15, 18; 18:43; 19:38; 21:27;
23:47; 24:26. Since the angels are associated with the heavenly bodies,
they speak of God's glory in the highest, that is, among the hosts of
heaven (cf. Psalm 148:1, "in the heights"). Thus first the majesty of
God is given expression. The question is, will man be able to stand
in the presence of such glory? This tension is resolved by the second
statement. On earth forms a contrast to "in the highest." Luke will
make a big point of this in a subsequent narrative (cf. 5:24). The
majesty of God does not preclude the possibility of an encounter favorable to man. Peace is the assurance that God does not seek to crush
man but to establish a relationship between himself and people (see on
1:79). The phrase among men does not refer to international or inter-
personal relationships, but to people as the recipients of God's benefits. This thought is amplified by the concluding phrase, with whom he
is pleased (cf. Psalm 149:4). There is general agreement that the meaning of this phrase is now beyond all controversy.

   These words in Luke 2:14b do not mean that God is pleased with men
because of their status as respected people in a religious community.
Not national origin, nor descent from Abraham, nor conformity to ceremony
determines their acceptance by God. For God takes 'no delight (pleasure)
in sacrifice' (Psalm 51:16), but in those who fear him (Psalm 147:10-11;

cf. 34:18, and note the emphasis on salvation; 51:17; Isaiah 66:2).
The oppressed and the needy will see God's salvation (Psalm 69:29-32),
and they are heard in the acceptable time (that is, the time of God's
good pleasure, Psalm 69:13). Thus the angels' message reiterates the
theme of the Magnificat. The mighty are brought low and the lowly exalted, and the shepherds are among the latter. Related thoughts on
God's 'good pleasure' were expressed at Qumran (cf. I QH 4:32-33; 11:9),
but the perspective differs somewhat from Luke's theology. A similar
juxtaposition of the majesty of God and favor displayed to the humble
is found in Isaiah 57:15 (cf. 66:2):

> 'I dwell in the high and holy place,
> And also with him who is of a contrite and humble spirit.'

In sum, to have the assurance of God's favorable intention is equivalent
to having the peace of God (cf. Isaiah 57:17-21), and the Messiah is the
point of demonstration for that peace (cf. Isaiah 9:6; 62:4). The
angels' song echoes the promise of 1:79 and anticipates the acclamation
recorded at 19:38.

15-17. The faith of the shepherds is revealed by their decision to
proceed to Bethlehem to see this thing (cf. Acts 10:37). 16. Like Mary
in an earlier recital (Luke 1:39) they went with haste. What they found
at Bethlehem is spelled out in detail in order to emphasize the nature
of the response that follows. Depth of spiritual commitment is determined by the quality of one's fidelity after the majestic voice is no
longer heard. They find an ordinary Jewish couple and the child who
lies in the manger. 17. Instead of being disappointed they published
the angelic interpretation of this child (cf. 1:65). Thus they are the
first evangelists. Characteristic of the literary restraint in this
recital is the absence of a reference to an act of worship by the shepherds.

18. Their listeners wondered, a normal response to description of
divine actions (cf. 1:21, 63), but not necessarily indicative of faith
(cf. Acts 3:12). Wonderment can even be associated with unbelief (Luke
24:41). The contrast with Mary's response (vs. 19) suggests that the
person of Jesus will be subject to misunderstanding (cf. 4:22-24; 8:25;
9:43-45; 11:14-16).

19. Since angelic manifestations are a characteristic of apocalyptic,
although of course not limited to such writing, Luke describes Mary's
reaction in language very close to that used in a description of Daniel
(Daniel 7:28 and cf. Luke 1:66). Similarly Jacob pondered the significance of Joseph's dreams (Genesis 37:11; cf. Testament of Levi 6:2).
How God's purpose will develop is not yet apparent. To receive a vision
is one thing. To understand its meaning in the concrete circumstances
of life is another matter (cf. 'kept all these things,' 2:51). But Mary
is a model for the community (cf. 1:45), and thoughtful hearing of the
word of God is a major theme in Luke's gospel (see 8:15, 19-21; 10:39;
11:28).

20. The shepherds return without depreciation of enthusiasm and add their praises to those of the angels. Luke has a high regard for these shepherds. They do not ask for signs, and they believe what they have been told by their heavenly visitor. The disciples will display far less faith and understanding when they hear the predictions of the suffering and death of this same one who was acclaimed by shepherds (cf. 9:45; 24:25-26).

The Naming of the Infant   LUKE 2:21

As in the case of John (1:59) the evangelist attaches greater significance to the naming of Jesus than to the circumcision. Lest there be any doubt about the divine purpose behind this child, Luke reminds his readers that this was the name decreed by the angel (1:31). All the deeper, therefore, is the mystery of his person. This one, heralded by angels, enters into the mainstream of Israel's history through the normal route taken by every male Israelite. But his life-and-death-style will put every norm under investigation.

The Presentation   LUKE 2:22-24

The translation obscures the form of introduction which is parallel to that of vs. 21. Both paragraphs begin in the Greek text with the phrase: 'And when the time came' (literally 'When the days were filled'). In the announcement to Mary, the child is also to be called 'holy' (1:35). Thus 2:21 corresponds to 1:31 and 2:22-24 corresponds to 1:35.

Combination of two different legal prescriptions complicates this paragraph for the modern reader. In accordance with the law of Moses, Mary had to complete a period of purification that continued thirty-three days after the circumcision (Leviticus 12:2-4). During this period the mother was not allowed to come near the temple. Thus Luke confronts his readers with the astounding circumstance that Jesus, who came to reunite man in fellowship with God himself now involves his mother in ritual impurity. St. Paul did not overstate the case: 'Born under the law' (Galatians 4:4). At the end of the period the mother was to present to 'the priest at the door of the tent of meeting' a year-old lamb as a burnt offering, and a young pigeon or a turtle dove for a sin offering (Leviticus 12:6). If she could not afford a lamb, she could bring two turtledoves or two young pigeons, one for each of the offerings. Mary is one of the 'poor' in the land (cf. Luke 6:20), and offers two birds. The second prescription (every male that opens the womb shall be called holy to the Lord; cf. Exodus 13:2,12,15) concerned the presentation of the first-born (cf. Luke 2:7 and see the comment on 1:35). Luke does not mention any offering made in connection with this action, but uses the occasion of Mary's offering for her purification as an opportunity to introduce Simeon's encounter with Jesus at the temple. The law of Moses did not prescribe appearance at the temple, but the presentation at that sacred place is itself especially meaningful, since Jesus, the Son of God, is presented to his Father, as Samuel was once dedicated to God

(1 Samuel 1:11-28). Thus the declaration of the angel (see Luke 1:35) is profoundly fulfilled. Acquitted of responsibility for the normal priesthood in Israel, Jesus will nevertheless be the one who marks the place of meeting between God and His people. Dogmaticians have argued at length whether Jesus was born with Mary's womb remaining closed. A glance at Luke 2:22-24 would have spared them much useless debate and 'imaginative enlargement' of the text (see on 1:35).

Simeon   LUKE 2:25-35

25. Luke marks the entry of Simeon (meaning '[God] has heard') on the scene with the words 'And behold' (rendered now by RSV). Resembling Job of old (Job 1:1) and Zechariah (Luke 1:6), Simeon is a righteous and devout man. That is, he was anxious to conform to God's will and showed himself conscientious in his religious obligations (cf. Acts 2:5; 8:2; 22:12). There is no proof that he was a very old man. Consolation of Israel was a technical term for the Messiah (cf. Isaiah 40:1-2). His expectation (cf. Luke 2:38; 12:36; 23:51) is emphasized in order to focus on the fulfillment at hand in the person of Jesus. At the same time Luke confronts his readers with the fact that a 'layman,' not Israel's scribes or chief priests, interprets the real significance of this child (cf. 10:21-24). The Holy Spirit was upon him means that he was empowered by God to understand what God was doing at this hour in Israel's history.

26. He has no independent knowledge of the peculiar circumstances surrounding the birth of the infant Jesus, but the same Holy Spirit who was responsible for the entry of Jesus into the world had communicated to Simeon in some way that he should not see death before he had seen the Lord's Christ. According to biblical and rabbinic tradition, the Holy Spirit would make His presence known especially in the Messianic age (cf. Isaiah 40:1; Joel 2:28-29; Strack-Billerbeck II, 126-127). Luke's heavy stress on the Holy Spirit in these initial chapters is in accord with such understanding and emphasizes that God himself gives this child all the credentials he needs. The fulfillment of Simeon's expectation is the answer to a poignant question once asked by an ancient poet (Psalm 89:48), and at the same time the realization of the prophecy made by Zechariah (Luke 1:79). The phrase the Lord's Christ admits of no doubt that the "consolation" of vs. 25 is the Messiah.

27. The Spirit had given him hope and now leads him to the realization of his hope, for Simeon comes to the temple inspired by the Spirit. Thus again it is clear that what he is about to say in the temple is of prophetic inspiration, without prior acquaintance with this child or his parents. Luke sharpens the reader's appreciation of this fact with the observation that he came in at the time they were carrying out the requirements of the law. To all appearances this was an ordinary Jewish child, but Simeon will interpret along different lines. Jesus will one day welcome children into his presence (Luke 18:15-17); now Simeon takes Jesus into his arms.

28. He blessed God. This means that he recognizes Jesus as a remarkable demonstration of God's goodness. Then he gives utterance to
the song known as the *Nunc Dimittis*. As an expression of hope that
finds fulfillment it rivals the words spoken by the watchman in Aeschylus' *Agamemnon*. Long he had waited for the signal-fire that would
announce the fall of Troy:

> Now would this sentry find release from toil,
> And see the murky-nighted beacon fire
> Beam with good news. O hail, bright light!
> That makes the night as day and brings to Argos
> Joy of dance and song in Fortune's hour.
> (Lines 20-24)

29. Now is the first word in the Greek phrasing of his song and
emphasizes that the present moment is the hour of salvation. Thus
Luke again refutes the popular apocalyptic doctrine. The word rendered
Lord occurs only here and at Acts 4:24 in Luke's twin-work and means
"Master" (see also Daniel 3:37 LXX; 9:8, 16,17,19; Revelation 6:10).
The term is appropriate as a foil for Simeon's own self-designation as
'slave' (RSV less accurately, servant). As a faithful Israelite Simeon
acknowledges himself as one who is completely dedicated to the service
of God (see on 1:38 and cf. Revelation 1:1; 2:20; 7:3; 15:3; 19:2).

The words now lettest . . . depart in peace might better be rendered:
'Now you are permitting me to take my departure in peace'. The word
for depart is a euphemism for death (cf. Genesis 15:2; Numbers 20:29 LXX;
Tobit 3:6). Similarly a pagan philosopher wrote: 'When God gives the
signal and releases you from this service, then you shall go to him.'
(Epictetus I,9,16) In peace is reminiscent of Luke 1:79; 2:14. Simeon
had been assured that he would not die before he had seen the Christ.
Now he expresses his confidence that the promise has found fulfillment
(according to Thy Word). In similar vein Jacob expresses his willingness
to die, now that he had seen Joseph (Genesis 46:30). The only alternative to this interpretation is to suppose that Simeon sees in this hour
a release from slavery. But this is improbable, since he loves God his
Master and would not seek manumission on any terms, for even in heaven
the redeemed are called slaves (Revelation 19:5; 22:3: RSV 'servants').
Luke might have had in mind the oppression experienced by the 'poor'
in the land, but this thought does not accord with the context. He is
able to depart in peace, for the time of the Messiah is the age of fresh
assurance of God's concern for his people. Thus Simeon's words begin
where the Benedictus had left off (Luke 1:79). Such expressions of hope
are in brilliant contrast to the despair expressed on countless headstones
of antiquity. This epitaph commemorating an unwedded woman exemplifies
many:

Lament, O passer-by, my short-lived hour
And stand a moment near my funeral urn.
From morn to night, for all my bitter fate
The ones who bore me shed a frequent tear.
They saw no wedding day come in its turn.
No singer played before my bridal bower.

30. Simeon now gives the reason for his statement on peace. Once salvation was a matter of promise, but according to Isaiah 40:5 (quoted at Luke 3:6) it would one day be seen. Simeon's function in the narrative is to establish the fact that Jesus is in his person the embodiment of the salvation spoken of in the Benedictus (1:69-71, 77).

31. God Himself has prepared this salvation in the presence of all peoples, a thought expressed in Isaiah 52:10 and.Psalm 98:2. However, the Greek version of Isaiah and the Psalm uses the term 'Gentiles' not 'peoples' (but see Psalm 98:9). The alteration here is in line with one of the main themes in the gospel, that the good news comes to all nations via Israel, and that no one nation, not even Israel, has a monopoly on salvation. Gentiles, in other words, also can lay claim to peoplehood under God, and Israel is only one people out of many peoples.

32. Now the term "all peoples" is divided into two separate groups: Gentiles and Israel. God's salvation is to be a light for revelation to the Gentiles (cf. Acts 13:47). Psalm 97:2 LXX (98:2 RSV), in combination with Isaiah 40:5 and 49:6 (cf. 42:6), suggests how the passage is to be understood. In the Magnificat (1:54) reference was made to Psalm 98:3, and the promise of mercy was limited to Israel. Luke 2:32 utilizes also the thought expressed at Psalm 98:2 and includes the Gentiles as beneficiaries of the light Zechariah had anticipated for Israel (1:78). This light brings revelation (the Greek word is the term for 'apocalypse') or salvation to the Gentiles. And for glory to thy people Israel. Instead of for glory it is best to render 'and as glory,' making glory stand with light in apposition to salvation (vs. 30). Simeon sees Jesus as the light and the glory. Isaiah 46:13 seems to be the source for the closing phrase. Jesus is the climax of God's revelations to Israel (cf. 9:4-5). Therefore he is her glory and the means whereby she can achieve her ultimate purpose as God's people. The Benedictus expressed hope of rescue from those who oppressed her (1:71-73). Psalm 91:15 declares that one who is in trouble will be rescued by the Lord, who will honor (or, glorify) him. This thought is expressed at greater length in Isaiah 60 (see especially vs. 19). Once it was said of Moses that he was unable to enter the tent of meeting, lest he die, for the glory of the Lord filled the tabernacle (Exodus 40:35). Simeon now beholds the glory of the Lord and is prepared to make his departure, for he has found peace.

33. Despite the angel's revelation to Mary (Luke 1:31-35) and the news brought by the shepherds (2:17), the parents of Jesus respond with astonishment and perplexity (cf. 1:29; 2:18) at Simeon's prophecy. It is difficult for them to connect his words with their child. But if his own parents do not grasp the miracle of divine purpose, what is to be expected of Israel as a whole? This question is the theme of Simeon's concluding prophecy, and the dramatic tension that will finally break at a cross-crowned hill begins to tighten. Luke's statement, his father and his mother, is a hint of the mystery that will confound many, and the high court of Israel will condemn Jesus for claiming to be the Son of God (Luke 22:70-71). Mary herself will soon have more to ponder (cf. Luke 2:49-51).

34. Before announcing the coming of the gloom that is to put the light into question, Simeon blessed the parents. What is to come will be under God's direction and they are especially privileged participants in his purposes. Then he addresses Mary personally, for this child is not Joseph's but hers. Thus Luke stresses the prophetic power of Simeon. Behold calls Mary to attention.

This child is set for the fall and rising of many in Israel. To be set for the fall and rising means that Jesus is the point of decision for Israel. The words reflect the thought expressed in Elizabeth's Magnificat that the mighty are to be brought low and the humble exalted (1:52-53; cf. 6:20-26; 16:25). Those who consider themselves 'arrived' (cf. 3:8; 13:28) in the Kingdom of God will fall, that is, find themselves outside; those who are counted least likely in the eyes of the elite to succeed will rise, that is, be welcomed into fellowship with God (cf. 13:29; 18:13-14).

The language of Isaiah 8:14-15 applies to the first of these two groups. God himself, according to the prophet, is a 'rock of stumbling . . . and many shall stumble thereon; they shall fall and be broken.' Luke 20:18 applies a similar thought to these who are hostile to the 'stone which . . . has become the head of the corner' (Luke 20:17, quoting Psalm 118:22; cf. Acts 4:11). Micah 7:8 indeed speaks of the rising of those who have fallen and are ridiculed by their enemies, but the passage is no argument for viewing Luke 2:34 as a description of one class of people, who fall and then rise. At Luke 2:34 the falling lies in the future. Micah 7:8 pictures it as a present reality for the oppressed. Lowly people like that, says Simeon, are certain to have a rising, that is, a vindication from God. Israel will be surprised to learn that the Ninevites are to be included in this group (Luke 11:32).

The fact that the credentials of Jesus do not seem to measure up to Messianic specifications will prompt many to ask for a sign (cf. 11:29-32). Already the angel had declared a manger the sign of the Messianic presence (2:12). No other sign would be given. Jesus' message, his proclamation, would be his badge of authority (11:29). Another Herod will find that he cannot budge Jesus from that decision (23:8). Jesus being himself a sign will find himself spoken against. In Luke this expression occurs always in contexts expressing hostility from religious elements (20:27; Acts 13:45; 28:19,22). It was and remains the fate of Jesus that much of the opposition to him or to his principles comes from the ranks of those who claim allegiance to God. However, those who do the opposing also do the falling (cf. 20:18). And the fact that the division does take place is proof of the credentials of Jesu

He knew it well and sold nothing at bargain prices (cf. Luke 12:51-53; 14:25-33).

__35__. It is certainly a mistake to put inside parentheses the climactic words of Simeon's description. In form the prophecy preceding the statement of purpose resembles the more elaborate predictions by Jesus of his own death (9:22; 18:32). This veiled reference to the outcome of the call to decision in Israel makes more credible the introduction early in Luke's narrative of the hostility at Nazareth (4:29). Moreover, it is typically Oriental to describe the fate of a child through the sorrow of its mother. The figure of the sword echoes Ezekiel 14:17. The Greek term for this type of sword refers to a very heavy weapon, signalling terrible destruction.

That thoughts out of many hearts may be revealed. This final statement expresses the divine objective in all that Simeon has said about the child. The apparent failure of Jesus is no sign of divine displeasure. On the contrary, through him God strips man of all disguise. The word for thoughts appears frequently in Luke-Acts in the sense of hostile attitudes, usually resident in the religious leaders (cf. 5:22; 6:8; 20:14, but as a verb). Since the scribes and Pharisees, the core of the religious establishment, claim devotion to God, the genuineness of their claim will be tested in their response to Jesus. This is what it means to have the thoughts revealed (cf. 12:1-3; 16:14; 20:19; and see 1 Corinthians 14:25). (The high spiritual moment, the glow of the burning bush, the crescendo of full-throated choirs -- all this may give a feeling of walking in the presence of God. But the critical hour is the confrontation with the needs of the poor, the outcast, the forgotten ones; when the course lies to the right or to the left, to the safe and easy haven or to the dangerous, the creative and imaginative possibility. Then the integrity of the heart's devotion will be known. The sword that has gone through the land; the dreadful chasms in the social structure -- these have also at the end of the twentieth century laid bare the emptiness of much that lays claim to God.) Simeon began with a vision of large vistas for Israel (vss. 29-32). He closed with the hard reality of decision no man can evade.

Anna

__36__. The second witness in the temple precincts is Anna ('Grace'). She is one of a number of prophetesses who appear on the pages of Scripture. In the pre-Lukan cycle of the infancy narratives her father's name Phanuel may have suggested associations with Genesis 32:30-31. In the Old Testament passage the variant form Penuel means 'Face of God.' Phanuel is a transliteration of the Hebrew place-name. Anna, one would then infer, has a face-to-face encounter with God in this Messianic gift to Israel. Luke, however, could not have intended his readers to grasp such complicated etymological associations. If the meaning of a Hebrew name is important he translates it (cf. Acts 1:19) or replaces it with a Greek equivalent (Luke 23:33). Anna is of the tribe of Asher. Asher ('Happy') was eighth in line of birth (Genesis 30:12-13) but is mentioned

last in the list of Jacob's sons (Genesis 35:26). The political history
of the tribe was insignificant, and the name is omitted from the list of
rulers at 1 Chronicles 27:16-22.

37. She had been married for seven years and remained a widow for
eighty-four years (not, "till she was eighty-four"; see comment below).
Luke records the fact that she had never remarried in order to emphasize the integrity of her character. Gravestones of antiquity praise
spouses for renouncing a second marriage. This act of self-denial was
considered a mark of special piety (cf. 1 Timothy 3:2; 5:9). As a widow,
who had lost her principal means of support, she had cast herself completely on the mercy of God (cf. 21:1-4) and spent her time continually
in the temple precincts. There she worshipped God with fasting and prayer night and day (cf. Luke 24:53: Acts 26:7). This appraisal bears the
marks of what is called hyperbole, that is, literary exaggeration, designed to accent her profound piety. 1 Timothy 5:5 contains a similar
sketch of the model widow.

Luke's description on the whole bears a remarkable resemblance to
an earlier portrayal of Judith, a heroine of Jewish history. Judith
also was a widow, and she fasted all the days of her widowhood, except
on festival days (Judith, 8:4-8). She refused offers of a second marriage and died at the age of 105 (Judith 16:22-23). The high age attributed by Luke to Anna parallels that of Judith. Given fourteen years
as the age of marriage, seven additional years plus eighty-four would
add up to 105 years. Luke's ambivalent syntax not only permits this
view of a very advanced age, but seems even to demand it. Evidently
Luke, who displays other familiarity with the apocrypha, thought of the
parallel with Judith and assumed that his readers would do likewise. In
any case, the verdict on Judith applies to Anna: 'There was none who
spoke an evil word against her; for she feared God exceedingly.' (Judith
8:8)

Luke's interest in Anna's genealogy is now apparent. It is of importance to him that this aged woman is an Israelite born and bred.
Others will boast of Abraham as their father (cf. Luke 3:8; 16:19-31).
Anna not only has the lineage, but she is an Israelite good and true.
Her tribe may be insignificant, but God raises the lowly, and the mighty
fall. Jesus receives the attestation of prophets who have the finest
credentials. Zechariah, Elizabeth, Simeon, and now Anna -- all these
are Israel as Israel ought to be, and the reader will soon see how these
contrast with scribes and Pharisees and chief priests, one of whom bears
the masculine form of her name, Annas (3:2). Simeon's presence in the
temple was motivated by a special revelation. Anna requires no previous
notice, for she is in constant attendance in the temple area.

38. She gave thanks. The Greek word occurs only here in the New
Testament. It is used, however, in the Greek version of Psalm 79:13,
in a context that speaks of God's salvation for Jerusalem and deliverance of prisoners (cf. Luke 1:68-75). Simeon had been looking for the
consolation of Israel (vs. 25) and associated his expectation with the
infant in his arms. Anna spoke to those who were looking for the

redemption of Jerusalem (cf. Isaiah 52:9; Luke 23:51) and said, 'It is
here in the person of this child' (cf. 2:17). Isaiah 8:17 contrasts
those who wait for the Lord with those who stumble (vs. 15). Anna came
at the very hour Simeon had recited his prophecy of stumbling. Yet her
faith remains firm. Two men on the road to Emmaus (Luke 24:21) will
display less understanding than Anna. The place of Jesus in the family
of Israel has now been firmly nailed down. Jerusalem has heard the testimony. It remains to be seen how those who found refuge in tradition,
as they had been taught it, understood it and applied it, will respond
to that testimony.

Return to Nazareth   LUKE 2:39-40

39. His parents performed everything according to the law of the
Lord. Although he was brought up in Galilee and in a village despised
by religious circles, he shares in the traditions of his ancestors.
John had gone into the wilderness (1:80). Jesus remains with his parents.
But he will have his days in the desert (4:1-13).

40. Under the God-fearing tutelage of his parents the child grew
physically and inwardly. The description in this verse is similar to
that of Luke 1:66 and 80 (cf. Judges 13:24; 1 Samuel 3:19), for Luke
has now concluded his story of the parallel infancies of John and Jesus
and established for his readers basic difference between the two. At
the same time he introduces a fresh factor. John was empowered by the
Spirit, as prophets normally were, for his prophetic task. Jesus is
fathered by the Spirit and will receive the credentials of the Spirit
for his Messianic assignment, but after his baptism (3:21-22). At this
point, therefore, Luke notes that he was filled with wisdom (cf. Wisdom 7:7). Wisdom is understanding of the will and purpose of God, reflected in performance according to the law of God (cf. Proverbs 1).
Thus Luke sets the stage for his recital of the trip to Jerusalem, where
Jesus will display not only exceptional intelligence but understanding
of God's favor (1:28,30). That same favor rests on the child. And with
this note the apocalyptic aura of the annunciation blends into the
routine of a Jewish child's upbringing.

Jesus at the Age of Twelve   LUKE 2:41-52

Since Luke set out to write neither edifying legends nor a biography
of Jesus, but rather to establish certainty concerning things 'accomplished among us' (1:1-4), he ignores much detail that might interest
a biographer. He attaches great significance, however, to the tradition
of Jesus' visit to the temple and notes that this took place when he was
twelve years old. At the end of the thirteenth year a boy was obligated
to observe all the commandments, including the ritual regulations. The
fact that Jesus is taken to the temple at his twelfth year indicates
that his parents are concerned that in addition to his previous training
he be introduced to other responsibilities that await him as a fully
grown Israelite (cf. Strack-Billerbeck II, 144-47). Luke locates this

fact within a larger perspective. Jerusalem is the locale where God
begins and brings to a climax his redemptive purpose. Jesus goes to
Jerusalem in complete harmony with the traditional law of Israel, yet
more profoundly implicated than any Israelite in his obligation to One
whom he recognizes as his Father, for he is the Son of God, declared
so by an angel (1:35).

41-42. Whether women and children (with the exception of boys who
had reached the age of thirteen) were to be excused from attending the
three great feasts prescribed by Moses, was a matter of debate among
rabbis. The three feasts were Unleavened Bread (or Passover); Weeks,
marking the end of the grain harvest; and Booths, commemorating the
wandering in the wilderness (see Exodus 12 and 23; Leviticus 23; Numbers 28-29; Deuteronomy 16). In any event, the piety of Jesus' parents
is expressed by the observation that they went every year at the feast
of the Passover. This feast is particularly noted since the visit by
Jesus anticipates one other trip that Jesus will make to Jerusalem,
beginning at 9:51 (the visit described at 4:9 is of a different order)
and climaxing at the time of Passover.

43. Despite their poverty (see on 2:24), the family stays for the
entire period. They cut no corners. Jesus, however, stayed on longer.
For the first time he is identified as the boy. As a person who is
about to become a full-fledged Israelite, the term child (vs. 40) no
longer properly applies to him. But Luke appears to be sensitive to
further implications in the term. Earlier he had used it in description
of Israel (1:54) and of David (1:69). Isaiah 41:8 and 42:1 apply the
term to Jacob (=Israel) in the sense of 'servant.' The second of these
passages is especially significant, for it speaks of Israel's receipt
of the Spirit. According to Luke, Jesus is the boy or Servant of the
Lord in a sense that transcends Israel's mission. Jesus comprehends in
his person the identity of Israel, and this is demonstrated by his subsequent declaration of identity to his parents (Luke 2:49). Luke's usage
in the Book of Acts confirms this line of interpretation (cf. Acts 3:13,
26; 4:27,30). It is probable, therefore, that boy is to be understood
as a double entente.

44-45. Inferences concerning possible neglect by the parents or
thoughtlessness on the part of Jesus are irrelevant and obscure the
literary function of Luke's reference to the parent's ignorance. Not
only are they unaware of his whereabouts, but they do not understand the
situation. In the original there is no object to the verb know(vs.43).They
took it for granted that he would be with kinfolk and acquaintances.
But he, from whom acquaintances would one day remain at a distance (23:
49), stands in a much closer relationship to Another, as he will be
quick to inform his parents (2:49).

46. Like the Marys who failed to find the body of the Lord Jesus in
the tomb (24:3), the parents looked for their son in the wrong place.
After three days they found him in the temple. The phrase after three
days parallels Luke's use of 'the third day' in reference to the resurrection of Jesus (9:22; 18:33; 24:7, 21, 46). Luke's readers, who know

how the story finally ends, would recognize the subtle hint of that lifting of the sword that was one day to pierce Mary's heart (2:35). They found him . . . sitting among the teachers (cf. Wisdom 8:10), even as he would on the third day be "among" the disciples (24:36). On this occasion, and on this occasion only, is Jesus described as being in the presence of teachers. Hereafter in the gospel Jesus will be the teacher (the one exception is John the Baptist, 3:12). Here Jesus is not a teacher but a pupil, for he was listening to them and asking them questions. One day his questions will pierce to the very core of the religious establishment, and he will give answers to his own questions (cf. 11: 19-20; 13:2-5 etc.).

47. All who heard him were amazed at his understanding and answers. Commentators have drawn attention to the parallel between this recital and other accounts of precocious children. Plutarch relates the following about Alexander:

> When legates sent by the king of Persia came to Philip's court during the latter's absence, Alexander his son served as their host and engaged them in conversation. Such sagacity did he display that he put to them no puerile or petty questions. He inquired rather about distances and means of transport in the upper regions of Asia Minor. He expressed his curiosity about the king of Persia, especially how he treated his enemies. And he asked about the Persians' courage in combat and the strength of their forces. So impressed were they that they concluded that the legendary shrewdness of Philip was nothing compared to the zeal and thirst in this young lad for the performance of great deeds. (*Alexander*, 5)

Similarly Josephus wrote of himself:

> When I was a child, about fourteen years of age, I was commended by all for my attachment to learning. For this reason high priests and leading men of the city came frequently to me in a body, to determine my opinion about precise interpretations of the law. (*Life*, 2)

Luke may have been influenced by such type of narration to include from his sources a related story about Jesus, but his primary interest is theological. Luke had said that Jesus was filled with wisdom (vs.40). The composer of the *Wisdom of Solomon* observed: because of wisdom 'I shall have glory among multitudes, and honor in the sight of elders, though I be young.' (8:10; see also Sirach 47:14) Subsequently Luke will point out that a greater one than Solomon is here (11:31), and the residents of Capernaum will be astounded at the instruction of Jesus (4:32). But wisdom is not a goal in itself. For an Israelite the summation of wisdom is to know and love God and to do his will (cf. Proverbs 28:7). Luke makes it abundantly clear that what the centurion observed one dark hour (23:47) was true of Jesus from the very beginning.

48. His parents on this occasion display a similar reaction and demonstrate that they do not comprehend the destiny of this child. The focus, however, is on Mary and her relationship to Jesus. Therefore she is the one who enters first into the dialogue. It was natural for Mary to address her child with the word Son (the Greek term here is the normal expression for 'child'; in Luke 1:32, 35 the customary term for 'son' is used), but in a sense, suggests Luke, it was a misunderstanding on her part, intensified by her further words: Behold, your father and I have been looking for you anxiously. The rendering anxiously does not bring out the force of the original, which speaks of pain, such as that experienced by those who are faced with the prospect of never again seeing their loved one (Acts 20:38). Luke is the only writer in the New Testament to use the expression, and the two other instances occur at 16:24, 25, in the story of the tormented rich man. In the context of Luke's total work, the term is well chosen, for Simeon had predicted that a sword would pierce Mary's heart (2:35), and the three-day interval would one day be repeated.

49. At the grave two men asked the women: 'Why do you seek the living among the dead?' (24:5) Jesus asks his parents: How is it that you sought me? The words echo the language about the search at vs. 44. There is good reason for addressing this and the next question to both parents. They must learn to live with the fact that he, their son, is a stranger and a guest in their house, for he is under orders from Another. I must be in my Father's house. The Greek syntax is ambiguous, and Luke may have intended a double entente: 'In my Father's house' or 'with my Father.' The RSV, however, renders correctly a common Greek idiom, and there is no doubt where the emphasis lies. Jesus is totally committed to God, his Father (1:35; cf. Psalm 27:4). The word must characterizes his entire life (cf. 4:43; 9:22; 13:33; 17:25; 19:5; 22:37; 24:7, 26, 44). Only the Son knows the Father, and only the Father really knows the Son (10:21-22). And into the Father's hands he will one day commit his spirit (23:46).

50. Jesus displayed profound understanding (2:47) in the temple. His parents, on the other hand, do not understand what he has just told them. The future disciples of Jesus will not have less difficulty (18:34). But finally Jesus himself will expound all (24:45), for he is the Teacher of the community.

51. Once again Luke draws the veil. Jesus, who was soon to reveal an extraordinarily free and creative mind and spirit that would shock all Israel, returns to Nazareth to be obedient to parents who do not understand the fire that burns within him. This return to Nazareth may appear to be in contradiction with Jesus' interest in staying at the temple. But Luke's technique of anticipating future developments must be kept in mind. Jerusalem is the ultimate goal, and one of Jesus' first acts on his arrival at the city will be the cleansing of the temple (19:45-46). There he will spend his time teaching (cf. 19:47; 20:1; 21:37). Again religious leaders will ask him questions, and he in turn will question them (20:1-8; cf. 22:53).

The experience at Jerusalem had an apocalyptic ring to it. Mary's response is appropriate: <u>She kept all these things in her heart</u> (cf. Daniel 7:28, and see on Luke 2:19). The shepherds' recital and now this! But why does Luke stress the fact that Mary, of all people, lacks fuller understanding? The answer is suggested by his critique of popular apocalyptic. The credentials of Jesus are not to be determined by spectacular signs. The word of God, spoken also through the mouth of Jesus and through his chosen apostles, is the vehicle for communication of God's purpose. Despite the unusual experience of a visit from Gabriel himself, Mary is faced with the same problem that confronts all who hear the Word of God. Ultimately faith, independent of signs, is the single port of entry into the mystery of Jesus' person. Mary is not relieved of that responsibility. Hence Jesus has no special comfort for those, including Mary, who claim a close physical kinship with him (8: 19-21; 11:27-28). Except for these last passages and a brief mention at Acts 1:14, Mary disappears from the pages of Luke-Acts. If, as some hold, Mary is representative of Israel, then her disappearance in the succeeding narrative is all the more understandable. Now Israel must do like Mary and ponder the word that Jesus will bring.

<u>52</u>. The description in this verse bears a close resemblance to that of 1 Samuel 2:21, 26 (cf. Proverbs 3:4), but Luke's addition of the word <u>wisdom</u> is a further example of his careful editorial technique. Jesus is a prophet in the tradition of Samuel, but he will be charged with breaking the laws of Moses. In advance the reader is reminded that not Jesus but the prevailing religious establishment is to be put into question. Neither from the side of men nor of God was any fault to be found with this young man. Pilate would be puzzled that Jerusalem should think otherwise, and a centurion would say the same thing in his own way (23:47). <u>Stature</u> is of God's making; man cannot add to it by anxious thought (cf. 12:25). <u>Favor</u> is God's gift to the humble (cf. Sirach 3:18). Jesus displayed humility in his self-subjection to his parents (Luke 2: 51), and the Lord would exalt him.

MINISTRY OF JOHN THE BAPTIST   LUKE 3:1-20
                                    (MARK 1:2-8; MATTHEW 3:1-12)

The Ruling Powers   LUKE 3:1-2

At 1:76 John was called 'the prophet of the Highest.' As in Hosea
1 and Jeremiah 1, the date of the prophet's public introduction is solemn-
ly recited. with emphasis on the contemporary rulers. The revolution
of the Kingdom of God will not be buried in a corner of history (cf.
Acts 26:26).

1. Tiberius Caesar, successor to Augustus, began his reign in
A. D. 14. His fifteenth year would date the beginning of John's ministry in 28/29. Pontius Pilate governed Judea as prefect, A. D. 26-36.
(On his official title, see A. N. Sherwin-White, *Roman Society and Roman Law in the New Testament*, 1963, p. 6.) Herod Antipas governed Galilee as tetrarch (4 B.C. to A.D. 39). Originally tetrarch meant 'ruler
over a fourth part of a region,' but in time the term was loosely applied
to petty, dependent princes, whose authority was lower than that of a
king. Philip, Antipas' brother, similarly had jurisdiction of Ituraea
and Trachonitis (4 B.C. to A.D. 33 or 34) and Lysanias controlled Abilene,
a region northwest of Damascus.

2. Annas was deposed as high priest in A.D. 15, and Caiaphas, his
son-in-law held the post A.D. 18-36. The term high priest is applied
honorifically to Annas. It was not necessary to specify that Caiaphas was
actually the office-holder. Similarly one might refer to 'the era
spanned by President Lincoln and Wilson'. In other passages in Luke the
term chief priests also includes the presidium of the Sanhedrin (cf. 9:22;
20:19; 23:13; 24:20).

Luke's recitation of names is not without design. All except Lysanias
play some role in the succeeding narrative. Tiberius Caesar at 20:20-26.
Pontius Pilate at 13:1 and in chapter 23. Antipas, 3:19; 8:3; 9:7,9;
13:31; 23:7-15. Philip at 3:19. The chief priest(s), 9:22; 19:47;
20:1,19; 22:2,4,50 (Caiaphas), 52,54 (Caiphas), 66; 23:4,10,13; 24:20.

Following the style of Old Testament writings (cf. Jeremiah 1:4)
Luke says that the word of God came to John. This is a solemn way of
asserting that God signally intervenes at this moment in history, so

carefully defined against the background of imperial and ecclesiastical systems. Reference to the locale (in the wilderness) anticipates the use of Isaiah 40:3 at vs. 4 (see also 1:80).

Prophetic Fulfillment   LUKE 3:3-6
                                            (Mark 1:2-6; Matthew 3:1-6)

John's mission is not limited to a narrow area, but covers much of the valley of the Jordan, apparently west of the river. Nor does he invite his hearers to an isolated life, such as that at Qumran. Verse 3 does not emphasize that he baptized, but that he proclaimed a baptism of repentance, the aim of which is the removal of sins. Without repentance a washing would only spell disaster for those who used it as another ritualistic device to manipulate God. The word baptism is a transliteration of a Greek word meaning 'a washing' or 'cleansing.' 'Wash' is used by Luke also of experience of death (12:50) and of receipt of the Holy Spirit (3:16). Here it is applied, also without primary stress on water, to the experience of repentance, that is, a change of mind and attitude. He who then received John's 'baptism' would thereby give visible expression to the revolution within himself. Without repentance there can be no receipt of forgiveness, and forgiveness is the primary ingredient of the New Age that has dawned (1:77). The prophets repeatedly assert that Israel's sins have separated them from God and that a right-about-face is required (Isaiah 46:8-9; Jeremiah 8:6), usually described as a turning back to the Lord. Without such repentance, the coming of Jesus as the end-time bearer of salvation will be of no benefit to Israel. In subsequent narratives Luke will describe the Savior as one who offers forgiveness (5:23; 7:47-49; cf. 17:3-4; 23:34). For him who is repentant the baptism, as God's own action, is the seal of that forgiveness (cf. Acts 2:38).

4-5. Luke's quotation from Isaiah 40:3-5 recapitulates the meaning in vs. 3. There is no mention of ritual cleansing, for 'baptisms' were common in the Jewish community (cf. Luke 11:38; Mark 7:4). Rather, the emphasis is on moral alteration. The words describing the preparation of the way of the Lord are typical of the pains taken to clear the way for a visit by an Eastern potentate. In their context in Isaiah they refer to Israel's deliverance from captivity under the imagery of a second Exodus. Luke applies them to the moral change Israel must undergo for reception of God's new action in connection with Jesus. Lord is used of God or Jesus Christ in the New Testament. In verse 4 God, as understood in the Old Testament, is meant (cf. 1:17, 76). A reference to Jesus first appears in the concluding clause: and all flesh (including the Gentiles) shall see (that is, be invited to share) the salvation of God (cf. 1:69,71,77; 2:11,30-32). Jesus, as the content of God's rescuing action, is that salvation.

Important for the understanding of Luke's presentation is the manner in which he departs from Mark's use of the Old Testament in this account about John. Mark begins with a citation from Exodus 23:20, a reference to God's special messenger sent to guide the Israelites on their journey.

As the messenger went before Israel so John goes before Jesus Christ, to prepare his way. Luke deletes the words 'Behold, I send my messenger before thy face, who shall prepare thy way' (Mark 1:2), reserving them for a later stage in his narrative (7:27). Association of the deleted words (Mark 1:2) with Malachi 3:1-4 apparently gave rise to the speculation that John's task was that of a second Elijah, to announce as imminent the Great Day of the Lord, the climactic wind-up of history; Jesus as the Messiah, was to usher this in immediately. Mark himself attempted through his secrecy motif to explain the puzzling delay and at the same time discourage speculative apocalyptic. Only after Jesus' death and resurrection and extensive publication of the Good News would the spectacular appearance take place. But how long must the church wait? Mark explained that the destruction of Jerusalem would spell the birth-pangs of the end of the end-time (Mark 13). After Mark had written, Christians remained perplexed by continuing delay in the wind-up of history. Luke's answer to this problem is that John is not really a second Elijah and was not meant to be construed as the first of two end-time installments.

6. His job is not to prepare the nation for the sudden advent in power of the messianic deliverer. He prepares the way for God so that God may announce his salvation for all flesh. That salvation is Jesus, in whose person the forgiveness of sins, the display of God's good pleasure, becomes reality. Since Jesus does not measure up to popular messianic expectation, repentance is all the more required. Only a complete reversal of national and religious thought will make possible proper appreciation of God's program in connection with Jesus.

Luke's omission of the phrase, 'and the glory of the Lord shall be revealed' (Isaiah 40:5), reinforces this interpretation of his thought. Inclusion of the phrase at this point might have suggested that an apocalyptic demonstration of a spectacular sort is about to take place. Luke, however, had earlier transposed the phrase to his account of the shepherds: 'and the glory of the Lord shone around them' (2:9). Jesus, in the humble circumstances of His birth (2:12) and as a sign to be spoken against (2:34), *is* the apocalyptic event. The child in the manger, the child in Simeon's arms -- this is the Savior, this is the scandal of the New Age. By dissociating John from Malachi 3 and therefore from traditional speculations about the return of Elijah, Luke intends to eliminate doubts concerning Jesus' messianic credentials. Even though the apocalyptic time-table, as popularly understood, was not followed, Jesus is nevertheless the fulfillment of Israel's and the world's hope. John comes in the spirit of Elijah (1:17); cf. Malachi 4:5), but Jesus is the real second Elijah, that is, if one is to speak at all of a latter-day Elijah. No signs as traditionally understood are needed to document his credentials, and the refining function described in Malachi 3:2-4; 4:1-2 is reserved for Jesus not for John (cf. Luke 3:16-17).

Call to Repentance   LUKE 3:7-14
                                                   (Matthew 3:7-10)

Luke omits Mark's description of John as a second Elijah wearing
camel's hair and a belt of leather (cf. 2 Kings 1:8). In Mark, the
association has point, but in Luke's time, because of popular misunderstanding, a fresh approach must be taken. The statement in Zechariah
13:4, that in the latter day a true prophet would not put on a hairy
garment, may also have influenced the evangelist.

7-8, Since Luke is not yet ready to introduce indictments of
specific religious groups, he does not spell out, as does Matthew,
that Pharisees and Sadducees come under critique. Instead, he simply
uses the word multitudes. This general term for 'crowds' replaces
Mark's reference to 'all the country of Judea, and all the people of
Jerusalem' (Mark 1:5). Encounter with Jerusalem is preserved for Jesus,
and at a later time. The news of John's 'baptism' had spread. The
implication is that the crowds understood this as another ritual cleansing. Like the prophet Isaiah, who addresses the people as a 'sinful
nation, a people laden with iniquity, offspring of evildoers, sons
who deal corruptly!' (Isaiah 1:4), John does not use complimentary language. Brood of vipers, he calls them, a description for which there
is precedent in Isaiah 59:5 (see also Jeremiah 46:22-23).

His question is satirical and means: 'From whom, in the world, are
you getting your directions to escape the impending wrath? You want
another wash? Then do it right. Bring out fruits that really show
repentance.' Isaiah 1:16-18 says 'Wash yourselves; make yourselves
clean; remove the evil of your doings from before my eyes . . . Though
your sins are like scarlet, they shall be as white as snow.' These
admonitions are preceded by the Lord's request to have 'no more vain
offerings. . . . Your new moons and your appointed feasts my soul hates'
(Isaiah 1:13-14). Ritual is meaningless without true repentance, that
is, a turning from wickedness. Therefore John is critical of a populace
that misinterprets his proclamation of a washing of repentance as an
invitation to another bit of ritual. 'Your iniquities have made a separation between you and your God, and your sins have hid his face from
you,' said Isaiah (59:2), and the chapter from which his words are
taken is the best commentary on Luke's meaning.

'Do not even begin to say to yourselves: But our father is Abraham!' That slogan plunged one rich man into flames (16:24). Traditional securities are of no avail in the New Age that now dawns. It is
not enough to recite the proper religious words. One must deal with
God in depth. For God is able to raise up children for Abraham out
of the very stones (cf. Romans 4:17). In brief, criteria of birth,
national identity, class, status mean nothing to God. The attitude
and disposition of mind and life is central. This is radical apocalyptic,
in a truly theological and moral dimension.

9. The ax is laid to the root of the trees. Hosea 10:1-2 describes
Israel as a 'luxuriant vine,' but headed for destruction. Jeremiah

2:21-22 says Israel is a 'choice vine' but though she 'wash (herself) with lye and use much soap,' she could not remove the stain of her guilt. No mere ritual washing will save these crowds. The ax is heading not only toward the base of the tree, but toward the very roots ---- total destruction! Such was the word of Amos concerning the Amorites (Amos 2:9). And the ax is in its downward stroke. No wonder John asked, 'Who was it who misguided you?' Trees without good fruit on them are headed for the flames. Luke will have more to say on *that* subject (6:43-49).

10-11. In response to the frantic question: 'What are we to do?' John answers simply: 'He who has two undergarments, let him share one with a man who has none. Do the same with your food.' (cf. Job 31: 16-20) In the wake of the overpowering apocalyptic and prophetic rhetoric that precedes in vss. 7-9 these words appear colorless. No unusual activities are required. No recital of religious obligation is made. Merely a call to unselfishness (cf. Acts 2:44-45; 4:32-36). Yet the words in Luke's context are revolutionary. The haves are to share with the have-nots, for God exalts the poor and elevates the rich (Luke 1:52-53). He who refuses such direction will, like the rich man, see Lazarus at Abraham's side and himself, while calling Abraham father, forever removed from the presence of God (16:26; cf. 13:28). The ax is heading downstroke in any society that thinks these words are an invitation merely to distribute Christmas food-baskets, handouts of castoff clothes, and dollar bills. Prophets did not risk their necks for petty moralizing of that sort. A call to repentance, an across-the-board review of 'respectable' resources for injustice, prejudice, and indifference to the needs of brother men, this is what separated true prophets from the phony.

12. Tax collectors also came to be baptized. Since one of Luke's main themes is the place of religious outcasts in the program of the New Age, Luke skillfully separates their arrival from that of the 'crowds.' Besides, it would have been inappropriate to suggest that these people, who were considered outside the religious establishment, should in complacency claim Abraham as their father. By introducing them at this point Luke is able to contrast them with those who were in fact the complacent ones.

Some measurement of the emotional impact Luke's reference to these detested representatives of Roman fiscal policy made on his readers can be done at the hand of other documents. Lucian, a non-Christian writer in the second century, summed the sentiment of both Jew and Greek when he lumped 'adulterers, pimps, tax collectors, yes-men and informers' as part of a vast 'crowd of people who only stir up huge confusion.' (*Descent into Hades* 11) St. Paul, in 1 Corinthians 6:9-10, submits much the same list as he looks back on his first membership class at Corinth, but omits reference to tax-collectors, who are mentioned in the New Testament only in the first three gospels. Such, then, are the candidates for participation in the program of the New Age. But unlike the fate of many who have lost much sense of worth as persons and fall easy victims to entrepeneurs in personality cult under the guise of idealistic goals, these people are not exploited in the interest of promoting John's ego. They get no patronizing sympathy, but hear a manly invitation to become persons in their own right, with identity, and to become new as the Age that is dawning. They come indeed to be washed, but not merely to get a feel of the water. Their first question is: Teacher, what shall we do? The complacent claimed Moses as their teacher. These men listen to one who has interrupted 'business as usual.'

13. Once again the directions are simple. Nothing is said about dropping their profession. But the ax comes down on the system. Collect no more than is appointed you. These simple words cut through roots of graft, the pay-off, the kick-back, the torn-up ticket -- all the tentacles that reach out to destroy the health and substance, the moral fiber and ethical backbone of an individual and his nation. Simple! Fair and just dealing, without attempts to aggrandize oneself at the expense of another -- this is the expectation of the Kingdom. Not many moons later a short man will climb a tree and volunteer such deeds without command (19:8).

14. Soldiers are given similar direction. Their entry on the scene is not unusual in a narrative that deals with a revolutionary figure. Rome would want to know what was afoot. Besides, Luke must give some account of the Church's attitude toward imperial policy. Does Christianity spell the end of the military establishment? The answer: Soldiery can be an honorable profession, but force and false accusation must not be used to shake down the weak. The appearance of soldiers in the narrative next to tax collectors suggests that military force, combined with oppressive systems, comes under special indictment.

Note: In line with this statement about the proper function of the military Luke is at pains to single out for special mention examples of Roman justice and consideration. The centurion in 7:1-10 is a model of the occupation. Pilate's soldiers are spared connection with the humiliation of Jesus (22:63-65; 'the men' who hold him in custody are from the temple guard). A centurion is the first, after the robber, to clarify the status of Jesus (23:47). Even Pilate is let off as gently as is possible (chapter 23), and the gossip about his cruelty is softened in the story of Nicodemus' request for the body of Jesus (23: 50-56). Luke 13:1 is no exception, for Luke has a special purpose in recording the bulletin about the Galileans' blood shed by Pilate (see on 13:1). Luke's Jesus is no threat to imperial authority. But imperial authority that does not recognize the validity of his claims ultimately signs its own expiration warrant, for the mighty will be brought low. Luke permits no skepticism about that! Justice is the bond of security for the people and the State. The final word to the soldiers, 'be satisfied with your wages,' would be especially noted in a period when soldiers were notoriously disgruntled about their daily stipend of money and grain. Theophilus can inform his superiors that the Christians are no trouble-makers, but let Caesar know that there are limits! Paul's record of imprisonment is testimony that Christians will not tolerate infringement of their allegiance to Jesus as Lord. Not Luke, but the later church, time and again capitulated to establishments that claimed more than their dues.

After reading John's speech, Theophilus might have asked 'Is this what all the fuss is about?' Some revolution, this!' But he would have missed the point. John's preaching emphasized the importance of individual decision, not dependence on the rules of the Scribes, or the stuffy moralizing of the Pharisees. The Pharisees held certain jobs to be degrading; John upgraded jobs to the level of human responsibility. That tack could be dangerous once moved to a high pitch of authority by the One who waits in the wings, a threat to those who resist change with automatic reflex. On the other hand, those who expected the Messiah to produce spectacular signs must be disabused of their misconceptions. Jesus will give no signs, and he will repeat in various ways much of what John said. Yet there is a hard-hitting radicality in Jesus' words, as reported by Luke, that pales John's expression into comparative insignificance. By underplaying John, Luke prepares the way for Jesus' ministry.

The Stronger One   LUKE 3:15-17
                                    (Mark 1:7-8; Matthew 3:11-12)

Since debates on the mission field and also within the longer established churches (cf. Acts 18:24-19:7) included the question of the relation of John and Jesus to the end-time program of God, Luke moves into the Messianic issue. Since Jesus was an apparent failure, rejected by the top religious leadership, some claimed that he could not be the Messiah. Others said that John was a kind of Messiah, but perhaps someone else would follow. In any case, some argued, Jesus might be merely another teacher or prophet. Especially potent was the opinion that John was a second Elijah. When the second Elijah came, the Messiah was shortly to appear. Jesus, perhaps some arguments ran, was clearly not the Messiah. Some other figure who would introduce the scenes described in John's preaching, the cleansing of the threshing floor, the burning of the chaff with fire, would come out of the horizon. As pointed out earlier, one of Luke's main objectives is to quash the idea that Elijah reappears in some way in the person of John, so that only the final stage in the apocalyptic timetable is left -- the spectacular demonstration from heaven of the Deliverer, whose arrival is to be preceded by catastrophic events in nature. Luke therefore has been at pains to dissociate Jesus' mission from too great dependence on John's appearance. The infancy narrative aimed to do justice to the importance of John, but left no doubt that he is definitely subordinate (see also Acts 1:5; 11:16; 18:25). Luke's inclusion of 3:15-16, not found in Mark, reinforces this interpretation of his intention. In any case, there emerges out of Luke's endeavor to aid the Christian community in discovery of truth, a picture of intense theological vitality. The church can move to fresh levels of understanding without disintegrating under the heat of controversy.

15. The initial words, as the people were in expectation, have a messianic orientation (cf. 7:19-20, where the word "expectation" recurs). Of special interest is the shift from the word 'crowd' or

'multitudes' (vs. 10) to the people (the Greek term is the source of the word 'laity'). "The people" in Luke's Gospel are usually presented as favorable to Jesus. Here they are viewed as expecting the Messiah. They debate within themselves about the role of John, but conclude: 'This man isn't the Messiah, is he?' The negative form of the question is Luke's way of disqualifying John for the office. By stressing that the question was in the minds (hearts) of the people and not overtly expressed, Luke is able to secure a double rejection of the hypothesis, for John replies of his own accord to their unworded question, thereby eliminating all doubt about the matter.

16. The Stronger One (mightier) is on the way, and John is not worthy even to perform a slave's deed for him -- to untie his sandals. (Matthew 3:11 highlights the slave's action with the word 'carry'). The distance between John and Jesus is strikingly affirmed in Luke's account by what he does not include, namely the Markan phrase 'after me' (Mark 1:7). As in the infancy narrative, John and Jesus appear at approximately the same time. John has only a minor chronological priority (cf. Acts 13:25). According to Jeremiah 50:34, God is the 'Strong One' who ransoms his people (see also Isaiah 11:2). Luke clearly wants the words of John about the Stronger One to be understood in reference to Jesus. John washes with water only. The Stronger One will wash them with the Holy Spirit and with fire (understood here as in Acts 2:1-3; cf. Isaiah 4:4; Ezekiel 36:25-27; Psalm 51:9-11; 1QS 4:20-26). With these words Luke aims to correct misinterpretations of the Messiah's mission as one of spectacular apocalyptic demonstration. Emphasis on the Spirit dominates his twin work (cf. Acts 1:8 and especially 2:1-3). [Note: In Acts 2:16-21 Luke applies Joel 3:1-5 (an apocalyptic text promising an outpouring of the Spirit) to the event of Pentecost that had been recited a few verses earlier. Luke 3:16 anticipates this moment that is already part of the Church's history at the time Luke was writing. Thus the evangelist is consistent in his approach to apocalyptic as he shows that apocalyptic terminology can be used to express not only future hope but events that lie in the past, for Pentecost spelled not the wind-up of history but rather the acceleration of God's ongoing mission. To state it theologically, Luke gave apocalyptic an ecclesiological dimension.]

17. Luke intends the words of vs. 17 to be understood in the light of 3:16, thus offering a corrective to those who used John's words as an endorsement for their own traditional apocalyptic viewpoints. Instead of sending fire immediately to demolish the opposition (a course rejected by Jesus at 9:54), Jesus will accomplish the separation in Israel through bestowal of the Spirit. The criterion will be sincerity of claim in recognizing Jesus as Lord (cf. 6:46-49), resulting in abundant fruit (8:15). The chaff, that is, those who rest on the pillow of meaningless liturgy, theological jargon and religious ease, will be cast off as refuse (cf. 16: 19-31; 17:25-37) in the apocalyptic moment that puts the possibility of present choice beyond recall. In brief, despite his apparent lack of credentials, Jesus is the Messiah, and words once spoken by John are to be understood in the light of God's subsequent mission carried out through Jesus and the apostolic community.

Exit of John   LUKE 3:18-20
                                          (Mark 6:17-18; Matthew 14:3-4)

The preceding analysis of Luke's interpretation of John's ministry
and preaching is confirmed by the summary in vs. 18. The key word is
in the phrase preached good news. In the original this entire phrase
is one verb, from which evangelize is derived. Luke uses the noun only
at Acts 15:7, 20:24. To Luke the good news is not a static statement of
belief that people can control (as in clever theological debate); rather, the good news breaks out in various patterns of expression as
human beings are confronted with God's rescuing action.

That John's words, some of which sound like the thunder of judgment,
should be called good news seems strange. But one man's lightning is
another man's anticipation of life-giving rain, and what John spoke of
as future became reality in Jesus' presence and at Pentecost. But even
more remarkable is the statement that his exhortation (or "encouragement"), which consisted also of moral precepts, was good news. It was
good news, for the words are a part of the pattern of the New Age. That
publicans and soldiers could be included in God's purposes without the
detours of fussy scribal guidelines -- this was a revolutionary idea
for the time. The 'multitudes' (vs. 7) heard bad news; the people (vs.
18; cf. 1:77) heard good news. It is the way in which one hears the
voice of God that spells the difference. John was impartial. To soldiers he said, 'Do your duty honorably.' To Herod Antipas, high representative of an ego-centered establishment, he said: 'You did wrong
to marry your brother's wife.' But that was only one item on the list,
and Herod could not stand the light. On top of everything else (on
the phrase, see Colossians 3:14), he clapped John in jail. It was the
finishing touch. With this brief sketch of John's last days in public
life Luke succeeds in clearing his church of any charge that its involvement with John the Baptist is subversive. John was not anti-Rome.
He was a preacher of righteousness.

Many months elapsed between John's first public appearance and his
arrest (cf. Matthew 14:3-4 and Mark 6:17-18, where the arrest is noted
as taking place during the course of Jesus' ministry). But Luke, with
the exception of one longer glance (7:18-30) and a number of brief re-
trospective references (9:7,9,19; 11:1; 16:16; 20:4,6; Acts 1:5,22;
10:37; 11:16; 13:24,25; 18:25; 19:3,4) is done with John. Like the Greek
actor who concealed his own power as he played a role subordinate to
that of the star in the performance, John gives way to the Main Player.

JESUS INTRODUCED

The Washing of Jesus   LUKE 3:21-22
(Mark 1:9-11; Matthew 3:13-17)

This episode is so important that it is introduced by the words
'and it came to pass' rendered now by RSV. Luke 16:16; Acts 1:22; 10:37
admit of no doubt concerning the importance Luke attaches to this moment. The rest of the syntax of Luke 3:21 is somewhat strained. Luke
wishes to emphasize the close association of Jesus with all the people,
in accordance with the angel's declaration (2:11), but is at pains to
separate the washing undergone by Jesus from the one received by the
people. Repentance was required of the latter, and Luke wishes to avoid
the suggestion that Jesus was included in this exhortation. In the
people's case, receipt of John's washing meant that they acknowledged
the supremacy of God in their lives; in Jesus' case it spelled his
total dedication to the Father's purpose.

His close relation to the Father is stressed through the observation that while he was praying the heaven was opened. Luke's accounts
of Jesus at prayer (5:16; 6:12; 9:18,28-29; 11:1; 22:41) usually indicate a crucial moment, and his language is emphatic on this point --
the revelation that follows did not take place during the washing. Attestation of the Messiah is made independently of John; in a way it comes
in answer to Jesus' prayer. With the heaven opened, the Holy Spirit
descends on Jesus. The people would see nothing unusual, for he makes
his presence known through some bodily form, something that looked like
(as) a 'pigeon' (the word used at 2:24). There was a voice from heaven, but again there is no suggestion that the people were aware of it
for the words are addressed to Jesus personally (in Matthew 3:17 in-
directly, 'this one'). Luke will explain later what is the purpose of
the Spirit's descent (4:18-19) but, as often in Jewish literature, his
presence signifies divine activity. According to Isaiah 42:1, Jacob is
God's chosen servant, and God gives his Spirit to him. In Psalm 2:7
the Lord says to the king: 'You are my son, today I have begotten you.'
The words addressed to Jesus are probably a composite of these and related statements, with the word beloved doing duty for 'chosen.' The
pronoun You is emphatic. Jesus and no other is the end-time Israel of
God, God's Servant, his chosen one. Nor is the present tense in the
phrase Thou art without significance. Not John's baptism, but the Spirit
himself has given Jesus his unique role. Once more Luke expects his
readers to recall a part of the infancy narrative: 'therefore the
child . . . will be called holy, the Son of God.' (1:35) As an infant
the grace of God was with him (2:40). At the age of twelve he recognized
his obligation to the Father. After his visit to the temple, he advanced
in wisdom and stature and favor before God and men (2:52).

In Jesus God is well pleased (cf. 2:14). This means, Jesus is at
the service of the Father who claims him as his own. The Spirit will
soon demonstrate that the claim is not misplaced (4:1-13), and at the
cross Jesus will terminate the first stage of his mission with the

surrender of his spirit (23:46). Thus without any spectacular apocalyptic fanfare Jesus enters on the scene, but his credentials are all in order. As Acts 10:38 affirms, the Spirit is the one through whom he is anointed (the verb in Greek is similar to the word 'Christ' which means anointed one, and this in turn corresponds to the Hebrew term that is rendered 'Messiah').

Genealogy of the Son of God
LUKE 3:23-38
(Matthew 1:1-16)

Through his separation of John from the subsequent narrative in verses 21-22 Luke focused all attention on Jesus, but to remove any doubt whether Jesus or John is the Messiah, he follows up the announcement of Jesus' divine sonship with a genealogy. In his infancy narratives (chapters 1-2) he had adopted a system of parallel presentations. By reserving Jesus' genealogy for the position it has in chapter 3, Luke is able to highlight further the essential difference between John and Jesus, for John does not merit a genealogy.

The translation Jesus, when he began his ministry is not accurate. Luke says, 'And he was Jesus'(cf. 19:2 'and he was a chief tax collector'). With these words he emphasizes that the voice from heaven was a personal address to Jesus, not to John, and at the same time he prepares his readers for the genealogical verification of Jesus as Son of God through David's line (1:31-32). The identification is amplified with a phrase that reads literally, 'beginning about thirty years.' The word 'beginning' is important, for Luke stresses at Acts 1:22 that a replacement for Judas must be found from among those who were associated with Jesus from the time he began to go in and out among them, namely from the time of his baptism. Similarly at Acts 10:37-38, the 'beginning' of Jesus' activity in Galilee is closely associated with the anointing by the Spirit which he received after his baptism. Not without design, therefore, Luke will introduce his readers to Galilean soil (4:14) immediately after Jesus' temptation (4:1-13), and the first witnesses will be gathered in Galilee (4:38; 5:1-11).

The choice of the word 'beginning' may also indicate a desire on Luke's part to modify slightly Mark's opening words -- '*Beginning* of the Good News of Jesus Christ.' Luke could not borrow such a statement, for his prologue (1:19 and 2:10) already contained announcements of Good News, and John had preached good news (3:18). Luke therefore suggests that the question of 'beginnings' can be viewed from another angle.

The words about thirty years old, reflect theological appreciation of Jesus' distinctive mission. In the early community Jesus was apparently viewed as a Messianic high priest. According to Numbers 4:3 men from thirty years old up to fifty are to be canvassed for service in the tabernacle. But it cannot be demonstrated that Luke made such a connection. According to Genesis 41:46 Joseph was thirty years old when he entered the service of Pharaoh; David was thirty years old when he began his reign (2 Samuel 5:4); and Ezekiel received a vision at the age of thirty (Ezekiel 1:1). Joseph plays a large part in the recital of Stephen's speech (Acts 7), and 2 Samuel 5:2 contains a personal address by God to David, Jesus' ancestor, along the lines of Luke 3:22. It is quite possible that Luke, who knew that Jesus was in his thirties when he made his appearance, uses the typical age to invite readers to assess the stature of Jesus at the hand of notable figures in the Old Testament. Like Joseph or David, he comes into Israel's history at a crucial moment, and with even greater credentials. If also as a prophet, then certainly greater than Ezekiel, even as he is greater than Jonah (11:32).

Matthew placed Jesus' genealogy at the beginning of his gospel and traced his descent from Abraham, thereby placing Jesus squarely in the mainstream of Israel's history. Luke begins his genealogy with Jesus and traces him all the way back to Adam, and through Adam to God. The names in Luke's and Matthew's genealogies do not all coincide, and it has been suggested that Luke gives the descent through Mary, and Matthew through Joseph. But such interpretation of Luke's list is based on slender patristic evidence. The fact is that no satisfactory solution has yet been found, and some of the differences probably have their origin in early Christological discussion.

But the genealogy as a whole is important for at least two reasons: 1. Merely on strict grounds of legal descent, Jesus can like Adam claim affinity with God in terms of sonship, and the voice from heaven has recognized him for his specific mission. Through association with Jesus *all* mankind can find the way of return to the Father, for Jesus' mission is MANKIND. 2. The parenthetical words as was supposed (vs. 23) represent clearly Luke's understanding that the mystery of Jesus' person is not solved by taking into account mere natural processes. Jesus enjoys a special relationship with God, but without having his identification with the human race thereby vitiated. John's mother bore him in her old age, and that was most unusual, but Zechariah was his father. Jesus was born of a virgin, fathered by the Spirit. The word of the Lord came to John, but Jesus hears the voice from heaven -- 'You are my son.' John was right -- here comes the Stronger One.

ENGAGEMENT IN THE TASK   LUKE 4:1-5:11

The Temptation of Jesus   LUKE 4:1-13
                                              (Mark 1:12-13; Matthew 4:1-11)

The Spirit that came down on Jesus at the baptism remains with
him, so that Jesus is fully under the direction of God (see 1:15, 41,
67; Acts 6:3, 5; 7:55; 11:24). Thus he is marked as a wise man (cf.
Wisdom 1:4-5; 7:7; Sirach 39:6). In view of the disappointing outcome
of Jesus' life, looked at from the perspective of nationalistic hopes,
it is important that Luke establish divine sanction for all that is to
follow. This is all the more necessary since Jesus' apparent failure
to carry out the messianic assignment, as popularly understood, is presented as the consequence of diabolic opposition. The tradition of the
conflict would probably be further illuminated for those who brought
to their reading of the Lukan account concepts of the messianic high
priest engaged in combat with the arch-adversary, the devil (Testament
of Levi 18; Testament of Dan 5:10). In any event, hostility against
Jesus is not to be viewed as a proof of Jesus' lack of divine credentials but rather as a testimony to the thorough-going nature of his
program.

He is here to destroy the works of the devil, and God has assigned
him the task, for he was led by the Spirit (vs. 2). According to Romans 8:14, those who are led by the Spirit are sons of God. This means
that they are the righteous ones, and according to biblical, as well
as rabbinic thinking (Strack-Billerbeck I, 135-36), the just can anticipate temptation or a time of testing. The centurion (Luke 23:47-48)
will pronounce the verdict after the final temptation: 'No doubt about
it, this man was innocent.'

2. In the reference to forty days, there may be an echo of the
forty days and forty nights (Exodus 34:28; cf. Matthew 4:2) that Moses
spent on Mount Sinai. This possibility is supported by the fact that
both Exodus 34:28 and Luke 4:2 (cf. Matthew 4:2) observe that time was
spent in fasting (in Moses' case also no drinking of water). However,
since Luke presents Jesus also as an Elijah-figure, one might with probability conclude that these words are an echo of 1 Kings 19:8, where
Elijah's fasting for forty days and forty nights is mentioned. But a
third option remains: Deuteronomy 8:2 refers to Israel's wandering of

54

forty years in the wilderness. There she was tested to determine whether she would observe God's commandments. Since Deuteronomy 8:3 is cited by Luke, it may well have been his intention to contrast Jesus' obedience with Israel's failure. According to Mark 1:13 Jesus was tempted *during* the forty days. Matthew and Luke indicate that the recorded temptations occurred at the end of the period of fasting (but Luke does not use the technical ritual word for fasting). Through emphasis on the weakness of Jesus the magnitude of his victory is enhanced.

<u>3</u>. The <u>devil</u>, a word meaning slanderer or adversary, renders the Hebrew word <u>for</u> 'the Satan.' In the Old Testament the Satan is presented variously as an inquisitor (cf. Job 1:6-7); as one who accuses (cf. Zechariah 3:1); and ultimately as a tempter (1 Chronicles 21:1); and during the intertestamental period as one who aims to disrupt relations between God and men. In the New Testament he appears variously as the accuser (Revelation 12:10), the power of darkness (Colossians 1:13), or the ruler of this world (John 12:31). To this last claim Jesus addresses his counter-claim of the Kingdom, and in the passion account the issues are clearly defined (Luke 22:3, 31, 53).

The first temptation begins with a reference to the words addressed to Jesus after his baptism. The phrase, <u>if you are the Son of God</u>, is not to be construed as a hypothetical assertion that awaits demonstration to validate it. Rather, the status of Jesus is made the starting point of the temptation. Granted that Jesus is the Son of God, as such he ought to exercise his powers and miraculously satisfy himself with food by turning stones into <u>bread</u> (literally, 'a loaf'). Just one loaf would turn the trick. Even Israel was given manna during its wandering of forty years in the wilderness (Deuteronomy 8:2-3). Surely God's own Son, the epitome of Israel, is entitled to similar preservation. The force of the temptation, therefore, is to use power for selfish ends.

<u>4</u>. As an obedient son of God, Jesus pays heed to the words of the law <u>in</u> Deuteronomy 8:3: Man shall (that is, does) not live by bread alone (cf. Wisdom 16:26). The thought is thematic in Luke, and the Lord who renounced the tempter on this issue will repeatedly warn his followers not to give in to similar temptation (see, for example, chapter 16).

<u>5-7</u>. In the second temptation the Kingdom of God and the Kingdom of Satan are set side by side. Since mountains are ordinarily reserved by Luke for revelations from God, he says simply that the devil <u>took him up</u> (in vs. 1 Luke uses the same verb minus the preposition; the <u>tempter</u> reproduces action of the Holy Spirit); Matthew (4:8) has: 'to a very high mountain.' In a <u>moment of time</u>, that is, in a 'split second,' he shows Jesus all the pomp and circumstance of the world. The devil claims jurisdiction over all of it and promises it to Jesus on one condition: 'Recognize my supremacy.' Before Israel entered the Promised Land Moses described the goodness of the land, its cities and fertile fields, but reminded them that they were not to forget God (Deuteronomy 6:10-12).

The warning was not heeded, and now Jesus as God's end-time Israel,

his chosen Son, is confronted with a similar temptation. Will he opt
for standard success-criteria, or will he choose God's directions? Will
he question the promise of Psalm 2:8 and attempt to realize at a dis-
count the donation guaranteed in Daniel 7:14 to the Son of man? Will
his career be a mere review of power struggles of the Pharaohs, the
Nebuchadnezzars and the Caesars? Or will he play for the highest stakes
and be able to say: 'All things have been delivered to me by my Father'
(Luke 10:22), and 'as my Father appointed a kingdom for me, so do I
appoint for you that you may eat and drink at my table in my kingdom'
(22:29)? 'We can have the coronation right now,' says the tempter. But
if Jesus renounces the offer, he must feel the full destructive weight
of the 'system,' and Caiaphas and Pilate, connivers in empire, will
crush him, for there will be other takers (on false Christs, see 21:8;
cf. Revelation 13:2), and the long history of the church will reveal
how difficult it is to keep distorted political ambition from contamin-
ating the church's mission. (Not government or administration as such
is here challenged by the evangelist, but any attempt to reduce God's
revolutionary action in Jesus Christ to power-grabs in the name of
churchmanship is here given its proper ancestry).

8. The die is cast in terms of Deuteronomy 6:13: You shall worship the Lord your God, and him only shall you serve. He who astounded
his teachers at the age of twelve and reminded his parents about the
identity of his Father, now gives lessons in statecraft! His is a decisive vote for the Kingdom of God, but also a certified invitation to
the cross.

In his *Dialogues of the Dead* (14), Lucian reports the following conversation between Philip of Macedon and his son Alexander, who had been
assured by Egyptian priests that he could not fail to be victorious
since he was the offspring of Zeus-Ammon.

> *Philip*: Surely you can't deny that you are my son,
> can you, Alexander? If you had been Ammon's
> son you would not have died.

> *Alexander*: There was never a doubt in my mind that you
> were my father. I accepted the word of the
> oracle only because I thought it was good
> policy.... I had no trouble defeating the
> barbarians once they thought they were en-
> gaged in conflict with a god.

No contrast could be greater than the decision of Alexander and that
of Jesus. Alexander was a king, but identified himself as a god with a
view to domination over many nations. Jesus was the Son of God, but
established his identity as king by refusing the standard well-marked
routes to political success. Thus Jesus once and for all declared exploitation obsolete and offered a fresh definition of power as opportunity to rescue those who appear beyond hope (see Luke 19:10). Alexander tried on the mantle of deity and lay naked in death at the age of
thirty-three years. Jesus renounced the way of self-aggrandizement and

invited death, but within three days reversed the verdict of Alexander's cheap imitators.

9-13. For the third and final temptation Jesus is 'led' (rendered took, but the same word appears in the phrase 'led by the Spirit' vs. 1) to Jerusalem, to take his stand on a pinnacle of the temple. Matthew terminates his record of the temptation with the vision of the kingdoms. For him this was the climax, since Jesus, by renouncing Satan's offer, inherited through his obedience all power in heaven and on earth (Matthew 28:18). Luke prefers to end the series with Jerusalem, for his gospel begins and ends with events taking place in the capital, and the principal event is the crucifixion just outside the city. Thus the third temptation raises the main question: Will Jesus accept the cross or will he avoid it? The first two temptations coax Jesus to defy God; the third invites him to show complete 'trust' in God.

Expectations of a spectacular messianic demonstration from the temple are described in rabbinic sources (see Strack-Billerbeck I, 151), but it is debatable whether Luke had this in mind. Once more it is a question of sonship, and this is the prime concern of Luke. Perhaps the fact that the second temptation did not and could not begin with the words 'If you are the Son of God,' was an additional factor in assigning the third position to this temptation. The basic question is: In view of the outcome of events, will Jesus appear to be the Son of God? If all goes well with him, then God is on his side. If disaster overtakes him, it will be quite clear that he was in the wrong: 'Cast yourself down! You have nothing to worry about, for you are God's Son. The Scripture says, 'He will direct his angels to protect you,' and 'They will lift you up and keep you from stubbing your toes against a rock.' (See Psalm 91:11-12) This temptation is an echo from Calvary (Luke 23:35, 37,39). There he would appear to be rejected by the Father. There his enemies would 'expose' his 'blasphemy' in calling himself 'the Son of God' (22:70).

In the devil's citation of Scripture the words, 'in all your ways,' are omitted. Some interpreters have seen in this omission an insidious trick of Satan. But such interpretation is irrelevant. Biblical citations in the New Testament are frequently contracted. The point is that Jesus is tempted to determine the outcome of his mission in terms of the world's criteria for success, and a cross is scarcely a success-symbol. Jesus retorts (vs. 12) with words from Deuteronomy 6:16: 'You shall not put the Lord your God to the test.' Here the omitted words are: 'as you tested him at Massah.' If Jesus suffers, he will suffer as a righteous one (23:47). Israel suffered much, but the Lord's anger was kindled against her because of her disobedience (cf. Deuteronomy 6:15). But there is no single rule of cause and effect. The righteous can suffer because God has a purpose to fulfill, and Jesus will be obedient to the rigors of sonship. Thus all three temptations suggest that Jesus avoid the path of suffering and take the easy road to success as determined by the standard criteria. For the readers of the gospel, these temptations are a reminder not to be misled by the ignominy of Jesus' death. It was all in obedience to his task. The devil now departs from Jesus and

LUKE 4:14-19

awaits a more convenient opportunity. He will not have long to wait
(22:3).

Jesus Returns to Galilee
LUKE 4:14-15
(Mark 1:14-15; Matthew 4:12-17)

These two verses are programmatic, announcing the first phase of
Jesus' ministry. In keeping with the renunciation expressed in the
temptation episode, Jesus returns to Galilee, not to Jerusalem, the
seat of Israel's traditional power. That city will become the objective beginning at 9:51. Galilee signals the world-wide mission of the
church (cf. Acts 10:35-37). Despite the fact that Jesus follows uncon-
ventional methods to achieve success he will be victorious, for he
accepts the guidance of God (in the power of the Spirit). Beginning as
a loyal son of Israel, he teaches in the synagogs; a pattern that will
be followed also by the Apostle Paul, for the promise is first to Israel. Because of his instruction, not demonstration of power, he is
glorified by all. He who renounced the 'glory' of the kingdoms (vs. 6)
now begins to gain what Simeon prophesied (2:32).

Temptation at Nazareth
LUKE 4:16-30
(Mark 6:1-6a; Matthew 13:53-58)

Verses 14-15 had suggested success. The episode at Nazareth now
puts into bold and dramatic relief the meaning of the temptations. Success alternating with rejection -- that will be the story of Jesus' life.
To highlight Jesus' ultimate fate, Luke here uses what appears to be a
variant version of what Mark recites in Mark 6:1-5. Luke's omission of
the account at 8:56 confirms this interpretation of his editorial technique.

16-19. Ordinarily the president of the synagog would invite another
Israelite to read from the Scriptures. But in Luke's narrative Jesus
appears to make the move independently. His 'opening' of the book was
literally the unrolling of a scroll. Whether the passage chosen by the
Lord was a fixed lesson for the day cannot be determined. Nor can the
exact words read on the occasion be recovered, for Luke's rendering of
the text from Isaiah is a composite of Isaiah 61:1; 58:6; 61:2. The
inclusion of the words from Isaiah 58:6 (to set at liberty those who are
oppressed) is prompted by Luke's connection of the episode with the
preceding account of Jesus' fasting and temptation. Isaiah 58 raised
a question about fasting. The prophet's complaint is that Israel fasts
but does not understand that fasting is to be accompanied with justice.
The fast God prefers is the loosing of the 'bonds of wickedness, to
undo the thongs of the yoke, to let the oppressed go free' (Isaiah
58:6). Jesus fasted, but now we see his purpose. Satan suggested a
selfish course. Jesus aims to carry out with precision the Isaianic
program of righteousness. He does what Israel was criticized for not
doing. And for this he is to incur rejection, as the sequel shows.
(Luke 4:28-29) The words taken from Isaiah will be expanded in the

58

beatitudes (6:20-23). Jesus' primary function is to proclaim the
good news to the poor. The poor are, according to traditional expression, those who look to God for help. Unlike the rich, those who are
at ease in Zion, the poor observe God's precepts. But they are despised by the bluebloods of Israel. These words about the poor and the
sight given to the blind will be recalled on a subsequent occasion (7:
22-23). In summary, it is the Messiah's task to proclaim the acceptable year of the Lord. This is the year of Jubilee (Leviticus 25:10),
when debts were cancelled. Jesus' ministry (distinct from that of
John's, cf. 16:16) is its practical expression. In line with that emphasis Luke omits the apocalyptic phrase, 'day of vengeance of our God'
(Isaiah 61:2).

20-21. With words such as these Jesus rolled up the scroll and
returned it to the attendant. He then sat down, a teacher's customary
posture (cf. 5:3; Matthew 5:1; 23:2). With all eyes fixed on him he
began (once again the thematic word; see 3:23; Acts 10:37) to deliver
an informal homily, introduced with the statement: "Today this Scripture has been fulfilled in your hearing." Today is an important word
in Luke's gospel, stressing the immediate action of the Kingdom in contrast to future apocalyptic fireworks (2:11; 5:26; 19:5,9: 23:43).
Similar to the response described in vs. 15 is the reaction at Nazareth.
In your hearing focuses attention on the authoritative call for immediate response to the royal proclamation. Jesus did not come to establish rabbinic or ecclesiastical debating societies.

22. All spoke well of him and "wondered at the gracious words
which proceeded out of his mouth." The word gracious suggests that
the words they have heard are the words of a wise man (Sirach 21:16;
cf. Acts 14:3; 20:24, 32), and the wise man according to Jewish thought
is one who observes God's will. Deuteronomy 8:3 says that man shall
live by 'everything that proceeds out of the mouth of the Lord.' Luke
had omitted these words from his citation of the passage in 4:4 (Matthew
includes them, 4:4) and reserved the thought for this occasion. Jesus'
ministry is the commentary on the words proceeding from the mouth of
God and is a strong refutation of all devilish attempts under religious
guise to manipulate people in the interests of egocentric objectives.
The words on his lips find living expression in his total dedication.
However, the observation Is not this Joseph's son? (cf. 3:23) evokes a
warning from Jesus. The misunderstanding of his parents (2:48) is
repeated in his home town, and the reader knows that they should have
exclaimed, 'This is God's Son!' It is apparent that Luke aims to express both the positive impression that Jesus gives of his real person
and the rejection he is to endure, but the rejection must follow Jesus'
own prophetic pronouncement.

23-24. In his programmatic words Jesus had not mentioned the
judgment of the heathen coupled with glorious news of victory for Israel over her enemies. And even his message of salvation for the poor
would be a disappointment. According to the War Scroll of Qumran (see,
for example, 13-14), the poor are said to be God's instrument of salvation at the end-time, and their enemies would be delivered into their

hands. Instead of offering such apocalyptic victory Jesus calls Nazareth to judgment. The words in vs. 23 are therefore words of strong indictment. Jesus will do deeds in Capernaum (cf. 4:31) that he will later refuse to do in Nazareth because of its unbelief. Gentiles and strangers will receive him, but not his own family circle (cf. 8:19-21). Note: Through the use of the future tense in the phrase You will quote Luke overcomes the difficulty posed by the fact that he has not yet spoken of Jesus' activity at Capernaum.

24-27. Rejection of Jesus by his own countrymen will ultimately force the message to be moved elsewhere, even as Elijah and Elisha performed their miracles outside the boundaries of the chosen people. There were many widows who might have been helped by Elijah, but a foreigner (at Zarephath) benefited from his services (1 Kings 17:9; cf. Luke 7:11-17). There were also many lepers in Israel, but only Naaman the Syrian was cured (2 Kings 5:14). On the phrase heaven was shut up, see Revelation 11:6; the phrase three years and six months suggests apocalyptic expression (cf. Daniel 7:25; Revelation 11:2; 12:6; 13:5; and see Strack-Billerbeck III, 760-761).

28-30. Through his association of Jesus' ministry with that of Elijah and Elisha, Luke once more emphasizes that Jesus' credentials are not validated by the appearance of some other Elijah-figure anticipated at the wind-up of history. As the apocalyptic language suggests ("three years and six months," "famine," "land"), the end-time is here in the presence of Jesus, but not as the end of the end-time, for no extraordinary signs generally associated with apocalyptic are given. Jesus' own share in the lot of the prophets is validation of his claim to fulfill the Isaianic program here and now. Simeon had talked of the sign to be spoken against, that the thoughts of many hearts might be revealed (2:34-35). Nazareth is a commentary on that prophecy. Satan had suggested that Jesus should test God's intention to preserve him. Jesus chose the way of obedience. At the same time Jesus, like Elijah, will be the object of official hatred. According to Deuteronomy 13:1-5 a false prophet was to be put to death. The citizens of Nazareth thought they had their man and were ready to carry out a threat once made against Jeremiah (Jeremiah 11:21). But the Father has arranged the schedule for Jesus, and the time will come when there will be no escape (cf. 20:15; 23:33). Jerusalem, headquarters of established religion, will not find challenged her monopoly on elimination of non-conforming prophets (13:33). Caiphas will let Judas 'finger' Jesus and Pilate will make the 'hit'. For the present, however, Jesus successfully evades the murderous intent of the angry crowd. And, suggests Luke, the devil was right, in a way, in what he said about 'stubbing one's toe' (see 4:10-11). Attempts to account for the departure on psychological grounds, such as 'the majesty of Jesus' bearing,' fail to do justice to the theological perspective.

Activity in Capernaum

A DEMONIAC HEALED

As stated in vs. 23, Jesus proceeds to carry out part of his ministry in Capernaum, specifically noted as a city in Galilee (see on 4:14).
As at Nazareth, he teaches on the sabbath, for his mission is first to
Israel. His word elicits astonishment, for he speaks with authority,
that is, as one who has first-hand knowledge of God. He has not learned
his theology by rote. Word, for Luke, is more than instruction. One
can be an eyewitness of this word (1:2), for it is attended with powerful action (4:36; 5:1; 7:7; 22:61; 24:19 and often in Acts). According
to Isaiah 11:4 the root out of Jesse will destroy the impious with the
breath of his mouth.

33. He who turned back the Tempter now encounters one of his
minions. The demon is described as unclean to differentiate his devilish origin from other psychic influences recognized in the Hellenistic
world. It is characteristic of Mark to describe demons as shouting with
loud voice, and Luke retains this expression.

34. Like the widow who asked Elijah whether he had come to cause
death in her family (1 Kings 17:18), the demoniac asks, What have you
to do with us?, that is, 'Why this interference?' With the citation of
the final words uttered by the demon Luke tells the reader explicitly
what Jesus' ultimate objective is -- the destruction of Satan (cf. 10:
18-19). Instead of 'Son of God' the demon says Holy One of God, a phrase
similar to the one used by the widow in her description of Elisha (2
Kings 4:9; cf. Psalm 106:16; also Judges 13:7 LXX, Vaticanus; Luke 1:
35). The word holy contrasts with unclean in vs. 33, and highlights
the conflict.

Luke's intention in his sketch of the proceedings in vss. 33-34 is
now clear. The demonized man is so controlled by the demon that he has
lost his individuality. The demon confuses the issue by suggesting
that the only way to get rid of him is to destroy the man in the process, hence the plural in the question Have you come to destroy *us*?
As the holy One of God, as one obedient to the Law (see his responses
in 4:4,8,12), Jesus should not tolerate the presence of an unclean person. In short, Jesus is put to the test. How will he preserve the
integrity of his own person and yet carry out the program of deliverance announced at Nazareth (4:18)? Either he must deliver on the apocalyptic dream and wind up history now or abandon the program announced
in his hometown. In either case the poor sufferer would be the loser.
But Jesus has resources for another option.

35. Jesus deals summarily with the demon. As one who makes a
noisy cur slink away he says: 'Quit your barking and get out of the
man.' Thus Jesus distinguishes between the man and the demon that

LUKE 4:36-40

possessed him. The demon's destructive power is engaged in a last
effort to overpower the man, but out he must come, and Luke notes that
the man was not harmed. Luke omits 'with a great cry' (see Mark 1:26),
so as to make more prominent the complete mastery Jesus has over the
demon. Thus Luke shows that delay in the arrival of the end-time is
not incompatible with the claims made for Jesus as the 'Holy One of God.'
The 'acceptable year of the Lord' (4:19) is not one spectacular moment
but the ongoing period in which God shows his deliverance through Jesus.
But let Satan know that his days are numbered.

36-37. In contrast to the people of Nazareth who looked at his
person and low position, the people at Capernaum concentrated on the
word he speaks. Satan had tried to detour Jesus, and he had good reason
for doing so, but Jesus made no 'deal' with the powers of darkness, and
he will be determined to see the battle through to the finish (cf. 10:
18-19; 22:28). For the benefit of Theophilus, who may have heard this
story (the word for report is related to the word 'informed' 1:4) Luke
has reinforced the depth of the truth contained in the report.

SIMON'S MOTHER-IN-LAW   LUKE 4:38-39
                                          (Mark 1:29-31; Matthew 8:14-15)

We are now introduced to the first of the witnesses who are to be
gathered in Galilee. As in 5:3, it is suggested that Jesus' movements
are by design. Simon's mother-in-law was afflicted with a high fever.

Jesus' fame has gone before him, and the family pleads with him to
heal her. Whereas Mark and Matthew say that she was healed at the
touch of his hand, without a word being spoken, Luke brings the account
in close connection with Jesus' mastery over the demon. Just as he had
rebuked the demon (vs. 35), so he rebukes the fever, here viewed as a
demonic effect. Thus Luke once more stresses the authority behind
Jesus' word. The cure is instantaneous, for not only does she immediately rise up (in all three synoptists there is a suggestion of resurrection power), but she also proceeded to wait on Jesus and the household.
According to Deuteronomy 28:22, fever is one of the curses Israel can
anticipate for breaking God's covenant. Jesus has come to proclaim
the good news and deliverance for the captives. Through him the curse
is removed, even as the chasm between clean and unclean was bridged
in the case of the demoniac.

MISCELLANEOUS ACTIVITY   LUKE 4:40-44
                                          (Mark 1:32-39; Matthew 8:16-17)

40. Both the healing of the demoniac and of Peter's mother-in-law
had taken place on the Sabbath day. But it would not be long before
the religious leaders got wind of it(6:7). Up to this moment there is
no hint of opposition to Jesus for healing on the sabbath. Yet awareness of the problem is evident in Luke's observation that at sundown,
that is, when the sabbath was past, the townsmen brought their sick to

62

him. Jesus, suggests Luke, is careful not to unnecessarily arouse hostility. At the same time the promise of 1:78-79 may be said to find fulfillment, but that Luke designed a connection between the passages is not certain. Luke's observation that Jesus put his hands on each of the sick points to the personal interest Jesus took in the sufferers, as well as to his lack of fear of contracting ritual defilement. (Acts 28:8-10 parallels the recitals of Luke 4:38-41.)

41. Once more demons are specifically mentioned (cf. Acts 19:12). Luke's addition to Mark's account, that the demons identified him as the Son of God, gives him an opportunity to equate this name with Jesus' role as the Christ (see on 2:11). Thus Luke suggests that the healings enumerated are in line with the program announced at Nazareth, where Jesus said that the Spirit of the Lord had anointed (literally, *christed*) him. In line with Mark's account, Luke observes that Jesus imposed silence (rebuked, as in vs. 35, 39) on the demons. Jesus refuses to receive any help from that source (cf. 11:14-20). Such advertisement could only lead to misunderstanding, and Jesus does not sponsor a personality cult. Moreover, Jesus as the Christ must suffer and die and rise again (9:22). Satan had suggested that Jesus bypass the cross. His refusal to permit the demons to identify him is a restatement of his resolution to resist the tempter. For this reason even the disciples were later forbidden to proclaim that he was the Christ (9:21). In brief, Jesus has no intention of making a spectacular apocalyptic demonstration. His real identity rests on the claims he will make before the chief priests (22:69-70) and on the cross (23:35-46).

43-44. In keeping with his practice of avoiding any popular messianic movement, Jesus resists the temptation to solidify his popularity in Capernaum. In his reply to the crowds, the words preach the good news and sent reproduce the program announced at Nazareth, for the same terms are used in vs. 18. The expression kingdom of God occurs for the first time. Some hint of it appeared in 1:33, but now, in the light of Jesus' encounter with demonic forces and in view of his program announced at Nazareth, it is clear that the Kingdom of God is a major assault on the forces of evil and a realization of Isaianic expectation. Let Theophilus know that this King is no tool to be manipulated by nationalistic interests! A divine necessity rests on him. He must (see also 9:22; 13:33; 17:25; 19:5; 22:37; 24:7, 26,44) preach the good news.

44. The concluding geographical reference, Judea, is a remarkable departure from Mark's 'Galilee' (Mark 1:39). Galilee is important to Mark as a locality, but not to Luke. In Luke, Galilee is significant primarily because of the witnesses who are gathered from that region, whereas Jerusalem is the central locale for much of the decisive action described in Luke's twin work. Reference to 'Judea' suggests activity that takes in all of Israel. 'Other ancient authorities read *Galilee*,' says the margin of RSV, but the reading 'Galilee' is apparently an attempt to bring Luke into harmony with Mark. Acts 10:37 echoes Luke 23:5 in the stress laid on Judea. Israel cannot claim lack of opportunity. It is also probable that Luke aims in vs. 44 to exonerate Jesus of subversive charges. Galilee was the hot-bed of the Zealots' liberation movement. Jesus, suggests Luke, did not limit his ministry to that area and, what is more, he disclaimed popular misconceptions of his mission. The Kingdom of God is not a demonstration of patronizing political power. Jesus renounced that in his rebuff of Satan (4:8). The Kingdom of God is God reaching out to claim what is properly his: the poor, the estranged, the outcast -- all who by established religious or social custom have been excluded from association with God. Jesus, the obedient Son of God, has come to lead men to the understanding that God is a Father who cares for them and invites them to obedient recognition of his Reign. There will be trouble only if the establishment with headquarters in downtown Jerusalem resists the validity of that claim.

The First Disciples
LUKE 5:1-11
(Mark 1:16-20; Matthew 4:18-22)

The Kingdom of God is defined more explicitly in this chapter as one of fresh relationships between God and people. Prophets viewed the basic problem of Israel as one of elimination of the sin that separated them from God. In contrast to Jesus' experience of rejection at Nazareth is his own reception of outcasts. The acceptable year of the Lord (Luke 4:19) has indeed arrived!

Mark's recital (Mark 1:16-20) of the call of the first disciples is expanded by Luke, who gives greater prominence to Peter in the narrative. Luke appears to be aware of special problems raised in the early community by those who questioned this apostle's credentials, for he had denied the Lord and had also embarrassed the mission to the Gentiles (cf. Galatians 2:11-14). Luke's account of his call therefore underwrites the legitimacy of his apostolic office. Peter qualifies as one of the witnesses required for the proclamation of God's action in Jesus Christ, and Luke suggests that he has known Jesus for some time (5:3; cf. 4:38). Since Peter was prominent in the church, it is possible that he might have been suspected of subversive activity. If such had been the case, Luke's account clarifies for Theophilus the nature of Peter's interest in One who was accused of insurrection.

1. At 4:40 the crowds came for healing. Now the emphasis is on the power of Jesus' preaching. The word of God is equivalent to the good news of the Kingdom of God (4:43). Luke will soon offer a sample of the content of Jesus' preaching (6:20-49). The press of the crowd forces Jesus to adopt the strategem of delivering his message from a boat. 2. But Luke's chief interest is in Jesus' encounter with Simon. This is apparent from Luke's emphasis on the two boats, and the fact that the fishermen (for the names of others, see Mark 1:16) were washing their nets. The night's work was over. 3. Luke suggests that Jesus chose Simon's boat by design. From this boat he kept on delivering his message to the crowds (the posture of sitting is borrowed from Mark 4:1, as indicated by the omission at Luke 8:4 of any reference to Jesus' presence in a boat). This instruction is now the setting for the episode that follows.

4. The dialogue is very compressed. Jesus tells Simon to head the boat for the deep. Simon, it is to be inferred, does so. At the deep point Jesus gives a second order: 'Men, let down your nets for a catch.' (The plural in the Greek verb is not translated by the RSV).

5-6. The picture up to this point is that of one in command of the situation. The Greek word for Master is used only by Luke (5:5; 8:24,45; 9:33,49; 17:13), and with the exception of 17:13 is found only on the lips of disciples ('teacher' is the usual expression employed by those outside the immediate circle; see 7:40; 8:49; 9:38 etc.). The term was applied in the Empire to holders of various types of administrative post. Jesus' word, Luke implies, is one of authority. But now Simon the professional informs an amateur that the fishing is simply no good, and his remarks about the long night's fruitless labor are a foil for the description of the great catch soon follows. Once more, however, the dialogue attests the authority of Jesus, and Simon orders the nets dropped. 'Blessed are those who hear the word of God and keep it' is one of Luke's repeated themes, and the fishermen have their reward, but it is more than they can handle.

7. They make frantic motions to their companions, who are still apparently on shore (vs. 2). Now both boats are so full with fish that the water laps at the gunwales. Luke's economy of description focuses all attention on the immensity of the catch in order to explain why Simon Peter reacts as he does. A normal professional experience can be taken in stride. But this Amateur finding fish in this quantity at a most unlikely hour! It can mean only one thing. He must have a first-hand contact with God -- and Simon wants no trouble from that source. Simon is not a bad man, but certainly not a model of piety, and he confesses 'I am a sinner' (cf. 1 Samuel 6:20). The term sinful man describes a mass of people classified by the Pharisees as outcasts, not entitled to God's favor (see above on 3:12).

8. Instead of 'Master' (vs. 5) Simon terminates his request with the word Lord, a clear link of the confession of the Christian community with the history of Jesus. **9.** But the main point is missed if Simon's confession is traced to awareness of the sinlessness of Jesus. Luke plainly says that the confession was prompted by astonishment over the catch of fish. (According to Acts 17:25-28 and Romans 2:4 the *goodness* of God aims to bring man to repentance.) Simon's confession is one of unworthiness of such signal demonstration of God's favor. But the proclamation of the Kingdom declares that such favor is not extended on the basis of worth, and that the distance between the unclean and the holy is bridged in the person of Jesus, the Lord of the community (see on 4:33-34).

10. Luke mentions the names of Simon's partners (i.e. business-partners) who were also impressed by the catch, but Simon is singled out for a specific consolation. The words do not be afraid appear frequently in Isaiah. Instead of encouraging Simon's departure, Jesus takes him into his own profession -- catching men alive (this contrast to the threat expressed in Jeremiah 16:16 is striking). The roles are now reversed. Simon has become the amateur! By inviting him into his own program Jesus pronounces an absolution that would never be superseded. Not a word is spoken about assurance of forgiveness. Such words would be superfluous after an invitation like this. (It is a reminder that the Gospel is more than words and syllables. When the church, due to inadequate attitudes and status-patterns, fails to communicate the forgiving presence of Christ, it is questionable whether liturgical pronouncement will convince the sinner that God has better intentions.) In any event, Simon, who became an instrument of prosperity to his few fellow-fishermen, will be a source of blessing to many of God's people inside and outside Israel. On this occasion Luke introduced the name Peter ('Rock-man') (vs. 8) into the narrative. Matthew (16:13-20) will view the confession of Simon at Caesarea Philippi as the crucial moment to display the contrast between the inadequate religious establishment and the informed apostolic community. Luke sees this incident on the lake of Galilee as the moment in which the far-flung mission of the church begins to crystallize. The Kingdom of God is in action. The church's missionary movement is seen rooted in this kind of invitation to join what will soon be the apostolic circle.

   11. It is remarkable that these fisherman at the height of their most striking professional success leave all to follow Jesus (see also 5:28; 14:33). Luke could not display more forcefully: 'He taught as one having authority, and his word was with power.' (cf. 4:6) The call of Jesus is the authentic way into the presence of God. But Nazareth relied on traditional rights (4:16-30)!

COLLISION COURSE   LUKE 5:12-6:16

   A Leper Healed   LUKE 5:12-16
                                          (Mark 1:40-45; Matthew 8:1-4)

   12. At this point Luke returns to the Markan order of events for his second outcast, a leper. Just as Simon Peter had confessed himself outside the normal religious patterns of Israel, so this man is unable to participate in the liturgy of his people. The generic term 'leprosy' is recognizable especially in translations of Leviticus 13, which contains the specific order that the 'leper' is to cry out in warning, 'Unclean, unclean' (Leviticus 13:45). Unfortunately most readers of the Bible conclude that the term 'leprosy' found in most translations refers to very specific types of a disease that is associated with *Hansen's bacillus* and known clinically as *Bacillus leprae*. The latter, known as 'true leprosy', is characterized either by the formation of nodules that ultimately lead to degeneration especially of the extremities, or by loss of sensation in the nerves serving such parts of the body, or by a mixture of both. It is extremely doubtful that Leviticus 13 or the story of Naaman the Syrian in 2 Kings 5 refer to this specific disease. However, the sufferer from *Bacillus leprae* has during much of the history of the disease borne the brunt of the social and religious ostracism practiced in the name of fidelity to Moses. As if this were not enough, popular insensitivity has

also associated leprosy with sinfulness, but the Bible nowhere states that leprosy is a type of sin.

Peter had grasped the knees of Jesus as a suppliant. This man fell on his face in most humble petition and, like Peter, uses the term Lord, the form of address used by the early community in its liturgy. He asks for cleansing, a request that goes beyond a mere cure. Once more the emphasis is on Jesus' power to restore interrupted relationships, whether with God or man. The statement if you will prepares the reader for Jesus' response I will (vs. 13), with stress placed on Jesus' initiative. Luke omits Mark's reference to the anger of Jesus.

13. The fact that Jesus reaches his hand out to touch the leper is another reminder that Jesus does not contract defilement but removes it. Officialdom of course would expect 'the Holy One of God' to uphold Moses and warn the man to keep his distance. But Jesus approaches no one gingerly, and tradition, no matter how rock-ribbed, must make way for the compassion of the New Age. Since Jesus' word is one of power, the leper is cured in the instant. But Jesus does not seek notoriety for cures. His healings are but one facet of a total ministry that seeks return of the person to the Father (see Luke 15).

14. Whenever possible, if it does not jeopardize that overriding concern, Jesus observes traditional ordinances. Therefore he tells the man to show himself to the priest and perform the required ritual described in Leviticus 13-14. The phrase for a proof to the people is difficult. Literally it reads: 'as a testimony to them.' Similar expressions occur in 9:5; 21:13. Since the words that precede this phrase emphasize legal performance, Luke evidently understood the plural form 'them' in Mark 1:44 as a general reference to the religious authorities. And since the very next episode raises the question of Jesus' sense of legal responsibility, it is probable that Luke understood the phrase to say that Jesus' fidelity to the Law is beyond criticism: 'let headquarters know that we do not undermine Moses (cf. 16:31).' Some of the readers, might, of course, have understood the further implication that Jesus' deed ought to prompt appraisal of his real identity as the Messiah for, according to rabbinic thought, the healing of a leper would be tantamount to raising the dead (Strack-Billerbeck IV.2, p. 745).

In any event, Luke has again fulfilled his promise to give an orderly account (1:4). Through this incident, coupled with the story of Simon's call and the cure of the demoniac, he has sketched the basic outlines of Jesus' ministry. He could not postpone indefinitely encounter with the religious establishment. But Jesus has been guilty of no overt criticism of the priests. Even John's remarks (3:7) were addressed to the 'crowds,' without singling out the religious leaders as is done in Matthew's account (Matthew 3:7). Moreover, the ministry of Jesus and that of John have been scrupulously kept separate. Any hostility that emerges must be the result of Jesus' own peculiar activity, that of one who bridges the chasm between God and the outcast. Only in that sense can Jesus be called subversive, but the responsibility for the misunderstanding will rest with Jerusalem's presidium.

15. Whereas Jesus has been proclaiming 'the word of God' (5:1), now the 'word' (report) about Jesus goes out everywhere. Word and action are again viewed in connection, for many hear and are healed.

16. With his final sentence concerning Jesus at prayer in the wilderness (a note absent in Mark 1:45) Luke alerts his readers to a fresh phase in the ministry of Jesus. He had heard the voice from heaven in answer to his prayers. Before the series of temptations he had fasted. Now, before encountering the Pharisees and Teachers of the Law, he communes with heaven. All his work is to be understood in terms of performance of the Father's will.

A Paralytic Healed   LUKE 5:17-26
                                        (Mark 2:1-12; Matthew 9:1-8)

Although this episode initiates a new phase, the words 'and it came to pass' (omitted by RSV also in vss. 1 and 12) link the narrative to the two preceding accounts. Simon Peter, the unnamed leper, and the paralytic all have the same basic problem. From a religious standpoint they are outcasts.

17. The narrative begins with emphasis on Jesus' teaching. Word and action again join in the person of Jesus, and the subsequent miracle is not so much a revelation of Jesus' ability to heal as an interpretation of his total instruction. God is demonstrating through this contact with sinners that the forgiveness of sins spoken of in 1:77 is divine reality. It is evident that Luke attaches great importance to this incident, for Mark's 'many' (2:1) is expanded by Luke into an impressive group of personages -- from every village of Galilee, and Judea and Jerusalem. In order to focus attention on the issues raised by Jesus' activity, Luke specifically mentions 'Pharisees and teachers of the law.' In this recital we are to see matched one lone scribe against the nation's best legal experts.

The teachers of the law are also called 'scribes' and 'lawyers' in this gospel. During the Exile the Law, or Torah, became the center of attention for Israel. Gradually a special class of interpreters or scholars gained prestige and became the recognized experts. Their task was to determine practical applications of the written law, teach in the temple precincts or synagogues, and serve as judges in court of law. Writing of laws was limited to copying of the Old Testament. Attracted to their ranks were many laymen who dedicated themselves to practical observance of the law. Because of their notoriety in the New Testament they have as a class received a bad press, but their contribution to the continuity of the moral and religious life of Israel was enormous. Without them Israel might well have been assimilated beyond recall. These laymen were called Pharisees, a term variously explained as 'interpreters' (of the Scriptures) or 'separated ones.' The latter term need not carry an unsavory connotation. Rather, their zeal to observe the precepts of holiness prompted them to isolate themselves from all ritual and moral contamination. Like the Puritans and many Victorians,

who have also been maligned, they tried to stem what they considered a
secularistic tide. In the same spirit rigorous people today resist
dirty-books avalanches, obscenity in other visual media, and attempt to
hold the line for well established social, political or religious tradition. As then, zeal often begets censoriousness, invasion of personal
liberties or refusal to recognize legitimate differences in point of
view. The result is resentment toward those who question such rigorous
application of inherited precept or moral theory. The hostility toward
Jesus described in the subsequent recital is understandable. Moral
fascism is a perennial disease. And no one who interferes with the
'system' goes unscathed.

The phrase and the power of the Lord was with him to heal is unparalleled in Luke (4:14; 6:19; 8:46 display a modified form). The word
Lord is ambiguous. It could refer either to Jesus or to God, but the
context, which raises the issue whether man or God has the right to
forgive sins, suggests that God is in mind here. God is behind the
healing that is to take place, and this will mean that the forgiveness
pronounced by Jesus is validated from the same source. There is the
further suggestion that Jesus is conscious of the power available to him.
He does not proceed on his own initiative, and the bold step he is about
to take has the Father's sanction.

The solemnity of the hour is further highlighted with the words
And behold, old English for 'Now note!' The popularity of Jesus is
suggested not only by Luke's repeated reference to crowds, but by the
fearlessness of the four men who ignore the presence of the dignitaries
and let their sick friend down toward the Center of attraction. (vs.18)

19. In place of Mark's description of a thatched roof (Mark 2:4,
'made an opening' = 'dug through') Luke observes that tiles were part
of the roof.

20. Jesus saw their faith, which stood in such contrast to the un-
bending legalism of the religious leaders. The pronoun their certainly
includes the paralytic. The point is that the man and his friends are
linked in a relationship of trust that ought to characterize Israel.

Jesus responds to their faith with the words: Man, your sins are
forgiven you. The reader must infer that the sick man is here addressed.
In the popular mind sickness and sin were intimately associated (cf.
John 9:2; and see the modification of Isaiah 53:4 in Matthew 8:17), but
there is no hint in the text that the man had been guilty of some great
sin, nor that he is overwhelmed with a feeling of intense guilt. It
should be noted, furthermore, that Jesus does not explicitly say: 'I
forgive you your sin.' The words are to be rendered: 'Your sins have
been forgiven you.' This could be understood as an objective declaration
of God's absolution.

21. The scribes (experts in the Law of Moses) and Pharisees are
quick to make assumptions. Their legal minds told them, suggests Luke,
that this man could not be pronounced forgiven, for he still remains

paralyzed. Forgiveness must mean the removal of sickness (see the Qumran scroll 4Q Nahum 4). In any case, the pronounced forgiveness remains in question, and Jesus, they conclude, takes too much on himself. He must be guilty of blasphemies, for only God can forgive sin; that is, only God can determine whether a man is forgiven. The best man can do is observe the Law and hope thereby to secure God's favor.

22. All this is going on in the minds of the Pharisees, so Luke points out with the words question in your hearts, that is, 'within yourselves.' The fact that Jesus understands what is going on within them is quite a blow to their reasoning, for they question the ability of Jesus to deal with an unknown quantity. They fail to realize, however, that he had already seen another unknown quantity, the faith of the other men, and faith is a prerequisite for forgiveness.

23. Since the Pharisees have questioned the power of Jesus' words to effect a change that could not be perceived by man, Jesus asks, 'Which is easier, to *say* your sins are forgiven you, or to *say*, rise up and walk.' The point is that the one statement appears easy, for who can prove it? The second is subject to observation. Yet in either case an inference must be made. Thus all is resolved into one question: Does the word of Jesus have God's power behind it or not?

24. Jesus addresses his questioners with the words: But that you may know that the Son of man has authority on earth to forgive sins. The form of statement seems to contradict the previous interpretation that Jesus does not himself forgive sins. But this statement says that Jesus has the right to make such a pronouncement because his credentials are from God (cf. 2:14). His words are ratified not only at some future apocalyptic hour of judgment, but by God's own decision *now* on earth. (On Son of Man, see comment on 6:5.) Now for the second time he addresse the paralytic, directing him to rise and take up his bed. The command to return home is a further touch to emphasize his restoration to community. Jesus said not one word about healing. He gave the man an order such as one might give to one in good health. As in the case of the pronouncement of forgiveness an inference must be made. In and through Jesus' very presence and action God expresses his love for the individual

25. The man must have been made well, for on the spot he rose up, took his belongings, and went home. The Pharisees must grant that the same inference is valid concerning his word of forgiveness. As one would say, it must have taken effect. And all the more since it is a rabbinic axiom that God does not listen to sinners, but if one reveres God and does his will God listens to him (cf. John 9:31). The healed man glorifies God, even as the shepherds did on their return from the manger (2: 20).

26. Such amazement overtook all of them, including the Pharisees and legal experts, that they gave praise to God. Thus Luke points out that even those who later were hostile had to confess that Jesus possessed the authority he claimed. And this took place today (see on 4:21).

Banquet at the House of Levi   LUKE 5:27-39
                                         (Mark 2:13-22; Matthew 9:9-17)

ANOTHER DISCIPLE   LUKE 5:27-32
                                         (Mark 2:13-17; Matthew 9:9-13)

27-28. The story of the call of Levi continues the account of
Jesus' outreach to the outcasts. Jesus deliberately selects such a
man for his fellowship (on tax collectors, see comment on 3:12). At
the command Levi leaves everything and links himself with the fortunes
of Jesus (cf. 5:11). There is no indication that Jesus has known him
before. Once again the focus is on the power of Jesus' word to command
response. The identity of Levi has long been in dispute. Neither Mark
nor Luke mention him in their list of apostles (Mark 3:16-19; Luke 6:
14-16). Matthew 9:9 identifies him with the apostle Matthew.

29. Levi proceeds to hold a farewell party. Jesus has second
thoughts about delays of this kind (9:61), but apparently in this case
Levi is not presumed to be guilty of temporizing, and in any case a
banquet scene is desirable for the holding of such dialogue as Luke
presents in vss. 30-39 (for similar 'banquet' discourses, see 7:36-50;
10:38-42; 14:1-24; 19:1-10, and perhaps through vs. 27). Like Abraham's
celebration at the time Isaac was weaned (Genesis 21:8), this was a
great feast. Luke notes that many tax collectors were present. But in
place of Mark's 'sinners,' Luke simply records 'others who were with
them.' He lets the term 'sinners,' a contemptuous classification, come
on the lips of the Pharisees at vs. 30. Luke evidently realizes the im-
probability of Pharisees dining with tax collectors and does not include
them in the guest list. That they are in the vicinity is clear from his
narrative. Headquarters was unrelenting in its determination to get
as damaging a dossier as possible on the young upstart from Nazareth.

30. Instead of criticizing Jesus directly (as they do in Mark 2:16;
'why does *he* eat') they complain about the disciples' participation ("why
do *you* eat"). The word murmured echoes Israel's flagrant violation of
their covenant with God (see, for example, Numbers 14:26-35).

31. Jesus takes the heat off his disciples with a proverb known
in many ages of antiquity: 'The sick, not the well, require the services of a physician.' Then he explains it in terms of his own practice:
I have not come to call (invite) the righteous, but sinners to repentance.
The rabbinic classification of sinners included thieves, cutthroats,
liars, cheats, fornicators, as well as a long list of ordinary occupa-
tions. In fairness to Judaism it should be noted that rabbis did not
discourage fellowship with repentant sinners, but it is clear that Jesus'
liberality went beyond the bounds of rabbinic practice. Philosophers
were frequently charged with similar breaches of polite morality. In
defense of his association with undesirable elements, Antisthenes acidly
commented: 'Doctors associate with the sick but do not contract fevers.'

<u>32</u>. What is especially remarkable about his reply is the shift in initiative. Jesus speaks as one who does the calling or inviting. He is the host (see 14:16, where the same Greek word is rendered 'invited') even though he appears to be the guest. He chooses whom he wishes for his company, and the outcasts are especially welcome. He does not, as suggested by the Pharisees, thereby make light of or condone sin. He invites the sinner, not his sin; for he makes his invitation with a view to the guest's <u>repentance</u> (see on 3:3,8). One cannot accomplish that objective by <u>refusing</u> to associate with those in need of it (cf. 1 Corinthians 5:9-13). On the other hand, there is no need to urge repentance on <u>the righteous</u>, that is, those who are already (from the standpoint of <u>accepted</u> standards) conforming to God's will. God, of course, searches the inner being (16:15). Jesus did not encourage a phony radicalism that bought its own prestige at the cheap price of downgrading virtue.

Up to this point the Pharisees have not been a special object of attack and Luke depicts Jesus as still avoiding any ground for hostility. The Pharisees, if they are genuinely concerned about God's will, are entitled to the Kingdom, but they ought to congratulate Jesus instead of criticising him for his outreach to those they classify as 'tax collectors and sinners.' Luke speaks to his contemporary church through this account. Where the congregation complains that the minister spends too much time on reaching those outside the respected borders of the church, there the Word is being misunderstood. Both Pharisee and church are therefore warned against developing into a society of self-congratulators. And unless there is a sympathy with Jesus' stance, the Pharisee will find himself requiring repentance.

MISUNDERSTANDING: NEW VERSUS OLD   LUKE 5:33-39

The Bridegroom   LUKE 5:33-35
(Mark 2:18-20; Matthew 9:14-15)

Now Jesus is addressed directly. It is a matter of instruction, says the opposition. Other religious parties require frequent fasting and prayers, but Jesus' disciples always seem to be partying. (Despite their leader's arrest, John's disciples carried on; cf. 7:18 and Acts 18:25-19:5). In other words, Jesus violates the 'system.' In effect they charged, 'He's a liberal.' The fact is, Moses prescribed only one fast-day, the tenth of Tishri (Leviticus 16:29-34; 23:26-32; Numbers 29:7-11), but guardians of tradition increased the dosage and, as in every age, found threatening any challenge to custom by a non-conformist like Jesus. In support of Jesus' action, however, it should be observed that fasting was ordinarily thought of as a means to improve relations with the deity. But Jesus is himself the expression of God's good will; therefore banqueting rather than fasting is appropriate to the New Age that has dawned. In later times the same type of debate would take place over guitar versus organ, informal versus prescribed liturgical expression, and contemporary speech patterns versus King James English.

__33.__ At Oriental weddings the bridegroom and his relatives are the chief participants. Hence there is no mention of the bride in this account (nor in John 2:1-10).

__34.__ Jesus likens himself to a bridegroom, for the Messianic Age is a time of happiness, and a wedding is the supreme example of joy. Hosea had described Israel as a faithless wife (Hosea 2:5) and pronounced dire judgment (vss. 10-13). But there was to be a fresh betrothal in time to come (vss. 14-23). John had called for repentance in order to make that betrothal possible. Now it is bridal and festival time, and since Jews did not fast on sabbaths and festival days it would be inappropriate for the disciples to fast in the time of fulfillment for Israel's marriage to God (cf. Ephesians 5:25-27).

Jesus does not here enter into the question of prayers. Prayer and fasting are closely joined in Jewish thought, and the purpose of the fasting is to improve the praying. Jesus will later instruct his disciples how to pray (11:1-13). Whether the community will preserve habits of fasting is to be subject to local decision and not to the dictatorship of custom. Luke, by his juxtaposition of John's and Jesus' practice, suggests in vss. 33-35 that John's views on fasting are not authoritative, since Jesus disclaimed it for his own followers. Thus Luke aims to remove one other obstacle barring harmony in the church. To many the new order would at first prove confusing, for the average person finds it difficult to distinguish between the transient and the permanently valid in religious and theological matters. But responsible confusion is a small price to pay for growth in appreciation of the values of unity in creative diversity. To administrate such unity in diversity is the responsibility of the church's politicians.

The words in vs.35 on the removal of the bridegroom, followed by fasting in those days, are not introduced by Luke to support fasting practice in his time with appeal to Jesus' words. Rather, this is the first preview during Jesus' public ministry of events that will culminate at Jerusalem. As in 2:35, we have an oblique reference to Jesus' death (see also 4:29). Fasting here means that there will be great sorrow, implying the loss of their beloved associate. Luke is soon to write the words in 6:11. The gulf between Jesus and the religious leadership is widening. The latter are determined to save their pride by sacrificing the living to the dead. But beyond Jesus' own death lies the judgment on Jerusalem (cf. 17:22; 19:43-44; 21:6; 23:29). The fasting of her inhabitants will be longer than that of the disciples.

Incompatibility   LUKE 5:36-39
                                         (Mark 2:21-22; Matthew 9:16-17)

Two proverb-like illustrations point up the contrast between the New Age and the old legal system. According to Mark's wording of this saying (2:21), no one puts a patch of unshrunk cloth on an old garment, because it will pull away from the old fibers and make the hole larger. Coupled with the saying about the wineskins, this means that the old

cannot be patched up with the new, lest the old be in worse shape
than before. On the other hand, the old is not to be preserved at the
expense of the new. The new must be made available, but in new forms.
(On the figure of the garment, see Isaiah 61:10; Matthew 22:11-12;
Revelation 19:8.) According to Luke's interpretation of the saying
both the old and the new are in danger of being harmed if old and new
are mixed. Therefore he speaks not merely of a patch, but of a piece
taken from a new garment. Not only does the removal of the patch
spoil the new garment, but it does not fit in with the old. Fresh
wine put into old wineskins will ferment and break the old wineskins,
and both the wineskin and the new wine are lost. Thus two points
emerge: Lack of harmony and the loss of both. Then Luke adds a
saying not found in Mark, to the effect that tastes are difficult to
change. One prefers that to which he has become accustomed.

The point of all this is that the Pharisees should be content
with their adherence to tradition. If they wish to fast, well and good.
But they must recognize the need of a fresh approach for those who cannot share their inherited customs. The Pharisees, however, thought
their way was the only path to serve God. Their position is, of course,
understandable.

In the early church, composed also of converted Pharisees and
people who had been brought up under their tutelage, the liberalism
of Jesus would be threatening. However, an imposition of their customs
on the Gentiles would spell destruction of the fresh view of the
Gospel that made possible a broader outreach to 'tax collectors and
sinners,' who by circumstance were excluded from any hope of conformity
to the many neat distinctions of scribal law. St. Paul's approach
to the question of circumcision is an example of the application of
this principle. Let Jews within the Christian community be circum-
cised. No harm done! But Gentiles must be permitted to retain their
freedom in the Gospel. Thus both could worship together without dis-
harmony or loss to either (cf. Galatians 2:1-5; Acts 15). Similarly
in the church today old established congregations are accustomed to
certain liturgical forms or types of formulation of the truth. However,
these same formulations may be meaningless to the unconverted on the
many and varied social, economic, and intellectual fronts where the
Gospel must make its outreach. The new must not be forced on the old
and the old must not be permitted to halt the progress of the new, for
truth must never be frozen into form. Modern means of rapid communication complicate the problem, but exploration of the principles expressed
in the Gospel will, under the Spirit's direction, guide the church to
appropriate solutions. In place of division-making and sectarianism
the unity of the Spirit will be sought in terms of the creative possibilities described, for example, in Ephesians 4:12-16.

Further Misunderstanding:
    Controversy Concerning the Sabbath   LUKE 6:1-11

THRESHING OF GRAIN   LUKE 6:1-5
                                        (Mark 2:23-28; Matthew 12:1-8)

At Capernaum Jesus demonstrated his ultimate objective -- triumph
of the reign of God especially over demonic forces (4:31-44). In chapter 5 the stress was on the reception of outcasts and the questions
this would raise for traditional scribal thought. Luke 6:1-11 deals
specifically with legal issues concerning the sabbath and illustrates
the kind of freedom practiced by Jesus and the church. Thus the way is
prepared for the description of the break that eventually developed,
and which is highlighted by Luke in the selection of the 12 apostles
(6:12-16).

_1_. A marginal note in RSV calls attention to the phrase *On the
second first sabbath*, which is quite meaningless to a modern reader,
but may originally have been a reference to specifications in Leviticus
23:15-16. In any case, the action of the disciples takes place on the
sabbath. Their rubbing of the beards of wheat would therefore be tantamount to threshing and come under indictment of the sabbatical anti-
work regulation, as refined by the legal experts. Once again the liberal interpretations of Jesus threaten the security of the system!

_2-3_. Instead of approaching Jesus directly (as they do at Mark
2:24) for what appears to be a flaunting of tradition the Pharisees in
Luke's account address their rebuke, as at 5:30, to the disciples. In
the early Christian community there would be disputes between Jewish
Christians (including converted Pharisees) and Gentile Christians on
prescriptive legislation, and appeal to the Scriptures (in this case 1
Samuel 21:1-6) for justification of practice would be popular. Such
appeal to Scripture would involve some torturing of the texts, as witnessed by the admission in the *Mishnah*: 'The rules about the Sabbath .
. . are as mountains hanging by a hair, for (teaching of) Scripture
(thereon) is scanty and the rules many.' (Hagigah, 1,8).

David himself ate the bread that had been laid out on the table of
showbread facing the lampstand in the holy place of the tabernacle
(Exodus 40:22). The loaves were prepared overnight by the Levites
(1 Chronicles 9:32) and were replaced with fresh loaves each Sabbath
(1 Samuel 21:6). According to rabbinic tradition, David ate the bread
on a sabbath day (Strack-Billerbeck I, 618-619). The appeal to David's
example is therefore especially trenchant. In his reply to the Pharisees Jesus calls their attention to the fact that not only David ate,
but those who were with him. Jesus, as noted above, was not personally
charged with violation of the law, and Luke may be suggesting that
Jesus was often more permissive about the actions of others than of his
own. This, then, is the substance of the Pharisees' complaint: Jesus
ought to observe tradition and instruct his disciples properly. Thus
Luke's recital of the Pharisees' indirect attack through their rebuke

of the disciples has the added advantage (as at 5:31) of permitting
Jesus to take the initiative.

4. Jesus goes on to point out that David and his associates ate
the bread in the house of God. According to regulation, the bread was
to be eaten only in the sanctuary. But only by the priests! And this
rule is reinforced by Jesus, with the words not lawful for any but the
priests. The Pharisees in their rebuke had said 'Why are you doing what
is not lawful?' Jesus echoes their question and compels them to place
David under their own indictment. Touche!

5. Then he concludes his refutation: The Son of man is lord of the
sabbath, with "lord" in emphatic position. Members of the early community would have had no difficulty recognizing the point. The term "Son
of man" came to be understood in early Christian circles as a lofty
designation for the apocalyptic deliverer spoken of in Daniel 7 and
in the Book of Enoch. He is a royal figure, for he sits at the right
hand of God. It is possible, therefore, that this saying about the Son
of Man was included at this point as a definition or explanation of
Jesus' authority. At the same time the term Son of man in Luke's
account is an admirable double entente to express also the thought
that Jesus is distinctively identified with the human race (cf. 3:
23-38). The saying in connection with David's prerogative in the matter of the showbread would be especially appropriate since Luke has
shown that Jesus is a Davidian (cf. 1:32). According to Ezekiel 34:
20-24 a latter-day David is to feed his flock and be their shepherd.
God's sanctuary is to be set up in the midst of Israel, with David as
her prince (Ezekiel 37:24-28). Lukan genealogy with David as a pivotal
ancestor (Luke 3:31), had identified Jesus as truly one with human
kind, and therefore "The Son of man" *par excellence*. With such credentials Jesus is indeed Lord of the sabbath; and the church, guided through
him to fresh interpretation of the Scriptures, finds his authority sufficient to break with crippling tradition.

HEALING OF THE MAN WITH A WITHERED HAND
LUKE 6:6-11
(Mark 3:1-6; Matthew 12:9-14)

6. Luke modifies Mark 3:1 in such a way that the introductory words
to this episode, On another sabbath, conform to the wording of 6:1. Thus
the story recited in 6:6-11 is to be viewed as an extension of the issue
raised at vss. 1-5. Debate about the sabbath is not merely academic,
says Luke. Involved is the question whether man is more important than
the security of an establishment whose primary motives are power and
control without compassion. Once more Jesus is presented as a teacher.
As in other passages, the observation is not trivial. The basic question is about to be raised: Since Jesus breaks with tradition, can
his instruction be trusted? Once before he had healed a man on the
sabbath (4:31-35). But the present case is different. In emergencies
the rabbis granted exemption from the general prohibition against medical work on the sabbath. This man's life, however, was not in danger,
and Jesus could well wait till sundown (see on 4:40). Instead he 'makes

waves' by taking the initiative, without so much as a whispered plea
from the sick man!

7. For the first time Luke explicitly draws attention to hostility
from the ranks of the scribes and Pharisees. They watched him in the
hope of finding some facts on which they might ground an accusation.
8-9. But he knew their thoughts. Simeon had spoken of 'thoughts'
that were to be revealed (2:35). As at 5:22, Jesus uncovers their
unspoken plot. He is a prophet, yet more than a prophet. Then he
carries the battle to the opposition by ordering the man to stand as
the center of attraction and asks the experts what is lawful (the same
word as in 6:2,4; see also 14:3). His either-or inquiry focuses attention on the main purpose of the sabbath -- to preserve human beings
from harm and exploitation.

The first part of the question (vs. 9) deals with morality, the
second part with the physical well-being of another. According to
Isaiah 1:11-17, ritual observance, including observance of the sabbath,
means nothing unless attended by change of conduct and performance of
justice. Isaiah 56:2 pronounces a blessing on the man who observes
the sabbath with hands that refrain from evil. These prophetic statements are in harmony with Deuteronomy 5:12-15. The spirit of the sabbath ordinance is that man should be preserved from exploitation by his
fellowman and have the opportunity to ponder the goodness of God. Since
the sabbath is the day on which God's goodness is especially to be
noted, there is no better occasion for Jesus to display that goodness.
The church, Luke would suggest, cannot afford to debate ways and means
to preserve traditional protocol while fellowmen suffer for want of a
spokesman. Is it right to save life or to destroy it? The church
cannot avoid the summons to hear and act responsively to the groans of
humanity.

10. In the absence of any instruction from the experts Jesus
looked at all of them, evidently waiting for a response. Then he said
to the man: Stretch out your hand. It was a bold move. As in the
desert of temptation, Jesus moved in a direction from which there was
no return. To have capitulated at this moment would have meant resignation to the 'system.' Yet in the command there is no violation of
traditional rules. Jesus did not say, 'Be well.' But Jesus' word is
a word of power and the man obeys. However, it is not an automatic
reflex under the power of suggestion. Such an interpretation is typical
of rationalistic solutions proposed in the nineteenth century. His
hand was restored.

11. Now the Pharisees were in a dilemma. God does not hear sinners,
yet this man reached out his hand simply at Jesus' command. According
to their own principles God must have been at work on this sabbath day.
In any case, Jesus had not broken their rules, at least not technically.
And technicalities were their specialty! Faced with the stubborn facts,
with their own system called into question, they can respond only with
blind rage (fury) and discuss what they might do to him. The Russian
poet Yevgeny Yevtushenko, after an attack on his person on a fieldhouse

stage in St. Paul, Minnesota, complained bitterly: 'When I begin to
recite a love poem I feel hate.' He was making reference to the weird
combination of allegience to the high ideals expressed in the Bill
of Rights with denial of freedom of expression to those who are connected in some way and perhaps involuntarily with different points of
view. Jesus did not interpret Moses as a hindrance to love; entrenched
interests saw it differently. Mark concludes: 'And the Pharisees
immediately counseled with the Herodians how they might kill him' (Mark
3:6); piety was on their lips, but murder on their heart. Luke prefers,
however, to emphasize Jesus' initiative in the progress toward his
death (see 4:30; 9:22,51), and Herod's involvement will be demonstrated
in due course. The reader, however, would catch the dramatic under-
statement.

The Call of the Apostles

LUKE 6:12-16
(Mark 3:13-19; Matthew 5:1; 10:1-4)

It is apparent that Jesus must now make preparations for the survival of his mission. There is no real hope from traditional sources. To
emphasize this point Luke shifts Mark 3:13-19 ahead of Mark 3:7-12 (Luke
6:17-19). Connection with the two preceding accounts is indicated by
the phrase, 'and it came to pass' (omitted by RSV), and the words In
these days. In view of the fresh development noted at vs. 11, Jesus
ascends a mountain to pray. Luke herewith emphasizes that what follows
has divine sanction, for mountains in Luke (with the exception of 8:32)
are places of revelation. The succeeding phrase in 6:12b sounds superfluous, but since it is an amplification rather than abbreviation of
Mark 3:13, Luke, we are to infer, would have his readers note the solemnity and urgency of the recital about to take place (cf. Acts 1:24-26).

13. The events recorded in this and succeeding recitals bear resemblance to the account in Exodus 24 concerning Moses and the seventy
elders who went up a mountain to receive God's revelation of the Law.
Thus Luke again displays the continuity of Jesus' activity with the
history of Israel, yet without equating Moses with Jesus, for Jesus is
not a carbon copy of Moses.

Jesus summoned his disciples and selected twelve from their number.
In the early community "disciples" would be the church members, and
apostles the principal sponsors of the church's mission. Mark refers
to the chosen ones simply as the 'twelve,' but indicates with the verb
(rendered "Sent"), from which apostle is derived, that they have apostolic authority (Mark 3:14). Luke says that Jesus expressly named them
apostles, evidently to emphasize for the church of his day that Jesus
is the source of their authority, and that the church has its roots in
his ministry. As the center and supreme head of the kingdom operation,
Jesus selects men who will have plenipotentiary power in his name. Whether Luke was acquainted with the rabbinic term shaliach, that is, the
one who is sent as the sender himself, is questionable. But his view
of the apostolate is substantially similar.

14-16. Luke's list (like that of Acts 1:13) differs in some details from Mark's (3:17-19), owing perhaps to Luke's special researches (cf. 1:1-4). At the time he was writing not a little of the history of the church had become obscure, and the term apostle had undergone some fluidity. Not infrequently people went by two names, e.g. Saul-Paul and Simon-Peter, and this may account for some of the differences.

At 10:1 delegates are sent out two-by-two. Also here the apostles appear in pairs. Remarkable is the inclusion of Simon the Zealot. The zealots were a revolutionary party from Galilee. Mark (3:18) prefers the Aramaic transliteration 'Cananaean,' perhaps to avoid any suggestion of subversive activity within Jesus' band. Luke, however, exposes the problem and through his presentation of Jesus' message shows that also a Zealot could be used constructively by Jesus. The fact that Judas had been chosen by Jesus caused perplexity in the church. He is identified as the traitor in order to eliminate any confusion with others bearing the same name. But the identification serves also to contribute a dramatic dimension to the episode at hand in forecast of the climactic event. At the same time, the mention of his deed completes the theological focus of vs. 12. Jesus is under final orders from God. He had renounced the easy way out in the desert of temptation. Now he is led by his Father to select the one who would destroy him. Thus the church is consoled with the thought of God's providential direction. Jesus did not make a mistake. Judas was part of his destiny. Yet this does not mean that Judas was victim of a plot over which he had no control. The church is interested in the consolation, not in the ultimate question of theodicy, that is, the justifying of the ways of God with men. There is in all this the ingredient of a Greek tragedy. But Jesus' death is not viewed as a tragedy. Dramatic element, yes, but not tragedy.

KINGDOM CANDIDATES AND REQUIREMENTS   LUKE 6:17-49

Before the Sermon   LUKE 6:17-19
                                      (Mark 3:7-12; Matthew 4:23-5:1)

As noted above (see on vs. 12), Luke shifted Mark's account of the selection of the apostles in order to bring to a climax the issues raised in 6:1-11. But he also requires a place in the narrative for a sermon that will outline the type of instruction Jesus' apostles would present. The early community would, like Jesus, be harassed by the hierarchy and would therefore require authoritative guidance. Since mountains are reserved in Luke for special communication with the upper world, Luke has the sermon delivered on a level plain, *after* Jesus' descent from the mountain. Similarly Moses came down from Sinai (Exodus 34:29) and addressed Israel. Mark 3:7-12, especially in view of the crowds mentioned in Mark 3:7-8, offered the appropriate context for such a presentation. And Luke adds the thought that they came to hear (vs. 18). The great crowd of his disciples anticipates expansion of the church (cf. Acts 6:1). The recital of healings just before the sermon appropriately continues Luke's thematic demonstration of Jesus' authority in deed and word. The geographical names in 6:17 echo the list in 5:17 and make emphatic the point that this is a message for Israel as a people (cf. 2:10). Galilee, however, is not mentioned, perhaps for the reason that Mark 3:9 implies the lake of Galilee, whereas Luke shows Jesus on a level plain near a mountainside ("he came down... and stood," vs. 17). The mention of Tyre and Sidon (see Mark 3:8) may be Luke's way of hinting at the implications in the selection of an apostolic delegation. From Jerusalem to the Gentiles is a main theme of Luke's twin-work, and Tyre and Sidon suggest a broad outreach. Both at 5:17 and here at 6:17 the geographical lists add weight to what follows and emphasize the stature Jesus enjoyed as a teacher and healer. At the same time they preview the world-wide mission envisaged at 2:32 and described in detail in Acts.

18. As often, stress is laid on exorcisms. We are not permitted to forget that Jesus' battle is ultimately with Satan. Power went out from him (see on 5:17), that is, it was clear that despite the criticism of the Pharisees, God was with him. This was not magic.

19. He healed them all, without distinction and, Luke may imply, without hope of personal profit.

The Sermon on the Plain   LUKE 6:20-49

The sermon as recorded by Luke is largely paralleled in Matthew's Sermon on the Mount (Matthew 5-7). But much of Matthew's sermon is not in Luke 6 but scattered here and there in Luke's gospel (see the Introduction on the question of sources). Luke has thus far programmed his record to the stage where open hostility has flared out against Jesus. The issue of Jesus' authority and the validity of his teaching has been raised. His authority has been demonstrated in deeds. Now Luke presents his readers with a sample of his words, concluding with the strongest possible claim to authority. The basic theme of the gospel is here presented, the rich and the mighty are brought low and the humble exalted. But exaltation of the lowly does not mean apocalyptic victory, with enemies crushed in a nationalistic Armageddon. The humble can expect trouble and even persecution. Thus the apostolic community is encouraged to abide by Jesus' instruction to love the enemy and at the same time reminded not to commit the mistake of Israel in confusing formal liturgy with the performance of the divine will. A prophetic tone pervades the whole, revealing Jesus in continuity with the best in Israel's tradition, yet with the added conviction that in his person a greater one than any prophet has appeared. Thus Luke's historical sensitivity is once again displayed. What the religious opposition objects to is clearly revealed and thereby the failure of that 'system' is exposed. Thus the persecution suffered by the church is of a piece with the attack on Jesus.

WORDS OF PROMISE   LUKE 6:20-23
                                                    (Matthew 5:3,4,6,11-12)

And he lifted up his eyes on his disciples. Luke moves from the
apostles (12-16) to the crowds (17-19) and finally to the disciples.
These disciples, to be distinguished from the apostles, are of the
same order as the disciples in the early community. The instruction
they receive here is a pattern of the kind of instruction the apostles
had given to the church. The Epistle of James is an excellent example
of a parallel type of exhortation, and the inclusion of the rich in
that homily (James 4:13-5:6) suggests that the beatitudes are not
meant exclusively for the disciples, with the rest of the sermon intended for the people, as might be erroneously inferred from Luke 7:1.

    The beatitudes expand the message delivered at Nazareth. Isaiah 61
is the best commentary on these words. The word blessed in the context
means more than happy. It suggests people who are the privileged
recipients of God's special gifts. God is for them, not against them.

    Especially favored are the poor. This term, in the light of Old
Testament usage, has both an economic and a religious connotation. It
contrasts, first of all, the economically disadvantaged in Israel with
the more privileged members of the higher social strata located especially
in Jerusalem. Most of the poor were tillers of the soil or small trades-
men. Generally speaking, they observed the spirit of Israel's religion
more faithfully than did the elite in the cities. Hence they became
models of the faithful worshipper, the second connotation in the term.
They are frequently linked with the 'meek' in the Old Testament (see,
for example, Isaiah 29:18-19). This does not mean they are doormats,
but that they submit themselves to God for the purpose of carrying out
his will. Unlike many in the privileged classes, they resist the temptation to win riches through sin (cf. Luke 20:45-21:4). The nature of
their work would prevent many of them from carrying out the minutiae
stressed by the Pharisees, who were not infrequently men of wealth and
had greater leisure for religious duties. This circumstance, coupled
with the fact that the poor were often victims of oppression and had
only God to turn to for hope of rescue (see, for example Psalm 9:17-20;
70), made them special objects of compassion. Thus the term poor in
this passage is a kind of double entente, meaning both economically
poor and those who recognize their dependence on God. Matthew's 'poor
in spirit' (5:3) emphasizes the latter. But Luke uses the more general
expression because of the contrast expressed in vs. 24. Matthew's
'in spirit' may well be an interpretive addition. Josh Billings
summed the beatitude well: 'Piety, like bears, duz the best on a poor
sile.'

    In Matthew most of the beatitudes are expressed in the third person;
Luke's beatitudes are addressed in the second person; hence yours. Not
counted religiously successful by the Pharisees, the poor are here pronounced the favored recipients of the new reign ushered in by Jesus.
His frequent association with publicans and sinners is a practical demonstration of this beatitude. Thus the direct address is extraordinarily

81

authoritative. These disciples belong to Jesus. Precisely because
they are his disciples, the kingdom is theirs. By separating them from
the crowds Luke has also made it clear that the kingdom is not a 'crowd'
movement with competitive political overtones.

21. The thought in the second beatitude (cf. Luke 1:53) bears close
resemblance to themes in Psalm 37 (see especially vs. 19); 107:9; 132
(especially vs. 15); 146:7; Isaiah 49:10; 55:1-2; Ezekiel 34:29. The
third echoes Psalm 126 and Isaiah 40:1-2. In both of these beatitudes
the present misery of the poor is contrasted with a future reversal of
their lot. According to Jewish apocalyptic the fortunes of the poor
were to be redressed in a radical transformation initiated by God in
an end-time cataclysm that was to spell the downfall of the mighty. In
the popular mind this would inaugurate the long-awaited Kingdom. Luke
teaches that the Kingdom is present reality, being here in the activity
of Jesus' deed and word. Future benefits await the faithful, but only
as the climax of God's ongoing Kingdom demonstration. Of primary theological importance in these beatitudes is the assurance given to the
disciples that God's favor does not depend on external fortunes. The
theory that the quality of a man's morality could be determined by looking at his fortunes here and now ('you must be living right,' goes
the phrase) was a popular truism among writers of wisdom literature, but
was questioned also by Jesus (see Luke 13:1-9 for the sterner moral
perspective, and cf. John 9:1-3).

Obviously the beatitudes in Luke 6:21-22 are not an endorsement
for social or political inaction. They rather stress that Jesus' presence is the realization of what the psalmists and prophets in Israel
had proclaimed. Jesus is unjustly attacked by the 'system' for his
association with publicans and sinners and for what they considered his
unorthodox disinterest in their fasting regulations and sabbatical
ordinances. Yet his companions, the 'poor' in the land, are the very
ones to whom the dream for ultimate victory expressed in traditional
apocalyptic applies. As the balance of the sermon will display, Jesus
does not call them to lawlessness but to rigorous moral response.

22. Persecutions endured in the apostolic period at the hands of
Jewish opposition prompt inclusion of the fourth beatitude. Compared
with Matthew's account (5:11), two notable additions appear. The first
is the word men and the second, the Son of man. At 5:20 Luke had changed Mark's 'son' to 'man' in order to make the term Son of man (5:24)
more comprehensible. According to Jewish apocalyptic the Son of man
was a heavenly figure who would appear at the end-time. Luke's doctrine
is that Jesus is the Son of man, one who associates with man's situation here and now. This view does not exclude an apocalyptic function
but contributes to a solution of the problem of Jesus' relation to the
apocalyptic figure. That Luke identifies Jesus as the Son of man in
the present moment is clear from the nature of the consolation. Men
will excommunicate (exclude) Jesus' followers from the synagog (John
9:22; 12:42; 16:1; note also the fate of Stephen, Acts 6-7). Cast out
your name as evil means that they will be pronounced godless and impious
men (cf. Strack-Billerbeck IV, 293-333). And all this because of their

association with Jesus, the Son of man, the one who has identified
with them in their situation, and has preceded them in similar experience by being pronounced worthy of the most shameful death.

23. Despite the fact that the Son of man does not come to their
immediate rescue in an apocalyptic demonstration, the disciples are
to remain patient (cf. 8:15) and rejoice when such things happen. Indeed, they are to leap, or dance, for joy (the same word used of John
in Luke 1:41). Acts 4:23-31 records an incident in which followers of
Jesus did just that (cf. Jeremiah 31:12-14). The words for your reward
is great (cf. Jeremiah 31:16) do not intend to motivate their conduct
through expectation of a reward. Rather, the words are consolatory.
Their experience will be a sign that they are on the right road and
that they have God's endorsement (see again Acts 4:23-31). Reward as
motivation is condemned in Luke 17:7-10. In any event, the Kingdom
of God in all its fullness is theirs. As added encouragement they
have the example of the prophets, such as Jeremiah, Ezekiel and Amos.
The example of the prophets is important, for Jesus' followers might
ask themselves whether their sufferings are not in fact the consequence,
as the Pharisees would be quick to point out, of breaking faith with
Israel's traditions. Jesus, therefore, reassures them that they are
in good company. What they will experience is merely the result of
a habit in Israel, to persecute the righteous (see Stephen's speech,
Acts 7). Along such lines Jesus constantly overturned standard criteria
for success. He was not a sponsor of the going rate of exchange.

WORDS OF WOE   LUKE 6:24-26

24-25. Corresponding to the four blessings are four woes that
echo 1:52-53 and parallel Isaiah 65:13-15 and James 4-5. The word woe
expresses a sense of dreadful doom approaching. Hence in the context
it is a watchman's warning, appealing to hearers not to ignore the
inevitable summons to the bar of justice. The rich are not attacked
because they are rich, and Jesus' sermon does not pit poor against rich,
for according to Leviticus 19:15 one is not to be partial to the poor
or defer to the great. But in contrast to the poor who must rely on
God, the rich can be misled by their prosperity into neglect of God
(see Luke 12:13-21; 16:19-31). In their eyes the moral guidelines that
follow would appear ridiculous. They could not do 'business as usual'
with such precepts any more than those who think that the church's
business is to 'preach the Gospel' while refraining from criticism
of society's oppressions.

The rich have received their consolation. Like a buyer who gets
a receipt for money delivered on goods, they have their consolation
now, but it is not the 'consolation' of Luke 2:25. Hence all they can
await is lamentation. The community that heard these words looked
back on the destruction of Jerusalem and pondered their aweful fulfillment. As strife-torn cities attest, a society that lives at the expense of the future sows the wind and reaps the whirlwind. Apparent escape in the immediate moment is no proof of immunity to judgment.

83

26. Parallel to the words about persecution addressed to the poor is the warning that congratulations may be endorsement for disaster. False prophets as described here are not people who teach wrong doctrine, but are rather those who make hypocritical claim to being God's spokesmen. They operate under the guise of established tradition and are highly respected in their religious communities for maintaining the *status quo*. They make no waves and rock no boats. But they are nevertheless religious quacks, unable to offer a real remedy while they exploit people for their own ends. Bogus prophets have always enjoyed popular acclaim, for they promise peace when there is no peace. 'What you want to hear is what's right,' is their slogan. But ruin and confusion is their chief legacy to those who fawn them into deceit. Jesus does not speak like the phony prophets. He turns the people from their evil ways (cf. Jeremiah 23:21-32).

GENEROSITY IN LOVE   LUKE 6:27-35
                          (Matthew 5:44,39-42; 7:12; 5:46,45)

27. I say to you that hear. Two classes of hearers have been sketched -- the poor and the rich. The poor are receptive to God; the rich, self-sufficient. This spirit of receptivity is important, for without it there will be no response to the moral directions Jesus is about to give. Thus 'hearing' is more than catching syllables. It is openness to the Kingdom communication. It is not a wait-and-see attitude, but a conviction that the Kingdom makes claims that supersede all others. Once the stance of hearing is taken, then the doing follows. Thus the evangelist separates the demands of the Kingdom, expressed in vss. 27-30, from the grace pronounced in vss. 20-23, but in his subsequent recital, climaxed by vss. 46-49, demonstrates how interlocked are the hearing and the doing (see also 8:15,21).

Love and kindness to the enemy are enjoined in Exodus 23:4-5; Proverbs 25:21-22. Love in the abstract without performance is self-delusion. Romans 12:16-21 expands on the principle. The missionaries who returned to the Auca Indians after some of their band had been murdered required no extraordinary logic to persuade their hearers of the authenticity of their message.

28. Instead of calling God's curses down on those who vilify them, they are to ask God to channel his gifts to the enemy. Jesus' own rebuke of his disciples when they wished to rain fire down on the Samaritans (9:51-55), his concern for Jerusalem (13:34; 19:41), his prayer for his enemies (see on 23:34); Stephen's petition (Acts 7:60); and Paul's wish in behalf of his countrymen (Romans 9:3) illustrate the meaning.

In summary, verses 27-28 express a principle of non-retaliation, not non-violence. It must be kept in mind that the directions apply to a church that finds itself subject to social and religious persecution. The disciple ought to know before he takes to the road of discipleship what the cost will be (Luke 14:25-35). Having opted for

the consequences, he must be prepared to accept them. Retaliation
would defeat his profession of faith. Jesus' own attitude toward
his persecutors at his trial was a standard example for the early
community (1 Peter 2:21-25). These verses say nothing about self-
defence unrelated to religious persecution, nor do they speak to the
question of the use of legal resources when these are available. Acts
16:35-40 offers a sample of Luke's own thinking on the latter topic.
The Christian, in other words, is not to be a simpleton, but must
judge circumstances in the light of the principle that vengeance belongs to the Lord (Romans 12:19), and that he is called not to curse
but to bless.

29-30. There is a striking shift from the plural form of address
to the singular in these verses, another indication perhaps that some
of the sayings in this sermon derive from exhortations modelled after
popular types of preaching called *diatribe*. (A similar shift occurs
at James 4:11-12). Greek has separate forms for the singular and plural
in personal address. 'You' in English does duty for both.

Disciples have been called not to fasting but to righteousness,
and it may well be that the thought of Isaiah 58:4-7, even more so
than 50:6, lies behind Luke 6:29. The prophet complains that those
who claim to seek God daily (Isaiah 58:2) 'fast only to quarrel and
to fight and to hit with wicked fist' (vs. 4). The disciple is not
to perpetuate the quarrel by retaliation, much less initiate them.
Instead he is to share bread with the hungry and cover the naked
(Isaiah 58:7). The thought of sharing is reproduced in Luke 6:30.
Behind the words from him who takes away your cloak do not withhold your
coat as well may be the figure of the stern creditor who has taken
the debtor's garment as pledge (cf. Deuteronomy 24:10-13) but has not
returned it, and now comes back for the undergarment (coat) as well.
The undergarment would be the poor man's last resource. Without that
he would be naked. But he is told to give it up, an action suggesting
total reliance on God; for God is compassionate to the debtor who cries
to him in his helplessness (see Exodus 22:25-27 and Amos 2:7-8). The
creditor, in turn would stand out as a totally shameless man. Thus
these words of Jesus are an expansion of the beatitudes, for they describe the plight of the righteous, with God as his only recourse.

30. The phrase every one is more properly to be rendered 'anyone.'
This verse anticipates the discussion on motivation for lending (vss.
34-35). At this point Jesus says that the disciple is not to make
distinctions between friends and enemies, fellow-believers and unbelievers, or between those who have a good credit-rating and those who
are poor risks, perhaps because they are very poor. Begs is, therefore, too limited in meaning. Luke uses a more general term: 'asks,'
as one would do in petitioning a loan. Of him who takes away your goods,
do not ask them again. The phrase takes away does not necessarily refer
to use of force. In view of the succeeding remarks (vss. 32-35) that
express the principle behind these statements in vss. 27-30 and include
words about lending, it is probable that Luke had borrowing in mind
(so also Matthew 5:42). Luke 6:29 then describes the disciple as debtor

and vs. 30 views him as creditor. The Greek term behind the phrase do not ask them again is a commercial expression applied to one who makes demand for payment and should be rendered: 'Don't press continually for payment' That is, the disciple is not to harass the poor man, as the creditor described in the previous verse had done (cf. Sirach 20: 15).

31. The so-called Golden Rule is not original with Jesus. Homer, the epic poet (Odyssey 5, 188-189); Isocrates, the orator (Nicokles 49,1); and Seneca, Nero's chaplain (On Benefits 2,1,1) expressed a similar thought and in a positive form. Leviticus 19:18, 'Thou shalt love thy neighbor as thyself,' is akin to it. Rabbi Hillel put it in a negative form: 'That which you hate do not do to your neighbor; this is the whole law, and all the rest is commentary.' The negative form, however, permitted the priest and the Levite to pass by the wounded man (Luke 10:25-37). The rich man did not harm Lazarus, but neither did he show him any special consideration (16:19-31). On the other hand, even the positive form does not compass the possibilities of creative moral action. For I may do to another what I would wish for myself, but my need may not be his need, nor my interest his interest. Most people do in fact live by the Golden Rule: 'I want to be left alone so I leave others alone.' Or, 'I like to make my own way, and I'd like to see others make their own way, too.' Therefore, unless one has the motivation of the 'poor' (6:20), even the Golden Rule can become an instrument of self-congratulation and selfish morality. In any case, the 'Rule' is not a fundamental principle in Jesus' thought but a 'rule of thumb for the purpose of guiding those who already accept the fundamental principles of love to God and love to neighbor when they are puzzled about what to do for the best in particular cases.' (T. W. Manson, The Sayings of Jesus, 1954, p. 52). What Jesus himself understands by the Rule is shockingly radical, and vss. 32-35 cancel out most of those who crowd in to espouse it on a shallow prudential level.

32-34a. These verses cut through the bargaining system that characterizes much of standard ethics -- do good to those who can return the favor. 'He never did anything for me,' is a complaint often heard. To be seen 'in the right crowd' is the main social objective. 'But remember, I'm running a business, not a charity.' Jesus replies in withering words, even sinners do the same. Sinners, as usual in Luke, are those who from the standpoint of the Pharisees have no capacity for religion. Luke prefers the term to 'tax collector' and 'Gentiles' (Matthew 5:46-47). Even at the bottom of the scale, in the underworld, the firmest ethic is to be found. There is no stricter code, and violators may end up on the missing persons list, or eventually be found in a concrete coffin. 'Grease my palm, and I'll grease yours.' The graft changes hands, the bribes are taken, the votes are delivered, and the disciple who prides himself on what is merely the going ethical rate hears the indictment: What credit is that to you? That is, 'Why should you expect to be congratulated for that? It's normal, accepted practice' (cf. 1 Peter 2:20). Such words run counter to the standard thought of the times. Sirach 12:1-6 exemplifies the popular slogan: 'help a good man, not a sinner.'

34. Just as vss. 32-33 account for the manner of statement in vss. 27-28, so vs. 34 argues the case for liberal lending expressed in vs. 30. There is no special virtue in making a risk-free loan, says Jesus in defence of his earlier statement, 'Give to anyone who asks you.' Mosaic law forbade the taking of interest from a fellow-Israelite (Deuteronomy 23:19-20). The aim of the legislation was to protect the poor from exploitation. The godly man is one who observes this law (Psalm 15:5; Proverbs 28:8). It is clear, then, that Jesus has in mind the problem of permitting the use of money to people who because of their poverty may not be able to return it. Prudence dictates that one make a 'safe' loan that will be returned in full. But the disciple is expected to rise above the requirements of a sound banking system.

35. This verse summarizes the preceding discussion. Loving the enemy, non-partisan goodness, and willingness to lend without expecting a return are to be the characteristics of the poor, who rest their case with God (cf. Sirach 29:1-2). That directions of this kind should be given to the *poor* is itself an indication of the radical revolutionary character of Jesus' preaching. He does not aim to have the poor repeat what they themselves criticize about the rich. The phrase and your reward will be great echoes vs. 23. All this is a blow at the reciprocity system, under which favors received are a kind of I.O.U. held for payment. Much social, political, and economic injustice can be traced to the selective-favor and patronage system, with penalties for favors not delivered. Jesus disclaims the 'scratch-my-back-and-I'll-scratch-yours' or 'the now-we-owe-them' arrangement. Clearly Jesus' pronouncements are radical, running counter to all standard and accepted rules for so-called civilized existence. Yet they are largely repetition of Mosaic and prophetic pronouncement. The difference between Jesus and the prophets, however, is that Jesus in his person is the living embodiment of the validity of these sayings and expects his followers to be guided by them, for the Kingdom is here. You will be sons of the Most High, he says (cf. Sirach 4:10). In Jewish eschatological and apocalyptic writing (cf. Psalms of Solomon 17:27; Enoch 62:1) sonship with God is a privilege conferred in the New Age (see Romans 8:23; Galatians 4:5). The term "Most High" (1:32,35,76; Acts 7:48) expresses the majesty and sovereignty of God. Remarkable is the fact that Jesus identifies his disciples with a relationship attributed to himself by the angel at the annunciation (1:35). This promise is not valid only in the future but is a description of the authentic follower here and now. The Kingdom of God is God's lavish expression of himself, and Jesus is the proof of that generosity. God is kind to the ungrateful and the selfish. He who participates in the benefits of such a God through association with Jesus cannot endorse any other kind of behavior. Freely the disciple has received, and freely he must give. Experience of the Father's kindness is the source of his motivation (cf. 1 John 4:19). Thus the promise and 'reward' are really an invitation to personal identity.

ON JUDGING OTHERS   LUKE 6:36-38
                                                   (Matthew 5:48; 7:1-2)

36. This verse introduces the next major section of the sermon:
Cautious judgment of others. Verse 35b presented the motivating force
of God's kindness as a *conclusion* to the discourse that preceded it.
Now a similar motivation is offered for the discourse in vss. 37-45,
only this time the motivation *introduces* the discourse. Thus vss. 35b
and 36 are a kind of hinge on which the two major parts of the sermon
swing. In formal terms this is known as chiasmus, from the Greek letter
which looks like an 'x'. To be merciful means that one is not quick
to pounce on the evildoer, or to demand the last ounce of flesh, even
if one has a legal right to it. Matthew 5:48 is a variant form of
this saying.

37. Judge not does not mean that one glosses over sin or ignores
it. Nor are these words to be used by one who is caught in some
wrongdoing and then says to the one who admonishes him, Remember,
'Judge not!' Jesus aims to say that one is not to assume the role of
a keeper of other men's consciences. One is not to be a fault-finder,
a nit-picker, creating the impression that he shares none of the flaws
of humanity. This idea will be expanded in succeeding verses. A self-
righteous approach, therefore, is here condemned. The motivation lies
in the knowledge of God's own attitude (cf. Psalm 103:13), and you will
not be judged. God does not hunt man down, but is forgiving. Thus
these last words are parallel to those in vs. 36. On the other hand,
the words you will not be judged suggest that if one prefers to apply
an inexorable standard to his fellowmen, then he invites God to treat
him in the same fashion -- and from that judgment there is no escape!
In other words, one's attitude toward the brother does not make God
merciful to him, for Jesus plainly says, be merciful as your Father in
heaven is merciful, but to misunderstand God's forgiveness is to invoke
his judgment. To condemn not means that one does not pronounce a verdict on the other, as though he were morally or spiritually hopeless.
Expectation of better things from the other is to characterize the
disciples' approach, for God in his mercy gives sinners an opportunity
to repent. On the positive side, forgive and you will be forgiven.
Again, God's forgiveness is not the result of man's forgiveness of his
fellow man, but the one who is unforgiving shows that he does not understand forgiveness from God as an invitation to understand himself anew
in relation to others.

38. This verse sums up the preceding remarks. The picture is
taken from the oriental grain market. Grain is measured out to over-
flowing in order to insure the purchaser a full measure. The phrase
rendered will be put reads literally, 'They will give.' In the light
of the context, God is the subject. A similar use of this colloquialism
appears in 12:20,48. Our measure will become God's measure. That is,
if we deny mercy to the other we short-circuit God's mercy toward us.
A similar principle is expressed in the Lord's Prayer (11:4). A
different application of the proverb is made in Mark 4:24. In Isaiah
65:7 the figure is used of God's adverse judgment (cf. Psalm 79:12).

BLIND LEADING THE BLIND

LUKE 6:39-42
(Matthew 15:14; 10:24-25; 7:3-5)

<u>39-40</u>. This series of proverbs describes the false teachers and prepares the way for the understanding of the succeeding illustration in vss. 41-42. In one of his satires, the Roman author Persius (Satires 3,94-96) has the following dialogue:

> *Doctor:* You are quite pale.
>
> *Patient:* You look worse. Don't try your remedies on me!

The picture of the self-righteous person trying to improve others while he ignores his own weakness appears with many variations in the world's proverbial literature. Proverbs naturally do not take in the exceptions but sum up the general experience of the race. If a teacher uses incorrect grammar he can scarcely expect his pupils to become masters of rhetoric. In Matthew 10: 24-25 the pupil-teacher proverb is applied to experience of persecution, but here it refers to efforts at moral improvement. 'What you are speaks louder than what you say' sums the matter. Jesus is not opposed to tradition, but he wants the pupil to hand down instruction of first-rate quality. Luke 6:20-38 is of the essence of 'true doctrine.' Any departure therefrom falls under the indictment of 'false doctrine.' The great temptation is to debate intricacies of 'theology' rather than heed the instruction of Jesus and the apostles. 2 Timothy 2:16-23 echoes Luke 6:39 ff. by warning against such indulgence of the ego.

<u>41-42</u>. Jesus' proverbial speech was stocked with humorous contrasts. The picture is purposely overdrawn in order to make the point that any effort at moral improvement of others without taking stock of oneself is utterly ridiculous. His words do not mean that since the disciple is also a sinner he should live and let live and be blind to moral imperfections about him. Such a stance would give the green light to evil and spell the end of mutual admonition in the community. What is criticized by Jesus is the moralist's patronizing attitude, condemned also by Greek philosophers. Already in the 5th century B. C. Democritus had written: 'Better it is to correct one's own faults than those of others.' (*Fragments* 60)

<u>42</u>. Jesus sketches the approach: 'Brother, just let me get that splinter out of your eye.' But all the while this self-styled ophthalmologist ignores the beam blocking his self-assumed penetrating gaze. The follower of Christ who aims to improve others must make a frontal attack on his own moral problems, his foibles, his weaknesses, his sins. Again, this does not mean that he must first succeed in eradicating all that is sub-standard in his own life before confronting others. Rather, he must approach his brother-man as one who takes seriously God's call to repentance for himself also. Then what he says will be more convincing to others and not a matter of the pot calling the kettle black. A church, for example, that prides itself on doctrinal purity

89

and at the same time engages in division-making gouges an unbridgable credibility gap. Jesus uses the word hypocrite. Hypocrisy means to adopt a role. Disciples of Jesus are not to pose as judges when in fact they are themselves liable to judgment. The self-righteous person buys his own righteousness at the expense of denying it to others. Only the poor man in Jesus' sense of the term will be convincing to others. And he will be able to say to others,'Imitate me, as I imitate Christ' (1 Corinthians 11:1; see also 2 Thessalonians 3:9; 1 Peter 5:3; 1 Timothy 4:11-12). The reason: He sees clearly.

KNOWN BY THE FRUIT
LUKE 6:43-45
(Matthew 7:16-21; cf. 12:33-35)

These verses amplify the thought in the preceding illustrations. Good trees bear good fruit, bad trees bad fruit. "Tree" in Greek applies to a number of growing things, including what we would call plants or shrubs. A bad tree is therefore a plant that produces inedible or useless fruit. Bushes bearing beautiful berries but bitter to the taste would fall into this classification. Luke includes thorns and bramble bushes. The false teacher invites censoriousness, legalistic boot-strap lifting, judgmental and patronizing criticism (cf. James 3:10-12; Mark 7:21-22). The good, or poor man, dependent on the resources of a God whom he knows to be merciful to him, produces what is good (cf. Proverbs 11:30), for example, blessing instead of cursing, thanksgiving instead of complaint, commendation and encouragement of the brother, and honest expression of concern. The heart, the real spiritual mind-set of the individual, this is what determines goodness, and it has nothing to do with legal respectability.

It has been suggested that Jesus showed himself loveless by engaging in such critique of lovelessness. But it must be remembered that he did not discourage correction of the brother. Rather he attacked the spirit of isolationism that subverts, in the name of religion, the outreaching love of God. It may seem odd that Luke, who desired to bring together diverse parties in the church, should repeat such abrasive sentences. But forthrightness is no crime. To conceal one's own potential for evil is. Besides, no surgeon ever healed without a cut. But shun that man who enjoys the cutting more than the healing!

CONCLUSION
LUKE 6:46-49
(Matthew 7:21, 24-27)

46. This verse climaxes the preceding exhortation and serves as a transition to the concluding paragraph (47-49). The words Lord, Lord are an echo of liturgical practice. The community is reminded that it must take seriously the Lord's words. To go through the ritual without bringing forth the fruits expected from a supposedly good tree is phony religion (cf. Isaiah 5:4). If Jesus is Lord, then he is the controller of the disciple's life. And if *he* is the Lord of the disciple, then the

disciple is not lord over others. These words, then are the climax
of all that precedes. The poor are those who are prepared to make
of their lives a constant and real liturgy.

47-49. At vs. 27 Jesus said, 'I say to you who hear.' Now he
couples doing with hearing of his words (cf. 8:21; 8:15; 10:37). His
words are not theoretical statement. They are not presented as discussion themes, as theses for ecclesiastical committee work designed
to make the church think it is doing God's will because it is spend-
ing so much time talking about it. He expects his words to be carried
out. To build on rock means to hear and do. The builder on sand hears
but does not act. False prophets cause a wall to fall under a deluge
(Ezekiel 13:8-16). Jesus is God's true prophet, but more than a prophet,
for no prophet ever said,'He who comes to me is like a house built on
rock' (see also Matthew 16:13-20). His words have authority because he
is God's own Kingdom expression. His words address themselves to the
depths of man's existence. They are not interesting religious or humanitarian specimens, designed to entertain and arouse sentiment over 'such
idealistic thought.' They do not permit business as usual. An em-
bezzler caught in a crime said to the arresting officer, 'I prayed
hard.' The officer said, 'The way I see it, you tried to make a bargain. You weren't really interested in quitting.' God makes no
liturgical bargains.

JESUS' CREDENTIALS
LUKE 7:1-8:3

Recognition
LUKE 7:1-17

REMARKABLE FAITH
LUKE 7:1-10
(Matthew 8:5-10, 13)

Once more the words spoken at Nazareth (4:23) find fulfillment.
And once more Luke underlines the authority of Jesus' word with authoritative deed. Zechariah was chastised for his lack of faith (1:20) and
Mary was commended (1:45). The five men cited in 5:17-26 gained their
objective because of their faith (vs. 20). Now a centurion becomes a
model for the proper response to Jesus' authority, so eloquently asserted in 6:47-49. Matthew prefers at this point to stress Jesus' contact
with outcasts, of whom a leper is exhibit A. Unlike Moses who ascended
a mountain surrounded by barriers to keep the Israelites from approaching too closely to God, Jesus encourages such encounter. Luke, on
the other hand, had discussed Jesus' treatment of outcasts, including
the leper, in a series of recitals placed *before* the sermon. Here he
sees the issue as one of faith, and the centurion is his prize example.
Luke's recital is closer to that of Matthew 8:5-13 than that of John
4:46-54, except that in Matthew the centurion encounters Jesus personally
(in line with the motif expressed in Matthew's account of the leper),
whereas in Luke the centurion sends word through intermediaries. Through
this shape of the story Luke is able to show that even Jewish leaders

recognize Jesus' power and urge him to use it for the benefit of a
Gentile. The gesture fits Luke's Jew-to-Gentile theme and his concern
to establish continuity between Israel and the Gentiles (cf. Acts 10:
35). Not all in Israel, he suggests, shared Jerusalem's attitude
toward the Gentile mission. Matthew is concerned to show that the
apostles replace Jerusalem's hierarchy as teaching authority; therefore he naturally omits reference to any Jewish delegation.

2. The recital is marked with pathos. Centurions were officers
in charge nominally of a hundred men, although the number varied. Per-
sius, the Roman satirist, thought of them as uneducated, uncultured
blobs of humanity, totally unequipped for philosophy (*Satires* 3,
77-85; 5,189-191). Luke's refined compassion seizes on the man's
affection for his slave, a rather rare attitude in a world where slaves
were mere chattel.

3-7. At first the centurion had requested Jesus to come down
and heal his slave, but as Jesus comes near his residence he sends
a second delegation, explaining that he was neither worthy to approach
Jesus personally, nor to have him come into his house. The dialogue
captures much in few words. Jesus does not fear to contract defilement by entry into a Gentile's home (see on 5:13). On the other hand,
the centurion who would not hesitate to offend religious scruples by
entering a Jewish house if he suspected trouble, does not wish to
expose an eminent person like Jesus to undue criticism. But Luke's
chief interest in the reticence of the centurion is to highlight the
fact that Jesus heals the slave without a personal contact, and that
the centurion requires no sign but simply recognizes the authority
of Jesus' word.

8. Readers of the gospel would understand well what the centurion
meant when he said that his soldiers responded without question to
his commands. In Pompeii the body of a soldier was discovered in the
ashes, still at his post. Machine-like discipline was demanded by
Rome (see also 1 Esdras 4:1-12 on the Oriental despot). Through his
simile, then, the centurion was not equating himself with Jesus as an
authority-figure. On the contrary, his point is that if his orders
are obeyed, how much more Jesus' command (See Epictetus I,25,10 for
a Greek philosopher's viewpoint). Fishermen had learned that Jesus
was no amateur (5:1-11). But this centurion's statement is among the
finest tributes ever paid by one man to another. It was the acme of
professional courtesy. A representative of the most efficient military
machine of the time equates the power of a Galilean teacher with Caesar's
unalterable will!

9. Even Jesus marvelled (the only instance in the gospels) and
repays the courtesy with the finest compliment a Jew could give to a
Gentile: "I have not found faith like this in all Israel."

10. On their return, the messengers found the slave doing well.
Yet no specific command of healing is recorded. Not even a word was
necessary. The centurion did not require it. His faith secured the

benefit. Men like him would be among the 'poor' and they would be
living commentaries on the meaning of Jesus' word, 'Why do you call
me Lord, Lord, and not do what I say?' (6:46). Caesar was accustomed
to being addressed as 'Lord.' In Luke's account the centurion accords
this honor to Jesus (7:6). Luke 23:47 will echo this recital, and
Acts 10 is its epilogue.

RESURRECTION AT NAIN   LUKE 7:11-17

This story is peculiar to Luke and is introduced here in order
to prepare the way for the answer to John's question at 7:19. At the
same time, this account reinforces Jesus' call to faith in his word
that once more finds expression in a merciful deed. Since 7:18-35
deals with the problem of Jesus' credentials, Luke emphasizes here
that Jesus is himself an Elijah-figure, not to prove that Jesus is
therefore the Messiah, but to take the wind out of the sails of the
grossly apocalyptic-minded members of the Christian community. No
whirlwind-type apocalyptic sign is required to signal the Messiah's
arrival. Jesus in his person renders superfluous the end-time return
of Elijah. Elijah had raised the son of the widow at Zarephath, which
is located near Sidon (1 Kings 17:9-10, 17-24), and Elisha performed
a similar miracle at Shunem (2 Kings 4:32-39). Nain lies between
Endor and Shunem. Since Sidon lay outside Jesus' normal itinerary,
tradition prior to Luke appears to have fixed on Nain as the locale
for the miracle. Luke's narrative, however, is patterned in its wording
more after the account in 1 Kings than in 2 Kings. The original readers, however, would sense no problem, for Elijah and Elisha traditionally constituted two facets of a composite prophetic mission. As in
6:19-20, the disciples are distinguished from the crowd, perhaps to
set up a contrast with John's disciples (7:18).

12. Luke calls attention to the gate, for the dead were buried
outside the city. The word behold (cf. 1 Kings 17:10) calls attention
to an extraordinary circumstance. The centurion's slave had been on
the point of death (Luke 7:2), but this young man was already dead,
and his mother's plight is poignantly described. He was her sole
mainstay (cf. 8:42, 9:38; the expression only son is applied to Jesus
in John 1:18). In times when there was no social security, this was
an especially grievous calamity. We are to understand that the funeral, according to Eastern custom, was taking place on the day of the
young man's death, and probably toward evening.

13. The compassion of the crowd is superseded only by the concern
of the Lord, who meets the woman's need unasked. Luke's use of the
term the Lord is not accidental. In the presence of death, he who was
recognized by the community as Lord by virtue of his resurrection, is
about to display his mastery. His command that she stop her flow of
tears is remarkable in an Oriental setting where profuse lamentation
with hired mourners, was customary. On his lips it is a command with
promise, a call to faith.

14. Even more remarkable is the fact that he, a noted teacher in Israel, touched the bier, for contact with the dead defiles (cf. Sirach 34:25-26). But the Lord, who had previously invited himself to the centurion's house, does not contract defilement; he removes it. Great physician that he is, he encounters disaster at its depth, and his own body that will soon itself lie in death is the instrument of life. The 'bier' is a litter on which the dead man, concealed only with cloth, was being transported. As in other recitals of resurrection (cf. 8:54; John 11:43), Jesus addresses the dead man personally. The dead man is not merely a corpse, or a soul, but a person, and the pronoun you is in an emphatic position in the original text.

15. Elijah prayed three times to the Lord. Jesus speaks on his own authority, and the response is immediate. There is no delay in the restoration of the young man's powers, for he begins to speak. As Elijah had done, Jesus gives him back to his mother (1 Kings 17:23; cf. Acts 9:41). Death destroys relationships; Jesus restores them.

16. The crowd recognizes the power of God displayed in its midst (cf. Luke 2:20), for resurrection of the dead is God's prerogative. The word 'arise' that Jesus had addressed to the young man is now referred to Jesus: A great prophet has arisen among us, perhaps a reference to the popular expectation of Elijah's return. Others say, God has visited his people (see on 1:68, 78). The story circulates in all Judea, thus setting the eventual rejection of Jesus against a background of witness to his person as the instrument of God.

A parallel to this healing is frequently cited from the *Life of Apollonius of Tyana* (IV,45), a miracle worker of the second century. 'A girl had died just before she was to be married,' runs the account, 'and the bridegroom was following her bier, lamenting naturally his unfulfilled marriage. Since the girl belonged to a prominent family, the whole of Rome joined in his mourning. Apollonius, who happened to come by, witnessed their grief and said: "Put down the bier, for I shall put away the tears you shed for her." The crowd thought he would deliver a eulogy . . . but he did nothing of the sort. Instead he merely touched the girl, said something inaudible over her, and without delay awakened her. The girl spoke out loud and returned to her own home.' The biographer is skeptical, however, and suggests that there may have been a spark of life in the girl. Luke admits of no doubt that the young man was dead.

Perplexity   LUKE 7:18-50

JOHN'S QUESTION   LUKE 7:18-23
                                                          (Matthew 11:2-6)

How the functions of John the Baptist and Jesus related to one another was a heated subject of debate in the early church. According

to popular apocalyptic expectation, Elijah was to reappear at the
end-time. Some thought that John was Elijah, and therefore a fore-
runner of the Messiah, who was to make his appearance with extraordinary signs and wonders. Jesus had been acclaimed as the Messiah,
but had failed to fulfill the apocalyptic expectation. John had said
that One who was stronger than he would come and bring the refining
fire (3:16-17). Luke does not indicate that when he spoke those
words John had any idea that Jesus was indeed the Stronger One, for
the voice from heaven had spoken to Jesus, not to the people (3:22).
While he was in prison he heard about Jesus, who had a large following
and performed mighty deeds. But Jesus preached mercy, not judgment,
and associated with publicans and sinners. Could Jesus therefore
qualify as the Coming One? Luke now uses the occasion of John's perplexity to show that Jesus is indeed the Coming One. To do this,
he reinforces his doctrine that John is not Elijah (cf. the explicit
denial, John 1:21). On the contrary, Jesus is the one who carries out
the functions of Elijah; and his ministry, as sketched in the preceding portion of the gospel, is the badge of his messianic credentials.
Thus Luke eliminates John as an apocalyptic sign in the popular sense
of the term and shows that apocalyptic demonstration of the spectacular
kind envisaged for the wind-up of history is not a necessary ingredient of the Messiah's ministry. As the Coming One Jesus will enter
Jerusalem and head for death (Luke 19:38). But in due course he will
also come with apocalyptic splendor (21:27). John's mistake, like that
of many Christians in Luke's time, was to concentrate on the apocalyptic aspect. Luke corrects the error by focusing attention on the
less spectacular coming. The Kingdom of God, as Jesus will point out
later, is not subject to human verification (17:20), and it comes in
two stages. Even slight acquaintance with Luke's gospel could spare
the pains of many a calculator of the time of the second coming of
Jesus.

18. Luke had recorded at 3:20 the imprisonment of John, thus
making possible an interval in which Jesus preaches and performs acts
of mercy. Now John's disciples inform their teacher about these words
and deeds (all these things). John then sends two of his disciples
to secure an explanation from Jesus concerning his mission. Two is
the customery number of witnesses required by Mosaic Law (cf. Deuteronomy 19:15). There is no hint in the text that the disciples had
raised the question. John wants to know whether Jesus is the one who
is to come (cf. Habakkuk 2:3; Luke 3:16; the term is used of God, Revelation 1:4,8; 4:8; the imperative 'come' is addressed to Jesus in
Revelation 22:20). Put plainly, is Jesus the Messiah in the sense
John spelled it out during his ministry at the Jordan?

21. Jesus gives John's emissaries a demonstration before their
very eyes. It is now even clearer why Luke recorded a series of
sayings and healings before introducing this account concerning John.
But Jesus offers no spectacular signs, such as fire from heaven. The
miracles recorded here are similar to those presented prior to this
recital. They are rather routine for Jesus, but not earth-rocking or
heaven-shaking enough for those who looked for apocalyptic fireworks.

In other words, nothing is said or done beyond 'all these things' (vs. 18).

22. Since it is John who has the problem, the disciples are sent back to report to him what they have seen and heard. Once again the stress is on both deed and word, but the most important feature, that the poor hear the good news, climaxes the list. That Jesus performed deeds that transcend normal explanation is beyond question. That God was revealing his saving intentions through those extraordinary deeds is an affirmation of faith. Keeping these two basic propositions separate is important for resolution of debate concerning the relation of scientific and biblical truth. Christians who tend to use Jesus' miracles as props for their faith in his person need to heed the reminder that his proclamation to the poor is the primary badge of his messianic office. The authority of Jesus' word is independent of the ability of historians to establish whether an alleged miracle took place or not. God's activity is not subject to the limitations of human knowledge and any attempt to 'prove' miracles through scientific demonstration is itself a denial of belief in God's miraculous dealings. A geologist can hazard an educated guess about the age of the earth. He can neither prove nor disprove God's relation to observable phenomena. Precisely in an age that senses both the power and the futility of purely rational processes, Luke's interpretation of reality is particularly helpful.

The words of Isaiah 35:5 and 61:1 form the background for much of the recital in vs. 22, except that the curing of lepers and resurrections from the dead are not mentioned in these passages. These last two types of miracles, however, fit into the Elijah-Elisha tradition (cf. Luke 4:25-27). Thus Jesus stands clearly in the prophetic-apocalyptic anticipation, but with modifications. John is not to be 'offended' (the word for one who is caught in a trap). That is, he is not to be distressed over the absence of apocalyptic fireworks. Everything happens in its due course, but for the present, and that means also for the age of the church, the main evidence of Jesus' authority and messianic credentials is that the poor hear the good news. Those who were apocalyptically conditioned naturally expected the good news to be a promise of deliverance of oppressed Israel from her Roman enemy (cf. 1:68-74); instead Jerusalem was crushed in the revolt of A.D. 70. Luke corrects this misinterpretation by pointing out that the good news is a message of assurance to the "poor" (see on 6:20) and that they have as much title to a relationship with God as do the scribes and Pharisees. What, then, is the role of John? Luke answers this question in vss. 24-28.

JESUS' ANSWERS TO JOHN AND THE CROWDS　　　　　　LUKE 7:24-35
(Matthew 11:7-19)

The questions addressed by Jesus to the crowds are quasi-satirical.
Surely they did not go into the wilderness (see 3:7) merely to see
reeds blowing in the wilderness. Nor did they expect to audition
a prince who was dressed in fine robes. They went to see a prophet.
Yes, more than a prophet. John was a prophet's prophet. No ancient
prophet's coming had been foretold as was John's arrival. This is
the one who shares the credentials of the messenger who went before
the children of Israel in their wanderings (Exodus 23:20). Failure
to note the citation from Exodus has led many readers to think that
Jesus is referring to himself in the pronouns. But it is Israel's
way that the messenger is to prepare (cf. 1:17, the only other occurrence of this word in Luke). The voice cries out in Luke 3:4: 'Make
ready the way of the Lord.' Israel was to make ready for the arrival
of the Lord God by heeding John's call to repentance (cf. Exodus 23:
21). And John's task was to prepare the way before Israel, so that
Israel might be readied for God. In this sense he was indeed a fore-
runner. Thus by shifting Mark's citation (Mark 1:2) of the Old Testament quotation (note its absence at Luke 3:4) Luke is able to give
fresh significance to the pronoun you. The second line of the quotation is usually traced to Malachi 3:1, but it is doubtful whether Luke
so understood it; for this prophetic passage was popularly applied
to Elijah, and Luke questions popular equation of John with Elijah.
The sequence of wording does not match any passage in the Old Testament.

28. Since John's task is to prepare the people for God's demonstration of his salvation (cf. 1:76-77), revealed with finality in
Jesus, Jesus can say that John is the greatest mortal ever born. Yet
the person of least account in the kingdom of God is greater than he.
This does not mean that John is excluded from the Kingdom, but that
relatively speaking fulfillment is better than anticipation, and the
poor in Jesus' fellowship are the beneficiaries of John's proclamation to Israel. The logic is not Western but Eastern in its affirmation that the Kingdom is here.

29-30. This paragraph is found in a related form at Matthew 21:
32. In Luke's recital the words are to be understood as a continuation
of Jesus' remarks. Had Luke meant the words to be parenthetical he
would very probably have introduced vs. 31 with words such as, 'Then
he said' (cf. 19:12, following a comment by the evangelist). If Luke
construes the words as part of Jesus' conversation, then the word
this in the phrase "when they heard this" is to be dropped. In any
case, the word "this" has no counterpart in the Greek text.

The word "least" (vs. 28) prepared the way for the statement
about the tax collectors. John may be dismayed that the religious
leadership does not recognize Jesus, but their refusal does not affect
the validity of Jesus' own credentials. All the people (cf. 2:10;
3:21) and the tax collectors justified God (cf. Psalms of Solomon 2:15)

that is, declared him to be in the right and accepted John's baptism.
But Pharisees and lawyers (experts in the Law of Moses) secure in their
legal performance (cf. 3:8), rejected God's demand for a change of
heart. They refused to admit that they could be in the wrong and
declined to be baptized (cf. 20:1-8). God indeed exalts the lowly
and brings low the mighty (1:52). Hence the least becomes great (vs.
28).

31-35. Jesus now characterizes the men of this generation. The
word generation may be used simply to call attention to a particular
period in a nation's history, or it may be used in connection with
a moral judgment. Thus 'this generation' in Genesis 7:1 means 'These
wicked people.' Psalm 78:8 looks back on the fathers in the wilderness as a 'stubborn' generation. Similarly Psalm 95:10 speaks of
them as 'that generation,' loathed by God. Their unfaithful character
becomes a yardstick against which one's contemporaries may be measured.
In Psalm 24:6 the term is applied in a positive sense, and without
reference to any historical moment, to those 'who seek' the Lord, that
is, the righteous (see also Isaiah 61:3 LXX). The context always
determines the meaning. In Luke's context the words 'this generation'
are used in a negative sense, and 9:41 gives Luke's own definition:
it is an unbelieving and perverse kind of people, but not everyone
alive belongs to it (cf. Acts 2:40). The language is, of course, no
more anti-Semitic than similar statements by the prophets in the Old
Testament. Jesus is himself a Jew, proclaimed to Jew and Gentile
alike, and the revolutionary call to participate in God's salvation
beyond caste of nationality or birth is the point at which every man
is called to decision.

32. For his characterization Jesus draws on children at play who
cannot agree on the game. Some want to play wedding, others funeral.
One misses the point if the couplet is pressed and the identity of
the we is sought in John or Jesus or both. This would be Western
logic. The illustration merely focuses attention on the inability of
the participants to decide on what they want. But on one thing they
are agreed -- both John and Jesus betrayed the 'system.'

33. John is ascetic and they say he is possessed by a demon. 34.
Jesus, the Son of man (the Coming One!), joins mankind in normal patterns
of life and they heap on him obscenities (see the Targum on Deuteronomy
21:18), climaxing with the charge that he consorts with the worst in
society. Thus they endeavor to contradict the verdict expressed at
2:47. Jesus appears to shame his Father (cf. Proverbs 28:7). The fact
is, they want to be left to their own self-chosen ways. Or, to use
Luke's words, 'they rejected the purpose of God for themselves' (vs.
30).

35. The final saying, Yet wisdom is justified by all her children
(cf. Sirach 26:29 for the syntax), is best taken as a statement made
by the opposition, being a continuation of the criticism Jesus attri-
butes to those who cannot agree on the game. They stand on the side
of wisdom and declare that they will be vindicated. Jesus, they claim,

sponsors the way of the fool (cf. Proverbs 23:20-21; Sirach 15:1-8). Their judgment will be subject to scrutiny in the next account.

JESUS' REPLY TO A PHARISEE   LUKE 7:36-50

The conflict outlined in vs. 33-35 now breaks into the open. Jesus appears to be a fool, in the sense of the writers of wisdom literature, since he seems to endorse the life of harlots. The Pharisee appears to be on the side of wisdom (vs. 35; cf. Proverbs 2). The fact that a Pharisee invites Jesus to dine with him indicates that Jesus does not, as charged at vs. 34, limit his association to the worst. Jesus is no respecter of persons, not even of tax collectors and sinners.

37. The word behold calls the reader's attention to an unusual development and alerts him to the point to be made by the writer. The woman had a bad reputation in the town. Sinner is the usual equivalent for one who breaks the law of Moses. The fact that she dares to enter the house of a Pharisee is in harmony with the esteem in which Jesus was held by 'sinners.' He would not let highly-perched piety alter his customary sympathy.

38. Jesus, following the practice of the time, reclined while he was dining, and the woman stood behind him at his extended feet -- feet, it might be added, that had walked many miles to preach good news to people like her (cf. Isaiah 52:7). The translators obscure the sensitivity in Luke's choice of tenses. She did not kiss his feet once only (cf. vs. 45), and her use of the perfume was lavish. Ordinarily Pharisees were concerned about observing laws of cleanliness. Here it is the woman who, as the sequel shows, displays even more concern than the Pharisee.

39. Luke's qualifying remark, the one who had invited him, indicates that there are other Pharisees at this dinner (see vs. 49). The Pharisee's inward thought betrays his misunderstanding. A man who claims to be God's spokesman ought to know what sort of woman this is, and in that case he ought not permit this shameless display; for to be on the side of God means that sins of her kind are not to be tolerated (cf. Deuteronomy 23:18). There was no doubt about it. He had the Law on his side.

40-42. Jesus' reply to the unuttered thought is a further piece of irony in the account. He who challenged Jesus' credentials as a prophet now has his own inner mind exposed (cf. 2:35; 5:22). Jesus' urbane manner is demonstrated in his gentle treatment of the Pharisee, one of the few occasions in which a partner in dialogue is addressed by name. Respectfully, but with self-assuredness, Simon urges Jesus to have his say.

43. His response to Jesus' illustration is a grudging admission, but at least it is a response (on the silence of Jesus' opponents, see

6:9).

44-48. The content of his reply, and Jesus' verdict on it, is crucial for the understanding of the sequel. Forgiveness begets love. Simon does not understand love in such depth. Had he appreciated Jesus as an unusual gift of God he would have gone beyond expected social protocol and displayed all the courtesies that are ascribed to the woman. (On the use of oil for a guest at a banquet, see Psalm 23:5 and Amos 6:6; on the kiss, Luke 15:20; Acts 20:37; Romans 16:16; 1 Corinthians 16:20; on the foot-washing, John 13:4; 1 Timothy 5:10).

47. Jesus informs Simon not to judge in terms of traditional slots for people. The individual is to be judged not by labels but in terms of himself alone. It is evident, says Jesus, that the woman must have already received forgiveness, otherwise it would be impossible to explain such great love. And Jesus adds the phrase 'her many sins,' not in order to embarrass the woman, but to make her deed of love stand out in bolder relief. The addition also indicates that Jesus does not, as the Pharisees have complained, take sin lightly. Jesus concludes his remarks to Simon with the converse of Simon's verdict at vs. 43: The one who has experienced but little forgiveness loves little. Simon stands convicted out of his own mouth, but the rebuke is tenderly sparing in the presence of the other guests. It was, indeed, a most gracious invitation to the Kingdom, as gracious as the absolution pronounced on the woman: Your sins are forgiven (literally,'your sins have been forgiven').

49-50. The other guests now dialogue within themselves, as Simon had done earlier. Their problem is the same as that expressed in 5:21. Jesus' answer to them is a further word of benediction to the woman: Your faith has saved you; go in peace. Her faith in God's demonstration of his love through the ministry of Jesus has brought her the salvation promised in 1:71, 77; 2:11. The specifications for the New Age were clearly announced in the prologue. Jesus must meet them if he is indeed the Messiah. The words Go in peace echo 1 Samuel 1:17 and Luke 2:14. God's peace is the pronouncement of reconciliation, of a mending of the breach between himself and the sinner (cf. Isaiah 59:2). The Pharisees were correct; only God can forgive sins. But Jesus embodies in his person the divine intention. Who was the woman? Simon's name made Luke's history book. But ecclesiastical gossips have ignored Luke's genteel sensitivity in burying the woman's identity which remains unknown. In St. Louis, Missouri, a house for 'sinners' was named 'Magdala House.' There is, however, no reliable foundation for identifying the woman with Mary the Magdalene (see 8:2). In some respects the story parallels the account in John 12:1-8, and there are affinities with Mark 14:3-9 (cf. Matthew 26:6-13), especially in the choice of the name Simon.

Women Disciples

It is clear from the preceding account what Luke means with the comment that Jesus was spreading the good news of the Kingdom of God. The Kingdom is God in action claiming men for himself and breaking down the barriers of separation, whether those are sin or legalistic walls that divide the righteous from the 'sinner.' Luke's phrase 'and it came to pass' (soon afterward) signals a fresh development, reinforced by the express mention of the twelve. They, together, with the women in Jesus' company are the witnesses of his ministry that climaxes with his death and resurrection. The reference to the twelve and to the women again would suggest to Theophilus that this is scarcely a subversive movement. To the more discerning reader it would also be apparent that Jesus' choice of women for his company was highly unusual for a 'rabbi.' Women were equated with children as respects capacity for knowledge of the Torah. Some rabbis in fact questioned whether they should even be taught the Torah (Strack-Billerbeck II, 164). Non-conformist that he was, Jesus refused to permit tradition to make second-class citizens of women, whom he considered his sisters. His enemies would say, as at Luke 23:5, that it was poor judgment to flaunt custom in this way; Jesus would reply that those who hear and observe God's words belong to his family (8:21).

Among the women was Mary called Magdalene. Magdala was a little fishing village off the shore of Lake Galilee. Seven demons had been driven out of her, but there is no hint here, nor in any other portion of the gospels that she was the sinful woman mentioned in the preceding narrative. This piece of gossip was first circulated by Tertullian. Moreover, demon-possession was not construed as a sinful condition. The reference to Joanna indicates that Jesus has penetrated Herod's own establishment. Of Susanna we know nothing further. Luke's mention of many other women contributes further to our understanding of Jesus' proclamation. It was a word that reached beyond normal and accepted social restrictions. What people might think of his conduct was outweighed by his own forethought in the interests of people. Willingly the women helped provide for Jesus' company, not limiting their largesse to the leader. However, we are not to imagine that they were in constant attendance during the Lord's many travels.

EXPANSION ON THE THEME OF FAITH

Right Hearing

PARABLE OF THE SOWER
(Mark 4:1-20; Matthew 13:1-13, 18-23)

4. Luke's mention of the crowd helps prepare the reader for the significance of the recital that follows. Jesus does not accept a following in terms of sheer numbers. His Kingdom call is not propaganda

for the 'rabble,' but an invitation to accept the rigors of discipleship. No political innovator approaches his followers in such fashion.
The word parable was used earlier in 4:23; 5:36; 6:39. In those
passages it was equivalent to proverb. In 8:4 the word refers to an
extended type of illustration. Such illustration can express especially
some aspect of man's relation to God; it can also describe God's intention for, or critique of, man in general or of his people in particular. The hearer is expected to abstract from the illustration to his
own situation. Parables are not allegories, although some parables
may contain allegorical elements. In allegory there are two levels of
communication: the level that one perceives with the senses and the
philosophical or religious level. Each item on the one level usually
has a corresponding item on the other level. In most parables, however, there is a single point that the speaker or writer wishes to
make, and the individual items have no special meaning in themselves.
Parables may be explained allegorically, but if it was not the speaker's
intention to present an allegory, then such an explanation is not strictly an interpretation of the parable but an application. All of Jesus'
parables have in the course of history undergone allegorical interpretation, but a commentator has the obligation to interpret the text
as it was first meant to be understood.

5-8. Jesus' parable of the sower was not difficult to understand.
In ancient Palestine the field appears to have been plowed *after* the
seed had been broadcast by hand. Because of paths worn through the
field, rocky surfaces hidden by the remaining stubble, or patches of
weed, the sower of the seed does not have equal success with his seed.
Only that which fell on good soil amounted to anything. Jesus' concluding words, He who has ears to hear, let him hear (cf. Revelation 2:7),
bid the hearer at the very least to draw the conclusion that one must
take Jesus seriously. It is not enough to say, 'Lord, Lord' while
neglecting to heed his preaching (cf. 6:46). Anyone who heard Jesus
would know what was meant, and those who did not like the admonition
would indict themselves.

9. The request of the disciples for an interpretation of the
parable appears, in view of the simplicity of the simile, at first
sight rather remarkable. But the reader of Luke's gospel must not
forget that Luke is writing for the benefit of his contemporary church.

In Mark 4:10 the disciples ask Jesus about his parables in
general. Luke alters their question into a request for the meaning
of the parable, because he wishes to clarify further for the church
Jesus' use of parables. In the process he eliminates the uncomplimentary
remark addressed by Jesus to the disciples (Mark 4:13). Since Jesus'
parables had been misused by gnostics, who claimed special insight
into God's mysteries and looked with disdain on the untutored and less
'spiritual' members in the church, Luke aims to show that the parables were not given to conceal but to reveal the truth to all the disciples. Hence in Luke many of the parables are accompanied with some
word of explanation so that the reader might not be left in doubt about
their main intention.

__10.__ Jesus replies that there are two major classes of hearers: those who have been given the privilege of knowing the "mysteries" (secrets), and those who see but do not in reality see. The mysteries are not secret things, but the wisdom (cf. Wisdom 6:22) and purpose of God now ripening in the work of Jesus and the mission of the church (cf. Revelation 10:7; 17:7). Those who have been given the privilege to know them are the believers (cf. 6:20-23; 10:23-24; 1 Corinthians 2:12-15; Revelation 3:18). Those who see and yet do not see are the unbelievers (cf. Acts 28:23-28). The disciples therefore have the greater responsibility. Jesus' statement then means: 'You ought to know the meaning because you are the ones who have received the privilege of knowing the mysteries of the kingdom of God. The rest also hear them, as you do, in parables, but in their case a judgment takes place.' The latter think they are secure in their relationship with God and require no further enlightenment; therefore they cannot really see nor hear. In other words, the message goes past them. The fact that many in Israel had rejected the apostolic message required some explanation. Luke's wording of Jesus' reply is one form of the answer to this perplexing development. Thus the words 'in order that' (so that) do not express purpose but tragic realization (see vs. 18).

__15.__ Since application of Jesus' instruction was made by teachers in the church in accordance with the mind of Christ, under the guidance of the one Spirit, Luke does not hesitate to follow Mark in attributing the explanation to Jesus, for he is the authoritative Teacher (cf. 24:32). The four classes of hearers suggest types of response encountered by the apostolic proclamation. The word patience in vs. 15 especially points in that direction. "Patience" means endurance or perseverance and describes the disciples who hold out in the face of opposition (cf. 21:19), not succumbing like the shallow-rooted people of vs. 13, who fall away in time of temptation. The fact that the word 'patience' does not appear in Mark's recital points to Luke's editorial activity or familiarity with a variant version of sermonic material. Certainly the parable and its explanation are thoroughly in concert with Lukan thematic emphases, including faith (cf. 7:9), steadfastness in time of temptation (cf. 22:28), resistance to the enticement of material things (cf. chapter 12), and especially an undivided heart dedicated to the performance of the word that has been heard (cf. 13:22-30).

LUKE 8:16-18

"TAKE HEED HOW YOU HEAR"

LUKE 8:16-18
(Mark 4:21-25)

16. Little oil-burning lamps, notorious for their wretched
light, here serve as a lively point of departure for the subsequent
description of the revelation that takes place through Jesus.

17. The words in vs. 17 further explain the point made in vs. 10.
It may be Luke's intention to stress that Jesus has no secret communication (cf. 22:53). He has taught openly, and there is nothing subversive in his activity. But it is more probable that the words originally echoed Deuteronomy 29:29: 'The secret things belong to the
Lord our God; but things that are revealed belong to us and to our
children for ever, that we may do all the words of this law.' With
the advent of the Messiah God reveals the mysteries, that is, his
plans for the end-time, expressed without reservation in Jesus (cf.
1:78-79). However, Wisdom 6:22 may have been in Luke's mind as he read
the Markan version: 'But what wisdom is, and how she came into being,
I will declare, and I will not hide mysteries from you; but I will
trace her out from the beginning of creation, and bring the knowledge
of her into the clear light and I will not pass by the truth.' This
passage comes from a book ascribed in ancient times to Solomon (see
also Sirach 39:1-3). In 11:31, Luke reports that the queen of Sheba
came to hear Solomon's wisdom, but that a greater than Solomon is
now here. Jesus, as the supreme Wisdom-figure, reveals God's will
also to the most untutored in his following (cf. 10:21).

18. Since the revelation is so open, the hearer has all the
more responsibility to take heed how he hears. Wisdom multiplies
to the one who comes for instruction, not confutation (cf. Proverbs 1:
2-6; 9:9), and this is the meaning of the phrase, to him who has will
more be given. The mysteries of the kingdom have been given to the
disciples. These mysteries become even more meaningful to them as they
ponder their responsibility in the light of the message. The words
from him who has not . . . will be taken away express the opposite
experience and restate the thought of vs. 10b. The Markan rendering:
'and he who has not, even what he has will be taken away from him'
is rephrased by Luke to read: even what he thinks that he has will
be taken away. The sentence means: A person who is complacent, resists further instruction, and does not explore himself in the light
of Jesus' message, will experience collapse of the foundations on
which he built his false life. Thus Jesus says in 19:41-44 that the
Fall of Jerusalem was hidden from Israel's eyes. They thought they
possessed knowledge, but he was the instrument of the peace and security they thought they had in their temple. They rejected him and
lost the temple and their city. Now, in the apostolic age, Luke
recites Jesus' warning to his first disciples. The church's disciples
are not to make the same mistake that Jerusalem's inhabitants once
made. The word of Jesus calls for responsive and responsible hearing,
of the type commended by Elizabeth (1:45). In addition to this note
of admonition, the proverb conveys a forceful consolation for the
Christian community. The fact that much of Israel's religious leadership

104

rejected the apostolic proclamation led to much heart-searching.
Had the church perhaps made a mistake? Luke answers: If some do not
respond, it is not because they lacked the light. They did see, but
they did not like what they saw. Instead, they preferred their own
vision and brought their city down in ruins.

JESUS' TRUE FAMILY   LUKE 8:19-21
                                         (Mark 3:31-35; Matthew 12:46-50)

    Luke returns to Mark 3:31-35 for this account about the family
of Jesus. He omits entirely one of Mark's parables (4:26-29) and
postpones another (Mark 4:30-32; see Luke 13:18-19). Nothing is
permitted at this point to detract from the main theme: Responsive
Hearing. There is no reason to understand brothers in any other than
the usual sense. A basic rule of interpretation requires that unless
there is evidence in the text for a less customary understanding of
a term (see e.g. John 20:17, where the disciples are meant) the more
usual sense of the term is to be accepted. That Mary should not have
had other children stems from a gnostic line of thought, according to
which sexual relations are inferior to ascetic discipline. James was
one of the brothers and became leader of the church in Jerusalem (see
Acts 12:17 and ch. 15). John 7:3-5 relates the earlier hostility of
the brothers toward Jesus. The fact that in 11:28 Luke reproduces the
thought of 8:21, followed by an indictment of sign-seekers in 11:29,
suggests that the phrase desiring to see you is perhaps to be understood from the same perspective. Like Herod, Jesus' own family demands signs. Luke's inclusion of the criticism would be in harmony
with his earlier treatment of Mary at 2:48-51. Moreover, the passage
endorses the knowledge of his divine sonship possessed by Jesus at
his visit to the temple (2:49). He had heeded his Father's word (4:
1-13), and all those who through him hear and do God's word are his
family. Together with him they share the Father (6:36). Thus the
passage does not record a rejection of his own family by Jesus, but
corrects a basic misunderstanding. Whether the problem of factions
in the church, with some rallying around members of Jesus' immediate
family, lies behind Luke's record, cannot be determined with certainty.
The thought of the passage is in harmony with Luke's frequent emphasis
on the precedence of the Kingdom of God over family obligations (cf.
9:59-62; 12:51-53; 14:25-26).

Word of Power   LUKE 8:22-56

OVER THE STORM   LUKE 8:22-25
                                         (Mark 4:35-41; Matthew 8:18,23-27)

    This account continues the theme of responsive hearing. The disci-
ples (Luke does not say how many) were warned through the parable of
the sower about falling away in time of temptation (vs. 13). Now in
a moment of trial they betray the lack of faith described in the parable.

That is, they do not apply to the present situation what they have
heard from Jesus' lips.

23. Jesus fell asleep. He seems unconcerned about their peril.
And he is! For even in sleep he is in command. It is quite possible
that the recitation of this story was designed to console the church
in its conflicts and sufferings at the hand of the opposition. At
times it would appear that the Lord was not in charge.

24. Not realizing that Jesus is in their presence and that with
him they are safe, the disciples cry out, We are perishing. Instead
of Mark's 'Teacher, do you not care if we perish?' Luke allows the
twice-repeated "Master" (the same word in 5:5) to express the disciples'
agitation as well as their dissatisfaction with Jesus. There is no
hint that they expect unusual help from him. He awakens and the
word rebuked, used earlier in the recital of the demoniac (4:35)
and of Peter's mother-in-law (4: 39) is applied to his command to the
wind and wave. The response is immediate. He who tells the storm to
be still is the one who urges the disciples to hear the Word of God
and keep it.

25. Mark reads: 'Why are you afraid? Have you no faith?' Luke
omits the suggestion of cowardice (Mark 4:40) and while granting that
the disciples do have faith, Jesus asks 'Where is it?' They ought to
be watchful in the time of temptation (8:13). Their concluding question,
Who then is this? betrays the misunderstanding which prompted Jesus
earlier to say of the centurion, 'I have not found such great faith
in Israel' (7:9). If the winds obey him, how much more ought the
disciples obey him! The question also prepares the reader for the
Messianic inquiry at 9:20.

In the Psalter God is frequently pictured as having mastery of
the sea (cf. Psalm 29:3-4; 65:7; 89:9), and Luke's account practically
reproduces Psalm 107:23-29. He also may have had Psalm 78 in mind.
This psalm begins with a statement about parabolic instruction and
then goes on to describe rebellious Israel. Yet God showed his mighty
deliverance, overwhelming their enemies in the sea (Psalm 78:53). Again,
when they were suffering under their chastisements, 'the Lord awoke
as from sleep' (vs. 65; cf. Luke 8:24). They are not to be like that
part of Israel which thinks it sees, but does not see.

WORD OF POWER OVER A DEMON
LUKE 8:26-39
(Mark 5:1-20; Matthew 8:28-34)

26. The story of the Gerasene demoniac is a thematic complement
to the preceding account, for association of demons with water would
be readily grasped by Luke's readers   (Luke 11:24; cf. Strack-Billerbeck I, 493). Jesus has power over sea and demons, that is, over all that
is hostile to man. The fact that the man is associated with Gerasa,
a city two days' journey from the sea of Galilee, is an expansion
of the theme in 8:16-18. Jesus' new relations are to be found also

in an area heavily populated by Gentiles. For the outreach of the
apostolic mission this account would be especially stimulating.

27. The symptoms of the man relate to those of a manic depressive,
but such disorders are declared a part of the demonic usurpation
now being halted through the action of the Kingdom of God. As at
Acts 19:16, nakedness is one of the conditions into which men are
forced by demons.

28. He is as one among the dead, for he inhabits the tombs, a
favorite haunt of demons (cf. Strack-Billerbeck I, 491-492, with references to Deuteronomy 18:11 and Isaiah 65:4). The desperate conflict
within the man is described in terms of the great cry he emitted and
his falling at Jesus' feet. The demon, as in 4:35, seeks to gain the
mastery of Jesus by unveiling his identity. He knows that Jesus has
come to consign him to the apocalyptic pangs. Therefore he says,
'Do not torture me.' There is also a suggestion of pathos in the
man's encounter with Jesus. Will Jesus' mastery over the demon spell
the destruction of the individual who is possessed? Again, as in
1 Kings 17:18, the words What have you to do with me express the anxiety
of one who encounters the holy. But Jesus, like his prototype, comes
not to destroy, but to heal.

29. Luke accounts for the cry with the words for he had commanded
the unclean spirit to come out of the man. Mark states: 'for he
had said to him' (Mark 5:8). Luke uses the imperfect tense of the
verb: 'he was about to command the unclean spirit,' wishing to avoid
the implication that Jesus' word could be ineffectual. By shifting
Mark's description (Mark 5:4) of the unsuccessful efforts to bind
the man (Luke 8:29), Luke is able to account for the delay in the demon's
departure and prepare the ground for the subsequent dialogue. The
drama has reached a point of tension.

30. Jesus, in turn, asks the man his name. The demons, however,
assert their authority over the man and say Legion. This is not a name,
but a statistic. It is the Roman military term for a regiment and expresses the man's total bondage. Modern views of disintegration of
the man's personality are not interpretations of the text, but homiletical applications. Luke's point is that the demons have met their match
and are now suppliants.

31. They do not wish to be sent to the abyss, a word for the
depths or pit to which the dead (Romans 10:7) or evil spirits (Revelation 9:1-21) are consigned. In apocalyptic writing this fate of the
demons at the end of all things finds repeated expression (cf. 2 Peter
2:4; Jude 6; Revelation 20:1-3). Luke shows that the end of the end-
time will be but the consummation of what has already been experienced.

32. Demons are not content to wander about without inhabiting
something (cf. Luke 11:24). Since the demon spoken of in vs. 29 was
"unclean", it is appropriate that the demons request to enter the herd
of swine.

33. Deprived of their victim, the once-united legionary force
breaks up, and the swine leap into the sea. Mark says there were
about two thousand (5:13), undoubtedly one for each of the demons.
Some readers have been disturbed by the fact that Jesus' miracle
caused such wholesale destruction to helpless animals. But observations of the 'Society for the Prevention of Cruelty to Animals' are
irrelevant and contribute little to the understanding of Luke's account.
The text does not say that Jesus commanded the herd to plunge into
the sea. Both Mark and Luke clearly establish the fact that demons
can only destroy, but Jesus brings salvation (see vs. 36). And, as
is stated elsewhere, a man is worth more than sparrows (12:6-7).
Throughout the story there runs a strain of kingdom-humor. The demons
end up in the sea, but Jesus had just demonstrated his power over that
sector of the creation! Job 5:13 says that 'the schemes of the wily are
brought to a quick end.' Jesus proved it to be true also in Satan's
case.

34-37. Through the succeeding description of the reaction of the
swineherds and the citizenry, the miracle gains in power. The cured
man, now clothed, is the center of attention. Luke modifies Mark's
phrasing to get in one of his favorite words, 'saved' (healed, vs.
36). That the citizens care more for their swine than for the cure
of a townsman is not stated. Luke says great fear lay behind their
request for Jesus' departure. They are alarmed at the evidence of
powers beyond their comprehension (cf. 5:8).

38-39. At this point in the narrative Mark suggests that the
man makes his request of Jesus while Jesus is taking leave (5:18).
Luke in effect separates the departure from the subsequent dialogue.
The word return is the clue to what at first seems an unusual departure from Luke's normal practice of smoothing Mark stylistically.
This is Gentile area. Jesus returns to his own sphere, Israel, but
the man is to return to his own place. There he is to declare what
God has done for him. Luke's alteration of Mark's 'the Lord' (5:19)
is not accidental. The man "proclaims" (a standard word for apostolic
preaching) what Jesus had done for him. Luke emphasizes through his
change of wording that God is at work in Jesus. The Gerasenes, like
Israel, misunderstood Jesus. But the Gospel comes back both to Israel
and to the Gentiles through the apostolic proclamation. The man had
requested to be with Jesus (vs. 38), an alternate expression for 'follow.' Following Jesus, however, means to hear and do his word. This
can be done outside physical association with him. For the apostolic
mission this understanding was important. Preachers of the Gospel
were not to be limited to the disciples or their circle (cf. 9:49-50).

OVER SICKNESS AND DEATH   LUKE 8:40-56
                                          (Mark 5:21-43; Matthew 9:18-26)

40-42. At 7:19-20 the question was asked 'Are you the coming
one or are we to expect another.' The word waiting (8:40) is the
same word rendered 'expect' in the earlier passage, and the succeeding series of miracles is a further answer to the question. Not
all the religious leaders reject Jesus, for this president of a synagog
pleads for Jesus' help. Luke picks up at this point Mark's later
observation that the girl was 'twelve years old' (Mark 5:42), with the
slight modification "about." Thus he anticipates the woman's malady
of twelve year's standing (vs. 43), as well as suggesting perhaps that
she was ready for marriage. The father's request is for healing; the
girl, his only daughter (cf. 7:12; 9:38), is not yet dead.

43. Luke condenses Mark's discussion of the woman's problem with
the medical profession, but since he abbreviates elsewhere in the story,
it cannot be ascertained whether he does so out of professional courtesy,
especially since he declares her case medically hopeless (compare his
language in 8:27). More probably his stress on the seriousness of the
malady focuses attention on the greater power of Jesus.

44. According to Leviticus 15:25-31 a woman with a chronic case
of bloody discharge was ceremonially unclean, and strict separation
from the body of Israel was required. The woman's approach to Jesus
and her fear of discovery relate to this regulation. Superstition
and belief in magic were especially common, and not only among the
uneducated classes. The woman, therefore, thinks that she must touch
something that belongs to Jesus in order that his power might reach out
to her (cf. 5:17 and Acts 19:12). Yet her confidence in Jesus' person
is a tribute to her. She does not want to defile Jesus by touching
him personally. Instead she fixes on the most meaningful part of his
garment. Following the precept of Numbers 15:37-41, pious Israelites
wore tassels terminating in a cord of blue to remind them of God's
commandments. Jesus, from the standpoint of the 'system', was a liberal
and a non-conformist, but as a true 'son of the law', he does not protest in meaningless disregard of tradition. The woman's choice of
the fringe of his garment is remarkable, but the formulators of the
tradition behind Luke's account may have wished to emphasize that Jesus came not to judge but save. To understand this would require great
faith (see vs. 48). In any event, at her touch her malady was cured.

45. In the dialogue that follows, Peter replaces 'the disciples'
mentioned in Mark 5:31, for he is an acknowledged spokesman for the
apostolic band. 46. As at 5:17 and 6:19, power (cf. Acts 8:10) is
viewed as coming out of Jesus, that is, something of him is involved
in the healing process, even in the presence of ritual uncleanness.
Her cure is not to be ascribed to fortuitous circumstances, or to God
in the abstract.

47-48. The woman's confession is made before all the people. But
instead of a reprimand she hears an absolution, similar to the one

pronounced on the sinful woman (7:50). Not confidence in magic, but faith (cf. 8:12) had overcome ritual obstacles, for Jesus spells a New Age. The word daughter is a reminder that she is to be accepted in the family of Israel. A similar word will be spoken at 19:9 over Zacchaeus.

49-56. One problem of defilement has been overcome. What will Jesus do with the next case? 49. Again, as in vss. 42-43, there is a link between one account and the second installment of the other. One daughter has been saved, now Jairus' daughter has her turn. 50. In words that echo Isaiah 41:13, Jesus says, 'Fear not.' The program spoken of at Luke 7:22 is still in movement. The faith of Jairus is now required to secure his daughter's salvation, that is, return from the dead. In such language the community's faith in Jesus as the bringer of ultimate salvation through resurrection from the dead also finds utterance. Salvation for Luke is rescue from all that separates man from man, or mankind from God (cf. 2:11; 8:12; 8:36; Acts 16:31). Jesus accepts the ultimate challenge!

51. Luke's reference to the three disciples, Peter, John and James, prepared for the account of the transfiguration (see 9:28). Whereas Mark 5:40 records the expulsion of the mourners (usually hired), Luke omits this detail as well as some of the satirical humor in Jesus' rebuke as recorded by Mark: 'Why are you causing such an uproar? You act as though she were dead. She's sleeping.' The implication is, 'Are you trying to wake her up?' (Mark 5:39)

52. Through his briefer account Luke brings into sharper focus the picture of Jesus in full command of a most desperate situation. For him the girl is as one who sleeps -- but too soundly for those about her. 53. The only laughter comes from those who ridicule Jesus for his simile. They knew better. She was dead! But this mockery, itself short-lived, will highlight the fact of Jesus' greater power. 54. Isaiah's God took Israel by the hand (Isaiah 41:13; 42:6). Jesus takes the young girl by the hand and, as in 7:14, calls out in personal address. 55. Not only did she rise (got up, a word used of Jesus' resurrection), but her recovery was complete. They were not 'seeing ghosts' (cf. 24:36-43).

56. In response to the astonishment, Jesus forbids the parents to recite the miracle. It is but a small part of a much larger message -- the proclamation of the good news. His directive is not out of harmony with the command given at vs. 39. There the recovery of the demoniac had become well known, and Jesus' encouragement of the demoniac to return and relate what he had experienced was a sign that Jesus bore no resentment to the citizens. They had yet another chance to understand God's message at work among them. More significant is the contrast between the directive of vs. 56 and the procedure cited in vs. 48. In the case of the woman's healing Jesus could well have preserved anonymity. But he did not choose to do so. It was important that she be restored to the larger family of Israel. In the second case it was a restoration to the immediate family. From

such varied observations one strong picture emerges: Jesus did not
seek notoriety for himself. He was a man on a mission, sent to do
the Father's will. Resurrection is God's work (cf. Strack-Billerbeck
I, 523), and God will more fully reveal what he himself is up to
after he has raised his own Son from the dead. Peter, John and James
are among those entrusted with the full story. After Pentecost no
power on earth will seal their mouths.

PARTNERS IN THE KINGDOM   LUKE 9:1-50

Sharing the Mission   LUKE 9:1-17

MISSION OF THE TWELVE   LUKE 9:1-6
                           (Mark 6:7-16; Matthew 10:1,7,9-11,14)

Endorsement of the apostolic mission is once more located in
the ministry of Jesus. Since Luke had already recorded at 4:16-30
Mark's account of the rejection at Nazareth (Mark 6:1-6), he picks up
immediately Mark's recital (Mark 6:6-13) of the sending of the Twelve.
Mark makes no mention of the proclamation of the Kingdom. Luke enlarges on this aspect. He does not share Mark's preoccupation with a
secrecy motif, but to avoid the clash, undoubtedly noticed by Mark,
between the proclamation of the Kingdom of God and the interests of
Herod the King, Luke calls Herod a tetrarch (9:7).

Verse 1 states that Jesus gives the Twelve power (the word used
in 8:46) and authority (used in 5:24) to exorcise and heal. Verse 2
is not a repetition of vs. 1. Rather it affirms that the authority
given by Jesus is coincident with God's interests. The Kingdom of
God they are to proclaim is to be accompanied by the healing power
they have just received from Jesus. Once again word and deed are cor-
relatives, and Jesus' ministry is viewed as God's action.

3. The standard equipment for the traveler is not for them.
They are to rely completely on the resources of the King. Mark's
text permits them a staff (Mark 6:8; cf. 2 Kings 4:29). 4. Unlike
itinerant philosophers who brought their philosophy into disrepute
by begging from house to house (see the warning in 10:7), the church's
missionaries are to find hospitable quarters and remain there. How
the injunction was carried out may be learned from Acts 9:43; 16:15.

5. Wherever they are not favorably received they are to make the
gesture of the prophet who declares himself free of the judgment about
to overtake those who reject God's message. This is the meaning of
the phrase, as a testimony to them (see on 5:14). 6. The summary
account prepares for the introduction of Herod. The word villages
(compare 'town,' vs. 5) suggests outreach to the 'poor' in Israel.

HEROD'S PERPLEXITY
LUKE 9:7-9
(Mark 6:14-16; Matthew 14:1-2)

7-8. Who *is* Jesus? The answer to this question is the burden of the succeeding recitals. Luke's revision of Mark's account about Herod's superstitions concerning John is in harmony with his own distinction between the ministry of John and the ministry of Jesus. Certainly Jesus is not a reincarnation or second edition of John. His function as an Elijah-figure will be taken up in the subsequent narratives.

9. Like the family of Jesus (8:19-21) Herod seeks to see him, but the opportunity will come first in the Passion narrative (23:8). Herod's hostility toward Jesus is taken up at 13:31, but Luke points out that in the final encounter Herod exonerates Jesus (23:15). Thus the evangelist endeavors to guard the Christian movement against a charge of subversion. Mark's narrative suggests that John is a latter-day Elijah, for he is the victim of a second Ahab and Jezebel (cf. 1 Kings 18). Luke, however, does not interpret John as a second Elijah. Instead he parallels some of Jesus' activity with that of Ahab's enemy. Therefore he omits Mark's story of the beheading of John the Baptist (Mark 6:17-29) permitting immediate presentation of the feeding narrative with its Elijah-Elisha associations.

THE RETURN OF THE TWELVE AND
THE FEEDING OF THE FIVE THOUSAND
LUKE 9:10-17
(Mark 6:30-44; Matthew 14:13-21)

10-11. The village of Bethsaida, which means 'Place of Satisfaction,' is appropriate for the story of the feeding of the five thousand. Luke had stressed the preaching of the Kingdom and healing of the sick in Jesus' injunction to the disciples (vs. 2). Now Jesus preaches the Kingdom of God and cures the sick. Thus his own practice underwrites the activity of the church. Response will vary, however, and Jesus will have something to say later about the quality of faith at Bethsaida (10:13).

12. This verse begins with a phrase that will be echoed at 24:29 ('the day is now far spent' = 'wear away'). It is a way of saying: 'It was meal-time.' Luke abbreviates the preliminaries to Mark's account (6:30-31) of the feeding of the five thousand, perhaps with the intent to eliminate the suggestion that Jesus seeks to escape the crowds, for Luke emphasizes that Jesus "welcomed them" (vs. 11). By doing so, Luke obscures the easy transition Mark had made for the 'desert' place (Mark 6:32) and leaves his readers in perplexity over the shift from Bethsaida. Luke also omits Mark's observation that they were as sheep without a shepherd (Numbers 27:17; Ezekiel 34:5), for Jesus is the shepherd who has *welcomed* them. The reference to the 'wilderness' (lonely place) in vs. 12 makes the need all the more acute.

13. The Twelve, who are the basic resource for the Christian community (cf. Acts 2:42), are given instructions to feed the multitude.

Similar instructions were given by Elijah to a man from Baalshalishah (2 Kings 4:42). The reply is similar to the one in 2 Kings 4:43 (cf. Numbers 11:22).

14-15. The command to distribute the guests in companies of fifty may be an echo of ancient practice in Israel (Exodus 18:21; Deuteronomy 1:15). Jesus is the head of the latter-day Israel.

16. The blessing and the breaking of the bread anticipate two significant narratives (22:19 and 24:30), and what the Lord did near Bethsaida is continued in the apostolic community (Acts 2:46). Specific associations with the Lord's Supper are, however, not apparent to the degree found in the Fourth Gospel, where a parallel recital is used in place of an account of the Lord's Supper (John 6). The prayer of blessing suggests that the multiplication of the loaves is traceable to God's power invoked through the prayer. God's action is present in Jesus. The disciples, who are to nourish the Christian community, are the intermediaries for distribution.

17. In accordance with 6:21, all are satisfied. As in the case of Elisha's banquet (2 Kings 4:43-44), which itself mirrors the feeding recorded in Exodus 16, there was ample left over -- twelve full baskets, one for each of the apostles. The Kingdom of God does not terminate with Jesus' activity. The apostles continue to answer in full measure the question once asked in a Hebrew poem: 'Can God spread a table in the wilderness?' (Psalm 78:19)

Identity of the King   LUKE 9:18-36

WHO AM I? FIRST PREDICTION OF THE PASSION   LUKE 9:18-22
                                        (Mark 8:27-33; Matthew 16:13-23)

At this point Luke omits a large portion of Mark's narrative (6:45-8:26). Mark 6:45-52 could easily be construed as a doublet for Luke 8:22-25. Mark 6:53-56 contains accounts of miscellaneous healings. Mark 7:1-23 incorporates criticism of the Pharisees, which is taken up by Luke in 11:37-54. Mark 7:24-30 violates Luke's theme, to the Jew first and then to the Gentile (Luke 8:26-39, parallel in Mark 5:1-20, was a sufficient exception for Luke). Mark 8:1-10 is a doublet for the feeding of the five thousand. Mark 8:11-13 discusses the sign-seekers. These are taken up by Luke in 11:16 and 29 and 12:54-56. Mark 8:14-21 raises the question of the leaven of the Pharisees, discussed in Luke 12:1. Mark 8:22-26 relates the story of a blind man, which Luke omits in favor of the narrative preceding the entry into Jerusalem (18:35-43). Luke's primary reason, however, for omitting the section is prompted by his concern to bring the question of Jesus' Messianic office into immediate relation with the feeding of the five thousand. In that narrative Jesus was clearly revealed as an Elijah-figure. Now it is important to clarify Jesus' real identity.

18. As in 3:21; 5:16; and 6:12 the sight of Jesus at prayer introduces an exceptional communication. From vss. 9, 12, 14 and 16
one may conclude that the Twelve are meant by the term "disciples."
19. As in 9:7-8, the suggestion is made that Jesus may be John the
Baptist or Elijah, or one of the prophets, now resurrected (cf. 9:8).
20. Peter's reply, that Jesus is the Christ, or Messiah (cf. 2:11,26),
parallels a usage found later in the gospel (23:35) and aids in dis-
tinguishing Jesus from John the Baptist, or any other figures in Israel's past history. The association of Elijah with Jesus has served
its purpose. Now Luke is prepared to have Jesus examined in terms of
his messianic credentials.

21-22. Luke omits Mark's criticism of Peter's confession (Mark
8:33), but in this first prediction of the Passion (see also 9:44;
12:50; 13:32-33; 17:25; 18:31-34) shares with Mark the understanding
that Messiahship involves suffering, rejection, and death followed
by victorious resurrection (9:22; cf. 24:7,26). The word must (vs. 22)
emphasizes that this is of God's design (cf. Acts 2:23-24). Therefore
any announcement of Jesus' Messiahship before the culmination would
have been premature. Stated in Lukan thought: Jesus' death, perpetrated by the cream of the 'system,' does not invalidate his credentials as the Messiah. On the contrary, the path to apparent disaster
is the upward road to victory.

TAKING UP THE CROSS   LUKE 9:23-27
                                        (Mark 8:34-9:1; Matthew 16:24-28)

23. The words he said to all suggest that Luke is alerting his
community to the call of Jesus. In the evangelist's time it would
be a matter of identifying with Jesus' fate. Hence the disciple
must take up his cross. 24. Only thus will he be able to realize
Jesus' promise, whoever loses his life for my sake, he will save it.
Evidently Jesus did not consider it too high a price to pay for
bringing zest, vitality and spontaneity back into style. Jesus was
indeed the great master of the calculated risk.

25. The words in vs. 25 are a reminder of the second temptation
(4:5-8). 26. In his wording of vs. 26 Luke has eliminated Mark's
reference to 'this generation' (Mark 8:38), perhaps to retain a more
general application to the church of his time. Verse 26 affirms
that Jesus' ministry and words will be ratified by the coming of the
Son of man, who is to appear, according to apocalyptic thinking, at the
end of the end-time. Luke shares the view that Jesus and the Son of
man are identical, but in order to avoid the suggestion that an apocalyptic demonstration is required to validate Jesus' messianic mission Luke omits in vs. 27 Mark's words 'with power' (Mark 9:1). The
glory at the end of the end-time is of a piece with the glory into
which Jesus enters at his resurrection (24:26).

27. Therefore, there are some standing here who will not taste of
death before they see the kingdom of God. The Kingdom of God, present

now in Jesus' ministry (cf. 17:21), will be especially manifest at
the cross and recognized by the robber (23:42-43, with stress on
'today'). After that comes the period of the Church, followed by
the coming of the 'Son of man.' Thus vs. 26 is futuristic, and vs.
27 contemporary.

Since vs. 27 in the Markan context would suggest to the church
that the Parousia, that is, the second coming of Jesus Christ, could
be expected at any moment, Luke removes this source of embarrassment
for the church with his doctrine of a two-stage kingdom. His omission
of Mark's phrase 'with power' (see above on vs. 26) is a sure indication of his intent. The Markan view is apocalyptic. Luke's is
conditioned by emphasis on historical factors. Luke 21:31, which
speaks of the second stage of the Kingdom's manifestation, corresponds
to 9:26. It is therefore improbable that vs. 27 has reference to
the transfiguration scene, which took place only about eight days
later. The oath-like formulation in vs. 27 requires a more climactic
occurrence: namely, 23:39-43. The Transfiguration is but a preview,
which puts into focus subsequent developments and explains the two-
fold sense in which Jesus' Kingdom is to be understood: (1) Historical demonstration in suffering, death, and resurrection. (2) Apocalyptic fulfillment.

"THIS IS MY BELOVED SON" LUKE 9:28-36
(Mark 9:2-8; Matthew 17:1-8)

28. Luke's connection with the preceding discussion is more
explicit than Mark's (9:1), for Luke adds: after these sayings. The
phrase 'and it came to pass' (rendered now) introduces an important
development in the narrative. Luke's alteration of Mark's 'after
six days' may be an attempt to avoid the suggestion that Jesus' experience is a repetition of Moses's interview with God (Exodus 24:15-18).
In the latter account Moses hears the voice of the Lord on the seventh
day and remains on the mount for forty days and forty nights. Luke's
Jesus is not a second Moses. It has been suggested that the six days
in Mark may refer to the Feast of Tabernacles, described in Leviticus
23:33-43. Israel was to live in temporary booths for seven days and
observe a solemn convocation on the eighth day. Luke's awareness of
ritual is evidenced elsewhere and his phrase "about eight days" may
point even more precisely to this festival, and since the story of
the transfiguration does relate the suggestion of building temporary
shelters ('booths,'the same term used in the Greek text of Leviticus
23), there is something to be said for the interpretation. However,
it is odd that the suggestion should come at the end of the period,
rather than at the beginning. The most that can be said with certainty
is that typological considerations involving the Feast of Tabernacles
have entered into the tradition of the account of the Transfiguration.
At Jesus' time the Feast of Tabernacles was observed as a kind of
national recollection of ancient liberties, and Messianic hopes might
tend to rise to fever pitch. If the account of the transfiguration is
to be connected with the feast, then the synoptists are unanimous in

rejecting the false hopes generated during the festival. In the last analysis, however, Luke may simply be construing Mark's phrase as equivalent to 'about a week.' This writer has heard citizens of Greece use the phrase 'in eight days' in precisely that sense. Idiom of this type has a long life.

As at 8:51, Jesus takes Peter, John and James to witness his transfiguration. The mountain suggests a place of special revelation. Jesus at prayer is reminiscent of 3:21, and the answer out of the cloud (9:35) echoes 3:22.

29. Exodus 34:29-35 describes the supernatural glow of Moses' face. Expectations of a prophet like Moses were stimulated by Deuteronomy 18:15-18, and the passage is cited in Acts 3:22 and 7:37. Luke's account supports the view that Jesus is the fulfillment of the anticipation, but without endorsement of a second-Moses typology, which treats Jesus as a new lawgiver. The evangelist prefers to stress Moses' function as the leader of Israel's exodus (see on vs. 31). Thus Jesus is a replacement for Moses, not a new Moses. Luke 9:19-20 clearly indicates that Jesus is more than a prophet; he is the Christ. Coupled with the description of the shining garments, Luke's phrasing suggests not a reincarnation of Moses but the righteous one who comes through apocalyptic tribulation (cf. Daniel 12:3; cited in Matthew 13:43; Revelation 3:5). A centurion will judge correctly (23:47). Whiteness is the standard color in apocalyptic description (Revelation 2:17; 6:2; 20:11). Thus Jesus' kingdom is described as one transcending the standard suggested in the wilderness of temptation (4:6-8).

30-31. The word behold calls attention to an especially remarkable phenomenon. Moses and Elijah now appear and speak, not to the disciples, but with Jesus. These two prophets are often interpreted as emblematic of the Law and the Prophets, but Elijah was not in Jewish thought a representative of the prophets. Rather he was recognized as the one who would return and restore all things (cf. Mark 9:12). Luke retains Mark's mention of Elijah to endorse his own doctrine that John the Baptist is not a second Elijah. Jesus, more so than John, takes over Elijah's functions, but Jesus is more than Elijah, and there are aspects in Elijah's ministry that cannot be applied to Jesus (see on 9:54). Elijah therefore disappears, along with Moses, in the sequel. Moreover, according to popular thinking, Elijah comes to the rescue of the sufferer (cf. Mark 15:36). Jesus, however, must endure the last frontiers of disaster. Luke therefore eliminates Elijah from consideration as one who is to validate the appearance of the Messiah through apocalyptic revelation. Instead, both Moses and Elijah speak of Jesus' departure (an item not found in the account of Matthew or Mark).

The word "departure" translates a Greek term easily recognized in its anglicized form 'exodus.' Jesus is to accomplish through his own death a new exodus. Luke therefore will omit in his passion account Mark's reference to Elijah; it would be superfluous. Jerusalem is emphasized in accordance with Luke's doctrine, 'beginning at Jerusalem' (Luke 1-2; 24:47). The reader is not, however, to infer that Jesus is

dependent on Moses and Elijah for information concerning his suffering. At 9:22 Jesus had himself informed his disciples about his fate.
The heavenly visitants merely ratify what has already been determined
as the Father's will, and Jesus goes the route foretold by Moses and
the prophets (cf. 16:31; 24:25). Apocalyptic, says Luke, is to be
interpreted in terms of Jesus' own message, not Jesus from the standpoint of traditional apocalyptic. Thus his inclusion of apocalyptic
narrative and phraseology does not contradict his repeated rejection
of apocalyptic as the structure for communicating the mission of Jesus.

The appearance of the two in glory forms a contrast to their
conversation. According to Luke's doctrine, Jesus' suffering is
his way to glory (24:26). Hence 'two men' appear in shining garments
at the grave (24:4) and reappear in Acts 1:10 for Jesus' ascension.
Consistent with Luke's eschatological doctrine, their presence in both
instances is a way of introducing an apocalyptic dimension to Jesus'
action, while at the same time repudiating the doctrine that the
Messiah must make himself known in accordance with the popular apocalyptic hope. It cannot be asserted definitely that in the last
two passages Luke has in mind Moses and Elijah. However, the account
of the Transfiguration would probably be recollected by the reader.

32-33. The motif of the deep sleep is a feature of apocalyptic
narrative (cf. Daniel 10:9). The disciples are warned against sleep
in the face of the undetermined end (21:34). In the Garden of Gethsemane they are overpowered with drowsiness (22:45). It is to be
inferred that they were ignorant of the conversation between Jesus
and his heavenly visitants. They are pictured as ignorant of the
urgency of the hour, failing to note the intimate connection between
suffering and glory. The words but kept awake are an error in translation. The fact is that they awaken and take note only of the glory
and are distressed as they see Moses and Elijah slipping away (a Lukan
feature) from Jesus. Had they remained awake they would have been informed about Jesus' Exodus. Peter was a young man with old ideas and
did not see that the time was past for setting up booths. Out of ignorance he suggests that the disciples be permitted to make three booths,
one for each of the dignitaries. He was all for celebrating the apocalyptic wind-up then and there. The painstaking description vividly
illustrates his misunderstanding. Jesus is not merely one alongside
two prophets, nor do the disciples require the continuing presence of
these heavenly visitors to assure themselves of Jesus' authority. Besides, Jesus is the living manifestation of God's presence among men
(see Ezekiel 37:27; 43:7,9; Zechariah 2:10; Luke 19:6-10; Revelation
21:3). The disciples require no apocalyptic camp-out.

34-35. At this point a cloud overshadowed them (cf. Acts 1:9).
This cloud is no ordinary cloud, but the traditional indication of God's
presence. In Exodus 13:21 a 'cloud' guided the Israelites; in Exodus
24:15 a 'cloud' covered Mt. Sinai; in 1 Kings 8:10-11 a 'cloud' filled
Solomon's new house for the Lord. According to 2 Maccabees 2:8 the
cloud is to return to signal God's presence among the people.

God himself pronounces the correct interpretation of all that
has transpired: <u>This is my Son, my Chosen; listen to him</u>! The disciple's fear, <u>as they entered the cloud</u>, expresses the normal reaction
to divine intervention (cf. Daniel 10:7) and lends to these words an
additional solemnity. At his baptism Jesus heard a portion of these
words addressed to him personally (Luke 3:22). Now the words are
addressed to the disciples, and through them to the community. Noteworthy is the alteration of 'beloved' (in 3:22 and in Mark 9:7) to
chosen. Luke appears to draw on Isaiah 42:1, which describes Jacob
as God's chosen or elect one. The context of this passage speaks
of the light to the Gentiles (vs. 6; cf. vs. 4 and Luke 2:32) and
echoes the program outlined in Luke 1:79; 4:18; 7:22. Since Jesus
speaks with authority that far exceeds even that of Moses, the disciples must <u>listen to him</u> (cf. Deuteronomy 18:15; Acts 3:22-23). Not a
spectacular <u>apocalyptic</u> demonstration, but the continuing presence
of Jesus in the community is God's way of bringing his plans to com-
pletion for his people.

<u>36</u>. Jesus, the light of the Gentiles, has been separated from
Moses and Elijah. This is stressed by the fact that Jesus is found
alone, after the voice has spoken. The community is not to limit
its thinking to exclusively Jewish moulds. It is to heed the word
of Jesus, now authoritatively communicated through the apostolic
mission. Above all, the disciple must hear Jesus' word about his
approaching death (9:22).

The revelatory nature of the account is once more stressed through
the observation that the disciples were silent (cf. Daniel 10:15).
So overcome were they with the vision, that they <u>told</u> no man. But the
significant words <u>in those days</u> are added. After the resurrection of
Jesus the truth concerning Jesus' person would be better understood
(cf. 24:9). Mark's wording (Mark 9:9), that they should not relate
what they had seen until the Son of man had risen from the dead, is
eliminated. Luke 9:21 took care of this detail, and Luke's omission
here indicates that the recital of the transfiguration sums up his
christological doctrine (cf. 9:20).

Summary: The Transfiguration reveals (1) that God's tenting among
men does not take place through the observance of the ritual of booths
or the maintenance of other Old Testament ritual. God's promise to
tent among men is fulfilled in Jesus' presence. (2) Traditional
patterns of apocalyptic thinking are not applicable to Jesus. Jesus'
ministry is not validated by apocalyptic demonstration. His Kingdom
is a present reality, awaiting its consummation. Apocalyptic in the
strict sense of the term applies to the latter. (3) Jesus' suffering
and death is God's design for the Messiah. His credentials are in
no way invalidated by the verdict pronounced in Jerusalem. Rather his
glory begins at the cross. (4) Jesus' Kingdom is not of this world.
That is, it is not to be defined in terms of human criteria or pre-
vailing systems.

A final word needs to be said about the connection of this account
with the account of the resurrected Lord. It has been suggested that
a resurrection story has been retrojected into the narrative. Against
this view are the following: (1) In resurrection accounts Jesus
does not appear in white, nor is his glory observed. Luke, in any case,
does not promote the idea, for the two men on the road to Emmaus are
convinced through Jesus' word and action (24:30-32), having been ignorant beforehand of his identity. (2) Moses and Elijah do not appear
in the resurrection stories. If they are to be inferred in 24:4, it
is the result of projection from the Transfiguration account, not
vice versa. (3) The number six or 'about eight days' does not fit
a resurrection account, at least not Luke's. All of the events recorded in Luke 24 take place on Easter day. If the retrojection did
indeed occur, it must have taken place at a very early stage in the
tradition, for Luke displays no awareness of it. But in that event
the living witnesses were a strong control for the recital of experiences in the life of Jesus and the disciples.

Misunderstanding   LUKE 9:37-50

HEALING OF A DEMONIAC   LUKE 9:37-43a
                                     (Mark 9:14-29; Matthew 17:14-21)

Between the story of the transfiguration and the healing of the
demoniac, Mark (9:9-13) had introduced a discussion about Elijah and
John the Baptist's identification with Elijah. In Luke's time such
association of John with Elijah could be used to cast doubt on Jesus'
Messianic credentials, for the conclusion could be drawn that since the
expected apocalyptic fireworks had not taken place Jesus could not
be the anticipated deliverer. Luke therefore eliminates the recital.
Whatever John was or did, Jesus can be fully understood apart from him.

37-40. Mark's account of the healing suggests that the incident
took place on the same day as the Transfiguration, but it may have
been his intention to suggest a night scene. Luke, however, is very
definite in his chronology, on the next day, in order to make the incident stand out in bolder relief against the command given in the
account of the transfiguration (see 9:43-45). Thus the pattern of
mountain scene followed by encounter with demons (cf. 6:12-18) is
maintained. By eliminating the scene of disputation between the disciples (whom Jesus had left behind) and the scribes, Luke is able to
focus attention on the basic problem: The disciples are not heeding
Jesus' word. Hence they could not cast out the demon (vs. 40). It is
not a matter of legal technicalities. The man pleads with Jesus to
look upon (the Greek word is rendered 'has regarded' in 1:48) his child.
Luke adds in vs. 38 the words only child to emphasize the father's
plight (cf. 7:12; 8:42). The symptoms are those of epilepsy. Luke
emphasizes the weakness of a human being exploited by demonic forces.
Thus the unfortunate sufferer is not to be classed as a sinner but de-
serves all the compassion that can be mustered in his behalf. In view

of such hostility, the prediction concerning Jesus' own suffering is a natural development.

41. Jesus' reply is not, as in Mark 9:19, directed specifically to the disciples, but is a general statement on the type of response his message encounters (see on Luke 7:31). The word perverse, meaning 'crooked,' is an addition to Mark's text, and recalls Deuteronomy 32:5; Proverbs 6:14; Isaiah 59:8. It reappears in Acts 13:8, 10 (cf. Philippians 2:15). In the words bear with you Jesus speaks as does God in Isaiah 46:4 (LXX). Luke evidently intends to spare the disciples some embarrassment, but there is no doubt that the community is warned not to make the mistake of this "generation."

42. In the description that follows, Luke omits Mark's recital about the father's faith (Mark 9:21-24). Luke apparently considers it irrelevant, for the problem is the disciples' inability to carry out the injunctions given them by Jesus not long before the Transfiguration (9:1-2). It was their task to proclaim the Kingdom of God and to heal, yet on the mountain they wanted to prepare tents for Jesus, Moses and Elijah! They wished to retain Elijah, but like Gehazi, Elisha's servant (see 2 Kings 4:29-31), they could not carry out instructions.

Through his casting out of the demon Jesus once more reinforces his purpose -- to demolish the works of Satan. Luke relates that he healed the boy. The word 'heal' echoes the command in 9:2. Jesus does what he had given his disciples instructions to do. Once more an Elijah-motif enters the Lukan recital. He gave him back to his father (see on Luke 7:15). Jesus does not require the presence of Elijah for validation. He in his own person initiates the end-time. Or, to express it theologically, apocalyptic is Christologized.

43. The concluding words clearly indicate that God is at work in Jesus' action (cf. Acts 10:38). In like manner the voice from heaven (9:35) endorsed his total ministry. Mark 9:15 refers to astonishment of the crowds at the time of Jesus' descent from the mountain, Luke speaks of astonishment at the later moment spelled out in vs. 37. The word majesty is used in only one other passage in the New Testament (2 Peter 1:16), and there in the context of a reference to the Transfiguration. Luke affirms that Jesus' daily round of activity is his own authentication and a kind of continuing transfiguration. There in the 'routine' performance of his task is *the* sign, *the* proof that God is at work in Jesus. Such mode of revelation was too tame for those who had made up their minds that God would show his hand in more spectacular fashion.

SECOND PREDICTION OF THE PASSION   LUKE 9:43b-45
                                              (Mark 9:30-32; Matthew 17:22-23)

In view of Luke's economy of statement elsewhere, his repetition of the motif of the astonishment of the crowd is noteworthy. He is affirming that the majesty of God is indeed being revealed, but that

the climactic demonstration is yet to come -- when the Son of man
is handed over into the hands of men (see also 9:22; 12:50; 13:32-33;
17:25; 18:31-34). This is the ultimate in divine mystery and the
verbal assonance is striking. He who identified with man's situation
is to be rejected by men. The phrase put it into your ears parallels
the expression in Exodus 17:14. Since the Son of man was ordinarily
construed as a triumphant apocalyptic figure, the concept of suffering
would be difficult to understand. Once more the debate in the church,
whether Jesus is to be identified with this apocalyptic figure, is
reopened.

45. Luke adds to Mark's account (9:32) that the disciples' ignorance (cf. Acts 13:27; 17:23) is traceable to divine intervention --
it was concealed from them. They could have asked Jesus for details,
but they feared to make the inquiry. Jesus himself later removes
the misunderstanding of two disciples on the road to Emmaus (24:16-32).
Thus it is affirmed that Jesus' ministry transcends all normal patterns
of human expectation, and God himself through Jesus and the Holy Spirit
must open the minds of men for faith (cf. 10:21-22). The fact that
Jesus was rejected is no proof that he was not what he or the apostolic mission claims him to be.

ARGUMENT ABOUT GREATNESS
LUKE 9:46-50
(Mark 9:33-41; Matthew 18:1-5)

46. Mark (9:33) disconnects this account from the preceding prediction by introducing a fresh development at Capernaum. Luke preserves the association by eliminating that visit. In his recital the
dispute over prestige is a misunderstanding of the Kingdom, about to
be climaxed by Jesus' own rejection of standard greatness through
acceptance of the cross. The lowly are to be exalted, and the mighty
are to be brought low (Luke 1:52). Luke does not limit the discussion
to the circle of the twelve (Mark 9:35). The entire church is to learn
this lesson.

47. A child is an excellent illustration to use in teaching the
lesson of humility. It can do nothing for the disciple and cannot
satisfy the one who asks: 'What's in it for me?' All hollow status-
seeking is here brought under indictment. To some rabbis a child under
the age of twelve was incapable of knowing the Torah; to spend much
time with them was folly. (See *Theological Dictionary of the New Testament*, translated by Geoffrey Bromiley, V, 645-647). The disciple is
not to share the criteria of the old age.

48. Jesus identifies so closely with the child that reception
of the child is a reception of Jesus himself. And he who receives
Jesus receives the Sender -- namely the Father. Luke here omits
Mark's wording 'receives not me but,' for Luke emphasizes that Jesus
is intimately linked with the Father (cf. 10:22). He who learns
leastness learns greatness. The word least is a reminder of the words
in 7:28.

49. It is indeed remarkable how Jesus could 'talk past' his disciples. But 'in one ear and out the other.' Now it is a question of 'union rights.' Do others, besides the apostles, have the right to exorcise? The story echoes Numbers 11:26-30. The question would be asked for centuries to come, with the established churches zealously guarding their prerogatives and traditions against the encroachments of spiritual gifts that could not be subject to firm institutional control. Resistance to the 'charismatic movement' is symptomatic of the problem confronted by Jesus. Luke, who is the spokesman for division of labor in the apostolic community (cf. Acts 6:1-6), lays his finger on the malady--status - seeking. But Jesus' proclamation is not limited to one magisterial center. God's Spirit, to the dismay of many an ecclesiastical administrator, does not always go through channels! John's question may also reflect the early church's problem of recognizing the ministry of people not associated with the mainstream of Christianity as it emanated from Jerusalem. Apollos was one of these non-conformist preachers, being acquainted only with the baptism of John the Baptist (Acts 18:24-26). But he was graciously treated by others in the church, notably Priscilla and Aquila (Acts 18:26).

John had said to Jesus 'we tried to prevent him' (not as the RSV renders, we forbade him). Jesus answers: 'Stop preventing him!' (better than RSV, do not forbid him). The reasoning of Jesus does not at first sight strike a Western reader as particularly sound: He that is not against you is for you. It seems to encourage spineless neutrality, and appears to be in contradiction to 11:23. But from the Eastern point of view it means: "One who is not associated with you is not necessarily opposed to you. Let him carry on his activity." In similar vein Cicero pleaded with Caesar in behalf of a client: 'We have often heard you assert that, while we held all men to be our opponents save those on our side, you counted all men your adherents who were not against you' (In Behalf of Ligarius, 33; Loeb Translation). The church does well to recognize the value also of humanitarian effort that lacks a professed Christian base and ought not to belittle such contributions. The church's long sad tale of persecution of dissenters is only a reminder that the thick-headedness of the earliest disciples did not go out of style after Pentecost. The story is naturally not included in Matthew's Gospel.

PART IV: WE GO UP TO JERUSALEM
LUKE 9:51-19:27

FIRST PHASE   LUKE 9:51-13:21

Hazards of Discipleship   LUKE 9:51-62

IN SAMARIA   LUKE 9:51-56

51. With this passage Luke begins another major section of his
gospel, marked by the words "And it came to pass" (omitted in RSV).
The Gospel began in Jerusalem and it will terminate there, but only
to spell a fresh beginning (24:47). The experience of rejection by
the Samaritans parallels the rejection at Nazareth (4:16-30). Once
more the figure of Elijah haunts the narrative. The same word used
of Elijah's departure for heaven is used of Jesus (received up). This
reception actually takes place at the end of the gospel (Luke 24:50-51;
cf. Acts 1:1-2, where the verb recurs). It is Luke's intention, however, to show that the fate Jesus suffers in Jerusalem is the main
stage toward his enthronement as the son of David (cf. 1:32-33). Jesus has his face set (Jeremiah 44:12). The expression 'his face' is
a semitic formulation meaning 'himself.' But the total phrase expresses Jesus' fixed purpose. What is to befall him is no tragic set
of circumstances from which there was to be no escape. Satan had
offered a way out (4:6-8). But Jesus is obedient to the Father's
will (2:49). Just as Ezekiel's face was directed toward Jerusalem
(Ezekiel 6:2; 13:17; 14:8; 15:7), so Jesus heads for his city. Ezekiel was directed toward her in judgment. Jesus goes to seek her
peace (Luke 19:42), but also must pronounce prophetic judgment on her.
John went before God in the spirit and power of Elijah (1:17), and
he was sent as a messenger 'before the face' of Israel (7:27). Jesus
sends his own messengers 'before *his* face' (ahead of him). Since
Jesus is himself an Elijah-figure, he requires no Elijah to precede
him. John goes in the *spirit* of Elijah, but Jesus himself gives
content to the role of Elijah, and according to Luke's doctrine di-
vests the people of erroneous apocalyptic associations concerning
Elijah. Note: RSV includes the words "And he sent messengers ahead
of him" as part of vs. 51. In other translations these words form
part of vs. 52.

123

52. Luke has a special interest in Samaritans. This is the only instance recorded by him of their hostility (cf. 10:33; 17:16). The Samaritans were a mixed race with pagan ingredients (Ezra 4:2), the result of Assyria's repopulation of the northern kingdom after its destruction. Blue-blooded Jews refused to have anything to do with them (John 4:9). Jesus' directive to the disciples to prepare the Samaritans for his visit is a sign of things to come. The totality of Israel, north and south, is to be reclaimed for God. 53. But the Samaritans would not receive him, for he was headed toward Jerusalem. They would have preferred that he recognize Mt. Gerizim as the holy locale (see John 4:19-20).

54. James and John once again display their misunderstanding and are prepared to exceed earlier directions about shaking off the dust from their feet (9:5). At 9:48 Jesus had spoken of those who 'receive' him, but he had said nothing about those who rejected him. James and John, however, want to see apocalyptic fire rain down on the Samaritans. They share only too plainly the hostility of their countrymen. At the same time there is a suggestion that Jesus demonstrate that he is a 'man of God.' The marginal reading, *as Elijah did*, calls to mind 2 Kings 1:9-12. Elijah said: 'If I am a man of God, let fire come down from heaven' (vs. 12).

55-56. Jesus rebukes the disciples, even as he had to rebuke demons. Jesus is an Elijah-figure, but his pattern is not of destructive stripe (see Luke 19:10), and he is under no compulsion to *prove* his intimate relationship with God. His fire is of a different order (see 12:49), but grace spurned will elicit destruction (cf. 21:20; Revelation 11:5). Luke's recital would pave the way for the proclamation of the good news in Samaria (see Acts 8). Like those responsible for Jesus' death (see Acts 3:12-26), also the Samaritans are entitled to another chance.

ON RASH DISCIPLESHIP
LUKE 9:57-62
(Matthew 8:19-22)

The previous rebuke to the disciples discouraged the thought that the Kingdom is a demonstration of force. Association with Jesus is not entry into a popularity contest. The three sayings that follow amplify the rigors imposed on the follower of Jesus. In ascending order they link the Son of man with the Elijah-cycle, climaxing with a statement on the Kingdom.

57. The words as they were going along are Luke's editorial addition, in keeping with his travel motif. 58. Tiberius Gracchus once said of the poor: 'The wild beasts roam over Italy and each one has his own hole and lair, but those who fight and die for Italy have only the light and the air as their portion' (Plutarch *Lives*, 828c). Tiberius' use of the proverb evokes pathos. In the Lukan context the hazard of association with Jesus is stressed, more along the lines of Sirach 36:26: 'Who will trust a nimble robber, that skips

from city to city? Even so who shall trust a man who has no nest, and lodges wherever he finds himself at nightfall?' The Son of man, popularly conceived as an apocalyptic figure, is in Jesus' person a man who seems to offer nothing, and even a source of risk to his followers. His kingdom is not offered to the lowest bidder. He does not appeal to the baser motives of those who seek gain and advancement.

59-60. The second reply runs counter to the prudential ethic espoused in Sirach 38:16-17. The saying is not to be softened by the suggestion that the man's father was either elderly or on the point of death. Jesus' Kingdom-program permits no delays. The dead, that is, those who have no interests beyond their daily routines, can take care of the deceased. Like the Nazirite (Numbers 6:6-8), the disciple is to devote himself to the proclamation of the Kingdom. Mark was one who had to learn the lesson (see Acts 13:13; 15:36-40). Many a would-be follower of Jesus has pleaded the requirements of social obligation or prior business demands as an excuse for not meeting the imperative of obedience.

61. The third request echoes the plea of Elisha, who requested permission from Elijah to bid farewell to his parents (1 Kings 19: 19-21). Elijah gave him permission. Jesus tolerates no such delay. His authority is greater than Elijah's and the requirements of the Kingdom more rigorous.

62. The proverb of the plowman (used also in Greek literature, cf. Hesiod *Works*, 2,30) may have been stimulated by the observation in 1 Kings 19:19 that Elisha was plowing when Elijah cast his mantle on him. It is impossible to plow straight furrows while looking backward. Paul knew well the meaning of such words (Philippians 3: 13), which appear to express a wisdom motif (cf. Sirach 38:25). Taken together, the stern words of Jesus are also a reminder to the church to be wary of the volunteer. The policy in Acts is to *choose* people 'full of the Spirit' (Acts 6:3).

Mission of the Seventy LUKE 10:1-20
(Matthew 9:37-38; 10:7-16; 11:20-23)

Now that the requirements for the disciple have been defined, the stage is set for the massive propaganda offensive described in chapter 10.

1. Just as Jesus embodies, and yet transcends in his person the figure of Elijah, so he carries on his ministry as one who supersedes Moses. According to Numbers 11:16-17, Moses was to appoint seventy men of the elders of Israel to assist him in his work. The addition of Eldad and Medad (Numbers 11:26) probably accounts for the variation of seventy-two in the textual tradition of Luke. Corresponding to these figures are the variations in numbers of the nations cited in Genesis 10(70 in the Hebrew text; 72 in the Septuagint). Luke's recital

125

thus anticipates the empire-wide mission described in the book of
Acts. Jesus is on the way to Jerusalem, but from Jerusalem the
Gospel goes forth to the Gentiles. Luke 10 is the preview (see also
2:30-32; 3:6). The word others is important. Luke is at pains to
emphasize that the proclamation of the Kingdom is not limited to the
efforts of the Twelve. As Elisha did with Gehazi (2 Kings 4:29-31),
Jesus sends his disciples on ahead (see the same expression in Luke
9:51, 'And he sent messengers ahead of him', RSV = 'before his face.'
Other translations include this phrase as part of vs. 52 instead of
vs. 51 as in RSV. They go two by two, perhaps a way of emphasizing
their responsibility as witnesses (cf. Deuteronomy 19:15), but from
Luke's point of view this practice is a reproduction of the apostolic
custom described in Acts (see, for example, Acts 13:2).

2. The fruit to be harvested is bountiful, but the workers are
few. Yet Jesus did not lower the requirements for messengers (cf.
9:57-62). Success of the Kingdom is not to be bought at the mercy
of mediocrity. The saying also reminds the church that its orders
for messengers of the Gospel are not limited to the patterns set by
Jesus, whether those be the Twelve or the Seventy. Moreover, it is
not to be forgotten that the harvest belongs to God, not to the
church (see the warning in Acts 20:28).

3. Roman emperor Hadrian once remarked to a rabbi that Israel
was like a sheep among the seventy wolves (that is, the nations of the
world). Jesus' disciples are not invited to beds of ease. In advance they are warned of the hazards. 4. If they are concerned about
their possessions, then they have not read the job specifications.
The variations in wording from Matthew's parallels (Matthew 10:9-10)
reflect the homiletical application of Jesus' words in the preaching
of Luke's day. Naturally the details would differ according to the
situation. But the picture emerging is clearly that of a disciple
who lives and works in total dependence on the Lord of the harvest
(cf. Luke 22:35). Gehazi (2 Kings 4:29) was reminded by Elisha not
to greet anyone along the way. Oriental formalities can be time-con-
suming. Jesus, as the latter-day Elijah-Elisha, sends out his messengers with no less urgency. This is the point of the saying, not that
the disciple should pass up even a casual opportunity to share the
good news.

5. Jesus also tells his disciples what they are to say. The message
of the good news should be their first word. There is no mention of a
call to repentance, for the message is first of all good news of God's
reign for Israel. In place of the ceremonial greetings, he is to say
Peace be to this house. These were the instructions given by David
to part of his band who were sent to Nabal (1 Samuel 25:6). The word
house includes all the residents (cf. Acts 10:2; 16:15).

6. Son of peace is a semitic expression meaning one who is not
wickedly inclined, but concerned about righteousness (cf. Isaiah 59),
as would be displayed in his willingness to receive the messenger. Nabal
showed himself not a son of peace, but a son of folly (1 Samuel 25:25),

for he assaulted the messengers. Jesus, the Davidian (Luke 1:32), is at work wherever his disciples are. His work will bring out the secrets of men's hearts. Men will no longer be able to sit on the fence. For or against God? The reaction to Jesus' message will reflect where people really stand beneath their facade of religious ritual (cf. 2:35). The disciple's pronouncement of peace does not work magically. Only if there is a receptive mind will that peace be valid. If the mind-set is wrong, the peace he pronounces will return to the disciple. That is, the intended recipient will lose the benefit.

7. Unlike itinerant philosophers who begged their way across the country, the disciples are to accept, as did Elijah (1 Kings 17:15) and Elisha (2 Kings 4:8), the hospitality of *one* house. They are not to create the impression of peddling God's wares for personal gain. On the other hand, they can hold their head high as emissaries of the King. They need not be apologetic about accepting food and lodgings. Thus Luke clarifies for his own time the problem of the 'paid worker.'

8. Since Jewish dietary regulations would raise a problem for the church's missionaries (see Acts 15), Luke points out that Jesus' words envisioned removal of such scruples. The missionary is to eat whatever is set before him, for his journeys will take him to homes of Pharisees as well as those of the 'poor.' He is also to heal the sick (as did Elijah, 1 Kings 17:17-24) and accompany his deeds of mercy with the pronouncement that the Kingdom of God has come near them, that is, has made its presence known in their midst. Thus Luke again affirms that the Kingdom is not to be defined in popular apocalyptic terms, but can make its appearance even in the act of human proclamation.

10-11. Since the disciples displayed misunderstanding in the case of the Samaritan's rejection of Jesus, they require instruction on how to handle similar situations. Instead of calling down fire from heaven they are to use a prophet's symbolic gesture and shake the dust off their feet (cf. 9:5; Acts 13:51). To some readers this might have suggested that the city was viewed as a ritually unclean place. For those whose confidence was placed in Moses, this gesture would be most meaningful. The gesture is to be accompanied with the solemn announcement that they have had encounter with the Kingdom.

12. To reject encounter with the New Age is an awful invitation to judgment. Sodom, a synonym for depravity, would have an easier time than some of Israel's cities in the day of judgment. Israel's responsibility is all the greater, for her opportunities were unparalleled.

13-14. Chorazin and Bethsaida, cities within the land of Israel, would be called to sterner account than Tyre and Sidon, for the former had received in vain the witness of Jesus' mighty deeds. Sackcloth is a symbol of judgment (Isaiah 50:3). Ashes symbolize repentance (Job 42:6; Isaiah 58:5).

LUKE 10:15-20

15. Capernaum will suffer the fate of heathen Babylon (cf. Isaiah 14:13-15). These woes are a striking reminder of 6:24-26. 16. The disciples are not to take the rejection personally. Jesus accepts full responsibility for their mission, and it is he and the Father who are ultimately rejected (see also John 5:23; 15:23). Thus the apostolic mission is clearly viewed as God's own effort.

Luke's doctrine of the two-stage demonstration of the Kingdom comes out clearly in vss. 9-16. The Kingdom of God can be present without apocalyptic fanfare. Even after the departure of Jesus the Church is entrusted with the message of the Kingdom, and where that message goes the Kingdom comes. The destiny of man is ultimately decided in terms of his response to the message. Luke's primary interest, however, is to explain Israel's rejection of the apostolic message. Jesus himself anticipated it, he says, and the church is not to be disheartened. The apocalyptic moment will come -- but not until the harvest has been garnered.

17. The seventy return in good spirits. How thirty-five pairs of disciples happened to arrive at the same time is not explained. Their address of Jesus as Lord is appropriate to the dignity of their mission. And they are delighted with their power over the demons. 'It worked!'

18. Jesus' answer is a masterpiece of style: 'Yes, I was watching Satan falling like lightning from heaven.' In other words, 'You were really in good form. Satan toppled over before your advances' (cf. Isaiah 14:12; Revelation 12:9). But they say nothing about the proclamation of the Kingdom of God!

19. Jesus' own authority and power has been placed in their hands. Psalm 91:13 may be the source for the saying about serpents and scorpions (see also Genesis 3:15; Revelation 12:9). According to Testament of Levi 18:12, the Messianic high priest will bind Belial (Satan) and give his children power to tread on evil spirits. Ability to exorcise, is, however, not to be a disciple's major ambition. It is possible for an emissary of the Lord to do mighty works in his name and yet lose the Kingdom (see Matthew 7:22, and cf. Luke 13:26).

20. Possession of spiritual powers is no guarantee of salvation. One must have his name written in the book of life (see Exodus 32:32; Isaiah 4:3; Enoch 47:3; Daniel 12:1; Revelation 3:5). This means that one must stand in a proper relationship to God, and that means in Luke's language to hear and keep Jesus' word (8:21).

Jesus Rejoices

LUKE 10:21-24
(Matthew 11:25-27; 13:16-17)

The saying in vss. 21-22 is paralleled in Matthew 11:25-27, but
Luke omits from the common source Q the words of comfort for the
heavily burdened (Matthew 11:28-30). In Luke's context they would be
inappropriate, since his stress is on the disciples, whose names are
written in God's book, in contrast to representatives of Israel's
religious leadership who do not grasp the message. The succeeding
narrative about the lawyer exhibits their blindness, and 10:38-42 reinforces Luke's doctrine that Jesus is the source of true wisdom. See
also 11:29-32, which is followed by a saying on light (vss. 33-36) and
indictment of the Pharisees and scribes (vss. 37-54).

The Matthean form of the saying (11:25-30) follows Sirach 51 in
its pattern of thought: 1. Thanksgiving (Sirach 51:1), 2. God the
source of wisdom (vs. 17), 3. Invitation (vs. 23). A closer parallel,
however, is to be found in a gnostic Hermetic tract, which reads: 'I
believe and bear witness. Praise to you, O Father. You have delivered
to me, your Son, the fullness of your power. For you have permitted
yourself to be known, and through your revelation you have become
known. This knowledge I share with men of worth, in accordance with
your commandment. The unworthy close their minds to it.' (See E.
Norden, *Agnostos Theos*, p. 293). The anti-gnostic reformulation in Q
of what appears to have been a wide-spread formula was to Luke's
liking. God reveals his mysteries (cf. 8:10) through Jesus. And he
reveals them not to the sophisticated initiate, but to the unlearned.
See also Psalm 111; 1 Corinthians 1:21; and 1QH 7:26-27: 'I praise
you Lord, for you have given me understanding through your truth, and
you have given me knowledge through your wonderful mysteries.'

21. The word rejoiced is typical of the New Age (see on 1:14).
The Spirit is to be given in the Messianic age to God's servant (Isaiah
42:1). One way to assert the truth of something is to express thanks
for it (cf. Psalm 118:19-21 and, from a false perspective, the Pharisee's prayer in Luke 18:11). From the standpoint of Hebrew thought,
God is the ultimate source of good and evil. If the wise and prudent
(that is, the learned theologians among the Jews; cf. 1QH 1:35), and
the sophisticated of this world (cf. 1 Corinthians 1:18-25; 2:1-16)
do not accept the message, the disciple is assured that it is God's
doing, not a deficiency in the message or in the disciple. The word-
play of the original might be rendered: 'You have *concealed* these
things from the wise and prudent and *revealed* them to children.' The
phrase these things includes the understanding that it is more important to have one's name in the book of life than to perform dazzling
miracles (Luke 10:20). A sign-seeking generation would need to learn
the lesson (11:29). Stoics, who claimed that only a wise man could
be godly, would find it even more difficult. Christianity does not
invite renunciation of the intellect, but participation in the Kingdom
does not depend on intellectual resources. Jesus laid the ax on snob
appeal. 'Good pleasure' (gracious will), as God's outreaching love,
was used at 2:14.

22. Whereas the rabbis ascribed their teachings to the traditions of the fathers, Jesus receives his instruction directly from
the one Father in heaven. Since God's will comes to expression in
Jesus, the Son of God, only the Father knows the fullness of his intent in Jesus. Therefore the Father must reveal it. Conversely,
since Jesus is the chosen instrument to reveal the Father, only
the Son knows the scope of the Father's will (cf. 2:49). The first
of these propositions was supported after the baptism. At 3:22 God
revealed to Jesus his own understanding of Jesus. The second propo-
sition found endorsement at the Transfiguration. Jesus was pronounced the sole revealer of the Father, and the disciples are to
listen to him (9:35); for those to whom the Son wishes to reveal the
Father are the believers. In association with Jesus they become children of the heavenly Father (cf. 6:36; Romans 8:15; Galatians 4:5-7).
God's loving concern and willingness to share himself in forgiveness
with man is not an intellectual datum but a reality in Jesus Christ.
Hence Paul puts being known by God ahead of his own knowledge (1 Corinthians 8:3; 13:12; Galatians 4:9).

23. The words Then turning to the disciples, he said privately
are added to a Q passage (see Matthew 13:16-17). This addition suggests that Luke understands the prayer in vss. 21-22 as an unspoken
kind of meditation, permitting easy introduction at this point of a
related thought from another portion of his source. That Luke has
shifted attention here from the Seventy to the Twelve is by no means
certain. Luke's point is that the disciples -- and from his standpoint in the church this would mean the believers -- are the recipients of the revelation discussed in vs. 22. The formulation of the
beatitude is similar to those in 6:20-22.

24. The reference to the many prophets (e.g. Isaiah 9:1-7)
and kings (cf. Isaiah 60:3) focuses attention on the magnitude of
the blessing enjoyed. There is no esoteric knowledge yet to be revealed, no 'secrets of the pyramids.' Those who are associated with
Jesus and hear his word have the knowledge that counts in the New Age.
The subsequent account of the priest and Levite, who act casuistically
out of legal confinement, reveals how blessed the disciples are.

Misunderstanding   LUKE 10:25-42

A LAWYER   LUKE 10:25-37

A Lawyer's Question   LUKE 10:25-29
                                        (Mark 12:28-31; Matthew 22:35-40)

25. Lawyer is Luke's alternate term for scribe. It denotes an
expert in the Law of Moses. Luke's addition to Mark 12:28 put him to
the test ('tempting him') is derived from a second source and presents

the lawyer in marked contrast to the disciples who have been privileged to see.

26-27. In Matthew 22:36 and Mark 12:29 Jesus answers a question about the chief commandment. Here the lawyer asks about inheriting eternal life and is in turn queried by Jesus in typical rabbinic debate. The lawyer's answer is derived from Deuteronomy 6:5 and Leviticus 19:8 (see also Testament of Issachar 5:2; Testament of Dan 5:3). The various parts of man are not to be diagnosed separately. Verse 27 is thoroughly semitic in its expression of the totality of one's being. God is to absorb all our resources, and the neighbor is to be trusted with the love we have for ourselves. Thus self-love is not to be denied nor disparaged. However, the rule 'love your neighbor as yourself' can easily lead to casuistry. One can say, 'I do not wish my neighbor to interfere in my life, and I will not interfere in his.' Or one may, as the lawyer does, first try to secure a definition of neighbor. Prolonged debate, or referral to committee, is the time-honored method of shunning collective and individual responsibility.

28. Jesus now challenges the lawyer to action: Do this and you will live. This is in accordance with the Lukan doctrine: 'Hear the word and keep it.' The lawyer needs to learn, however, that in order to observe the will of God he must transcend the thinking of his own legalistic establishment. Otherwise he will remain on the level of self-justification. (cf. 16:15; 18:19-21). Objective yardsticks for behavior, with the rules closely defined, make it possible for any man to be a paragon of virtue. But on the basis of love God alone is in a position to judge. The lawyer seeks a more 'reliable' criterion. Once defined, the neighbor and a thousand other intrusions on one's privacy can be eliminated. All the bother of independent decision can be cleared out. How to extract oneself from the embarrassment of doing too much? That was the lawyer's problem. The Christian minister usually hears it this way: 'Don't meddle into social issues. Preach the Gospel.' In brief, 'I am willing to love my neighbor as myself, but don't get me involved with the wrong neighbors.'

Story of the Good Samaritan   LUKE 10:30-37

One might have expected Jesus to make a Samaritan the object of a Jew's concern but not the principal actor in the story. For according to much popular Jewish traditional law a neighbor was a fellow Jew, not a non-Israelite. But it is possible to lose national prejudice and not to have love. A *respectable* Samaritan might even merit one's help (cf. Romans 5:7). The problem of the lawyer requires a deeper probe. He needs to see the phoniness of cult without love, of legal adherence without awareness of the spirit. Eyes opened to the New Age would have no difficulty in seeing that the narrow definition of neighbor as a fellow Jew is old wine (cf. Luke 5:37). Hence the answer is confined to a problem within the lawyer's own peer group, priests and Levites.

30. The road between Jerusalem and Jericho was notorious for
its hazards. Attacks by 'punks' were frequent. From the fact that
Jesus makes much of the help of the Samaritan it is not difficult to
conclude that the victim was a Jew.

31-32. Both priest and Levite were travelling from Jerusalem.
Hence they were not on the way to discharge heavy religious obligations.
Whether they nevertheless feared contamination from a person who might
be dead (cf. Leviticus 21:1) the text does not say. Nor is it suggested that they feared being robbed themselves. Any speculation concerning their reasons is irrelevant. This is a story, and the story focuses
attention on their basic malady -- lovelessness. Luke may, however, aim
to point out that popular theories of retribution lead to callousness
toward one who in the judgment of religious experts must be a *sinner*.
The man's fate was proof of that! Independently of one another, both
priest and Levite pass on the other side to avoid encounter. Someone
has facetiously suggested that they were in a rush to attend a meeting
on making Jericho road safe for travellers. Hugh Clough in 'The Latest
Decalogue' captures the thought: 'Thou shalt not kill; but need'st not
strive officiously to keep alive.'

33-35. The Samaritan (see on 9:53) had good reason to keep moving.
He had an ass (beast) and money (denarii) and was therefore a man of
means and a target for robbers. He saw what the others had seen, but
he responds with compassion, as did his countrymen centuries earlier
(2 Chronicles 28:8-15), and as God did to Jerusalem when the city welter-
ed in her own blood (Ezekiel 16:5-14). Oil would serve as a salve, and
wine as a disinfectant. At the hotel (see on 2:7, where a different
word is used) he remains with the man. Inns of that time were worse
than American fifty-cent-a-night hotels. And innkeepers were not noted
for their humanitarian sentiments. Therefore the Samaritan makes a
generous down payment of what amounts to two-days' normal wages, with
the assurance that he will pay the balance on his return. The pronoun
I is emphatic: 'I, not the man, will pay.' He takes all precautions
to insure good service for the wounded man. Of Jesus it was said that
he loved his own to the end (John 13:2). A casual 'Good Samaritan'
will do the spectacular emergency deed as a kind of sentimental reaction,
but when the needy one becomes a burden or makes demands on time, then
a quick exit is sought. Public officials know the 'do-gooder,' the
self-serving humanitarian, who will not follow through, the 'baskets-
at-Christmas' type. But this Samaritan kept a vigil through the night
and did not leave this man to chance assistance. He acted as God did
toward Jerusalem. Divine compassion is the model for neighborly love.

36. Jesus corrects the initial question: 'Who was neighbor to that
man?' The lawyer's question had been wrongly phrased. Not, who is
qualified for my help? But, what need can I meet? Love, not law nor
social strata, determines the choice of neighbor. The lawyer has asked
what he might do to inherit eternal life, and Jesus had said 'Do this
and you will live.' Verse 37 is the commentary: 'Go, and you make a
habit of doing likewise.' The present tense of the imperative and the
emphatic *you* are of the essence, and both are obscured by RSV. Adopt

this Samaritan's way of thinking! It is a reminder of Luke 6:31-36.
Divine mercy does not ask the worth of the recipient. It only sees
the need. Herein lies the creative possibility for action not measured
by rules for neighborly behavior. The lawyer broke his own law through
his casuistry. The Samaritan kept it. He who hears and does Jesus'
word is like a man built on rock (6:47-49).

MARTHA: ONE THING NEEDFUL

38. Since the home of Mary and Martha was located at Bethany
(John 11:1), and since Luke is not yet prepared to announce Jesus'
arrival at this village located so close to Jerusalem, he speaks
vaguely of a village. The story of the Good Samaritan had dealt
principally with the question of the second table of the Law. This
account deals with the first.

39. In Acts 22:3 Paul is said to have sat at the feet of Gama-
liel. Here Mary sits at the feet of Jesus. He is the Teacher. The
lawyer learned his lesson from Jesus, and this account underlines the
fact that Jesus is the authoritative Teacher for Israel. The title
Lord would remind the community of the resurrected Lord.

40. Martha is a picture of the fussy legalist, preoccupied with
much apparent service but without thoughtful love and embarrassing
her distinguished guest by an obvious demonstration of the trouble
to which his visit had put her. Besides, she upbraids him for his
lack of consideration. He ought to have reminded Mary to help Martha.
But had Martha loved the Lord, she would have considered it a privilege
to do all the serving herself. However, like the legalist, she sees
her own performance against the lack of performance in others.

41-42. She would have to learn the lesson set down in the sermon
on the plain (6:41-42). St. Paul had a similar reminder for the church
(1 Corinthians 7:34). The double mention of Martha's name reflects
the sensitivity of the narrator. All this hubbub needs to be toned
down. The wit in Jesus' dialogue is a choice bit of stylistic 'relief'
of the tension built up in the narrative: 'There is need only of a
few things, or even one.' (This is the preferred text, rendered in the
margin of RSV: *few things are needful, or only one.*) That is, an olive
or two will suffice at present, for Mary has already had the 'best
course' (good portion), and it cannot be taken away from her. Jesus
has already dispensed the banquet of life, for Mary has been treated
to his word (vs. 39). And blessed are those who hear the word of God
and keep it (8:21). Martha made the mistake of thinking that she was
the host and Jesus the guest. It was the other way around (see on 5:
32). As 22:27 notes, the Son of man came not to be served but to serve.
The lawyer had come to find the answer to his legal problem. Jesus'
word to Mary and Martha is an answer also to the scribe and a constant
source of life for the Church. With this understanding the church can
avoid the impasse of activism without love. Thus Luke's association
of the story of Mary and Martha with that of the Good Samaritan

illustrates well his grasp of the challenge of Jesus' address to
legalistic dehumanization.

Of Good and Evil Spirits   LUKE 11:1-28

ON PRAYER AND THE HOLY SPIRIT   LUKE 11:1-13

The *Lord's Prayer*   LUKE 11:1-4
                                                       (Matthew 6:9-13)

1. The words 'and it came to pass' (omitted by RSV) and the fact
that Jesus is at prayer alert the reader to a fresh development in the
narrative. Legal casuistry and Jesus' authoritative word were contrasted in 10:25-42. Now dependence on God, with receipt of the Spirit, is
contrasted with the legalists' charge that Jesus is in league with an
evil demon (11:14-23). At 5:33 the Pharisees had said that John taught
his disciples to pray. Luke takes the present occasion in his travel
document to point out that Jesus also instructed his disciples on
this matter. Jews would be accustomed to some form of the Eighteen
Benedictions, or Shemone Esre, which was standard liturgy for the
synagogue. But special prayers, of which the Psalms are excellent
examples, would be composed for certain occasions, and rabbis were
accustomed to encourage their disciples in the discipline of private
expression.

Romans 8:15 and Galatians 4:6 may indicate that the Lord's Prayer
early in apostolic times became a liturgical formulation, but the evidence is inconclusive. The variations, as attested by a comparison of
Luke's version with that in Matthew and by the different readings of
the manuscripts, are the result of liturgical adaptation.

2. Personal address of God as Father was especially common in
hellenistic circles (cf. Sirach 23:1, 4; Wisdom 14:3;3Maccabees 6:3,
8). The older literature also speaks of God as Father, but ordinarily
as Father of the entire people (Deuteronomy 32:6; Psalm 68:5; Isaiah 64:
8; 63:16; Jeremiah 3:4; Malachi 1:6; 2:10). The writings of Qumran,
like the Old Testament, contain no example of personal address of the
type in Luke 11:2. In Aramaic the word here rendered "Father" is *abba*.
The preservation of the word *abba* in Romans 8:15 and Galatians 4:6
suggests that this expression was used by Jesus himself (see also Mark
14:36). Luke naturally avoids an Aramaic word in a document designed
for Greek-speaking readers. Jesus' use of the term reflects the revolutionary character of other aspects of his teaching. *Abba* is a child's
term, like 'Daddy.' Jesus encouraged his disciples to understand God,
not as one far removed from their existence, but as One who could be
known as intimately as their own fathers (see on 10:22). It is a term
in keeping with his stress on the faith of the child (18:15-17). Such
familiarity does not mean contempt, for the disciple is to pray that
God's name be holy (hallowed).

A name in antiquity meant more than mere identification. The totality of the person was understood in a formulation of this type. The nature of God's being is revealed through his associations with his people and through their response to his direction. When God's people violate his ordinances, they bring his name or his person into disrepute (see Romans 2:24; Isaiah 52:5; Ezekiel 36:20). At Isaiah 52:5 a word transliterated 'blaspheme' is used in the Greek version. Blasphemy is the opposite of treating God's name as holy, a subject to be taken up further in Luke 11:14-20. But Isaiah 52:6 also states that God's name will be known 'in that day.' Thus Luke's emphasis on Jesus' directions for prayer is a part of his doctrine that Jesus is the one who introduces the New Age, a distinctive mark of that Age being a fresh understanding of God as Father. He, the Son of God, is especially equipped to reveal the Father's purpose for them (cf. 19:21-22). Hallowed be thy name, then, is another aspect of Jesus' constant reminder: 'Blessed are those who hear the word of God and keep it.' Not to hallow God's name is to repeat the mistake of those in Israel who were unfaithful to him who wanted them to call him Father (Jeremiah 3:19-20). The death of God takes place when Christian profession is not matched by performance.

'Let your kingdom come' is another way of realizing the holiness of God's name. God's kingdom destroys the work of Satan (see Luke 11:17-20). God's kingdom is present in the person of Jesus and the proclamation of the good news, but the disciple is to pray for its realization especially in his own existence, and for its full consummation at the end of the end-time. Thus the petition is not out of harmony with Luke's two-stage view of the Kingdom. Some manuscripts have in place of this petition the words 'Let your Holy Spirit come on us and cleanse us' (see also 1QH 3:21). The thought is in harmony with Luke's subsequent stress on the donation of the Spirit, but the change may well represent post-Lukan clarification that subsequently gained liturgical status and displaced the petition for the Kingdom. More important, however, is the witness of this variation to the church's liturgical freedom and its boldness in revising even the words of Jesus. The Lord's Prayer was not meant to be a rigid formulation, but a guide for the petitioner. The church today is also at liberty to modify, revise, and restate the Lord's Prayer in terms that will not require such elaborate clarification as these comments aim to accomplish. Yet liturgical commissions know how strongly people can feel and react to any tampering with time-hallowed phrases.

3. In the petition concerning daily bread Jesus exhorts his disciples to live in complete trust and dependence on their Father. The Kingdom of God is opposed to the kingdoms of this world (4:6-8), and anxiety over things (10:38-42) will frustrate its objectives. Jesus had himself given the disciples a demonstration of God's concern for them when he sent them out without extra provisions (see 10:4 and cf. 22:35). Now he tells them to pray for the bread they need for the day, and no more. This daily bread is in contrast to the annual supply petitioned in the ninth and eighteenth *benedictions* of the traditional prayer in the synagog.

135

LUKE 11:4-8

What does the petition mean today? Churches saddled with heavy
debts find themselves unable to carry out more needed missions of
compassion. Potential income determines choice of vocation for young
man or woman. The applications are many. The wonder is that any one
today dares pray this petition! In subsequent chapters Luke presents
the commentary on the petition (see, for example, 12:16-21; 21:1-4).

<u>4</u>. The words of the petition on forgiveness are an echo of the
theme expressed in 6:36-38. The thought is not that God should be
as compassionate as the disciple is in his relations to his fellowman.
On the contrary, the disciple can pray for forgiveness from God only
if he understands that such forgiveness binds him to every man in
similar obligation. The word <u>every one</u> is emphatic. God makes no
distinctions; neither can the <u>disciple.</u> No one is to be excluded, and
no score is to be kept (cf. 17:1-4). The petition is, therefore a
promise to God to take care of unfinished business. The mercy of
God creates the climate for the disciple's growth in love.

The concluding petition is a reminder to the disciple that he
has good reason to ask for forgiveness, instead of keeping score of
wrongs done to him. Temptations are no light matter. Peter, like a
piece of wood snatched from the burning, found this out to his sorrow
(see 22:31-32; 22:61-62 and cf. 22:46). Humility, therefore, is
becoming to the disciple as he asks his heavenly Father to preserve
him from the consequences of his own self-confidence. The words are
a reminder of what was said at 8:13. Once again Jesus signalled the
advance of a New Age. Litany, he demonstrated, need not be sepulchral.
And to our own age, which *communicates* less even while it *talks* more,
the brevity is refreshing.

The Friend at Midnight   LUKE 11:5-8

<u>5</u>. The Lord's Prayer lists a series of requests that might appear
impossible to meet. Something more than human power is necessary. Luke
assures the church that superhuman resources are indeed available --
the Holy Spirit (vs. 13). The rhetorical question in vss. 5-7 advances
an extreme situation in order to make that assurance stand out more
strongly. The <u>three loaves</u> requested are a normal ration. Jesus'
sense of humor <u>is reflected</u> in the hilarious description that follows.

<u>6-7</u>. Palestinian homes were not large and a single bedroom would
suffice for the family. After stumbling over his children, the host
would have to remove the huge timber that locked the door, but not
without considerable effort and noise. The prospect is unbearable, and
the friend shouts out that he <u>cannot</u> come.

<u>8</u>. But the man persists with his request. Soon the whole town
will be up. Not friendship, but desperation to secure at least some
night's rest prompts the donation. The man has won his plea because
of his refusal to take 'no' for an answer. The translation calls it
<u>importunity</u>, but the Greek means 'shamelessness.' Luke does not, of

136

course, suggest that God is as hard to move with a request as was this groggy friend. On the contrary, as the following series of sayings is quick to point out, God is anxious to give.

Answer to Prayer

LUKE 11:9-13
(Matthew 7:7-11)

<u>9</u>. The three imperatives in this verse emphasize the urgency to ask now for God's gifts and thereby gain what is expressed in the Lord's Prayer. <u>10</u>. Should the disciples fail to ask for and utilize these gifts they will find themselves as beggars without recourse (see the warning, with similar terminology, in 13:25-30).

<u>11-13</u>. The word <u>father</u> in vs. 11 echoes the directive to address God as Father (vs. 2). The variant about the stone listed in the margin of RSV comes from the parallel account in Matthew 7:9. God, says Jesus, is not less fatherly than are the disciples. The argument is typical of rabbinic reasoning. One argues from the lesser to the greater, in the formula, 'If this, how much more this.' But, in fact, there is no comparison between God and the disciple. Even the non-Christian Juvenal said: 'Dearer is a man to the gods than to himself.' The disciple is <u>evil</u>. That is, in comparison with God he must say, as did Peter, 'I am a sinful man' (5:8). Yet he knows how to give good gifts. The Father in heaven, then, will most certainly give the best of all -- the <u>Holy Spirit</u>! But one must want that gift! The word "Holy" before "Spirit" is not a mere formality. The disciples have been declared "evil." The Holy Spirit comes to make the changes described in the Lord's Prayer. He is available not only to theological bluebloods, but also to the 'poor' in the land. Ultimately, not ritualistic observance, but obedience from one who is a hearer and a keeper of Jesus' word is the criterion of the New Age.

ON EVIL SPIRITS

LUKE 11:14-28

Controversy on Exorcism

LUKE 11:14-20
(Mark 3:20-26; Matthew 12:24-28)

<u>14</u>. Appropriate to the theme of petition is the introduction of a man who suffers from a <u>demon</u>, curiously described as <u>dumb</u>. The demon is characterized by the effects he has on the man. In Luke 7:22 the cure of the dumb is a sign of the New Age. This is in fulfillment of Isaiah 35:6. The dumb man had been kept from sharing Israel's liturgical life. Now he is able to speak. Matthew underlines the interruption in communication with the observation that he was also blind.

<u>15</u>. Despite his close relationship with the Father and his attack on the demonic world, Jesus is charged by <u>some</u> in the 'crowds' (<u>people</u>) with being in league with Beelzebul, one of the princes of darkness.

137

16. __Others__ ask for a __sign__. They want a special demonstration, such as Gideon asked of the Lord (Judges 6:36-40), to establish Jesus' credentials. A parallel in modern times is the criticism that the Christian message is invalidated by the fact that the church has been unable to eradicate war and injustice. The principal flaw in the criticism is a confusion of the message with institutional forms. Luke observes that the request was in the nature of a tempta- tion (__to test him__). Ironically, while Jesus casts out a demon this portion of the crowd takes over Satan's specialty (cf. 4:2).

17-20. Jesus uses three arguments to refute the complaint con- cerning alleged alliance with Beelzebul. The __first__ appears in vss. 17-18. Satan would not permit rebellion in his own ranks. That would spell the dissolution of his kingdom. By ascribing a kingdom to Satan, Jesus asserts his own superior kingdom claims. Verse 19 presents the __second__ argument. Other Jewish exorcists are at work (cf. Josephus __Antiquities__ 8, 2,5). But the opposition has taken God out of the picture. Very well, asks Jesus, 'If __I__ (the pronoun is emphatic) am using Beelzebul as an ally, whom do __your sons__ employ?' The succeeding verse suggests that the Lord has in mind the magicians summoned by Pharaoh to duplicate the feats of Moses and Aaron (Exodus 7:11). The sons of the opposition would not want to be placed in that category. __Therefore__, says Jesus, __they will be your judges.__ That is, they will instruct you properly. (On the judge as a possessor of wisdom, see Sirach 10:1,) The use of the present tense in the verb __cast out__, may refer to the frustrated attempts of the exorcists, who would use much mumbo-jumbo. Jesus effected his cures with a single command. Hence other exorcists would readily recognize his superior power. If, then, devils were to be expelled with the help of Satan, why do they come out with such reluctance when other exorcists are at work (cf. 9:40)? Furthermore, why was it Jesus who had to expel the demon from the dumb man? Why did __they__ not do it? The argument of the opposi- tion is patently ridiculous on any estimate of the circumstances.

20. The __third__ argument is to the effect that God is asserting his reign. Jesus replaces Moses. Pharaoh's magicians could duplicate only the first two plagues of blood and frogs (Exodus 7:14-8:7). The production of gnats stumped them (8:18), and they were forced to confess 'This is the finger of God' (8:19). Apparently they were making refer- ence to Aaron's staff. In Luke 11:20 the __finger of God__ refers to divine power, as in Exodus 31:18 and Deuteronomy 9:10. Jesus was to accomplish an exodus at Jerusalem (9:31). His exorcisms are among the signs that anticipate that climactic event. They are evidence that the Kingdom of God has made its appearance. In the context these words suggest that the Kingdom can spell either success or disaster. Those who oppose Jesus are moving on a collision course.

The Strong and the Stronger
LUKE 11:21-26
(Mark 3:27; Matthew 12:29-30,43-45)

21-22. In the Markan (3:27) and Matthaean (12:29-30) version of the first part of this series of sayings, Jesus is viewed as the one who enters the house of the 'strong' one, that is Satan, the thought being originally derived from Isaiah 49:24-25. Luke not only expands on the saying, but understands it differently and makes a fresh application of Isaiah 49. The strong one in his recital of the saying is Israel. If Israel guards her inheritance, all is well and her goods are in peace. But if she permits herself to become weak, a stronger one, comparatively speaking, can come and conquer her, take all the armour in which she puts her trust, and divide the spoil (an express allusion here to Isaiah 53:12 cannot be proved). Luke 19:41-44 pictures the tragic fate of Jerusalem which failed to take note of her source of peace and took refuge instead in her traditions. The stronger one, Satan, had blinded her eyes (cf. 8:12). Her leaders, who attributed Jesus' works to Satan, could have no other expectation (see also 14:29-32).

23. This second saying endorses the previous interpretation. The word gather is the theme of Isaiah 49, an indication that this saying was associated in Q with the preceding saying. Jesus is the one who gathers Israel. The hope of Isaiah 49:24-25 is that God will send help to the captives and deliver them from their strong oppressor. Jesus says in Luke's account that the reverse of this expectation can happen if one does not gather with him. In such case a scattering, that is, destruction takes place. And, as the preceding verses state, those who thought themselves strong will be overcome. The interpretation advanced here appears to ignore the usage of 'stronger' (RSV, 'mightier') in Luke 3:16. However, context takes precedence over verbal correspondence.

24-26. A comparison of the third saying with its placement in Matthew further confirms the interpretation given to the preceding sayings. Matthew has these words after the recital of the sign of Jonah (Matthew 12:39-42, 43-45). Luke appears to have shifted them from the position they held in the Q source in order to climax his description of Israel's basic problem, her failure to see that she could come under demonic control. Thus the three sayings (11:21-22, 23, 24-26) parallel the three 'if' clauses in vss. 18-20.

24. The desert is the standard locale for demons (cf. Isaiah 13:21; 34:14), but they long to take up residence in human beings. No description of self-righteous security can match this proverb-like statement. Israel was a chosen instrument of God. She was like a man from whom a demon had been expelled. But now her religious leadership rejects him who is Satan's most potent enemy (vs. 20).

25. Secure in her ritual and legalistic purity she becomes easy pickings for demonic forces. 26. Seven other spirits return, a number expressing total annexation (cf. Testament of Reuben 2-3). Thus the final condition is worse than the first (see John 5:14). Rejection of the Holy Spirit (vs. 13) invites invasion of the evil spirit (cf. 1QS 3:18-25). In Luke's total account the text also explains why demonic power was so apparent during the apostolic ministry. It is due

to failure to heed the word. Satan has been defeated, but he still
is operative in those who do not accept his defeat as real.

Flattery Rebuked   LUKE 11:27-28

The story of Mary and Martha (10:38-42) had accented the importance
of hearing Jesus' word as answer to legalistic lovelessness. Now a
logion on hearing the word terminates the indictment of those who
charged Jesus with being in league with Satan. It was customary to
praise the offspring through congratulation of the mother (cf. 1:28, 42,
48). Thus Ovid writes:

> O Youth, most worthy
> To be named among the gods. If god
> You be, then Cupid is your name.
> And if a mortal, blessed are those
> Who call you son. Blessed is the one
> Who boasts you brother, and she who calls
> Herself a sister. Blessed is the nurse
> Who tendered you her breasts.

(*Metamorphoses* 4, 320-324)

27. The womb is mentioned as the source of life, and the breasts
as source of nourishment. In Mary's case the mention of the womb would
be especially significant for the reader, since her offspring was the
result of the Spirit's descent (1:35). As at 8:19-21, Jesus disavows
an advantage based merely on natural association (see also 13:26). By
implication, distorted pride in temple and ancestry comes under indictment.

28. Jesus does not disclaim the woman's remarks, but through
his emphasis on the word of God draws attention to the importance of
hearing such words as have just been spoken, e.g., in vss. 23-26. Word
echoes 'while he was *speaking*' (RSV, as he said this, vs. 27). Jesus'
words are the authoritative message of God's Kingdom. Only those who
renounce the reign of Satan will receive the Spirit of God, the only
effective antidote to the powers of evil.

On Response to the Word   LUKE 11:29-54

SIGN-SEEKERS   LUKE 11:29-36

Sign of Jonah   LUKE 11:29-32
                                                            (Matthew 12:38-42)

29. Luke now introduces Jesus' answer to the sign-seekers of 11:16.
On this generation, see comment on 7:31; on sign-seeking, see 11:16.

Matthew (12:39) adds, or retains from his Q source, the expression
'adulterous,' a term readily understandable from the Old Testament
(see, for example, Hosea). Luke's readers might have found the term
puzzling. The generation is evil, for it seeks a sign of ratification instead of heeding the message presented by Jesus. Since Jesus,
in accordance with the prophetic program, invited Israel to share the
benefits of the New Age, there is nothing in his presentation that
should arouse opposition, unless it be that their claims to honor
God are not really genuine. Jesus, in line with Simeon's prophecy
(2:34-35), refuses to offer any other sign but his own person and
message. In this respect he is like Jonah. Jonah was God's instrument of salvation for Nineveh. Had they not listened to Jonah's
preaching, the Ninevites would have been destroyed. But they heeded
it and were saved.

30. The Son of man is likewise a sign to this generation. This
apocalyptic figure is present in Jesus of Nazareth, but instead of
being the victorious deliverer for Israel, he may turn out to be its
source of disaster -- that is, unless the nation repents. Thus the
sign is in the authority with which both Jonah and Jesus preached,
backed by the decisive action of God. In Nineveh's case, a stay of
execution; in the other, disaster.

31-32. Israel's response to Jesus is even more critical because
he, as the center of the end-time revelation, is greater than either
Solomon or Jonah. The Queen of Sheba (1 Kings 10:1-13) came to listen
to Solomon. Similarly the Ninevites, Gentiles, heeded the message
of Jonah. Israel therefore has two examples in her past history that
ought to shame her in the present hour. They will rise up in judgment
against Israel. Thus the ultimate disaster of Israel is here reviewed,
and the mission to the Gentiles is viewed as part of the judgment of
Israel's failure to recognize her hour of decision (cf. Acts 28:28).
Solomon, the epitome of wisdom, may be included in the narrative also
because of the reference to the Son of man, who is described in Enoch
49:1-3 as filled with the spirit of wisdom (see also Luke 2:47,52;
10:21-22). Moreover, it is quite possible that Luke was familiar with
the tradition that Solomon was deprived of the privilege of perpetuating
the Davidic dynasty through his descendants. 1 Chronicles 28:6-7
conditions the perpetuity of Solomon's house on his obedience, and 1
Kings 11:9-13 describes the disaster that befell him. Jeremiah 22:30
declares that no descendant of Jeconiah's (the last ruler in Solomon's
line) would sit on the throne of David. In his genealogy of Jesus,
Luke by-passed a long line of kings and traced the Lord's descent
through the obscure line of Nathan (3:31), another son of David (1
Chronicles 3:5). Thereby he avoided any mention of Jeconiah (Matthew
1:11) and also discouraged suggestion that Jesus' title to the throne
of David was suspect in view of Jeremiah's pronouncement. Jesus is
greater than Solomon also by virtue of his superior title to the
Davidic throne.

Two Sayings on Light   LUKE 11:33-36
                                                      (Matthew 5:15; 6:22-23)

In Matthew the first of these sayings appears at 5:15, the
second at 6:22-23. Luke used the illustration of the light and the
lampstand in 8:16. He reproduces it here almost verbatim, but in the
interests of a different application. This procedure is a reminder of
the extent to which traditional material was shifted about in the
recital of Jesus' life and freely modified in public preaching and
written records. Similarly in contemporary preaching the same text
will be handled differently by various preachers.

Verse 33 is not to be allegorized. It is true that in the Old
Testament both God and the Law are described as light. (On God as
light, see Isaiah 60:19; on the Law as light, Psalm 119:105; Isaiah 51:
4.) But the purpose of the illustration is to emphasize that the
function of a lamp is to give light.

34. In 8:17 the illustration was applied to God's unveiling of
his mysteries. Here it introduces a pointed critique of the religious
man, who frustrates the purpose of the light through insincerity. In
Jewish thought the eye is viewed as the light-bearing organ, flooding
the body with light, as through a funnel. If the eye is sound, the
body is in good health. If the eye is not sound, or bad, (the word is
the same one used to describe this generation, vs. 29), then the body
will be dark, that is, it will lack perception of the things outside
it and steer a course outside God's purposes (cf. Proverbs 4:19).

35. Luke now applies this experience of the physical faculty to
man's spiritual apprehension (as does Philo in his treatise *On the
Creation* 53). Only instead of directing the hearer to check his eye,
Jesus says that he must check what is within himself -- it may be
darkness instead of light. In that case the man has serious eye-trou-
ble. The word "sound" (vs. 34) is the key to the meaning. This word
is also used in moral discourse in the sense of pure, unalloyed,
sincere, single-minded. To be single-minded means that what 'appears on
the surface is matched by what is being actually thought (see Testament of Issachar, 4-5). A single-minded person, e.g., does a kindness
without privately wishing that he had not been obligated to do it.
The elder brother, who said to his father, 'All these years I have
been slaving for you' (Luke 15:29), was double-minded. His father
thought he was obedient because the son loved him. But soon his true
colors were shown. Similarly in the case of Jesus' opposition. They
go through the rituals of their religious tradition, and it would
appear that they are devoted to God. But then they charge Jesus with
a demon and request a sign. They claim to see, but do not see (cf.
Luke 8:10; Acts 28:26-27), and their vaunted boast in the Torah is
proved to be phony. The Semitic mind deals with concrete realities.
Hence Jesus' final statement speaks of the light that floods the body.

36. If the body is filled with light, then the eye must be sound.
The body, in the light of the context, is   the total personality.

If the religious man hears the word of God and keeps it, he qualifies
as a sound or sincere person. Israel's leaders are in danger of blindness (despite their confidence in the Law as light; cf. Psalm 43:3;
Proverbs 6:23), for they attribute Jesus' works of light to the prince
of darkness. With these sayings the thought in 10:21-24 is seen in
bold relief.

INDICTMENT OF THE PHARISEES   LUKE 11:37-44
                                                   (Matthew 23:25-26, 6-7,27)

37. The preceding discourses (11:5-36) spoke of true spirituality,
climaxing with inward light versus inward darkness. A banquet scene
continues this thought with a discussion of external rites and inner
goodness. Jesus' failure to follow the ritual practices of the Pharisees sets the stage for the dialogue. **38.** The word wash is the same
word used in 3:21, where it is rendered 'baptized.' Handwashing before
meals was a religious ceremony, not an anti-microbe action.

39. As the lamp can be a vehicle for expressing spiritual receptivity, so the cup and dish become a symbol of spiritual content (cf.
Jeremiah 51:7; Revelation 17:4). The Pharisees are more concerned
with outward appearances than with their inward condition. In the
Assumption of Moses (7) impious men are described as 'self-pleasers,
dissemblers in all their own affairs and lovers of banquets at every
hour of the day, gluttons, gourmands .... Devourers of the goods of
the poor .... And though their hands and their minds touch unclean
things, yet their mouth shall speak great things, and they shall say
furthermore: "Do not touch me lest thou shouldst pollute me in the
place (where I stand)."' Jesus' words, therefore, are a strong rebuke,
tantamount to classifying the Pharisees with the very publicans and
sinners they despised. As defenders of the Law they considered themselves among the wise, described in such literature as the Book of
Proverbs (see, for example, Proverbs 4).

40. Jesus addresses them with the opposite term -- You fools.
In the Old Testament a fool is a wicked man (cf. Proverbs 6:12),
and a godless person (cf. Psalm 14:1). Boasting a knowledge of God,
the Pharisees know little about him. Otherwise they would know that
the inside is more important than the outside. Luke does not include
any statement resembling Matthew 5:22, and his use of the term "fool"
in personal address (here and in 12:20) is unique in the gospels.

41. According to Proverbs 20:27, 'the spirit of man is the lamp
of the Lord,' followed by these words: 'Mercy and truth are the
bulwark of the king' (Septuagint version). The word mercy used in the
Greek version of Proverbs 20:28 is the word rendered alms in Luke 11:41.
Almsgiving is the practical expression of mercy (see 12:33 and cf.
Hosea 6:6). Mercy, then, is a characteristic of the man who is full
of light. Whether Luke was prompted by this association of light with
mercy to see a connection between this section from Q and the earlier
logion (11:34-36), is impossible to determine with complete certainty.

If the passages were already connected in Q, then Matthew has scattered them in his gospel, and there is strong probability that Luke sensed the connection. However, there is stronger probability for influence of Isaiah 1:10-31 (especially vss. 16-17) on the development of this passage. In Isaiah 1 Israel is indicted for emphasizing cult to the exclusion of justice and is invited to 'wash' herself (vs. 16) by removing 'wickedness' (cf. Luke 11:39) and by practicing 'justice' (Isaiah 1:17; cf. Luke 11:42). If Israel repents along these lines, she will be 'pure' (Isaiah 1:16). This also is Luke's meaning in 11:41. If the Pharisees practice mercy, then they need not worry about contracting impurity from external things (cf. Titus 1:15).

42. Deuteronomy 14:22-29 lays down the rules for tithing, but with strong emphasis on meeting the needs of the poor through a portion of the tithe. The Pharisees are at pains to carry out the provisions that deal with produce, even to the extent of tithing the smallest herbs, but they bypass the more important part of the legislation. The words justice and love of God echo the two tables of the Law (cf. Luke 10:27). To say that a Pharisee, who boasted of his delight in the Law of the Lord, did not love God, would be enough to shock him into apoplexy. Yet this is the trap into which his fussy ritualism had led him. Jesus does not suggest that Pharisees should turn their backs on tradition, but they ought to make their ritual a vehicle for reminder of the weightier requirements. Luke's retention of this saying reflects debate in the church between Jerusalem and the Gentile mission. It was generally agreed that Jewish Christians should practice their ancestral customs, but that Gentiles be permitted to develop in freedom (see Acts 15). Galatians 2:10, however, reflects the general concern -- ritual or not, the poor are the responsibility of all.

43. The pitiful name-dropping and scrambling for recognition by being seen in the right places and in the most advantageous company are under indictment in the second woe. The Pharisees enjoy the gaping esteem of the people, who marvel at these last outposts of truth and righteousness. Yet it is they who are the great hazard.

44. So concerned about ritual purity, they are like unmarked tombs over which the wayfarer walks in ignorance. Far from being clean, they make others unclean through their presence (cf. Numbers 19:16). In Matthew 23:27 the contrast is between a whitewashed exterior and decay within, thus displaying the Pharisee's fine outward show of piety against inner rottenness. Luke, however, is writing for hellenistic readers who would be familiar with landscape dotted by tombs. Therefore he emphasizes the thought that the average person is unaware of the deep-seated moral inadequacy of these religious practitioners. In other words, they are deceiving men, not God.

INDICTMENT OF THE LAWYERS   LUKE 11:45-54
                                    (Matthew 23:4, 29-31, 34-36, 13)

45. The lawyers correctly assess that they are also indicted in
the Lord's pronouncement over the Pharisees, for they are the experts
who interpret the mind of Moses for their generation.

46. They place men under heavy burdens of obedience, but through
their own casuistry excuse themselves from compliance (see, for example,
Mark 7:11-13; Acts 15:10). They are more concerned about asserting
their legal authority than to find ways and means of being helpful to
the individual. While impressing others with their conservatism, they
were liberal in satisfying themselves. Thus in contemporary society,
righteous churchmen and church-goers may have much to say about law
and order, but may do little to aid in the solution of the social ills
that lead to disruption.

47-48. At first sight the criticism in vss. 47-48 appears irrelevant. Why should the lawyers be criticized for erecting tombs in
honor of the prophets? This would not necessarily mean that they endorse the murders done by their ancestors. The text, however, emanates
from the church's reflection on her contemporary experience. Not only
was Jesus, prophet par excellence, executed (see a related critique in
Acts 7:52), but Stephen, a man full of the Spirit (Acts 6:3) was
stoned. Among those presiding over the verdict of execution were
scribes, that is, the legal experts (Acts 6:12). On Jesus' lips the
passage would mean: 'You like only dead prophets, not living ones.'
Thus Jesus exposes the hypocrisy of religious people who invoke the
authority of holy men of God from the past, while refusing to listen
to similar contemporary voices. The ancient prophet, he says, is 'safe,'
for his words embalm situations that belong to a remote age. But let
those same prophets rise from the dead and pitch their message to a
contemporary key, let them proclaim an end to protected seasons for
self-privileging economics and theology, let them name names as in
the time long gone, and they will soon find themselves charged with
libel and remurdered by the very ones who boast that they have no
equals as curators of tradition.

49-51. Even while building their memorials they plot against
Jesus (Luke 11:54). Their action is like that of the Egyptians,
cited in Wisdom 19:3, who interrupted their lamentations to pursue
the Israelites. Wisdom 19:4 goes on to say: 'For fate rightly was
bringing them to this end, and made them forgetful of their past
disasters, that they might fill up what was left of their assigned
torment.' Similarly Jesus says that God's emissaries are sent that the
blood of all the prophets, shed from the foundation of the world, may
be required of this generation. Thus in Wisdom 19:4 and Luke 11:50
judgment ripens for the oppressor.

Luke refers Jesus' words in vs. 49 to the *Wisdom of God*. But the
quotation is nowhere to be found in the wisdom literature. However,
2 Chronicles 24:19 reads: 'Yet he sent prophets among them to bring

them back to the Lord.' Immediately following this verse is the
recital of the stoning of Zechariah, the son of Jehoiada the priest
(vss. 20-22). Luke 11:51 would appear to have this Zechariah in mind.
How are we to account for this striking combination of thought from
2 Chronicles 24 and Wisdom 19? A common interpretive device used by
rabbis was called *midrash pesher*. Through this method of interpretation a contemporary application was read into the ancient text, and
the text would then be quoted in that updated form. Instead of drawing on Q at this point in his recital, Luke appears to use a variant
form of Q, from Hellenistic Jewish-Christian circles, which included
reflection based on a combination of the thoughts expressed in both
Wisdom 19:3-4 and 2 Chronicles 24:19-22. Such a view of Luke's text-
form would also account for the following facts. 1. The mention of
apostles (vs. 49), a term that reflects the church's apostolic mission.
2. The phrase, The Wisdom of God (vs. 49). Instead of referring to the
Book of Wisdom, this phrase takes it into account, but speaks more broad-
ly of God's providential wisdom in governing the affairs of the early
community. Jerusalem had fallen, and this would be seen as divine
wrath for the blood of the prophets (cf. Revelation 6:10) from Abel
to Zechariah. God, who spoke in time past, now interprets the present
in the light of the past. Hence "the Wisdom of God said." An alternative to Zechariah the son of Jehoiada is Zechariah son of Bariscaeus,
slain in A.D. 68 by two Zealots in the precincts of the temple (cf.
Josephus *Wars* 4, 5, 4). But this view leaves largely unexplained Luke's
peculiar handling of his Q source when compared with Matthew's treatment.

52. The Pharisees had three woes pronounced on them (vss. 42-43).
A third is here pronounced on the lawyers. They claim possession of
the key to open the door of knowledge, but they have no interest in
going through the door, and they keep others from entering. As a television critic complained about religious television programs, these
guardians of the past were facing the issues 'with all the force of a
marshmallow bouncing off a pillow.' 53. Encounter with the 'establishment' has reached a point of no return. Both scribes and Pharisees
now wait for Jesus to utter some incriminating word.

On Careful Choice   LUKE 12:1-13:9

ADDRESS TO DISCIPLES   LUKE 12:1-53

Fearless Confession   LUKE 12:1-12
                                    (Matthew 10:26-33; 12:32; 10:19-20)

1. In the face of Jesus' encounter with the multitude, which is
said to number 'tens of thousands,' the disciples are given special
instruction on the hazards of association with their Lord and the need
of single-minded devotion. Hence the stress on the word first. The
crowds have their turn at vss. 54-59 (see also Peter's question in vs.

41). Strict instructions on the removal of leaven during the feast of the Passover are given in Exodus 12:14-20. Jesus' illustrative use of the word is therefore a strong indictment. In Mark 8:15 the leaven is interpreted as hardness of heart. Luke understands it as hypocrisy (cf. 1 Corinthians 5:6-8). Hypocrisy is the opposite of the soundness or singlemindedness described in 11:33-36. The details were described in 11:37-52.

2-3. Verse 2 is related in thought to 11:33-35 and once again picks up the theme of 2:35. Matthew 10:26-27 applies the same illustration to Jesus' teaching, which is made available to the disciples and through them to the public. Luke, however, views the saying as a description of one whose interior character is brought to light (cf. Luke 2:35; Romans 2:16; 1 Corinthians 4:5). The hypocrite will not be able to hide his true colors, and the disciple will have opportunity to display the genuineness of his profession. The disciple needs the reminder because discipleship involves persecution; and in the critical hour, described in 12:4-12, it will soon be apparent of what stuff he is made. Will the profession of faith recited on beds of ease be maintained on the spikes?

4. The words my friends express Jesus' confidence in his disciples as men whose words are backed by action (cf. John 15:14-16). Hypocrites cannot be classed as true friends. Fear of what men may do is removed by emphasizing that once the body is killed the enemy has done his worst.

5. God, however, has power over the totality of man's being. He not only takes life, but can destroy the person in hell. This is the second death referred to in Revelation 20:14. The word for hell is Gehenna, a valley near Jerusalem where children were once offered to Molech (see Jeremiah 7:31-32). Josiah's reform turned it into a garbage dump (see 2 Kings 23:10). Thus the locale became a symbol of punishment reserved for the rebellious (cf. Revelation 14:7-13). The negative picture of God's ultimate authority derives from the discussion of fear. If one is to fear what another can do, it is wiser to fear God who can do the greater damage. This means, of course, that he can also destroy those who persecute the friends of Jesus. In effect, then, vss. 4-5 say: 'Do not fear what men may do. The enemy must ultimately reckon with One who can do far more.' Thus these verses are a source of consolation as well as of admonition (cf. 1 Peter 4: 17-19).

Verses 6-7 continue the description of God's concern for the disciples. Here is the perfect love that casts out fear. In typical rabbinic style Jesus argues from the lesser to the greater. Five sparrows are worth only a few cents. Matthew 10:29 says that their death does not go unnoticed. Luke does not speak of their death, but of God's providential concern. Life, as well as death, is under his direction. The illustration of the hairs, like the reference to tens of thousands in vs. 1, is an hyperbole. God does not spend his time counting hairs. This is a semitic way of saying that the disciple can rest assured that

the God of the sparrows is not oblivious to the disciples' needs
(cf. 1 Kings 1:52; Luke 21:18; Acts 27:34). Their names are recorded
in heaven (Luke 10:20).

8-9. In Mark 8:38 the Son of man appears as a judge. Here he is
first of all an advocate of the faithful and then judge of those whose
profession of religion is hypocritical (cf. Luke 9:26). In popular
apocalyptic the Son of man was to initiate a glorious day for Israel.
Luke emphasizes the continuity between Jesus' ministry and the onward
course of history, culminating in the final judgment. Any claim to
be made some day before the Son of man is conditioned by response
now to Jesus' message (cf. Revelation 3:5).

Verse 10 is to be understood in the light of the Church's missionary activity. After the resurrection of Jesus the apostles would
proclaim the significance of Jesus within God's redemptive plan for
Israel. But could those who rejected Jesus receive assurance of forgiveness? The answer is positive: Anyone who speaks against Jesus,
identified here as the Son of man, is eligible for forgiveness, but
God will tolerate no reviling (blasphemies) of the Holy Spirit. Through
the apostolic proclamation the call to repentance is once more issued
(cf. Acts 2:37-41; 3:26). But Stephen is compelled to acknowledge
that his countrymen resist the Holy Spirit (Acts 7:51; cf. 28:25-28).
At the same time, the qualifications of the apostles are here clarified.
They had deserted the Lord before his crucifixion, and Peter had
denied him with an oath. For this there was forgiveness; and the response of the disciples at Pentecost indicates that their repentance
was genuine.

11. Experiences of the apostolic emmisaries find expression in
this verse. In Acts 7:51-52 Luke associates resistance to the Holy
Spirit with persecution of God's prophets. A similar association
appears here in Luke 12:10-11 (cf. 21:12-15). Luke's point is that
negative response to the apostolic message is no indication that the
apostolic messengers are in default, either religiously or politically.
Nor should they construe such experience as a sign that Jesus was not
Israel's authentic Messiah.

12. Especially Israel's leadership must know that they are
dealing not merely with men but with the Holy Spirit, who speaks
through the disciples. Thus vs. 12 parallels the thought of Mark 13:11.
In the missionary situation the words find fulfillment in Peter's
response to the charges of the leaders (Acts 4:5-22), and Acts 4:8
expressly states that Peter was filled with the Holy Spirit.

Worldly Cares

Since attachment to things may lead to a denial of Jesus in the
face of the Establishment, the evangelist supports the preceding
consolation with sundry admonitions relating to possessions.

The Rich Fool   LUKE 12:13-21

13. The fact that disputes concerning inheritance (cf. Numbers
27:8-11; Deuteronomy 21:17) would ordinarily be handled by a scribe
(in Luke usually 'lawyer'), indicates that Jesus is viewed as one
well trained in the Scriptures. Hence the address, teacher. According to the law of inheritance the eldest would receive more than the
younger brothers. Perhaps the plaintiff is one of the latter and
either feels himself cheated in the division of property or urges
an immediate execution of the estate.

14. Jesus' reply is patterned after the words in Exodus 2:14
(cf. Acts 7:27), but in this case with a disclaimer of the role of
Moses (see on Luke 9:28-36). The saying contrasts with Paul's
admonition that disputes were to be settled within the fellowship,
not in the secular courts (1 Corinthians 6:1-6). Luke, who describes
the voluntary sharing of possessions in the early community (see Acts
2:44-45), would find the words especially appropriate and in harmony
with the appointment of almoners so that the apostles might concentrate on the proclamation of the Word (Acts 6:1-4). The saying, then,
does not provide excuse for Christians to ignore questions of social
justice. This man's plea reflected private concern. It is another
matter when the rights of others are involved. The fundamental priority of the Good News over personal aggrandizement is at issue. Values
are to be kept straight.

15. Covetousness, or greed, can displace God, for it is the
equivalent of idolatry (see Colossians 3:5, Ephesians 5:5). 'How much
is he worth?' This is the popular measurement of man in terms of
stocks and dollars. Jesus denies the validity of such equation.

16-21. The word soul (vs. 19) in the story of the wealthy farmer
requires special attention. In 12:19-20 it specifies man in his totality, possessing life as that which animates him and having a personal
identity that transcends and outlasts mere bodily existence. This
farmer made the mistake of confusing his real self with his body. He
is like a certain man who trained for the dental profession and at
thirty looked forward to retirement at forty so that he might enjoy
his country estate; he ignored the fact that his trained talents were
needed by people. Luke's brief description is that of the man who
forgets God (Psalm 14:1) and, content with his monopoly, refuses to
use his bounty for the benefit of others (Proverbs 11:26). Ephesians
4:28 offers a contrasting picture of men who do not think in terms
of larger warehouses. Since the man's action is typical of the fool
(Luke 12:20), as he is described in wisdom literature (see Sirach
11:18-19; cf. Enoch 97) and in the story of Nabal (the 'foolish'
one), 1 Samuel 25, he is addressed with this term (see on 11:40). The
words is required (vs. 20) are a circumlocution for 'God demands the
return' (see on 6:38).

The supreme irony in Luke's story is the rich man's address to
himself: Take your ease, eat, drink, be merry (vs. 19). These words

149

are found frequently, with some variation, on ancient gravestones. The rich man pronounced his own epitaph! With almost brutal sarcasm comes the question about the things that were to spell his joy: Whose will they be?(vs. 20). Frequent is the lament in antiquity that a foolish heir may lay hands on the fruit of one's labors (see, for example, Ecclesiastes 2:18-19). This farmer dies in so unexpected a moment that the question comes with a shock. Quintus Dellius, friend of the Roman poet Horace, had a little more time: 'You must leave the many groves you have purchased; you must leave your house and your Tiber-washed villa; and an heir will possess your highly-piled riches' (Odes II, 3,17-20).

In 1923 a group of the world's most successful men met at the Edgewater Beach hotel in Chicago. Assembled were: the president of the largest steel corporation; the greatest wheat speculator; a man who was to be president of the New York stock exchange; a member of the President's cabinet; the canniest investor on Wall Street; a future director of the World Bank for International Settlements; and the head of the world's largest monopoly. A few years later this was their fate: Charles Schwab died in debt; Arthur Cutten died abroad in obscurity; Richard Whitney became insolvent, did time in Sing Sing, and was blotted out of Who's Who; Albert Fall was pardoned from prison in order that he might die at home; Jesse Livermore, Leon Fraser, and Ivar Kreuger the match king committed suicide. All learned how to make money. None of them learned how to live. All the bulls became lambs, and Schwab's bleating in 1930 was the most pitiful of all: 'I'm afraid; every man is afraid. I don't know, we don't know, whether the values we have are going to be real next month or not.'

Have no Cares   LUKE 12:22-34
                                    (Matthew 6:25-33; 6:19-21)

22-23. The rich man's experience revealed that man receives his life temporarily on loan from God and that he cannot live only out of the resources that surround his bodily existence. The value of man's real being and body, says Jesus, is not to be measured by food and clothing. These words are misunderstood if they are interpreted as an encouragement to idleness or improvidence. Nor do they sound an attack on any economic system, for Jesus said earlier, 'The laborer is worthy of his pay' (10:7). The key phrase is do not be anxious. A deep-seated anxiety is reflected in the rich man's dialogue. But living is more than having. Seneca, Nero's chaplain, preached sternly on the hazards of wealth, but from the vantage point of a personal fortune, and some of his critics have accused him of hypocrisy. In the case of Jesus, the poorest of the poor, there was no credibility gap, and he probed far more profoundly than did Seneca the theological issue.

24. Ravens, being birds of carrion, would be considered unclean. Yet God supplies them and their fledglings with food (Psalm 147:9; Job 38:41). Once again Jesus argues from the lesser to the greater.

25-26. The word rendered span of life is used by Luke in 2:52 and 19:3 in the sense of 'height.' A number of ancient copyists understood the word in the latter sense, for they include in vs. 27 the words how they grow. Since RSV also includes this addition in vs. 27, it is inexplicable why the translators use "span of life" instead of 'height' at vs. 25. The conditional statement in vs. 26 at first sight suggests that an addition to one's span of life would more easily qualify as a "small" thing, relatively speaking, than an addition of a cubit to one's height. But the proverbial saying must be viewed from the Semitic point of view. The growth of an individual is dependent on the nourishment he receives. The disciple has not grown to his present height through anxious thought. It is a natural process and a small thing (vs. 26), because it is taken for granted in human experience. One might render: 'Who grows by worrying about his height?' Such an interpretation clarifies the meaning of vs. 26. A significant part of the disciple's growth, ironically called a small part, has been achieved without his own preoccupation. Need he then be anxious about the maintenance from that point on?

27. The lilies mentioned in vs. 27 are the colorful wild anemones that dot the Galilean countryside in springtime. They grow in splendor outrivalling Solomon's grandeur. Corresponding to man's work of sowing and reaping (vs. 24) is woman's work of spinning and weaving (margin, RSV).

28. Wild flowers, for which no man displays a moment of concern, blooming today and used for fuel on the morrow, are God's extravagant hobby. But his chief business is man. O men of little faith calls the disciples to the realization of their true identity as God's chief concern. Lack of faith means that one identifies security under God's providential hand in terms of material satisfaction.

29. This verse does not, as it might appear at first sight, encourage irresponsibility. Irresponsibility is not a mark of piety or faith. The syntax of Luke's Greek suggests an agitated mind asking, 'My goodness, what do I have to eat?' and 'What in the world is there for me to drink?' The word underlying be of anxious mind is different from the one in vss. 22 and 26. It pictures one suspended between sky and earth, that is, one who lacks security and a firm spot for his feet. Such attitudes are to be expected of people who lack the knowledge of God that is possessed by the disciples. Anxiety is a species of unbelief, for it suggests that God abandons a man to his own resources. God is not stupid. He knows that his creatures require these elementary necessities. But they are not the staple of man's life.

30. In contrast to the 'Gentiles' (nations), these Jewish disciples are to show their superior theological understanding. 31. In accordance with what was said at 11:2, they are to seek God's Kingdom. Then these things will become a plus in their life, not the main interest. The non-believer seeks things, and that is all he has (cf. 6:24). The believer begins with God's reign, and the rest is extra. Hence, when

the disciples' things are taken away, only the plus is lost, whereas
the non-believer ends with nothing. Clearly, then, possession of
things is not in itself an evil. A prosperous person is not to feel
guilty because of his prosperity, unless his wealth is gained at the
expense of the Kingdom. Incalculable harm has been done by people
whose guilt feelings about possessions have prompted them to act
thoughtlessly toward others. Thus it is easy to dispense charity
at the expense of the unlucky recipient of misdirected alms. It is
much easier to buy garbage cans for a rat-infested neighborhood,
only to have them stolen and resold to the poor, than to move City
Hall to have more regular garbage collections. It is easier to give
a five dollar bill to a poor man than to go to the trouble of helping
him improve his laboring skills and to find constructive work for
him. Absurd welfare policies of a guilt-ridden affluent society
merely perpetuate the social dilemma.

32. This verse is not found in Matthew. The expression good
pleasure is typically Lukan (2:14; 10:21). Jesus is the head of a
little flock (cf. Matthew 9:36; Mark 6:34; 14:27; Luke 15:3-6).
Measured by human standards, his disciples are unsuccessful. And
they are to avoid acceptance of all accepted status symbols. The
Gentiles, that is, those who endorse the tyranny of things, seek control through wealth. The true power, or Kingdom, is God's to give,
and not to gain through standard channels. This is a minority viewpoint, but what seems folly to a self-satisfied establishment and the
mass of mankind is true wisdom.

33. To display his confidence in the heavenly Father and his
rejection of accepted criteria of human worth, the disciple is urged
to sell his possessions and give alms. The words echo Tobit 4:7-11
rather than the Matthaean version of Q. When material things are made
the standard of success, then tyranny, oppression, and social injustice are the fruits. Concern about property values, for example,
is a virus deeply imbedded in racism. The end thereof is destruction
of society. Jesus' disciples are to set their sights on that which is
permanent, and this is done through proper use of material things.
Varying social situations will determine the wisest type of almsgiving. Certainly the Lord does not advocate scaling heaven by making
poor people victims of selfishly motivated charity. In the United
States, Christians need to face up to the problem of an equitable
distribution of goods so that certain elements in the country do not
remain rooted in a poverty-crime-poverty syndrome. Political action
is necessary to achieve justice, and the Christian must accept his
responsibility to secure that end.

34. If one's bank deposit is made in Heaven First National,
then the real choices of a man's life will be governed from that perspective. That is having one's heart where the treasure is. Not
property values or political expedience, but concern for justice and
the true well being of one's fellow-man determine whether one has a
vision of the Kingdom. The Good Samaritan saw his man through to the
end (Luke 10:33-37). Stoicism endeavored to free men from anxiety but

displayed little interest in the poor. Ultimately such self-discipline was self-glorification. The Christian ideal is use of possessions, not ascetic rejection of things. Monasticism was the result of a misunderstanding. While the monks were praying, Russia ripened for revolution. Luke 12:22-34 is authentic commentary on the meaning of the Temptation of Jesus (4:1-13).

Watchfulness   LUKE 12:35-48
                                                      (Matthew 24:43-51)

35-36. The term Kingdom in vss. 31-32 suggests the second coming or Parousia, of Jesus. Since the Parousia may take place at any time, the disciple must be on the alert at *all* times. The girded loins picture a man with his full outer garment taken up at the waist. This would be done either to expedite travel (as at Exodus 12:11; Cf. Ephesians 6:14), or to equip the wearer for the task at hand (see the figurative use in 1 Peter 1:13). The latter interpretation is required by the context, which speaks of slaves being on the job. The burning lights remind one of the parable of the ten virgins (Matthew 25:1-12). The lamps would help the master enter his house at the late hour, and the slaves would be able to recognize him. That the disciple should be likened to a slave is not unusual (cf. Acts 4:29; Romans 6:19). The term is descriptive of God's people in Isaiah 65:8, 13-15; Ezekiel 20:40; Malachi 3:18, and expresses the total devotion of the disciple to his Lord's (that is, the Master's) wishes.

37-38. The blessedness (cf. 6:20) of the slaves is mentioned twice, once at the beginning and again at the end of the saying. Much of the language parallels Mark 13:33-37. To remain awake means to remain in touch with the Lord. To sleep means to interrupt the fellowship (see on Luke 22:45-46). So important is the theme of watchfulness that Jesus introduces his promise with the word truly (Greek, 'Amen'). In contrast to the large number of amen-sayings in Matthew and Mark, Luke has only six: 4:24; 12:37; 18:17; 18:29; 21:32; 23:43. The saying reflects the confession of the church that Jesus is among them as one who serves (cf. 22:27; Mark 10:45; John 13:1-11). Despite the late hour, the Master will treat his slaves to a banquet (cf. Luke 6:31). The uncertainty of the hour of arrival is repeatedly expressed (cf. Mark 13:35). He may come during the second watch (around midnight) or during the third one (early morning). In contrast to the rich man whose life terminated in Gehenna, the disciples will enjoy their returning Lord.

39-40. A second illustration is introduced. It is of course evident that no one will stay awake all night on the chance that some prowler will make off with the silver. But the disciples must do just that! They do not know when the Son of man comes. Hence, continuous vigilance. Overdrawn illustrations are characteristic of Eastern humor. The illustration of the thief recurs in 1 Thessalonians 5:2; 2 Peter 3:10; Revelation 3:3. The use of a morally reprehensible person or action for illustrative purposes occasions no surprise (see, for example, the unjust steward, Luke 16:8; the unjust judge, 18:1-6).

41. At 12:1 the disciples were addressed 'first.' Peter now asks whether the preceding parable was designed only for the disciples or for everyone. The nature of Jesus' reply indicates that Luke aims to accentuate the responsibility of the apostolic leadership, somewhat in the manner of 9:46-48. The fact that Peter, one of the important leaders in the community, is the questioner also points in this direction. Matthew follows Q without such editorial modification.

42. From Luke's stance the household is the serving staff in the church; and the portion of food, that is, the daily rations, suggests the administrative authority the Apostles and other leaders in the church are to exercise as stewards (see 1 Corinthians 4:1). **43.** The steward is also a slave (servant). The attribute of blessedness parallels 12:37. Those who discharge their responsibilities faithfully will be offered greater opportunities for service in the world to come.

45-46. The darker side of the church's life is depicted in these two verses. In his own time Luke saw how easily personality cultists could exploit those entrusted to their care. He noted the jockeying for position and development of bureaucratic control. Acts 20:26-35 is his commentary on the Lord's words, which in turn reflect the thought of Isaiah 5 (see also Amos, chapter 2). Included in Isaiah's indictment of the religious leadership is the charge of drunkenness (Isaiah 5:11-12). 1 Timothy 3:3 reveals that the picture in Luke's account is not overdrawn. And the architecture of the Middle Ages replied 'Amen.' Cathedrals, strong and durable as fortresses, said to the surrounding inhabitants: The church is powerful and here to stay.

47-48. In accordance with Jewish theology which distinguished between unconscious sins and those based on better knowledge (cf. Numbers 15:22-26; Psalm 19:12-13), Jesus places the leader of the community under heavier culpability. According to Luke 8:10 they have been granted privileged knowledge of the mysteries of the Kingdom (see also 8:18). The thought parallels Wisdom 6:6: 'The man of low estate may be pardoned in mercy, but mighty men shall be searched out mightily.' These verses do not aim to give detailed instruction on the after-life, nor do they speak of degrees of punishment. Rather, they emphasize the importance of understanding the principle that responsibility is commensurate with endowment and opportunity. Those who possess the greater gifts are not to use them as devices to manipulate others, but as instruments of service. The last words of vs. 48 are an indirect reference to God, who demands an accounting for endowments he had given. In brief, power-grabbing has no future. See 1 Corinthians 3:10-4:5 for further commentary on the passage.

Jesus, Source of Division:
Third Prediction of the Passion   LUKE 12:49-53
                                                         (Matthew 10:34-36)

The apocalyptic emphases in the preceding verses are brought to
a conclusion in vss. 49-53, which depict Jesus as the focus of decision. Precisely because Jesus' first coming is a call to decision
the disciple must be on the alert for his second coming.

49. According to 3:9, the advent of the Messiah is to usher in
the Great Day of the Lord, with the fruitless trees cast into the
fire. Luke's doctrine is that the Messianic fire burns now in the
time of the Apostolic proclamation. The disciples who requested fire
for the destruction of the Samaritans (9:54) misunderstood their Lord's
mission. Jesus does send down fire, but it is a fire that separates
the false from the true. Malachi 3-4 is the background against which
the Lord's words are to be understood. Jesus aims to refine Israel
so that they might present proper offerings to the Lord. Symbolic
of this refining fire are the fire-like tongues which were distributed
among the disciples at Pentecost (Acts 2:3). The Greek word for 'distributed' in Acts 2:3 is the same word rendered 'divided' in Luke 12:52.
Evidently Luke views the fire as an expression of God's activity, resulting in changed attitudes on the part of some and hostility on the
part of others. The popular apocalyptic program required a glorious
demonstration of Messianic power. Luke throughout his twin-work ve-
hemently opposes this conception and emphasizes Jesus' role as one
obedient to his Father's will. Although he is greater than all prophets,
yet he must accept a prophet's fate (cf. Luke 11:47-54).

50. The price for refining Israel is death. Hence Jesus, in this
third prediction of his Passion (see 9:22, 44) speaks of the baptism
which he must undergo. From Mark 10: 38-39 it is clear that he means
his crucifixion (on water as a symbol of great distress, see Psalm
42:7; 69:2). Thus Jesus' own experience is a foretaste of what will
happen when the Holy Spirit comes with full force through the apostolic
preaching. The consequences will be grave for Israel, yet God's will
must be done. Therefore Jesus feels constrained, that is, he cannot
wait for his "baptism" to take place. Only after his death can the
purifying action of the Spirit take place (see Acts 15:9). A notable
philosopher once said, 'We were not put on earth to be happy.' Another
said, 'Therefore let us work hard.' Jesus said: 'Let us squander our
lives in the opportunity of disaster.'

51. Since Isaiah spoke of the Messianic age as a time of peace
(Isaiah 65:25), the evangelist counters objections that Jesus failed
to qualify as the great deliverer. Jesus did not claim to bring peace.
On the contrary, he aimed to cause division (cf. Revelation 6:4). He
himself, in his own person, is the point at which man makes responsible
decision for or against God. The division is not his creation, but
of man's choice (see Luke 2:34-35 and John 3:17-21).

52-53. The word <u>henceforth</u>, that is, from now on, is repeated
in 22:69 and stresses the climactic character of God's communication
to Israel and mankind through the death and resurrection of Jesus Christ.
It must not be forgotten that these words are spoken on the way to
Jerusalem (see 9:51). The apostolic mission could take comfort from
this saying. Apparent lack of success in converting their kinsmen
was not to be construed as failure. Micah 7:6 used similar language
to describe the division of God's people. Matthew 10:35-36 is closer
to Micah's text, which speaks of the contempt of the younger generation for the older. Luke makes the responsibility mutual, but mentions
the older generation first (see on Luke 5:36-39). The revolutionary
character of the Good News does not permit acceptance of the *status quo*.

ADDRESS TO THE MULTITUDES:
ON INTERPRETING THE TIME   LUKE 12:54-59
                                               (Matthew 16:2-3; 5:25-26)

54-56. At 12:1-53 Jesus addressed himself to the disciples. Now
he turns to the crowds. The introduction of these sayings at this
point serves to underline the decisiveness of Jesus' mission described
in 12:49-53. The <u>present time</u> (vs. 56) is more than a chronological
moment. It is the critical hour in Israel's destiny. They are better
at forecasting the weather than noting the signs of God's activity
among them. They must come to grips with the hazards of hypocrisy,
or they will live to lament God's judgment on Jerusalem (see 19:41-44;
especially note the word 'time' in vs. 44).

Verses <u>57-59</u> are parabolic in form. The point is that God's people
ought to use at least as much wisdom in facing God's judgment as they
do in settling accounts with a bill-collector. As in 11:4, God is
viewed as a creditor. In the presence of such decisive call there is
no room for 'business as usual.' In Matthew 5:25-26 the saying is
applied to personal relationships.

CALL TO REPENTANCE   LUKE 13:1-9

1. The traditional chapter division obscures the intimate connection between 13:1-9 and the preceding sayings on the urgency of awareness. The first half of vs. 1 is a rhetorical device to stress the
subsequent lesson. On this incident we have no further information.
Josephus, however, records a related example of Pilate's repression
(*Antiquities* 18,3,2; *Wars* 2,9,4). Since Luke elsewhere is at pains to
depict Roman officials in a good light, it is probable that he considered these Galileans as Zealots, a group of anti-Roman revolution-
aries. His record of Jesus' attitude would reassure authorities that
the Christian community did not share such revolutionary aims. Luke's
reference to the occasion as a time of sacrifice suggests a conflict
between religious profession and illicit practice.

2. It was an axiom among some Jewish religious teachers that God

in this life rewards the righteous and punishes the 'wicked' (sinners; cf. Proverbs 10:24-25). Using experience as a criterion, it was easy for one who experienced no reverses to conclude that he must be righteous. As in John 9:1-3, Jesus rejects this popular theory. Quantity of guilt is not determined by quantity of suffering. 3. Repentance is required of all, without reference to accidents of life, or they will themselves ultimately perish (cf. 12:58-59; 6:24-26).

4. Verse 4 suggests a case of pure accident, not mentioned by any other historian. In place of the word 'sinners' in vs. 2 Luke here employs the term 'debtors' (offenders). Sin is indebtedness to God (cf. Luke 11:4). The reference to Jerusalem is designed. Galilee could conceivably be ripe for judgment, so the complacent would conclude. But not Jerusalem!

5. The Lord's answer to his own statement follows the formal pattern in vs. 3, but with one significant alteration, obscured in the RSV. In vs. 3 the translation 'likewise' is correct. In vs. 5 a different word is used meaning 'in the same way' (RSV again has likewise). The fall of the tower of Siloam was a prelude to the fall of the towers of Jerusalem (see Luke 19:44). Luke, writing after the fall of Jerusalem, impressed his readers with the urgency of the call to repentance. What was once spoken to Israel, is now addressed to the Church. The community is not to repeat the mistakes that led to Jerusalem's destruction.

Verses 6-9 explain the purpose in delayed judgment, which is erroneously construed by some as a sign of their own righteousness. If judgment does not immediately strike, this is indicative of God's mercy, not of his approval. To understand her relation to God in any other way connotes Israel's failure to know the 'time' (12:56). According to prophetic teaching Israel is God's vineyard (Isaiah 5:1-7). Fig trees were frequently planted in vineyards. Micah 7:1 includes a lament over a fruitless fig tree, and the succeeding verse explains that the illustration points up the absence of righteousness in the land. Luke evidently had the prophetic passage in mind, for Micah 7:6 is reproduced in Luke 12:53. If this interpretation is correct, we have a further indication that Luke 13:1-9 is an amplification of the argument in 12:49-59, and Luke's omission of Mark's narrative of the cursing of the fig tree (Mark 11:12-14) at the corresponding place in his own narrative (see Luke 19:44) finds cogent explanation.

7. The three years are not a reference to the length of Jesus' ministry but rather a typical Semitic expression for completeness. The owner has extended the time to its limit, only to experience complete frustration. He gives the order: 'Chop it down. It only takes up space.'

8. The plea of his gardener further emphasizes the mercy of God. A parallel illustration is given by Lucilius, a Roman satirist. He describes how God was pondering what measures to take in order to preserve the city of Rome; so great was the wickedness of a certain Lupus

and his followers. Finally five years was suggested as the limit for the testing of divine patience. In the case of Jerusalem, time was no ally. Judgment followed rejection of this earnest call to repentance. There can be no tampering with the grace of God. Luke's frequent reminder, 'Blessed are those who hear the word of God and keep it,' lurks in the shadow of this dramatic recital.

Success in the Face of Misunderstanding   LUKE 13:10-21

The nature of the problem discussed in 13:1-9 is further explained in 13:10-21. The contrast between the flourishing tree of 13:18-19 and the worthless tree of 13:6-9 is evident, and the point of the whole is that Jesus is successful, but Israel left to her own resources is a failure. From the legal questions raised in the narrative it is apparent that Pharisaic casuistry is a primary issue. The lack of repentance discussed earlier came out into the open in the refusal of the religious leadership to grasp what Jesus is about as he relates his ministry to the problem of suffering.

A CRIPPLED WOMAN HEALED   LUKE 13:10-17

10. The reference to Jesus' instruction in a synagogue is noteworthy. Luke records no other instance in his recital of the closing stage of Jesus' ministry. Evidently he meant the notation to be understood as an example of the mercy outlined in 13:6-9.

11. RSV omits the words 'And behold' at the beginning of vs. 11. In Luke's recital they alert the reader to an extraordinary occurrence. The profounder aspect of Jesus' ministry, attack on Satan's empire, is stressed by the description of the woman's malady as a spirit of infirmity. The term eighteen years may serve as a rhetorical device to connect the recital with the previous discussion (see 13:4 and compare 13:21 with 13:7). A similar use of repeated numeral to link narratives was made in 8:42-43. More probably, however, this chronological note is a conventional expression meaning 'for a long, long time.' 'Eight' appears frequently in the Old Testament in combination with ten or a hundred or a thousand, without any suggestion of mathematical precision. In Judges 3:14 and 10:8 'eighteen years' describes a long period of servitude or oppression. Conversely, *Testament of Judah* 9:1 applies the term to a period of peace.

12. Since a woman would be suspected of being cultically unclean, Jesus' initiative in addressing her is remarkable. 13. His word, which pronounces thorough release from her disability, is reinforced by his action. The power resident in his own person reaches out to the woman. He, as the servant of the Lord, is the instrument of her healing. At his touch she stands straight and gives all credit to God, thereby affirming the credentials of Jesus (cf. Acts 2:22-24).

14. The ruler of the synagogue appeals in protest to Deuteronomy

5:13 and Exodus 20:9-10, but lacks the nerve to address Jesus directly.

15. Luke accentuates the authority of Jesus with his reference to the Lord. The plural form hypocrites broadens the following words into an indictment of the total religious leadership. In his reply Jesus appears as an authoritative expositor of the Law. He who had declared that the disciples were worth more than sparrows (12:6-7), now pronounces the woman worth more than an ox or an ass (cf. 1 Corinthians 9:9). Jesus' warning about placing material things above the requirements of the Kingdom (see 12:29-31) is seen here in its brilliant necessity. Religious leaders permitted watering of their animals (see *Damascus Covenant Document* 13:22-23). To do this they would have to untie the halter.

16. Jesus plays on the word untie (vs. 15) and bound (vs. 16). The woman is entitled to more consideration than an animal. For eighteen years she has been, as one might say, in Satan's stall. It is quite apparent that there is no real connection between the requirement of water for an animal and a woman's malady of eighteen years' standing. After all, she could have been healed on the next day. Jesus' very playfulness in the dialogue indicates that he takes no stock in casuistry. He could not care less about such picayunish reasoning. As far as he is concerned, the sabbath day is an especially appropriate time to release this woman. Since she is a daughter of Abraham (see on 19:9) the oath sworn to Abraham (1:73) applies to her; for the Sabbath is emblematic of God's outreach to his people. It is the climax of God's creative activity (Genesis 2:1-3) and a day of special blessing for his people (cf. Hebrews 4:9-11; Matthew 11:29-30). The very purpose of the Sabbath was to protect the interests of man from exploitation by his fellowman. Legalists had turned it into a dreary prospect. Jesus' deed was in harmony with the spirit of the original ordinance.

17. As Jesus predicted (Luke 12:51-53), there is divided response. His enemies are frustrated, but the crowd rejoiced (cf. Luke 9:43). Isaiah 45 is the best commentary on vs. 17 (see especially Isaiah 45:16).

TWO PARABLES ON GROWTH   LUKE 13:18-21
                                 (Mark 4:30-32; Matthew 13:31-33)

18-19. The divided response leads naturally to the inclusion of the two parables that follow. Their common message is this: Jesus appears as one least likely to succeed. The leaders reject him, but God achieves his purposes through him. The presence of the Kingdom is made known through his deeds, as well as through his words (cf. 4:18-21; 7:22-23; 11:20). The disciples are entrusted with the mysteries of the Kingdom (cf. 8:10). The tree begins as a small seed, but develops into a refuge for the birds of heaven. This description is paralleled in Daniel 4:10-12,18; Ezekiel 17:23; 31:6. It speaks not of the growth of the church, but of the triumphant course of the Good News. The Kingdom is not the church. The church always remains small, but

God's Kingdom advances. The birds of heaven are symbolic of the Gentiles who share the promises made to Israel. But the tree that failed to produce fruit will perish (Luke 13:6-9; cf. 23:31). Jesus did not share the kingdom thinking of his contemporaries, but his renunciation of the way of Satan (4:5-8) led to the enthronement envisaged in 13:19.

20-21. Leaven is ordinarily used in a pejorative sense (cf. 12:1), but in this second parable it is used in a good sense. Looking in from the outside, God appears to have made a mistake in connection with Jesus. But just as leaven works in unseen ways, so God ultimately achieves his purposes through one rejected by Israel but exalted to God's right hand (cf. Acts 3:11).

SECOND PHASE OF THE JOURNEY TO JERUSALEM LUKE 13:22-17:10

Are Few Saved? LUKE 13:22-30
(Matthew 7:13-14; 25:10-12; 7:22-23; 8:11-12; 19:30; 20:16)

22. At this point Luke recalls his thematic note in 9:51: 'Behold, we go up to Jerusalem.' The reader is now prepared for another series of stories and sayings which will shed light on the meaning of Jesus' final action in Jerusalem. That Luke intends this section to be understood in the light of the foregoing sayings is clear from the parallel thoughts in 13:9 and 13:29-30. The stress on the Kingdom in 13:18-21 requires a further dismissal of apocalyptic misunderstanding.

23. As in 10:29; 11:45; 12:13, 41; and 13:1, questions are used to introduce authoritative replies of Jesus. According to 4 Ezra 8:3, 'Many are created, but few are saved.' Some rabbis, on the other hand, taught that only a few in Israel would enjoy immediately at death the blessings of heaven. The rest would wait in Gehenna. However, all Israel would share in the blessing of the world to come after the resurrection of the dead took place (see Strack-Billerbeck I, 883). Such types of speculation underlie the question: Will those who are saved be few? Jesus refuses to enter into such inquiries. Instead he takes up the prophetic note of decisive commitment.

24. Since vs. 24 speaks of the narrowness of the door, whereas vs. 25 lays emphasis on the fact that it is shut, it is probable that Luke has brought together words of Jesus spoken on different occasions, with the word door as the linking factor. The narrowness of the gate is stressed in order to express the fact that it is not made for crowds (see on 12:1). In 4 Ezra 7, 3-7, the narrow way must be negotiated before entrance can be made to the broad ways that lie beyond the hazardous water and fire. There is no national or collective salvation. Each one is called to responsible decision, without reliance on inherited religious association.

<u>25-27</u> The illustration of the locked door introduces a second motif -- obedience divorced from empty liturgical confidence. As in 6:46, the self-confident will use the proper address <u>Lord</u> and claim familiar association (see on 8:19-21), but the Lord will reply: <u>I do not know where you come from</u>. That is, he will disclaim any relationship. The reason is stated: They are <u>workers of iniquity</u>, a phrase taken from Psalm 6:8. It is not enough to hear Jesus' words with the ear, one must hear with integrity and perform accordingly (cf. Luke 6:47).

<u>28-29</u>. Not only will the hypocrites be locked out, but they will catch a glimpse of their venerable ancestors and the prophets sharing the Kingdom. Yet they have no real complaint. They were warned not to say, 'We have Abraham as our Father' (3:8; see also on 16:19-31). As the climax of their total frustration, they will see the Gentiles gathered in to share the blessings of the patriarchs and the prophets (cf. Isaiah 2:2; 59:19; Micah 4:1-2; Revelation 21:24). The Messianic banquet of Isaiah 25:6-8 is prepared for those who hear and do the Lord's word. The repetition of the phrase <u>kingdom of God</u> in Luke 13:28 and 29 draws attention to the inexorable triumph of God's purpose in Jesus (see 13:18-21).

<u>30</u>. <u>And behold</u> introduces the climactic summary. The Kingdom does not follow accepted standards of success. As a word to Jesus' contemporaries, these sayings were an urgent call to repentance. Addressed to the Church through Luke's Gospel they warn the community not to repeat the mistake of Israel. The principle is still valid: <u>Last</u> ones <u>first</u>, <u>first</u> ones <u>last</u>. Hence the previous warnings on watchfulness (12:35-59).

Misunderstanding in General   LUKE 13:31-35

WARNING FROM THE PHARISEES:
FOURTH PREDICTION OF THE PASSION   LUKE 13:31-33

The words <u>at that very hour</u> link this account with the preceding sayings. The religious formalism described in the previous verses receives a climactic refutation in the indictment of Jerusalem (vss. 33-35). At the same time, the import of Jesus' words in 9:51 is caught in more ominous perspective.

<u>31</u>. The warning of the <u>Pharisees</u> points to the *status quo* which Jesus is disturbing. Herod liked things quiet (see Josephus *Antiquities* 18, 7,2), a characteristic of petty men who are frightened by anyone who raises questions or rocks boats. In Palestine the fox is an insignificant predator next to the lion, the king of beasts. Jesus will be done in by greater powers than Herod. Some readers may have caught an allusion to Ezekiel 13:4, which speaks of foxes among the ruins. Herod governs in a land which is soon to experience terrible disaster. The timetable in vs. <u>32</u> does not refer to a three-day period. Like the

numeral in 13:7, the three-day period connotes completeness. Jesus
is on his way to Jerusalem, but not to escape from Herod, for his backbone was never curved with fear of any man. He carries out his healing ministry as a part of his prophetic function (cf. 7:22; 24:19),
but also heads toward Jerusalem to endure the fate Israel has in store
for her prophets (cf. 4:24; 11:47-52). This is his fourth prediction
(see 9:22; 44; 12:50). His suffering will spell the end of his <u>course</u>
(cf. 12:50; 22:37).

ADDRESS TO JERUSALEM   LUKE 13:34-35
(Matthew 23:37-39)

The repetition of the name of the city accentuates the solemnity
of the address (cf. 19:41). In Matthew these verses are recited after
Jesus' entry into Jerusalem. Luke's omission of the words 'from now
on' found in Matthew 23:29 was necessary in order to facilitate the
transfer, for Jesus is in Luke's account still on the way to Jerusalem.
In their present position these verses explain the total absence in
Luke's previous account of any ministry in Jerusalem. He, their
Messiah, would have loved to offer them the protection of a mother
hen (cf. Psalm 17:8; 57:1; 61:4). But their hostility has made this
impossible (see Luke 13:4-5). The word <u>behold</u> in vs. 35 echoes the
word in vs. 32. Despite his mighty works Jesus is rejected. The words
<u>your house is forsaken</u> echo Jeremiah 22:5 and are a reference to the
total dissolution of Israel's hope for the restoration of the Davidic
dynasty as a reigning power in Jerusalem. Jesus' words take on the
solemnity of an oath (cf. Judith 6:5) as he says, '<u>You will not see me
until you say, "Blessed be he who comes in the name of the Lord."</u>'
These words anticipate the acclamation on Palm Sunday (Luke 19:38).
Jesus is the legitimate heir to David's throne (1:32). But tragic
irony pervades the entire recital. The reader now knows what is meant
by the words <u>your house is forsaken.</u> As the patron of Greek theater
would be horrified while watching Agamemnon invite certain doom by
treading on the carpet laid out for him by Clytemnestra, so Luke's
readers would say to themselves at this point: 'But that's the week
in which they killed their King!' Through his skillful handling of
his sources Luke penetrates his recital with profound pathos and prepares the reader for the conjunction of acclamation and lament in 19:
38-44. King of Israel he is, but Pilate will publish the fact (see
23:38). A young French laborer on strike rushed jubilantly into his
house shouting, 'There's not a light burning in Paris tonight!' only
to see his daughter dying as a doctor struggled to perform an emergency
operation by candlelight. Jesus had warned his disciples. The things
we love the most are at the mercy of the things we ought to love the
least.

Specific Misunderstanding at
a Dinner with a Pharisee   LUKE 14:1-24

Chapter 13 developed the thought that misunderstanding of Jesus'
mission would ultimately bring disaster to those who relied on traditional religious association without real commitment. Chapter 14 advances this theme to another plateau. As in 13:10-16, Luke introduces
a chain of sayings and parables with a controversy concerning the
sabbath (14:1-6). In 13:18-21 statements on the Kingdom precede the
recital of the locked door at the Messianic banquet (13:22-30). Similarly 14:15 introduces the subject of the Kingdom, followed by a
parable about the Messianic banquet (vss. 16-24). The concluding series of sayings in vss. 25-35 sketches the total commitment of the disciple in contrast to Jerusalem's misplaced self-assurance (13:34-35).
Like Jerusalem, the false disciple may find himself rejected (14:35).

HEALING OF A MAN ILL WITH DROPSY   LUKE 14:1-6

<u>1</u>. In his reply to Herod Jesus spoke of the healings he had yet
to perform (13:32). The saying offered an easy link for the healing
narrative in 14:1-6. But Luke's choice of the particular type of
healing, together with the specific reference to the sabbath, was
prompted by his apparent desire to establish a relationship between
this stage of his narrative and the discussion begun in 13:10-17. It
was customary to have a festive meal on the sabbath, for which the
preparation would be made on Friday, with the food merely kept warm.
In accordance with Jewish custom, distinguished religious leaders
would be invited. The host in this case is himself a man of account
in his community and quite possibly the leader of a group of Pharisees.

<u>2-3</u>. Earlier in 6:7 and 11:53-54 scribes and Pharisees were
pictured as hostile. This appears to be Luke's intention also here
in the phrase <u>they were watching him</u>. Fresh light is now shed on his
reference to the Pharisees at 13:31. There they appear to be concerned
for his safety. Yet they, not Herod, suggests Luke, are the very ones
who must share a large part of the responsibility for Jerusalem's ultimate disaster. Their legalistic casuistry eats at the very vitals of
Israel's religious life. As at 13:11, the word <u>behold</u> alerts the
reader to a significant development. This time we have a man afflicted
with <u>dropsy</u>. Man was said to consist of two parts, water and blood.
When a man sins the water predominates. Dropsy, said rabbis, would
be especially indicative of some heinous sin (Strack-Billerbeck II,
203-204). Jesus, does not hesitate, however, to take hold of him (vs.
4). There is no indication in the text that the man, any more than
the woman at 7:37, was planted by the host or other guests. Jesus'
question cuts through a tangled mass of casuistry on the question
whether medicine could be practiced on the sabbath. In a later period,
perhaps reflecting a long established tradition, an exception was
made in cases where life was at stake.

<u>4</u>. Like wily candidates for political office these representatives

of the religious establishment are not about to expose their system
to attack. Instead they retreat into cowardly silence. Since they
refuse to express themselves Jesus proceeds on his own authority. True
to his own counsel given earlier to the disciples (12:4), Jesus does
not play it safe by telling the man to wait a day. That is the kind
of prudence one might expect from a slave to the 'system.' Jesus
heals the man and sends him off. The question in vs. 5 parallels 13:
15 (cf. Matthew 12:11-12). It is another example of the formula 'if
that, how much more this.' The word immediately is the cue. While
theologians spend time in debate, urgent matters are tabled and needs
left unfulfilled. Churchmen act as though they have forever, Jesus
has only today, tomorrow, and the next day (13:33). In the face of
his first query (vs. 3) the opposition retreated into silence. Now
they could not reply, for they would have had to acknowledge their
hypocrisy.

A LESSON ON KINGDOM MANNERS   LUKE 14:7-11

Once more Luke gives evidence of his profound insight into human
nature. A man given to casuistry is usually personally insecure. Status-seeking is the further seal on his pettiness. The dinner party
to which Jesus had been invited provides the framework for the parable
about the first seats. Customarily the seating would consist of three
couches, with three places on each couch. The place of honor would
be at one end of the center couch. All guests would recline. The
guest in the parable is advised to take a lower position; for more important guests, who often came later, would displace him to his embarrassment (cf. Proverbs 25:6-7). That the story is illustrative,
and not meant by Luke as a piece of social etiquette, seems clear
from vs. 11, which is repeated at 18:14. The thought is in line with
1:46-53 (cf. 1 Peter 5:5; James 4:6). Those who view the story as a
leaf from Elizabeth Post forget that many serious economic and political problems take shape in accepted social routines. Law can enforce
a black man's right to purchase property where he wishes, but social
patterns may still isolate the purchaser and encourage hostilities. The
seeking of chief seats leads to graft and corruption which further encourages exploitation of the poor and the oppressed. That Luke makes
the connection between self-advertisement and selfish disregard of the
needy, is clear from vs. 13 (see also 10:25-37).

ON PLANNING THE GUEST LIST   LUKE 14:12-14
                                                               (Matthew 22:1-10)

12. The first parable was addressed to the guests. Jesus now
turns to the host. Accepted social practice is once more exposed in
terms of its potential to exploit and isolate less fortunate members
of society. Inherited social patterns can become barriers to responsible encounter. It is easy to retreat into relationships that meet
one's own needs and satisfy one's own interests. The 'now-we-owe-them'
approach parallels the lending policies criticized in 6:34. Knowing

the right people, cultivating those who may 'do one some good' --
these are the stepping stones to success, but stumbling blocks for
those who would enter the Kingdom. For every-day social habits have
a way of rubbing off on one's religious thinking, but God makes no
bargains.

13-14. The directive in vs. 13 is in the spirit of Deuteronomy
14:29, but contrary to the policy expressed in 2 Samuel 5:8. As in
Luke 6:23, the reward is delayed to a moment outside history -- the
resurrection of the just. The doctrine of the resurrection of the
dead, developed in the intertestamental period, found strong support
among the Pharisees. In Daniel 12:2 the resurrection of both righteous
and unrighteous is anticipated. So also by Paul (Acts 24:15). Luke
20:35 speaks of those who are 'accounted worthy' to attain the resurrection. In 14:14 these are the just, or the righteous. The assurance
of reward is not designed to redirect the disciple's thinking into
commercial channels. Rather, by placing the reward outside the
boundaries of his present experience, the disciple is called to exercise faith. Faith, without evidence of return on the investment, is
the way of the Kingdom. Since the way described is God's way, as
reflected in Jesus' own reception of the poor, the disciple has no
viable alternative. However, to use unfortunate people as a device
to secure entry into paradise would be a misunderstanding of Jesus'
words. The name for such self-servers is 'do-gooders.' Like many
'do-gooders' in the public welfare system who lack creative understanding of the needs of people, they are more interested in projects
than in persons.

THE RUDE GUESTS   LUKE 14:15-24
                                                    (Matthew 22:1-10)

This parable about excuses enlarges on the theme of invitation and
brings the preceding discussion into more immediate relation to Jesus'
own ministry and revelation of the Kingdom. The recital parallels 13:
22-30.

15. Silence is hard to bear at a dinner party. No matter how
vapid the comment, the stillness must be broken. Evidently the guest
who pronounced the beatitude cited in 14:15 aimed to smooth an awkward
moment. But his inane statement is useful only as a literary bridge
from the statement on candidates for the resurrection (vs. 14) to their
share in the Messianic banquet (vs. 16-17). The guest's remark
suggested smugness. Jesus therefore calls him and others to more
serious appraisal of their religious thinking. 16. The greatness of
the feast emphasizes the generosity of the host. Since the story is
beyond question a parable of divine kingdom activity, the feast refers
to God's feeding of his people, as in Isaiah 25:6-8 (cf. Psalm 22:26).

17. In the Orient, as in the West, loose invitations are often
given: 'We must have you over sometime.' Custom in some cases dictated that no one go to a feast without receiving two invitations, for

the second would show that the first was meant seriously. Israel received her first invitation through the prophets. Now through Jesus and the apostolic proclamation she hears the final call to participate in the Kingdom.

18-20. As if in concert, all excused themselves. Three samples are cited. The first two are at least politely stated; the third is curt. All three reveal disinterest in the feast and concentration on the material side of life (see the warnings cited in chapter 12). In the third excuse Jewish readers would have noted a relation to the directive in Deuteronomy 24:5). A bridegroom was to be relieved of any communal responsibility for one year. There may be here a suggestion of legal correctness as a block to appreciation of the Kingdom. Luke 14:1-6 is the nearest illustration of this hazard. In any case, the Pharisees and other religious leaders are clearly envisaged as the recipients of the second invitation, for vs. 21 mentions the same types of guests as those named in vs. 13 and in precisely the same sequence.

21-22. The anger of the host suggests a strong note of judgment. He will have his feast, and his banquet hall must be filled. The double invitation stresses the liberality of the host. His guests come from the city and from the cross-roads of commerce. Luke evidently understands these to include the poor in Israel and the Gentiles, all outside the established religious grouping.

23. The command to compel them to come in was in time past taken literally by some churchmen as a directive to use force on the mission field. We have here, of course, a bit of vivid Oriental language. It is polite for the invited guest at first to refuse. This gives the host an opportunity to sound more generous and really in earnest as he repeats his invitation. As in Genesis 19:3, the thought is that those who are invited need to be urged. A Tamil proverb reads: 'He who is anxious to give will strike people on the cheek' (that is, compel them to receive).

The closing verdict in vs. 24 would express appropriately the contempt of the host for those who had despised his invitation. But since this is a parable of the Kingdom, the words are to be understood as an expression of judgment. It is a strong way of asserting that those who claim an interest in God but are in fact no different from the first group of guests will not share in the end-time blessings (cf. 13:28-29).

Proper Response   LUKE 14:25-15:32

KINGDOM COST-ACCOUNTING   LUKE 14:25-35
                                          (Mark 9:50; Matthew 10:37-38; 5:13)

In 14:15-24 God's disappointing experience with Israel was depicted.

The note of hostility is now extended to the experience of the disciples, who must count the cost of following one whose destiny was the cross. Unless radical decision is made, the disciple will repeat the mistake of those who rejected the invitation to the banquet.

25-27. The RSV obscures the fact that Luke continues his theme of the journey toward Jerusalem: literally, 'as many crowds were journeying with him.' They need to be warned of the price of association. Verse 26 is to be understood from the Semitic perspective, which places more emphasis on the observable fact than on the emotion. The disciple must put Jesus so strongly in the center of his thinking that he will appear to others as one who despises or hates his closest relatives. That is, when confronted with a conflict of loyalty he will give priority to the requirements of the Kingdom, and even his own life will be disposable (cf. Deuteronomy 33:9; Luke 12:4; 16:13). The stress on parents may suggest that proclamation of the Good News had attracted many young people. This means that the early community felt strongly the tension of the generation gap generated by the radical nature of Jesus' preaching. Nothing short of opting for the cross will satisfy the totalitarian demand of the Kingdom. In time of persecution family pressures would be brought to bear. Parents and siblings would urge the disciple not to endanger the family through stubborn allegiance to a suspected revolutionary. Matthew places these sayings in the mission directive (Matthew 10:37-38).

28-33. The two illustrations in these verses are found only in Luke. A poor cost accountant must be prepared to hear the verdict of fool pronounced on his life. Sempronius, a Roman general, faced the consequences of his foolhardy haste against Hannibal (Livy 21:54). And Juvenal warns that once the helmet is on it is too late to repent of the fight (*Satires* 1, 169-170). Following Jesus is no invitation to an ice-cream social. A church that encourages its followers to play it safe and to conform with the sub-standard practices of surrounding society not only invites disaster but loses all claim to association with the revolutionary cause of the Kingdom. The invitation to commitment expressed in vs. 33 is as total as any dictator could wish. Everything depends on the decision. A church that does not spell this out clearly to prospective members or to its constituency proves false to the Good News. Indeed, failure to do so has led the church to pussyfoot on issues of race and prejudice and economic exploitation. Even pagan philosophers caught something of the vision expressed in these sayings. Epictetus writes:

> Do you suppose that you can do the things you do
> now, and yet be a philosopher? Do you suppose
> that you can eat in the same fashion, drink in
> the same fashion, give way to anger and to irrita-
> tion, just as you do now? You must keep vigils,
> work hard, overcome certain desires, abandon your
> own people, be despised by a paltry slave, be
> laughed to scorn by those who meet you, in every-
> thing get the worst of it, in office, in honour,

in court. Look these drawbacks over carefully,
and then, if you think best, approach philosophy,
that is, if you are willing at the price of these
things to secure tranquillity, freedom, and calm.
Otherwise do not approach; don't act like a child -
now a philospher, later on a tax-gatherer, then a
rhetorician, then a procurator of Caesar. These
things do not go together. You must be one person,
either good or bad (III, 15,10-13, Loeb translation).

34-35. Since the nature of the disciple's commitment will determine whether he is a good or a bad man, a man of integrity or a hypocrite (cf. 6:43-45), he may be likened to good or bad salt (see also
Matthew 5:13; Mark 9:50). Salt that is hopelessly mixed with impuri-
ties is useless. It is good neither as a condiment nor as a fertilizer
(for the land). The disciple must be totally dedicated. The closing
words about hearing are not an invitation to debate (cf. 8:18). To
count the cost means to be prepared to risk all, even life itself, in
commitment to the Kingdom.

FINDING THE LOST   LUKE 15:1-32

Luke joins three stories linked by a common theme: Rejoicing over
the lost. The entire chapter is an expansion of the banquet motif presented in chapter 14, for Jesus is shown to be feasting with tax-collectors and sinners (vs. 1). This is in accordance with his own advice
to the Pharisees (14:12-14).

2. However, they construe it as a violation of the instruction laid
down, for example, in the book of Proverbs, that one is not to associate
with evil-doers (see also Psalm 1; Isaiah 52:11; and 2 Corinthians 6:14-
18). If Jesus were a true prophet, they would argue, he ought to
support holiness, and not appear to sanction sin (7:39). What they forget is that Jesus does not sink to the immoral level of sinners, but
meets them where they are in order to raise them. This grumbling is
therefore an ominous sign of misinterpretation of God's intentions at
work in Jesus' ministry. Israel of old was punished severely for her
grumbling in other circumstances (cf. Numbers 11:1; 14:27, 29). Jesus
would like to spare the Pharisees a repetition of disaster and, as he
had done earlier (5:29-30; cf. Mark 2:15-16; Matthew 9:10-11), invites
them to share his own interest in reclamation of the lost.

The Lost Sheep and the Lost Coin   LUKE 15:3-10
                                        (Luke 15:3-7 = Matthew 18:12-14)

With superb gentleness Jesus tries to bring the Pharisees to God's
point of view. The theme of the shepherd is common in the Old Testament. Ezekiel 34:11-16 is programmatic for Jesus' activity as the
shepherd of Israel (see also Jeremiah 31:10-14; Isaiah 40:11). What
Jesus does in behalf of the sinners is no different from God's concern

for rebellious Israel in the period of the Old Testament (cf. Isaiah 65:1). Jesus appeals to common practice. The owner of a hundred sheep will leave the ninety-nine and restlessly search until he locates the one that is lost (vs. 4). Thus the lost one is not treated as one outside the flock. Similarly the woman who has lost a coin (vs. 8) raises the dust in her earthern-floor home. There is no hint in the text that the coin is part of a necklace, or the like. It is simply one coin out of ten, and she will not rest until she finds it. Be the owner rich or poor, great energy is expended on one lost item. Can Jesus do less when human destiny is at stake?

Affluent Westerners smile at all this fuss, but the idea of a lost-and-found party over one mangy sheep or even a small coin seems utterly ridiculous. But that is just the point. Religious people expect God to be less concerned about lost sinners than they themselves are about some trivial possession. Values are completely perverted. God's most precious possession is *man*! And he rejoices over the return of the lost (cf. 2:10). Heaven rings with the laughter of the feast (vss. 7 and 10). Against so much that is drab in religion, Jesus depicts the happy laughter of a Father who invites the angels to the home-coming festival. Somber, morbid religiosity has no place in the Kingdom. Dancing, the blowing of trumpets, beating of drums is a legitimate part of the church's worship (cf. 2 Samuel 6:5). The cult of respectability must give way to the cultivation of the art of joy over God's delight in reclaiming the refuse of humanity. In worship the Shepherd is congratulated, not the sheep. God does not commend the righteous for remaining righteous (vs. 7), and Jesus has not come to compliment them for what they ought to be in the first place. Nor has he criticized their standards. Their position is not made less secure by Jesus' outreach to publicans and sinners. All he expects of them is that they share his joy over the return of the lost. In the ministry of Jesus they are to see the God of their fathers at work. Not Jesus through his association with sinners, but the scribes through their lovelessness discredit God.

Some commentators have looked for subtle differences between the two parables. The sheep, it has been suggested, was lost through its own stupidity; the coin by the carelessness of its owner. The shepherd and the woman, it has been claimed, represent the church. This is all beside the point. The church comes under rebuke in these stories. It is precisely in the church that arrogant loveless attitudes toward the fallen and the disenfranchised disply themselves. A ditty runs to this effect:

> We are the choice selected few
> And all the rest are damned.
> There's room enough in hell for you,
> We can't have heaven crammed.

Black clergyman Cecil Williams, in his complaint about people who only mouth their evangelism, put it this way: 'If Jesus saves, why doesn't he save that poor welfare recipient who has to wonder day after day

where her next meal is coming from? Why do we not have justice and
mercy for all people of our land? Why do we have a racist society?
... If you believe Jesus saves, why don't you act that way?'

The Parable of the Reluctant Brother   LUKE 15:11-32

Among the papyri found in Egypt is a letter from Antonios Longus
to his mother Neilus:

> Greetings: I hope you are in good health; it is
> my constant prayer to Lord Serapis. I did not
> expect you to come to Metropolis, therefore I did
> not go there myself. At the same time, I was
> ashamed to go to Kanaris because I am so shabby.
> I am writing to tell you that I am naked. I plead
> with you, forgive me. I know well enough what I
> have done to myself. I have learned my lesson.
> I know I made a mistake. I have heard from Postumos
> who met you in the area of Arsinoe. Unfortunately
> he told you everything. Don't you know that I would
> rather be a cripple than owe so much as a cent to
> any man? I plead, I plead with you . . ."
> (Signed) Antonios Longus, your son.

The story related by Jesus evidently recites a familiar tale of woe,
but in Luke's form it goes far beyond any experience of a wayward
son. For Jesus' story, as recorded in Luke, speaks not so much of
the waywardness of a boy who fell on bad times, as of the waywardness
of a young man whose body stayed home, but whose heart was lost in
misunderstanding of a father's love. Like the parable of the lost coin,
this story is found only in Luke.

12. According to laws of property it was possible for children
to receive a divison of the father's capital during his lifetime (cf.
Sirach 33:19-20). 13-15. The young son gathered all he had, that is,
he turned his holdings into cash. After he squandered his fortune, he
was reduced to feeding swine, a degrading occupation for a Jew. 16.
To say that he would have been happy to eat of the pods fed to the swine
is a way of saying that he was in the most desperate circumstances. New-
ly found friends flew with the speed of his money.

17. Then he came to himself. He saw what a fool he was. His
instinct for survival coincides with his memory of the parental hearth.
Exploited by his boss, he thinks of his father's hired servants who
are paid enough to be able to keep themselves in food and other necessities, with money to spare. The contrast between his generous father
and the tight-fisted man for whom he works is sketched with pathetic
economy.

18. His speech is prepared. The content is reminiscent of Isaiah
63:16-19. Inclusion of heaven, a round-about expression for God,

reemphasizes for the reader that God is a forgiving Father, acting through
Jesus, who invites publicans and sinners to the banquet. In a less theo-
logical vein Cicero put a similar plea to Caesar in behalf of a client:
'He blundered, he behaved recklessly, he is sorry. I find refuge in your
clemency, I plead indulgence for his fault, I implore that he be pardoned.'
(*Ligarius* 30)

Verse 19 introduces a fresh thought. The son does not expect to be received back as a member of the family. He does not even ask for the status
of his father's household slaves, who enjoyed the constant companionship of
a kind master. The hired servant, to be distinguished from a slave, did his
work and went to his own quarters. But at least the young man would have
some contact with his father.

20. The picture of the father waiting for his son is an echo of Jeremiah
31:18-20; God longs for the return of erring Israel. 21. The son is unable
to complete his prepared speech, so great is the father's compassion (cf. Luke
1:78). There is not one word of recrimination. It is not a matter of worth-
iness, but of the father's affection.

22. The father now gives orders to his servants, in this case 'slaves.'
The robe is of the best quality. The ring confirms full sonship and right
of inheritance. The shoes (sandals) -- a pathetic note, erasing the son's
humiliation. 23. The fatted calf would be the animal saved for a special
feast. And this is the moment! 24. Once Ezekiel asked whether the dry
bones of Israel could throb again with life (Ezekiel 37). God's forgiving
mercy assures the resurrection of one who is lost. The rich man had said
to himself, 'be merry' (12:19), and courted disaster. There is, however,
a place for merriment -- when one celebrates not himself but the return of
the lost.

25-26. The elder brother is an important feature of the story. His
attitude reflects the grumbling of the Pharisees (vs. 2), who could not
bear to see social sanctions and status go by the board. 27. The reply
of the slave is carefully worded. He reminds him that it is his brother
who has returned, and that his father is holding a party because the young
man returned safe and sound. Emphasis is again placed on the feelings and
attitudes of the father.

28. But the elder brother has no conception of what lies on his father's heart. His anger contrasts with the Father's pleading. 29. With
his word served (literally 'slaved') the mask drops, revealing the frigidity
of his soul. The father thought he had a son! But to the older son the
father's house spelled slavery. And he was a good slave, never disobeying a
command (the word usually used of God's commandments). Yet not so much as
a little goat did his father give him for a barbecue-party! 30. With contempt he says, this son of yours. He should have said 'my brother,'
but he aims to cut a father's heart to shreds. How does he know
that his brother spent his time with whores? Was his heart in

the far country, while his body stayed home in obedience?

31. No father ever appealed more tenderly to a wayward son. Son, you are always with me. The word rendered son means 'child.' Thus the prophet spoke of Israel (Isaiah 60:9). Was it not enough for the older brother that he was with the father. Another man would one day welcome such assurance (see 23:42). The father thought he was loved for himself, not for the prospect of a kid. Besides, all that is mine is yours. He was free, not a slave. He had only to ask, and the father would have been more than glad to give (cf. Luke 11:9). Moreover, he had received his part of the inheritance. He had no complaint. The younger son returned to be *with* the father. What more does the older brother want?

32. In his final word the father pleads necessity. The word rendered fitting is used frequently in Luke's gospel of salvation-necessity (2:49; 4:43; 9:22; 13:16, 33; 17:25; 19:5; 22:37; 24:7, 26, 44). Joy is the only option if the sinner returns. Gently the older brother is reminded, not 'this your son' (vs. 30) but this your brother. The 'far country' does not invalidate relationships. The older brother, like the righteous, needed no repentance (vs. 7). Only one thing was lacking, willingness to share a father's joy. But like the instruction to the young man in 18:22, it was a call to decision. A lost sinner is no less precious to God than a sheep is to a man or a coin to a woman. One's ability to rejoice with God over the return of the lost measures the validity of his claim to understand and know God. The best commentary on the entire chapter is Ephesians 2:1-19, but a paragraph in *The Christian Century* (July 17, 1968) illustrates well the point of Jesus' pronouncement. The writer had requested help from a pastor and his congregation for the rehabilitation of a parolee. After a series of disappointing attempts to interest Christians he told his story to a friend who dealt professionally with troubled people. His friend reminded him that 'the church is not for sinners.' It 'has become the place where people can come together once a week to reaffirm a sense of wellbeing and acceptance in society. They come not out of a sense of guilt or sinfulness, but to make overt manifestation of their righteousness and goodness. Most church goers,' he said, 'look on the fallen with scorn and distrust; they would find it practically impossible to speak to the needs of a recognized sinner.' The fact that the church has turned much of its own work over to the Y.M.C.A., family service and social welfare agencies, the writer went on, is proof that his friend was right.

Ultimately the elder brother was like the son in another parable (Matthew 21:28-32) who promised to work in the vineyard but never showed up. Another son disclaimed all interest in the vineyard but later on repented and began to work. Jesus concluded that parable with these words: 'Tax collectors and harlots go into the Kingdom of God before you.'

Urgent Appeal: Wisdom and Folly   LUKE 16:1-31

The parables in chapter 15 were addressed to the Pharisees. Chapter 16 begins with address to the disciples, and continues the theme of a proper sense of values. Possibly Luke also aims to correct a misunderstanding that might arise from the previous stress on forgiving mercy. The young son, as respects the squandering of his possessions, is not a model for the community, and forgiveness is not an invitation to irresponsibility.

THE CROOKED STEWARD   LUKE 16:1-9

The story of the crooked steward is simple enough, but one must be on guard not to concentrate on the character of the steward. His dishonesty is clear at the beginning, but gaps in our knowledge of ancient economic practice make it impossible to determine with certainty whether his terminal action was of the same order. Nor is it of any consequence. The point of the story is prudence.

1-4. Ordered to surrender his books, this man has a cool head in the crisis. Succinct phrases describe his predicament: 'What shall I do?' 'Digging's not for me!' 'Begging's not my style.' 'Ah, I have it!'('I have decided what to do.) His mind pulls a fast trigger. Already he sees the welcome mats laid down. He may have been in charge of the annual receipt of rental from tenant farmers who would pay in kind, or he may have kept accounts of his boss' dealings with merchants.

5-7. In any case, he invites the debtors to alter with their own hand the figures on the contracts in his possession, thus clearing the debtors of any obligation beyond the stipulated amounts. Naturally their gratitude would be immense (see 6:32). Variation in the figures was part of the plot.

8. The owner is not deceived, but why the comment of the master should have caused so much perplexity is one of the curiosities in the history of interpretation. And many readers have boggled at the verdict and missed the main point. Like many a judge or warden who has scratched his head in amazement over the ingenuity of a 'client,' this master was forced to admit that his clerk was extraordinarily shrewd. And just as leaven could be used as an illustration of the Kingdom (13:20-21), or an unjust judge in an encouragement to prayer (18:1-8), so this crook's cool thinking is used as a model for the disciple. Unfortunately RSV obscures the point by offering two different English words (prudence and wiser) for the one Greek root used in both cases and having the general meaning of 'shrewd.' The sons of this world (a semitism for 'the people of this world') are more shrewd among their own 'kind' (generation) than are 'God's people,' the sons of light. This last expression occurs in the scrolls of Qumran (1QS 1,9; 2,16; 3,13; see also Ephesians 5:8) and may indicate a thrust at the Pharisees (vs. 14) who boasted in the Law as their light to life.

173

This story is not so much a parable of the Kingdom as an illustration of the principle expressed in 6:30-35. In the everyday world of business, prudence is exercised to secure temporary advantage. God's people, who have higher goals and expectations, ought to display at least as much prudence in relation to God and their future hope. Yet when it comes to material possessions, they often forget that the proper use of those possessions is an integral part of their total religious experience.

9. Mammon, an Aramaic term for wealth, is termed unrighteous because it is often used as an instrument of injustice (cf. Mark 12: 40, in an indictment of the Scribes). Disciples of Jesus are to use it in the interests of justice. It is improbable that with the words make friends Luke limits the application to poor people who will greet their benefactors. Rather, the phrase is a reminder to the disciple that he must grasp the principle expressed in the illustration. A speaker, for example, may use an illustration drawn from athletics and point the moral: 'Play a good game' (cf. 1 Corinthians 9:24). As in Luke 6:38 the indefinite they is not a pronoun in the original, but a part of the inflected verb form and apparently refers to God. Eternal habitations are the living quarters of the righteous (cf. Enoch 39:4). These are eternal as opposed to the temporary advantage on earth. Thus the fate of the disciple will not be that of the rich fool (Luke 12:21). Instead of wealth being viewed as a criterion of success, its absence may be a stronger guarantee of a reception into heaven.

MAMMON AND THE KINGDOM   LUKE 16:10-18
                                              (Matthew 6:24; 11:12; 5:18,32)

Other sayings of Jesus spoken on various occasions are brought together in reinforcement of the message on proper use of wealth. Again there seems to be a thrust at the Pharisees who claimed to be the guardians of God's interests. But the problem is perennial, and the Pharisees had no monopoly on a common vice of religionists. See again the warning in 1 Timothy 3:3 and note the depreciation, since Vatican II, of emphasis on pomp and ecclesiastical extravagance.

10-11. Lest the reader infer that the unjust steward is a model with respect to his misuse of his master's property, the disciple is reminded that he will be judged on the basis of faithful use. The word little is used to describe material possessions, thus making the true riches stand out in contrast. These true riches are of the same order as the treasure promised in 6:20-21, 38.

12. Should the disciple conclude from the Lord's story that he has a right to use other people's property, perhaps to make 'friends' for himself, he is reminded that faithless use of property belonging to another will jeopardize his own attainment of the promised hope. Verse 13 expresses the single mindedness discussed in 11:34. Life is of a piece, and the disciple is to view the whole from the perspective

of God's interests. The manner in which the material benefits are used will determine the integrity of one's religious claims. This saying is included in the Sermon on the Mount (Matthew 6:24).

14. The reference to the Pharisees draws further attention to the problem of divided allegiance. Behind the mask of culture, fastidious taste and tradition there lurks icy decadence and greed. (On the greed of Pharisees, see Strack-Billerbeck I, 937.)

15. They justify themselves before men, that is, they impress men with their religiosity, but God is the One with whom they have to do. They give alms, but principally to win the esteem of men, or without any real sacrifice involved (21:1-4). The last part of vs. 15 expands on this thought. Congratulations of their contemporaries only increase their guilt before God, for God is not impressed by what men consider exalted (cf. 1:52). He searches the inner man (cf. 2:35; 1 Samuel 16:7; Psalm 7:9; Proverbs 17:3; 21:2; Jeremiah 11:20; Revelation 2:23).

Verse 16 (Matthew 11:12) appears to be a quotation of a charge levelled against the church's proclamation of the Kingdom. The Pharisees complain that the law and prophets were in force until John the Baptist, but since his time the Kingdom of God is being proclaimed and everyone, with no distinctions between good and bad, forces his way in (see the related criticism at 15:2). In other words, the Gospel lowers religious standards, that is, from the Pharisee's point of view.

17. Jesus replies that the standards of the Kingdom are as high or higher than the Law. The single-minded devotion he urges does not detract from Moses but takes seriously every pronouncement of the Law. Matthew's version of this saying (5:18) is put even more strongly. Verse 18 declares that in fact the Pharisees, not Jesus, undermine the Law. Through their own casuistry in dealing with the question of divorce, they accommodate the Law to their own interests. In Jewish law only the man had the right to secure a divorce. Divorce, says Jesus, is bad enough, but remarriage to another woman is adultery. Thus Jesus' standard is higher than his contemporary legalists, and his instruction on the proper use of wealth is in harmony with the strongest demand. Variations of this saying in Mark 10:12 and Matthew 5:32 reflect ecclesiastical debate, owing to the special problems developing as a result of the Gentile mission.

THE RICH MAN AND LAZARUS   LUKE 16:19-31

In view of the shift back to the disciples in 17:1, the story of the rich man and Lazarus is probably to be viewed as addressed to the Pharisees (see 16:15). The story carries out the theme of the gospel, namely, exaltation of the poor and humbling of the rich (1:51-53; 6:20-26), but with an additional warning to those who demand signs. According to Pharisaic viewpoint, riches would be a stamp of God's approval on a righteous life. Jesus' story overthrows this traditional view.

19-21. Unique in Jesus' parables is the use of a specific name for
the poor man. Later tradition supplied one also for the rich man --
Neues, read in a text of the second century. Lazarus, however, means
'God helps' and it may have been Jesus' intention to emphasize by the
use of only one name the contrast between the self-sufficient rich
man and dependent Lazarus. It is also possible that the name was
included in order to expedite the succeeding dialogue. In any event,
the rich man has no real identity; poor Lazarus enjoys personhood.
In a few bold strokes the ostentatious affluence of the rich man is
made to contrast with the degradation of Lazarus. The one is clothed
in garments worthy of a king, a connoisseur of the finest cuisine; the
other, too weak from hunger, cannot even ward off the pesky dogs who
lick his sores. These unclean animals not only increase the distress
of the poor man, but sharpen the contrast between the rich man, who
is secure in his ceremonial purity, and poor Lazarus who can make
no claim on God for ritual conformity. Lest the point of the story
be misunderstood, it is important to note that the rich man is not
accused of refusing a minimum of alms to Lazarus. Lazarus lay in front
of his door. Beggars are not directed to the homes of skinflints. And
the Greek text says that he was desirous of getting his fill of the
scraps that 'were falling' from the rich man's table. In contrast to
what is stated in 15:16, there is no indication that he was denied
the scraps, but the text does suggest that Lazarus never really got
his fill. In accordance with the promise in 6:21 it was not long in
coming, for now the reversal begins.

22-23. The text indicates that Lazarus was taken away bodily
into the realm of the blessed to enjoy the intimate fellowship of
Abraham, the hope of every pious Jew (see 1:73). The picture suggested
may be that of a feast, where people recline at table. Lazarus has
the place of honor, and is able to lean closely toward Abraham, even
as the beloved disciple did on the night of Jesus' betrayal (see John
13:23 and cf. Matthew 8:11; Luke 13:29-30). The rich man also died,
but that was his only point of identity with Lazarus. The simple statement, and was buried, does not suggest an elaborate funeral contrasting
with that accorded to Lazarus. On the contrary, nothing is said of
Lazarus' burial. In contrast to the rich man, who received the normal
rites due a pious Israelite (and this he was, as the sequel shows),
Lazarus was carried to Abraham's bosom. The subsequent narrative does
not aim to give information on the furniture of heaven or the temper-
ature of hell. Dialogue and description is all designed to point up
the contrast in the conditions of the departed and to reinforce the
Lukan doctrine that external circumstances on earth are no criterion
of moral worth.

24. The rich man begins his plea with Father Abraham. This is
precisely what John the Baptist had warned against (3:8). The phrase
was a part of the rich man's liturgical pattern while he was in this
world. His lips spoke to God, but his heart prayed to Mammon. Still
the same arrogant self, he gives Abraham orders to send Lazarus as

his lackey. He knows the poor man's name; he does not know Lazarus. His alms were cast-off clothing, toys that were no longer needed, time that satisfied a temporary curiosity, a five-dollar bill to ease his conscience. But to become involved with one inadequate person, to really share his problems, to live his heartache with him, and perhaps to endure the disappointment of failure -- that was not to his liking. The rich man was one of those ninety-nine righteous who needed no repentance (Luke 15:7). He made only one mistake, he did not invite Lazarus in!

25. And now it is too late. To Abraham the man remains a son ('child' as in 15:31), in response to the word "Father.' But the rich man has cut himself off from the fulness of the relationship. Verse 25 reproduces the thought of 6:21,24. The rich man had thought as a Pharisee and viewed his wealth as a verdict of divine approval. But God's ways are not man's judgments. Riches *per se* are not condemned, but misplaced confidence can keep one from having treasure in heaven (see 12:33-34; 18:22).

26. The chasm is fixed. Life on earth is the place for decision, but the rich man had created the chasm before his arrival. And now there is no bridge! Enoch 102-103 is an eloquent commentary on the relative fates of the two men.

27-29. The rich man then takes a different tack, with a plea for his five brothers. In the economy of the story this figure suggests the large number of people in Israel who claim formal association with Abraham, but are in peril of suffering the same fate as the rich man.

30-31. The rich man's final request and the reply of Abraham are to be understood in the light of Jesus' and the church's mission experience. Jesus' contemporaries demanded signs as ratification of his credentials (see Luke 11:29). But the main sign is that the poor hear the good news (7:22; cf. 6:20). The apostles proclaimed the resurrection of Jesus, but there was no wholesale repentance on the part of Israel. Luke gives the reason in 16:29-31. Many in Israel claim allegiance to Moses and the prophets, but their ears are shut to the testimony of their Scriptures (see on 8:10). If they are not ready to hear them, no amount of signs will persuade them, not even the resurrection of Jesus. Thus vs. 31 suggests an explanation for the fact that Jesus did not reveal himself as resurrected Lord to anyone but the disciples. The Scriptures are open to faith, and Jesus is the authentic teacher in Israel. Through the apostolic interpretation of the Scriptures Jesus' death and resurrection are seen in proper perspective (cf. 24:25-27; Acts 2:37-42; 8:26-35). He who senses his need will understand. A Tamil proverb reads: Though one pulls out his eyes and throws them before him, the other will only say, 'it is jugglery.' There is none so blind as the one who *will* not see. The rich man felt no need, for he was secure in his wealth, and his religion was purely formal. About the worst that could be said of him is that he was engaged in no widespread plot to enhance the glory of God. Therefore his reservation in hell was assured.

Moral Responsibility and Faith   LUKE 17:1-10

ON OFFENSES   LUKE 17:1-2
                                          (Mark 9:42; Matthew 18:6-7)

   1. The Lord now shifts his instruction to the disciples. Behind the phrase temptations to sin lies the word from which 'scandal'
is derived. Traps or snares to sin rather than stumbling-blocks are
meant. A woe is pronounced (as in 6:24-26) on those who ought to know
better, namely the Pharisees and the Christians in the community.

   2. Little ones are people of no account in the eyes of man, such
as those behind the figure of the lost sheep and lost coin, the prodigal
son, and poor Lazarus. For such as these Jesus came, and those who
are better informed have a larger responsibility.

ON FORGIVENESS   LUKE 17:3-4
                                          (Matthew 18:15, 21-22)

   3. Take heed to yourselves is not, as the semicolon in RSV suggests,
to be connected only with the subsequent saying. Rather, these words
serve as a bridge between vss. 1-2 and vss. 3-4. As at 12:1; 21:34;
Acts 5:35; 20:28, this phrase reminds the disciple to be conscious of
the great peril confronting him. Not only may he expose others to en-
trapment but, forgetting his own liability to sin, he may act arrogantly
toward his erring brother (cf. 6:37). If his brother sins, he is to
rebuke him. The story of the prodigal son does not mean that sin is
to be taken lightly.

   4. *But* (this is the force of the conjunction and) if he repents,
he is to be forgiven. The prodigal son returned submissive to his
father. To berate him would have been unconscionable. The expression
seven times is not to be taken statistically, nor does it encourage
light-hearted repentance. But Jesus here confronts the disciple, not
the erring brother. Members in the church would ask whether, for example, sins committed after baptism could be forgiven. The principle
expressed in 6:37-38 and 11:4 is to be followed. No scores are to be
kept; the door to the erring is always to be kept open. Thus vss. 1-2
remind the disciple to maintain the highest standards for himself, and
vss. 3-4 discourage any pride or arrogance that might result from preoccupation with one's own piety.

ON FAITH   LUKE 17:5-6
                                          (Mark 11:23; Matthew 17:20; 21:21)

   These verses declare that the attitudes described in vss. 1-4 require faith. And the illustration in vs. 6 aims to point out that the
solution is not merely a matter of *added* faith but of faith pure and
simple. Both Matthew and Mark use a related form of this saying, except

that in their versions a mountain (cf. Zechariah 4:7), not a sycamine tree is to be moved. Mark 11:23 and Matthew 21:21 are part of a story dealing with Jesus' cursing of a fig tree. Luke does not include this account in his gospel, but uses in altered form the saying imbedded in it. The simile as a grain of mustard seed is used in Matthew 17:20. A sycamine tree, or black mulberry, has an extensive root system. Hence telling a mulberry tree to be uprooted would display unusual resources. Furthermore, trees are not usually planted in the sea. Thus the point of the text is that faith accomplishes what is beyond the normal scope of man. It scarcely needs to be said that Jesus does not encourage the disciples to spend their time watching sycamine trees leap into the sea.

ON PUTTING GOD INTO DEBT   LUKE 17:7-10

7-9. These verses describe the character of the faith required to bear the burdens of the other. It is especially important for the understanding of this passage to note that the word for servant means 'slave.' Once again Jesus' sense of humor finds expression. Any listener would at least smile at the thought of a master telling his slave: 'See, I have supper ready for you. Sit down,' or saying to him, 'It was very kind of you to plow up the fields today.' Slaves did their assigned tasks and that was the end of it. Woe to the slave who disobeyed! This illustration would, of course, be misunderstood if one were to make inferences about the character of God, who is most frequently described as Father. Quite evidently the attitude of the disciple is the point of comparison. Just as the righteous of 15:7 were not to anticipate congratulations for remaining in the fold, so the disciple is not to expect a pat on the back for doing his assigned task. St. Paul once said that he awaited no laurels for preaching the gospel (1 Corinthians 9:16). A cavalryman once asked his commanding officer, Papirius Cursor, for some relief from a difficult campaign. 'You are relieved from patting your horse,' replied the Roman officer curtly. A Tamil proverb asks: 'Should one's stomach be honored for digesting food?'

10. Originally the Lord's saying appears to have been directed at wealthy land owners who possessed slaves. Many Pharisees were men of wealth, and their bookkeeping type of religion comes under frequent scrutiny in Luke's gospel. The disciples are to beware of their leaven (Luke 12:1). Instead of imitating them, they are to evaluate themselves as unworthy servants, that is, as the text goes on to explain, one who has merely done his duty. He who works for reward will never get it, for the reward is a plus given freely and lavishly by a generous Father (see 6:23). Rabbi Johanan B. Zakkai underlined the words of Jesus: 'Even though you have been faithful in carrying out the Law, claim no special merit; for to that end you were created.' (Strack-Billerbeck II, 235).

LUKE 17:11-18

THIRD PHASE OF THE JOURNEY TO JERUSALEM   LUKE 17:11-18:30

A Grateful Samaritan   LUKE 17:11-19

Once again Luke reminds his readers that Jesus is heading toward
Jerusalem, but the geographical note is vague and confusing. Such
reminders appear at intervals since 9:50, and always as a corrective
of misunderstanding. In 9:51-56 the misunderstanding concerned Jesus'
role as Elijah. The recital in 10:38-41 put into larger perspective
the question of mercy discussed in the story of the Good Samaritan. 13:
22 is followed by a question about salvation. 13:33 is imbedded in a
context describing Israel's hostility. And 14:25 introduces a series
of sayings on decisive discipleship designed to cool rash enthusiasm.
Luke's introduction of the motif of the journey in 17:11 indicates that
he views the story of the lepers as an important illustration of basic
misunderstanding in Israel. At 17:5 the disciples asked Jesus to
increase their faith. The present story reveals that faith properly
conceived is faith in *Jesus*. 17:7-10 emphasized humble recognition of
obligation, without sense of merit. The Samaritan who returned in
gratitude contrasts with the nine Jews who accepted the Messianic benefit as something owed them by God.

12-13. Since the lepers were not allowed to enter the village
they meet him at the gate, yet maintaining the distance prescribed by
Moses (Leviticus 13:46).

14. Instead of speaking a word of healing (as in 5:13), Jesus tells
them to show themselves to the priests (see on 5:14). The point is important for the understanding of the sequel, for the lepers are not yet
healed. But when they do find themselves healed, will they attribute
their good fortune to Jesus, or go on their way without one word of
recognition? The text does not specify the precise moment when the
lepers were healed. But it was while they were on their way (as they
went).

15-16. One of them, as soon as he saw that he was healed, returned.
His praise to God, like that of the shepherds (2:20), is accompanied
by recognition of the instrument of his healing -- Jesus. That he
should understand is all the more remarkable, for he was a Samaritan
(see on 10:33).

17-18. All the lepers had asked Jesus for mercy, and thanksgiving
is, according to Psalm 30:10-12, the proper response to mercy received.
But the nine lepers, like the religious leadership of Jerusalem, fail
to understand the meaning of mercy and that God's most eloquent expression of it takes place in Jesus. Hence the nine are not criticized for
failing to give thanks to Jesus, but for failing to return and give God
the glory, that is, the credit for making himself known in and through
Jesus, their Messiah. This is faith -- to recognize the point at which
God's glory is revealed, namely in Jesus, who welcomes the lowly, the
poor, the leper. This Jesus invites all to shed their legal self-confi-

dence and their self-aggrandizement at the expense of others.

__19.__ The Samaritan is told: <u>Your faith has made you well</u>. The
words <u>made you well</u> are a double entente, for the Greek word for 'make
well' is the word ordinarily rendered 'save.' The Samaritan now is
confirmed in his faith. He came to the right place. Thus these words,
"your faith has made you well," do not say that exertion of faith
spells healing, but that the one to whom the faith is directed has
spelled the difference for this man. Faith without an agent who can
respond to the faith is only a psychological phenomenon. Therefore
his return to Jesus was of great importance. He saw the Giver in
the gift. The other nine also had faith that Jesus could heal them
but they exploited Jesus for the gift; they were not in the market
for inward change. A plus accompanied the Samaritan's faith. He was
made well in the profounder sense of the word (see 7:50; 8:12; 9:24;
9:56; 13:23; 19:10). Through Jesus God extends the assurance of his
love and desire to have man in fellowship with himself. Once the disciples wished to rain fire down on the Samaritans (9:51-56) because of
their rejection of Jesus. But like the owner of the vineyard (13:6-9),
the Lord was patient, and now a Samaritan becomes, like Naaman of old
(2 Kings 5; cf. Luke 4:27), a model for Israel and a symbol of the
Church's outreach to aliens (see Acts 8:14).

Coming of the Son of Man   LUKE 17:20-37

THE KINGDOM OF GOD IS HERE   LUKE 17:20-21

The attitude of the nine lepers is reflected in the misunderstanding that lies behind the question of the Pharisees concerning the
arrival of the <u>Kingdom of God</u>. In Luke the Kingdom is viewed in two
stages. It is now present in the word and work of Jesus and will be
realized in its fulness when the Son of man comes. Thus no apocalyptic
demonstration is required to determine the validity of Jesus' credentials. To the Pharisees,therefore, Jesus replies that the Kingdom does
not come subject to man's ratification through observance of signs
(cf. 11:29). The revisers have done well in adopting the rendering
<u>in the midst of you</u> in preference to the marginal interpretation *within
you*. Luke never views the Kingdom of God as a psychological reality.
It is always God's reigning action. The thought is related to that of
Isaiah 45:14 LXX: 'God is in you' (that is, present among you). In
the same context Isaiah speaks of God's salvation (cf. Luke 17:18-19).
Being in the midst of them, the Kingdom is something from which they
can benefit; that is, it lies now within their grasp or power.

THE DAY OF THE SON OF MAN:
  FIFTH PREDICTION OF THE PASSION   LUKE 17:22-37
                    (Matthew 24:26-28, 37-39; 10:39; 24:40,28)

22-23. The disciples must be on their guard against false reports concerning the Parousia. Under pressure from hostile religious and social forces, Christians will long for (cf. Amos 5:18) one of the days of the Son of man. The plural days is a general term for the period in which the Son of man makes his appearance and for the New Age that follows this appearance. In the prophets the plural term 'in those days' is frequently associated with the singular 'in that day' (cf. Amos 8:11, 13; Zechariah 14:1,4,7). To long for one of these days means that the community will be in desperate straits and find little consolation in a vague and undetermined period of time. When they do not see their hope fulfilled, they will be tempted in their impatience to listen to those who fix on a particular time and say: Lo, there! or, Lo, here! But they are warned not to follow the false voice.

24. The Son of man does have one day, his day, but it comes with the dispatch of lightning.

25. Nor are the disciples to be dismayed by the fact that Jesus, who is here identified with the Son of man (cf. 9:44), suffered many things and was rejected by this generation (see on 9:22: 11:29). Such experience does not invalidate his credentials, and he is still the Son of man even though his Parousia appears to be delayed. Moreover, if such is the fate of the Son of man, the community can scarcely expect less from the opposition, for the disciple must take up the cross and follow Jesus (9:23; 14:27). Even though all signs of deliverance for the community are lacking, the followers of Jesus are not to search for someone else (see 7:19). For Jesus and the Son of man are one and the same. (Other predictions of the Passion precede in 9:22; 44; 12:50; 13:32-33.)

26-31. To discourage all sign-seeking, Jesus declares that the days, that is, the time of the Parousia, will be preceded by completely unspectacular phenomena. Dining, marrying, trading, farming, building -- all normal every day activities. Nothing is said about religious activity, for the judgment is not based on the formula 'Father Abraham' (see 3:8; 16:24). Only Noah's and some of Lot's family escaped the two catastrophes that presage the day when the Son of man is revealed (the Greek word is the word from which 'apocalyptic' is derived). Matthew 24:37-39 cites only the example of Noah. Luke includes a reference to Sodom in order to paint as darkly as possible the fate that befalls those who defy God. If it will be 'more tolerable on that day for Sodom than for that town' which rejects the emissaries of Jesus (see Luke 10:12), what a dreadful fate must be in store for the disciple who attempts to keep a foot in each of two offered worlds. Precisely because everything goes on as usual, the disciple cannot carry on business as usual. Mark 13:15-16, which speaks of the destruction of Jerusalem, is used in Luke 17:31 in reference to the Parousia. Since the Parousia may take place at any time, and without advance signs beyond the customary phenomena in nature and society (see 21:25-26), the disciple must be prepared in every instant.

32. Lot's wife is mentioned because she looked back on the city of

Sodom and became a pillar of salt (see Genesis 19:26). Jesus earlier had warned a would-be follower about laying his hand on the plow and looking back (9:62). Preparation for the Kingdom to come is made in singleminded response to the Kingdom that is reality now. Such response, precisely because there are no signs to document the validity of that to which one responds, is equivalent to faith.

33. This verse is paralleled by Matthew 10:39. There can be no divided allegiance, not even to the point of seeking to gain one's life (see Luke 12:4-7). Losing it will be the means to preserve it (more accurately, 'make it live').

34-36. The decision is everything. Two people engaged in the same activity have totally different destinies (parallel in Matthew 24:40). Like the house of Israel, deserted by God (13:35), one in each case is left, that is, abandoned, and the other taken. This latter word is used in 9:10,28; 18:31 of one who takes another into close association (see also Colossians 2:6, 'received Christ'; 1 Thessalonians 2:13, 'accepted').

37. The Pharisees had asked 'When?' (vs. 20). Now the disciples ask Where? The Kingdom comes neither 'there' nor 'then.' The disciple must be so prepared that he is never like carrion waiting to be devoured by an eagle or vulture. Throughout the hearing or reading of the entire paragraph, early Christians would think also of the fate of Jerusalem, and Luke's reference to the eagles may be a symbol for the Roman standards. The disciples are not to repeat the mistake of her inhabitants, or they will be as unprepared for the second coming of Jesus as Jerusalem was for the first.

Preparation for the Kingdom   LUKE 18:1-30

The theme of salvation is continued in 18:1-30. The story of the 'Unjust Judge' (18:1-8) is an expansion of the exhortation in 17:22-37, for 18:1 indicates that the disciples are still being addressed, and the reference to the Son of man in connection with the question of the vindication of God's elect (vss. 7-8) clearly echoes 17:22,24,26. 18:8 raises the question of faith. Misplaced confidence in self (18:9-17) or in riches (18:18-27) can keep one from entry into the Kingdom. Those who are prepared to renounce everything for the sake of the Kingdom will have a share in the life to come (vss. 28-30).

SPIRIT OF ACCEPTANCE   LUKE 18:1-17

Persistence in Prayer   LUKE 18:1-8

1. The parable of the Unjust Judge is an answer to the problem of survival in the face of persecution (see 17:22). Hence the point of the parable is not that persistent prayer will guarantee the petitioner

anything he wants. Verse 1 unequivocally states that the disciples' prayers are to offset cowardly resignation in the face of the hazards they will run (cf. 11:4b and 22:46). One is not to grow weary because of apparent lack of interest on God's part. He will not fail the disciples. The woman did not receive immediate redress of wrong, but her persistence won a favorable verdict.

2-6. Luke's description of the judge has parallels in non-Christian literature. Livy (22,3) calls attention to a Roman consul who was 'fearful neither of the laws nor the senatorial majesty, and not even of the gods.' Sirach 35:12-15 discusses God's function as judge in behalf of widows. The judge's dialogue is more vigorous than the translation in RSV suggests. He says in effect: 'I shall avenge her, or she will give me a black eye!' This woman will not take no for an answer. He is more afraid of her than he is of God. Luke does not aim to suggest through this dark portrait of the judge that God is like that (see comment on the "Unjust Steward" at 16:8). The point is rather, if even a judge like this grants a widow's petition, how much more will God, to whom widows are a primary concern (see Isaiah 1:17), grant the petition of the disciples. This interpretation is borne out in the subsequent application of the story.

7-8. The syntax of the original is difficult, but the sense appears to be: 'And will not God avenge his own elect who cry to him night and day? Is he patient with them? I tell you, he will avenge them speedily. But the question is, will the Son of man, on his return, find faith on the earth.' In this paraphrase, it should be noted, the words delay long are replaced by the more usual rendering of the Greek term for patient restraint or mercy (see Sirach 18:11; cf. Matthew 18:29). The formal structure of the reply is a cue to the meaning. Verse 7 consists of two questions: 1. 'Will God avenge His elect?' (Cf. Revelation 6:10) 2. 'Is he patient with them?' This second question deals with the problem of divided allegiance. In 17:5 the disciples had asked for an increase in faith. 17:7-10 defined faith as an attitude of unqualified acceptance of responsibility, without a feeling of merit. 18:9-17 will expand on this theme. God is indeed concerned about the disciples, but the disciples in turn are reminded that single-hearted devotion is required of them (cf. 2 Peter 3:9). Is God merciful to the disciples in the face of their own weakness of faith? Verse 8 gives answers to this and the first question: 1. God will avenge His elect speedily (cf. Isaiah 13:22-14:1; 51:5). 2. The Son of man will have difficulty finding faith on the earth. The implied thought is: God must indeed be merciful, for he displays not wrath but patience, despite the fact that faith nearly runs out before the Son of man returns.

Humility

Jesus' reply in 18:7-8 spoke of high spiritual demand in a context of consolation. The addressees in 18:9 are sufficiently indefinite and do not exclude the disciples. Since a Pharisee appears as one of the principal characters in the story, it is doubtful that the remarks were

addressed specifically to Pharisees. Preparation for the coming of the
Son of man means understanding of the basic principle of the Kingdom:
The mighty are to be brought low and the humble are to be exalted (1:
51-52). Jesus' contemporaries and the church must recognize this fact.
It is the faith of the lowly for which the Son of man will be looking.
He who prays (vs. 1), must pray in the right spirit, if he is to hope
for vindication (vs. 8; cf. Psalm 17:2; 34:6, 15-21). The prayer of the
Pharisee follows the thought of Psalm 17:3-5. Psalm 34 shapes the pray-
er of the tax collector.

9-10. Trusted in themselves expresses the smug complacency of those
who think that everything within them is in order before God. The liturgical stance of the two men is similar. Both stand as they pray, and
both address the deity directly: God. One offers a prayer of thanksgiving, the other a petition for mercy. Both use accepted forms of
liturgy. Nor is the Pharisee to be criticized for thanking God that
he was not rapacious. A psalmist prayed in similar fashion (Psalm 17:
1-5).

11-12. But the Pharisee's prayer soon deteriorates. Instead of
remaining on the level of thanksgiving, he makes odious comparisons and
glorifies his performance at the expense of another man's defects. He
boasts of his fasting (on Mondays and Thursdays), but fasting ought to
go hand in hand with humility (cf. Psalm 35:13). His tithing is based
on all his income, including garden herbs (see Matthew 23:23), far
beyond the requirements of Deuteronomy 14:22-23. With such boasting he
exceeds the psalmist's catalogues of virtue (Psalm 17:3-5).

13. The publican takes the same stance as the Pharisee. But there
the comparison ends. Not only does he not bore God with a long recital
of his humility, but he omits giving thanks that he is not like 'those
hypocritical Pharisees.' 'Pharisees' are also found among 'publicans'
who excuse themselves from responsibility by citing the hypocrisies of
'churchmembers' without making appropriate applications to themselves.
The publican's prayer is that of the poor man in Psalm 34:6,18, and is
accompanied by gestures that suggest one who is deeply agitated by lamentation (see Homer *Iliad* 18:30-31; cf. Luke 23:48). He describes
himself with the odious label pinned on him by Pharisees -- sinner.

14. This man, like the elect of 18:7, cried to God and his prayer
was immediately answered for he went to his home with God's approval
(justified or 'righteous'), whereas the other failed to secure it (cf.
Psalm 34:15,17,19, 'righteous'). Unlike Paul, who discusses the *process*
of justification (see Romans 3), Luke describes the nature of the
recipients of God's verdict of approval. The justified are the humble,
those who recognize that no righteousness of their own can be so great
that they could stand successfully before God with it (cf. 1 Corinthians 1:27-29). Thus they leave judgment to God. The Pharisee pronounced
judgment on himself and for the moment seemed to win his case. But he
was wrong. The publican was wiser -- he called on God to be both judge
and defender. In Psalm 34 the poet states that the Lord's deliverance
is open to the righteous. Luke 18:9-14 has defined the identity of the

righteous. But they are few (see 13:23-24), and the Son of man will not find many of this breed (see 18:8).

Receive the Kingdom Like a Child   LUKE 18:15-17
(Mark 10:13-16; Matthew 19:13-15; 18:3)

At 9:50 Luke had dropped the Markan narrative. Now he resumes Mark's order of events, with some adaptation. Like 9:43-48, this second recital of Jesus' acceptance of children is associated with the climactic events in Jerusalem (see 18:31-34). Luke clearly indicates that the death of Jesus will not be understood unless one has the faith of a little child, for the Passion of Jesus is the supreme illustration of the truth that the mighty are brought low and the lowly are exalted (18:14).

15. In his modification of Mark's account (Mark 10:13-16) Luke omits reference to Jesus' displeasure over the disciples and in place of Mark's first reference to 'children' reads <u>infants</u> (the word used in Luke 2:12,16). Not only children but *even* infants were brought. The omission is in harmony with Luke's rather consistent removal of features that are unnecessarily embarrassing to the apostles, and the alteration is prompted by his interest in the theme of total dependence on God.

16. According to rabbinic thought, children could not be models of righteousness, for they were incapable of knowing the Law. In his story of the Pharisee and the Publican Jesus put Pharisaic legal confidence under question. The Publican laid himself open to the mercy of God. Precisely this attitude of receptivity is required for entrance into the Kingdom, and children, like birds and flowers (12:24,27), are models of faith for the disciples; for faith in Luke is not intellectual assent, but openness to divine generosity (see 17:11-19). The thought is in harmony with Jesus' instruction to address God with the familiar term Abba, 'Daddy' (see on Luke 11:2), and with the prophetic identification of Israel as the 'child' of Yahweh (see Isaiah 41:8; 42:1; 44:1, 2,21; cf. Proverbs 4:1).

17. So basic is the pronouncement that a solemn *amen* (<u>truly</u>) prefaces the final saying. Entrance is possible only for those who come to God in the spirit of children approaching their fathers (see Luke 11:11-13), eagerly waiting to <u>receive</u>.

These words of Jesus appear to have helped resolve disputes in the community over the question of candidates for baptism. Luke's specific reference to infants may reflect such controversy, and his language in Acts 8:36; 10:47; 11:17 suggests that the principle expressed in these sayings found a broad application that broke through legal and sectarian isolation.

EXPEDITING FOR THE KINGDOM

Rid of Excess Baggage

The two recitals in 18:9-17 focused attention on receptivity, distinguished from legal self-determination, as primary requisite for
entry into the Kingdom. In 18:18-27 the last bulwark of the self-made
religious man comes under attack, namely material goods.

<u>18</u>. Mark's 'man' is called a <u>ruler</u> in Luke's recital, either
to account for his great wealth, or to focus attention on the type of
authorities who were responsible for Jesus' crucifixion (see 23:15,35;
24:20, and note the dialogue on the approaching passion, 18:31-34).
Matthew identifies the inquirer as a 'young man' and therefore omits
from Mark's record of the man's boast the words 'from my youth.' The
man's manner of address and the nature of his request betray a basic
misunderstanding. He views Jesus as a teacher of righteousness, who
might be able to supplement what Moses had said. Moreover, he does
not come like a child waiting to receive *now*, but in the future, and
on the basis of his own performance. He was in error on the first
count, for Israel has Moses and the prophets, and he should heed them
(see 16:29). And he was wrong on the second, for the Kingdom of God
is present, as well as future, reality (see 18:30).

<u>19</u>. Luke, unlike Matthew (19:17), is not disturbed by the Markan
phrasing of Jesus' question: <u>Why do you call me good?</u> This question,
together with the affirmation <u>No one is good but God alone</u>, is not a
disclaimer of personal goodness in the sense of moral rectitude. The
term <u>good</u> in this context connotes extraordinary distinction (see Strack-
Billerbeck II, 24-25). Any distinction possessed by Jesus must be viewed
from the perspective of God, who is the ultimate criterion of the good.
Jesus renounces any shallow appraisal of his own person (see 11:27-28,
where the focus is, as here, on God's word). Jesus has come to do the
Father's will (see on 2:49). Everything has been handed over to him by
the Father, and only he who understands the Father will understand
the Son (10:21-22). Hence Jesus disavows any claim to special revelation
beyond that of his own person as the embodiment and climactic demonstration of what had already found expression in Moses and the prophets (16:
29). <u>20</u>. Jesus therefore reminds the ruler of the <u>commandments</u> given
by God through Moses (see Deuteronomy 5:16-20; cf. Exodus 20:12-16).
These are repeatedly endorsed by the prophets (see, for example Isaiah 5;
Hosea 4). According to Deuteronomy 30:15-20, obedience to these and
other commandments would spell life for Israel.

<u>21</u>. The ruler's reply is to be taken at face value. Jesus recog-
nizes the righteous who need no repentance (15:7). And there is no
special virtue in confessing sins that one has not committed. <u>22</u>. But
now Jesus puts him to the ultimate test. The ruler had asked for further
guidance. Jesus takes him at his word. He strikes first at the center
of the man's security -- his material possessions. Here the very issues

of existence are determined (see Romans 1:18-25). Sell all that you
have and distribute to the poor. He had asked how he might inherit
eternal life. Jesus equates this goal with having treasure in heaven
(cf. 12:33-34). This means that one is invited to expose himself
totally to God's verdict, without the support of material blessings.
According to popular conception wealth would be a sign of personal
goodness (see Proverbs 15:6). But even such self-denial is not enough.
The ultimate decision must be made. Come, follow me. Jesus comes as
a Giver, not a Demander, but his self-giving involves the strongest
demand possible. Thus Jesus does not disclaim goodness but rather
links his life and work with the One who is good. And his command is
as absolute as any commandment of God. To be associated with him is
to accept the most dangerous assignment, without command over anything
that one can call his own. Thus the sincerity of anyone who claims to
be interested in God is called into question by the way in which he
responds to God's climactic revelation of himself in Jesus (see Luke
6:46-49).

23. The ruler had expected something else. He did not anticipate
a directive that went so contrary to all he had been taught to believe.
Entrance into the Kingdom is indeed difficult, for it belongs to the
poor (6:20). 24. But a rich man, when confronted with a call to decisive action that jeopardizes his capital, will be tempted to choose
temporary security ahead of treasure in heaven. Thus concern for property values outraces justice during racial crises in the United States.
Expensive church structures have taken precedence over responsibility
to the poor.

25. A camel, despite its hump, will go through the eye of a needle
before a rich man with his money bags enters the Kingdom. This lively
proverb should not be deflated by attempting to find a 'Needle's Eye
Gate' in Jerusalem. Jesus was fond of exaggerated pictures to make a
point (see, for example, 6:41).

26. Those who heard the proverb grasped it -- Then who can be saved?
Verse 27 answers: It is God's doing, for the Kingdom is God's gift.
And from the context it is clear that the faith of a little child makes
possible the impossibility (18:15-17). Zacchaeus would know the answer,
but only after he had seen and heard the generosity of Jesus who communicated the love of a Heavenly Father (19:8). St. Paul learned it well
(Philippians 3:7; 4:12). For the disciples it was a repetition of an
earlier warning (Luke 9:24-27; cf. 14:25-35).

Future Reward   LUKE 18:28-30
                                          (Mark 10:28-30; Matthew 19:27-29)

Jesus' response to Peter's question is a modification of the Markan
form (Mark 10:29-30). In Mark, what the disciple parts with is restored
in parallel form. Luke replaces this idea with the more general mani-
fold more (vs. 30). The Kingdom of God is present as well as future
reality. In his association with Jesus the disciple has much more than
he previously renounced (see 6:20; cf. 12:22-34). And in the age to come,

that is, after the Parousia, he will enjoy what the rich ruler longed to find but lost. Thus the Lord answers Peter with a further demand for faith. But the disciple dare not forget an earlier reminder of Jesus, that they are "unworthy servants," that is, 'useless slaves' (17:10). For the Kingdom is *received*, not gained through calculating trade.

FINAL PHASE OF THE JOURNEY TO JERUSALEM   LUKE 18:31-19:27

Sixth Prediction of the Passion   LUKE 18:31-34

Jerusalem is the focal point in Luke's gospel. In Luke 1 and 2 the city is mentioned repeatedly, climaxing with Jesus' visit to the temple (2:41-50). The temple is mentioned in the third temptation (4:9). At Jerusalem Jesus must carry out the exodus (9:31). At 9:51 the journey to Jerusalem had begun (see also 13:22; 17:11). And in 13:33 it was observed that no prophet perishes outside Jerusalem. The reminder of Jesus' destination is especially appropriate at this point, for the fate of Jesus involves the disciple in a call to decision that requires singleminded devotion, unhampered by misdirected concern about family or material possessions. Association with Jesus means readiness to part with standard status symbols or criteria of success.

Verses 31-34 present the fourth of a series of predictions concerning the suffering of the Son of man (9:22; 9:44; 17:25). Other predictions, minus "Son of man," were made in 12:50 and 13:32-33. This, then, is Jesus' sixth prediction of his Passion. Since the Passion story is about to be recited, 18:32-33 gives more details than the previous predictions. Another additional feature is the statement that the prophetic predictions about the Son of man will find fulfillment. Nothing, in fact, is said in the prophets about the suffering of the Son of man. However, in the Markan source, and elsewhere in Luke's gospel, Jesus and the Son of man are equated. The fate that ultimately befell Jesus was then understood in the light of such a passage as Isaiah 50:6, in which is found Luke's additional note that the sufferer would be spat on. Hosea 6:2 appears to have offered the pattern for the emphasis on the third day.

34. Since the popular view of the Messiah and of the Son of man did not include expectation of suffering, the disciples could not fathom Jesus' premonition of the fate in store for him in Jerusalem. As at 9:45, they understood none of these things (see also 2:50 and 24:16-21). Luke's variation in the phrasing of the last two clauses in vs. 34 ("this saying was hid from them" and "they did not grasp what was said") points to his blend of early Christian proclamation with Jesus' own statements about his approaching death. RSV obscures the distinction in the clauses by the rendering this saying. The Greek word for this expression is used frequently in Luke in the sense of 'this thing' or 'this event' (1:37; 1:65; 2:15; 2:19; 2:51; Acts 10:37, 'What happened,' NEB). In brief, such an outcome as Jesus described

lay outside the comprehension of the disciples. But Luke offers a
theological interpretation. This thing or event was hid from them,
namely by God. The second of the two clauses is corectly rendered
in RSV. Since the necessity of his death was hidden from the disciples, they could not understand what was said. But nothing is hidden
which shall not be revealed, Jesus observed in 8:16-17, and knowledge
of the mysteries of the Kingdom of God is granted to the followers
of Jesus (8:10). Thus the motif of ignorance sets the stage for
the enlightenment given by Jesus himself in 24:25-27. He is the
authentic Teacher for Israel and the church. The church's emissaries
are entrusted with the correct appraisal of the events that took
place on Good Friday and Easter Sunday (see Acts 3:12-18); for what
God hides he can also reveal. Thus Luke provides at least one solution for the problem of the disciples' earlier misunderstanding of
Jesus compared with the continuing misunderstanding on the part of
Israel's religious leadership. Disciples are spared the verdict:
'seeing they might not see' (Luke 8:10). Their ignorance is viewed
on a different level from that of the leaders who later rejected the
apostolic proclamation (see Acts 28:25-27).

A Blind Man Sees   LUKE 18:35-43
                                (Mark 10:46-52; Matthew 20:29-34)

Luke's account of the blind man healed near Jericho, together
with the account of Zacchaeus' conversion, climaxes his exposition
of the Kingdom. Faith is the eyesight required to understand what
God does in connection with Jesus. Disciples, as well as Israel in
general, must approach Jesus as did this blind man. To sharpen this
truth, Luke omits Mark's account of the request of the sons of Zebedee
(10:35-45), reserving part of the passage for his recital at 22:25-27.

35. In Mark the event takes place on the way out of Jericho (10:
46). Luke has his reasons, however, for relating the story of Zacchaeus
(not found in Mark) after this account, and therefore places the healing *before* Jesus' entry into the city. 36-37. The crowd proclaims that
Jesus of Nazareth is passing by. 38. The blind man 'sees' much more.
This is the Son of David. The title is strongly messianic. 39-41.
According to Isaiah 35:5 sight will be restored to the blind in God's
time of deliverance (see Luke 4:18; 7:22). The blind man recognizes
in Jesus the fulfillment of this anticipated messianic age, and the
Davidic affirmation is in harmony with 1:32; 1:69; 2:4,11; 3:21; 6:3
(misunderstanding of the title will be taken up in 20:41-44). His
request for removal of his blindness is a bold invitation to Jesus to
validate his credentials as Messiah.

42. As in the case of the Samaritan leper (17:19), Jesus declares
that the man's faith has 'saved' him (made him well). Jesus is the
one who gives sight to the blind and he will aid the disciples to see
(cf. 24:16,31) the significance of his person as the link between God's
past action in Israel and his continuing activity in the Christian commu-
ity.

43. Unlike the ruler who lacked such faith and refused to follow Jesus (18:22-23), the blind man is like the disciples who forsook all (18:28). And like the Samaritan (17:15), he glorifies, that is, praises God. The words echo the response of the shepherds in 2:20 and anticipate the climax pronounced in 24:26. Isaiah prophesied the glory of the Lord which was to be 'seen' (Isaiah 61:1-5 LXX; 40:5; 58:8). Zechariah proclaimed the coming age as a time of light (Luke 1:78-79). The Kingdom is really present in the work and person of Jesus of Nazareth and those who had before discouraged the blind man (vs. 39) now endorse the man's verdict (vs. 43; cf. 19:37), and again the phrasing echoes 2:20. If nevertheless Jesus goes to his death, let no one construe it as a collapse of messianic hope. Blindness remains in Israel, and her leaders who do not 'see' must accept the responsibility for the execution of the Messiah (see 18:32). Messiahship and death are not mutually exclusive.

Jesus Brings Salvation to the House of Zacchaeus

With his recital of the Lord's reception of Zacchaeus, Luke rounds out his exposition of the Kingdom and clears the way for proper understanding of Jesus' suffering and death about to take place in Jerusalem. The parable that follows (vss. 11-27) reinforces the doctrine expressed in this story: The Kingdom does not come accompanied by spectacular signs. Salvation is its basic characteristic. The blind man pronounced Jesus Son of David and heard the verdict: 'Your faith has saved you.' The Kingdom now comes to Zacchaeus (for the name, see Ezra 2:9; Nehemiah 7:14).

2. Zacchaeus is described by the unusual term a chief tax collector which suggests that he was a kind of overseer in charge of collection of a variety of taxes. He would therefore be all the more despised by the native populace. Luke's account of the ruler (18:18-25) had stressed the hazard of wealth as a barrier to entrance into the Kingdom (see 18:25). By emphasizing that Zacchaeus was rich, he prepares the reader for the answer to the question: 'Who then can be saved?' (18:26).

3-4. The observation that Zacchaeus was small of stature is not mere descriptive detail. At 12:25 Jesus had spoken about the futility of attempting to add a cubit to one's stature (see also on 2:52). Zacchaeus, despite his lack of height, finds real 'stature' through the welcome extended him by Jesus.

5. It was not necessary for him to elevate himself, for Jesus knows who he is and calls out his name, without any suggestion in the text that he had made inquiry as to Zacchaeus' identity. Zacchaeus had to see Jesus, but Jesus was already on the search for him (vs. 10). Jesus must stay at his home. This is the thread of necessity that weaves Jesus' career (see 2:49; 4:43; 9:22; 13:16,33; 15:32; 17:25; 22:37; 24: 7, 26,44). The word today echoed in vs. 9 is the second major thread

(see 2:11; 3:22; 4:21; 5:26; 13:32-33) climaxing at 23:43. Present
encounter with Jesus spells Kingdom reality. Jesus had instructed his
disciples to *remain* in the house where they were welcome (9:4; cf.
10:7), and his self-invitation to Zacchaeus' home indicates that Zacchaeus is a privileged recipient of the Kingdom (see also 24:29). 6.
This invitation, which is at the same time an absolution, marks the moment of conversion. His joy is a fulfillment of the promise expressed
in 2:10 (see also 1:14; 10:20; 13:17; 19:37; 24:41,52).

7. As at 5:30, Jesus faces criticism for his action. But this
time all, not only scribes and Pharisees, 'grumbled' (murmured). Their
characterization of Zacchaeus as a sinner provides a stark background
for the subsequent picture of the 'new' Zacchaeus. Once a Pharisee
stood in the temple congratulating himself on his tithes (18:11-12).
Later a ruler had turned his back on the Kingdom when he was directed
to sell all he had and give the proceeds to the poor (18:22-23).

8. In contrast, Zacchaeus addresses the Lord (the community's
term for Jesus as their recognized ruler) in words that demonstrate
how man's impossibilities become God's possibilities (18:27), and how
one is to have treasure in heaven (18:22). In contrast to the customary
limit of 20% of one's fortune (Strack-Billerbeck IV, 546-47), Zacchaeus
promises to give half of his possessions to the poor. In cases of
extortion (see 3:14) the normal practice was to make restitution, plus
20% (see Leviticus 5:16; Numbers 5:7). Zacchaeus goes far beyond such
expectation and binds himself to the law imposed on rustlers (cf. Exodus 22:1), who were liable to a fourfold penalty for theft of sheep. In
the eyes of rabbis, such promises would be indicative of true repentance
(Strack-Billerbeck II, 250). In Luke's recital he is a living definition of the word 'repentance' (see 3:8). Thus Zacchaeus now lives up
to his name, which means 'righteous' or 'pure' one, and becomes a living
illustration of what Jesus repeatedly stated on the subject of wealth.

9-10. Jesus himself amplifies his earlier absolution with words
that were originally aimed at the grumblers. Today echoes vs. 5. Salvation in Luke includes release from the anxieties that hamper one's
appreciation of God's outreaching love. Jesus, as the guarantor of God's
concerned love, spells rescue for Zacchaeus, and the latter's repentance indicates that the circle is complete. His entire household is
the beneficiary. With him they were implicated in guilt, according to
Jewish thinking (see, for example, Joshua 7), and with them they share
the benefits of the Kingdom (cf. Acts 10:2; 11:14; 16:31; 18:8). Thus
salvation also means assurance of God's desire that even the worst of
sinners be included in his family. It was appropriate for Jesus to include Zacchaeus, for he is a son of Abraham contrasting with those who
merely invoke Abraham as father (3:8; 16:24). Like the sheep, coin and
son (chapter 15), he was lost, but now a cherished member of the family
of Israel has been found. The Son of man comes not only as judge in
apocalyptic splendor at the end of history, but in the present moment
as Seeker and Savior of the lost (cf. Ezekiel 34:2,16). And what was
done for a lost Israelite will be done for Gentiles who are aliens in

the commonwealth of Israel (Luke 7:1-10; Acts 10), 'for we all are God's offspring' (Acts 17:28). Expressed in theological jargon, the story of Zacchaeus resolves the problem of apocalyptic soteriologically.

The Kingdom -- Present and Future   LUKE 19:11-27
                                                              (Matthew 25:14-30)

<u>11</u>. In place of Mark 10:35-45, omitted after 18:34, Luke presents the parable of the pounds. Similarities to the story of the talents in Matthew 25:14-30 suggest that an original parable about trading has undergone modification in the instruction of the community. In its present context in Luke it climaxes the contrast between the ruler (18:18-25), who is representative of Israel's formalistic leadership, and Zacchaeus, who despite his lowly status in the eyes of religionists was found faithful in response to the Kingdom. The parable also summarizes Luke's doctrine of the two-phase Kingdom. Luke does not deny that the Kingdom is present reality, but he uses the parable to correct a misunderstanding. Jesus is near Jerusalem but the Kingdom does not make its appearance now in a spectacular demonstration, as it will at the Parousia. Thus Luke's recital anticipates the corrective issued in Acts 1:6-8 and is a further answer to the question raised in Luke 17:20. Jerusalem will be the site of consummation of the Kingdom in its first stage, but this will take place in the suffering, death and resurrection of Jesus, a fact of which the disciples are ignorant (9:45; 18:34). Rescue of people like Zacchaeus exacts its toll, for it means crossing swords with an establishment that cannot tolerate such liberal practice, and it is only a matter of days before 2:35 finds fulfillment.

The parable in its present form contains allegorical elements, but there is no strict correspondence between characteristic features of earthly kings and those of Jesus as a royal figure. The king in the story bears marks of a tyrant. But unsavory characters have elsewhere been used as a base of comparison for truths relating to the Kingdom of God (see 16:1-8; 18:1-8). Money and rewards of cities are part of the scenario, appropriate to the royal theme. The reader is expected to abstract from them the principles that govern relationships between himself and the Lord of the Church. The comments that follow represent an attempt to do justice to the meaning of the parable through application not explicit in the text, a procedure supported by unmistakable echoes of thoughts expressed elsewhere in the gospel.

<u>12</u>. The hearers would be familiar with examples of rulers going to a distant capital to secure their positions. In 40 B.C. Herod the Great went to Rome to bolster his throne (see Josephus *Antiquities* 14, 14,1-4) and on his return executed some of his opponents (*Antiquities* 15, 1,2). However, the activity of his son Archelaus seems to have suggested some of the more explicit detail in the story. His interest in the throne was challenged by the Jews, who sent a deputation to Rome. Philip, Herod's third son, supported Archelaus in his plea before Augustus, while Antipas, who had also gone to Rome, spoke out against Archelaus (See *Antiquities* 17 and *Jewish Wars* 2,2,1-3). On his return

to Palestine Archelaus deposed the high priest Joazar in favor of
Eleazar.

Jesus is like such a noblemain. Between his first appearance and
his Parousia (see Acts 1:11) lies an indeterminate period of time,
described in terms of a journey to a far country. Jesus does not take
over the Kingdom, or kingly power, in terms of popular expectation at
Jerusalem, but receives it from the Father (cf. 1:32-33) by entering
into his glory, as spelled out in 24:26. After a time he will return.
Thus the Kingdom is an on-going reality, but it will appear (vs. 11)
in a climactic phase at the end of history.

13. Whereas Matthew enumerates three servants (that is, slaves!),
Luke begins with ten (see 17:12), but brings three of them to the fore
in the dialogue. In Matthew the slaves receive varying amounts, but
the monetary value is considerable. In Luke's recital each receives
one pound, that is, a *mina*, worth less than $20.00. This trifling
sum makes more cogent the reference to 'very little' in vs. 17. The
criterion of success is not to be based on varied endowment, with a
one-for-one return, as in Matthew. Faithfulness and shrewdness, measured by varying returns on the original investment, which is the same
for all, is the standard whereby the disciple is judged.

In vss. 14 and 15 the contrast between Jerusalem's hostility and
the faithful apostolic community is clearly drawn. Jesus, like Archelaus, is rejected by many of his countrymen. But on his return (his
Parousia) Jesus calls his disciples to account. Association with him
does not spell automatic success any more than does invocation of
Abraham as father (3:8). Faithfulness, as specified in 16:10, is the
criterion.

16-17. He who is faithful in very little is entrusted with much
(cf. 16:10), here spelled out as authority over ten cities (cf. 22:30;
12:32). Thus the contrast between the trifling amount and the responsibility now entrusted to the slave points to the surpassing generosity
of the King (see 18:30).

18-19. The second slave earned only half the amount of the other
and is entrusted with commensurate authority. Neither slave congratu-
lates himself, but only the first receives a special accolade from the
Lord, 'Well done, good slave!'

20-21. A third slave is chosen out of the ten as illustration of
total failure. He took no chances, risked nothing. He was not as
wise as the 'sons of this world' (16:8). Given freedom to act, he lived
in fear of his master, whom he viewed as a rigorous financial inspector.
Today one would say that he is typical of the disciple who retreats from
the world and involvement in the decision-making that goes on around him;
typical of the disciple who confines the good news in a deposit-box
of tradition, for fear that he will incur the wrath of the Lord if he
braves fresh frontiers of communication and creative enterprise. The
first slave was congratulated. 22. But this man hears the opposite

verdict: <u>You wicked</u> slave! <u>23</u>. His own conception of the Master should have prompted him to gain a return on the investment.

<u>24</u>. Why the man with ten pounds should be interested in one more pound after being entrusted with ten cities is not clarified. The point is that the faithless slave loses what he had. <u>25</u>. Those who <u>stood by</u> are quite surprised by the Master's order, but their remark serves to introduce the principle expressed in the next verse.

<u>26</u>. The man who <u>has</u> is one who views his possessions as a trust from the Lord. He who <u>has not</u> is one who functions in such a way that one would suspect he had been entrusted with nothing. Such is the condition of the religious man who boasts that he has a relationship with God, but fails to bear good fruit (see 6:43-45). Like the other two slaves, the third man said 'Lord' (vs. 20), but it was as empty a liturgy as the rich man's 'Father, Abraham' (see also the warning in 6:46). But to everyone who <u>has, more will be given</u> (see 6:36-38; 8:18). This is the principle of the plus. No special punishment is meted out to the third slave. He is simply not entrusted with the program of the future. The Master will not permit the experience of history to be repeated. Mediocre, middle-of-the-road, play-it-safe disciples will not be permitted to retard progress in the New Age yet to dawn. Luke is not interested in details of the final judgment. St. Paul holds out more explicit hope that such people will be saved as respects their persons but will lose much opportunity that might have been theirs (see 1 Corinthians 3:15).

At vs. <u>27</u> the citizens of vs. 14 come back into view. Like Agag (1 Samuel 15:33) they are to be slaughtered before the King's eyes. This bloody description is not to be taken as a literal representation of events at the Parousia but is again part of the scenery associated with ancient generals and kings. In Luke's recital it means that Jesus' presence in history is crucial. It was especially crucial for Israel, for much had been given to her. The language of 19:27 anticipates Jesus' lament over the city (vss. 41-44), and the reader is prepared for the entry described in vss. 28-38.

THE KING'S CLAIM   LUKE 19:28-48

The Royal Procession   LUKE 19:28-38
                                                  (Mark 11:1-10; Matthew 21:1-9)

28. The words <u>when he had said this</u> clearly indicate the relation
between the preceding parable and Jesus' royal entry into Jerusalem.
The 'journey' begun in 9:51 now nears its end and Luke again takes up
the Markan account (Mark 11:1), but with some variations. After the
story of the entry he inserts a dialogue between the Pharisees and Jesus. In Mark the cleansing of the temple takes place on the day after
Jesus' entry; in Luke apparently on the same day. Luke omits Mark's
narrative of the cursing of the fig tree and condenses the Markan
chronology of the first part of the last week into a general statement
(vs. 47: cf. 21:37).

29. The village of Bethphage (meaning 'house of unripe figs')
has disappeared. It was located on the Southeast slope of the Mount
of Olives. Closer to Jerusalem was <u>Bethany</u>. The meaning of this name
is uncertain, but some interpret it as 'house of the poor,' or 'house
of the afflicted.' The site is mentioned also in Luke 24:50; Matthew
21:17; 26:6; Mark 11:1,11; 14:3, and is today called Azariyeh or
Lazaiyeh, 'the place of Lazarus.' To early Christian readers the reference to the Mount of Olives would have been especially significant,
for this was to be the locale of end-time events. According to Zechariah 14:4 the feet of the Lord were to stand at this place and the
mount would be split in two. 'Then the Lord your God will come, and
all the holy ones with him,' (Zechariah 14:5), and 'the Lord will become King over all the earth' (Zechariah 14:9). The association may
have been also in Luke's mind, for Zechariah 14:21 declares that 'there
shall no longer be a trader in the house of the Lord of hosts on that
day' (see Luke 19:45).

Throughout the proceedings Jesus appears as master of the situation.
His prophetic powers are integral to the total picture. His approaching
death is no tragic accident. He has been aware of the divine intention.
Now his instructions concerning the colt lend further confirmation to
the conviction that he proceeds with unmistakable design. To suggest,
therefore, that Jesus had made previous arrangements with the owners
of the colt is to miss the theological intention of the text. The

196

observation that no one had ever ridden the colt heightens the impression of Jesus' mastery.

31-34. In the succeeding dialogue RSV unfortunately obscures the word-play in the original. The Lord has need of it (vs. 31) would be the normal interpretation of the text. But in vs. 33 the words its owners (literally, 'masters') parallel the phrasing in vs. 31, which by analogy can be rendered 'Its Master has need.' Greeks loved such word-play (see also Luke 10:42), and even an unsophisticated reader would have caught the double entente. The text, in effect, suggests that Jesus is a sovereign who claims all property as his own.

35. Parallel to this stress on lordship is the use of the name Jesus (vss. 34-35). In 1:31-32 this name and the fact of Jesus' kingship are linked. Luke 2:11 had added the reminder that Jesus is the Anointed One and Savior. Luke's literary artistry in drawing attention to his infancy narrative through repeated stress on the word 'lord' and now with the name 'Jesus,' is supported by his clear echo of 2:14 in 19:38. It is not improbable that he was also conscious of Isaiah 1:2 which states that the ass knows 'its master's crib; but Israel does not know, my people does not understand.' The context of Isaiah 1 would account for Luke's inclusion of the criticism made by the Pharisees (Luke 19:39) and Jesus' lament over the ignorance of Jerusalem (Luke 19:42).

36. Luke, more pointedly than Mark or Matthew, continues with the disciples as subject of the action. Like the servants of Jehu, who proclaimed their master as king (2 Kings 9:13), they spread their garments in Jesus' path (cf. 1 Kings 1:32-40; see page 141).

37. The verb draw near echoes the adverb in vs. 11 and the verb in vs. 29 (see also vs. 41). In one sense the Kingdom has arrived, but the disciples are not yet aware of the somber truth expressed in the previous parable (vss. 12-27). As at 18:43, the participants give praise to God. The mighty works of Jesus are the measure of his royal benefactions, and the reaction of the multitude of the disciples is in harmony with the message sent by Jesus to John the Baptist (7:22).

38. John had asked, 'Are you he who is to come?' (7:20). The multitude provides the answer with the cry in vs. 38 (see on 13:35). Once again Luke's literary artistry is obscured by the RSV. Mark (11:9) had written, 'Blessed be he who comes in the name of the Lord,' reproducing the wording of Psalm 117:26 (LXX). Luke retains this part of the acclamation, but adds two words: the King. His sentence reads: 'Blessed be the coming one, the King, in the name of the Lord.' Jesus is the 'coming one' of John's query (Luke 7:20). His royal credentials are in order. The conclusion of Mark's recital read: 'Blessed be the kingdom of our father David that is coming! Hosanna in the highest!' (Mark 11:10) Luke deletes the first part of this statement in favor of his simple reference to the king, thereby preserving the doctrine expressed in 19:11-27. Luke does not deny that Jesus is a Davidian (see on 18:40), but Jesus does not usher in the type of kingdom expressed by

the phrase 'the coming kingdom of our father David.' He is not a
competitor on the same level with Caesar. In place of the words
'Hosanna in the highest!' Luke repeats the song of the angels, who
like the multitude gave praise to God. 'Hosanna,' meaning 'God, save,'
would not have been understood by Luke's readers. The word peace
not only communicates a vivid concept of salvation (cf. 1:79; 10:5-6;
24:36), in the sense that nothing disruptive stands between God and
his people, but also prepares the reader for the pronouncement in 19:42.

Lament over Jerusalem   LUKE 19:39-44

    Luke's introduction of the Pharisees provides a cogent setting
for the lament that follows. Their approach to Jesus is respectful.
And their concern is legitimate. They want no disturbance of the
delicate balance between their religious interests and Roman power.
In his reply Jesus adopts a vivid semitic expression (cf. Habakkuk
2:11). So great is the crisis, that in the absence of any other
voice inanimate objects must cry out. The reference to stones is
filled with pathos, anticipating as it does the terrible doom predicted
in vs. 44.

    41. Within sight of the city, Jesus breaks into a tearful lament.
It is the weeping for the dead and for the fool whose understanding
has failed him (see Sirach 22:11). The very syntax reveals the
agitation of his heart.

    42. Heedless of the truth expressed in such passages as 12:56-59;
14:28-32, Jerusalem does not realize that the presence of Jesus had
placed her at a crossroads of national destiny. The meaning of Jesus'
earlier words, 'from him who has not, even what he has will be taken
away' (19:26), finds tragic fulfillment: Now they are hid from your
eyes. He who *will* not see, *shall* not see (Isaiah 29:10; Luke 8:10).

    43-44. Details of the disaster that followed in A.D. 70 recall
descriptions in Isaiah 29:3; Psalm 137:9. The words not . . . one stone
upon another are hyperbolic. Actually parts of walls and buildings
were left standing. The phrase is simply a rhetorical device to paint
in bold lines the ruin of a great city. The words, because you did not
know the time of your visitation, are a refrain of the first words. Israel knows how to predict the weather, but she does not know the critical moment in her history (12:56-59). Legalistic traditionalists like
the Pharisees had misled Jerusalem into thinking that there was peace
when there was no peace (cf. Jeremiah 6:14), and they are out to destroy Jesus, the city's only hope (Luke 19:47). For Jesus is the manifestation of God's visitation. Zechariah had spoken of this visitation
(1:78) and the people had glorified God for it at the resurrection of
the young man at Nain (7:16). God had kept his appointment with the
city, but downtown Jerusalem did not show up at the banquet (see 14:
15-24).

Cleansing of the Temple

LUKE 19:45-46
(Mark 11:15-18; Matthew 21:12-13)

At the age of twelve Jesus had claimed the temple as his proper province. As King of Israel his objective was not political control, but reclamation of Israel for God. Mark lays stress on outreach to the Gentiles (Mark 11:17). Luke omits this motif and emphasizes the default of Israel's religious leadership, whose ancestors were severely castigated in Isaiah 9. There is to be no trader in the house of the Lord in the day anticipated by the prophet Zechariah (14:21). The temple is for prayer, for expression of dependence on God. No amount of sacrifices can substitute for surrender of the self (see Isaiah 1:10-17). False religionists had made of the temple a place to trade in livestock and pigeons, and on the side devoured widows' houses (see 20:47). A non-Christian, Gaius Cestius, condemned the practice of grasping an image of Caesar after committing outrages on the reputations of fellow citizens. (Tacitus *Annals* 3,36) But these religionists, like robbers who return to their hideout to divide their ill-gotten gains, use the temple as a place of refuge, a kind of bomb-proof shelter from the divine wrath (see Jeremiah 7:1-11). No mistake was ever so fatal.

Jesus Teaches in the Temple

LUKE 19:47-48
(Mark 11:18)

47. Isaiah complained about prophets who taught lies and led the people astray (9:15-16; cf. 29:13). In Luke's gospel only Jesus appears as teacher. Now in the temple he does what Israel's leaders failed to do and gives proper instruction to the people. Liturgy is meaningful only when accompanied by an understanding of God's purposes and objectives for those who worship him. The chief priests, scribes, and leaders (principle men) of the people sense the rebuke and seek to kill Jesus. They were so accustomed to their own orthodoxy and strict patterns and established procedures that Jesus' powerful originality had a profoundly jarring effect on them. There was no longer room for both them and Jesus, and their choice was predictable - Jesus had to go. But Israel as a whole has not renounced its right to the blessings promised to the fathers, and many hung upon his words. In the course of the apostolic mission Jesus will continue as the authoritative instructor of God's people.

MISUNDERSTANDING

LUKE 20:1-21:4

The Scribes

LUKE 20:1-26

A QUESTION ABOUT AUTHORITY

LUKE 20:1-8
(Mark 11:27-33; Matthew 21:23-27)

1-2. Luke appears to allow for a longer period than does Mark for the events recorded during the last days. Jesus, according to 19:47, was teaching daily in the temple. On one of these days the recital recorded in 20:1-19 takes place. Jesus is questioned by members of the Jewish high court, the Sanhedrin, concerning his authority. They want to know his credentials, for he lacks official recognition as a rabbi. In Mark the question arises relative to Jesus' protest against trade in the temple precincts; in Luke the question is aimed at Jesus' activity as a teacher. Luke alters Mark's phrase 'as he was walking in the temple' (Mark 11:27) to as he was teaching the people in the temple and preaching the gospel. Mark refers only to his 'teaching' (11:18). Luke adds 'Telling the good news,' a favorite verb in his gospel, with emphasis on 'the people.'

3-4. Such instruction, if earlier samples are any indication, would be contrary to official guidelines and policy. Jesus counters with a question concerning John's baptism. This is not an attempt to dodge the issue, but simply a refusal to play into the hands of the opposition. Unless the leadership faces up to the basic problem raised by John, they could not possibly understand Jesus' own conviction that he was sent by God to bring to fulfillment what had been begun by John. The question deals with a vital theological consideration. Was John motivated by God? If so, how can they conclude that the message of Jesus conflicts with John's call to repentance?

5-6. The hierarchy betrays its own hypocrisy. Their fear of the people takes precedence over fear of God, and they plead the fifth amendment. Determined to charge Jesus with heresy, they are not interested in discussing the real issues, and *they* prefer to ask the questions. Luther experienced a similar refusal when he attempted to engage his ecclesiastical superiors in debate. Anything Jesus might say would be misunderstood, and if his questioners cannot grasp what the people had long ago concluded (cf. 7:26) nothing would be gained by continuing the discussion. Luke signals this point by a slight alteration of Mark's phrasing (Mark 12:1). Mark has the following parable addressed in the main to the inquisitors. Luke says that it was addressed to the people (vs. 9), but of course its bite was meant for the establishment (see vs. 19).

PARABLE OF THE VINEYARD   LUKE 20:9-19
                                            (Mark 12:1-12; Matthew 21:33-46)

9. This parable, like the one in 19:12-27, contains allegorical elements, but Luke does not appear to have had in mind precise historical correspondence for each of the three slaves. They are rather representative of a long succession of prophets. The picture of Israel as a vineyard is derived from Isaiah 5:1-7. Luke, as at 19:46, omits part of Mark's Old Testament quotation. Not the quality of the vineyard, but hostility toward the messengers is Luke's concern. His addition of the phrase for a long while is perhaps a way of indicating the interval between God's calling of Israel and the present time of

fulfillment of the promises made to the fathers. It may also be a
stylistic device to account for the various times in which the messengers were sent.

10-12. The three slaves are all treated with violence, but they
all escape with their lives (in Mark the third slave is killed). Luke,
in keeping with his artistic sensitivity, reserves the climax for the
third messenger and also omits Mark's reference to the murder of 'others'
who were sent.

13. Fine literary tact is apparent in his further description of
the owner's deliberation before sending out the last messenger. The
actual dispatch is not mentioned, and the pathos is more profound than
in Mark's phrasing, especially in the addition of the words translated it may be. The words my beloved son may echo the divine address
at the baptism (3:22).

14-16. Both Luke and Matthew reverse Mark's sequence in their
recitals of the fate of the son. He is first cast out and then killed
(cf. Hebrews 13:12). The Lord answers his own question concerning
the fate of the tenants and the vineyard. In Luke's account this can
only refer to two things: the destruction of Jerusalem and the shift
of the Good News to the Gentiles. At this point Luke inserts the
words: When they heard this, they said, 'God forbid!' They refers
again to the people (vs. 9).

17. The addition of the dialogue in vs. 16 helps bridge two
patches of text in Mark (12:9-10). As they stand in Mark it is unclear
how the quotation of Psalm 118:22, which speaks of an exalted stone,
ties in with the conclusion of the parable. In Luke, the response of
the people permits a clearer explanation. Luke then cites Mark's quotation, but in abbreviated form, and in place of the omitted portion
introduces a pithy statement that echoes the note of judgment in vs. 16.
The quotation from Psalm 118:22 appears also in Acts 4:11 and in 1
Peter 2:7 as a messianic endorsement for Jesus. The figure is taken
from procedures on construction projects. A stone with a flaw would
be rejected by the foreman. Jerusalem's theological experts disquali-
fied Jesus from Israel's highest office, that of Messiah. But the
church knows that he was exalted (cf. Luke 24:26). Psalm 118:17 declares: 'I shall not die, but I shall live and recount the deeds of
the Lord.' And the same Psalm (vs. 26) contains the acclamation used
in Luke 19:38. Luke's earlier correction of misunderstanding concerning
the Kingdom (19:11) is here ratified. Jesus is the Coming One, the
King, but first he must be rejected. After this comes the exaltation.

18. To reinforce this truth, Luke adds the words in vs. 18, which
may be derived from some Greek text of Daniel 2:44 or Isaiah 8:14-15,
or even an unknown document. A rabbi once said: 'Should the stone fall
on the crock, woe to the crock. Should the crock fall on the stone,
woe to the crock. In either case, woe to the crock!' (Strack-Billerbeck I, 877). Jesus is the point of decision. Response to him determines one's destiny.

LUKE 20:19-24

19. Since Jesus had entered into scribal territory with this
use of Scripture, the Scribes are mentioned first. With the help
of the chief priests (that is, the ruling board of the Sanhedrin, see
on 3:2) they would have arrested him on the spot, but their fear of
the people was stronger than their outraged theological sensitivities
(cf. 19:48). Theophilus would not fail to grasp the issues. Jesus
was 'framed' by the religious establishment.

A QUESTION ABOUT TAXES   LUKE 20:20-26
                                          (Mark 12:13-17; Matthew 22:15-22)

20. Foiled in their attempt to get rid of the troublemaker in
Israel, the hierarchy takes a fresh tack. Unwittingly they implement
Jesus' own prediction that he would be handed over to the Gentiles
(see 18:32). The governor, that is, the prefect (Pontius Pilate) will
be taken into the dirty business. A slip of the tongue on Jesus' part
will turn the trick. But the chief priests and scribes cannot endure
another debacle by tackling Jesus personally. Their experiences depicted in vss. 1-19 were already more than they could absorb. And
Luke, who is keenly aware of the seamy side of political-ecclesiastical
life, exposes a common tactic. These enemies of the future engage
others, who could not be suspected of vested interest, to investigate
Jesus. They would pretend to be sincere (literally, righteous), that
is serious inquirers. Jesus has been teaching the people; let him
now teach these pupils who feign interest in God's way. "Way" is a
favorite term in Luke's vocabulary. It refers not only to a set of
truths, but to behavior in harmony with religious affirmation.

21. We know that you . . . show no partiality. Every man has
his price, the spies say, but not you! You let the chips fall where
they may and tell it how it is. With such flattery they invite him
to his doom and themselves to Belshazzar's feast. Their question about
payment of taxes to the emperor had a short fuse. Yes or no! It is
the cheap trick often played by those who have no interest in probing
the real issues, but only seek to retain waning power while ostensibly
aiming to find the facts. 'Damned if you do and damned if you don't.'
Should Jesus say 'Yes,' then his magnetic hold on the people would be
broken. Taxes, in any event, are unpopular, but for a Jew to pay
taxes to Caesar -- this was the supreme indignity. Should he say 'No,'
that would be the end of the matter, for Pilate would see to it quickly.
Should he say neither 'yes' nor 'no,' he can be accused of *evading*
the issue.

23. Jesus knows the deck is marked, but there is a kind of
challenge in the game. 'Show me a denarius' (a silver coin) he
commands. The request is at the same time an exposure of their hypocrisy. They act profoundly concerned about God's loss of prestige
through the domination of their nation by a foreign power, whose chief
of state had his image incused on coins. Pious Jews abhorred graven
images (cf. Deuteronomy 7:5). 24. But these hypocrites, affecting to
come concerned about theological principle, produce a coin with Caesar's

image on it. A good spy would have said 'We don't carry them.'
Theologians who speak of love with a snarl indeed make a sorry, confused
sight.

25. Since they have Caesar's coins in their possession, they should
give them back (render) to Caesar. If they have scruples about graven
images, let them toss the scruples away by returning the coins. This,
of course, they would not do, for many of their kind were'lovers of
silver' (cf. 16:14; 18:25; 20:47). Jesus' wit and profound sense of
humor are here at their best, matched only by the profound moral sensitivity expressed in the clinching phrase, to God the things that are
God's.

Actually Jesus did not answer the question whether it was lawful
to pay tribute to Caesar. Stupid questions, not to speak of motivation,
do not deserve recognized answering routes (see Proverbs 26:4). However,
his reply suggests that if Caesar's coins are used for normal business
transaction and accepted for payment, as indeed they would be, for example in trading done at the temple, then their use in payment of
taxes would not be incompatible with allegiance to God. The chief
priests, however, will hand Jesus over to Caesar's representative
(23:1) and the scribes will continue to take advantage of widows under
a snug blanket of liturgy (20:47). All this in conflict with the reminder: to God the things that are God's. The disciples will do better.
Peter and John replied to the same authorities who sent these men:
'Whether it is right in the sight of God to listen to you rather than
to God, you must judge; for we cannot but speak of what we have seen
and heard.' (Acts 4:19-20) Caesar will also learn his limit (see the
Book of Revelation). Luke, who is at pains especially in Acts, to
show the quality of Roman justice, clearly understood the principle.
God is not so insecure as to see in Caesar a threat to his own claims
(see also Romans 13:1-7; 1 Peter 2:13-17). In any case, Jesus is not
a political revolutionary. Luke knows that the identification of Jesus
as a King had raised eyebrows in Rome. This story should clear the air.
'Down with the establishment' was not his theme song. There is nothing
wrong with 'establishment' as such. Establishment is necessary especially
to protect the weak. The error lies with those who use power to serve
their own interests and attempt to eliminate competition from the direction of truth. Not Jesus, but the chief priests and rulers are in fact
guilty of connivance with insurrection, for they will demand the release
of one 'who had been thrown into prison for insurrection and murder'
(23:25).

26. The spies had failed to drive a wedge between Jesus and the
people. They had received more teaching than they bargained for. Like
an earlier audience in the temple (2:48) they were astounded by his answer. Like the lawyers and Pharisees on a certain sabbath (14:6), they
have no reply. Jesus, the wise man, confounds the foolish (cf. Wisdom
8:12; Sirach 20:1-8).

The Sadducees   LUKE 20:27-44

A KNOTTY PROBLEM   LUKE 20:27-40
(Mark 12:18-27; Matthew 22:23-33)

27. The Sadducees are the next victims of their own skulduggery.
They are mentioned only here in Luke's gospel. Their name is derived,
with some probability, from the Zadok who was priest under David (1 Kings
2:35). In the book of Ezekiel only the 'sons of Zadok' are recognized
as legitimate priests (Ezekiel 40:46; cf. Sirach 51:12). The Sadducees
emerge as a party during the Maccabean period (2nd century B.C.). Their
chief interest was the preservation of priestly prerogatives, which
included interpretation of the law. Against the Pharisees who attempted
to update Moses through transmission of an oral law adapted to circumstances, the Sadducees appealed to the first five books of Moses. Thus
any interpretation imposed by tradition could be challenged by appeal
to the primary source. It is improbable, however, that the Sadducees
limited their canon to the Pentateuch, as was alleged by such Fathers
as Hippolytus and Epiphanius. They merely limited legal sources to the
first five books of the Bible. In a sense they were the 'fundamentalist-
conservatives' of their time and the Pharisees 'liberals.' Their god
was *status quo*. They viewed with alarm what they criticized as 'new-
fangled' doctrines of the Pharisees: the resurrection, future rewards
and punishments, and the existence of angels and spirits (see Acts 23:8;
cf. Enoch 15:6-9). The dialogue in vss. 27-39 revolves mainly about
the first of these doctrines -- the resurrection.

28-33. According to Deuteronomy 25:5-10, if a brother dies childless, a surviving brother is to take the widow, but not necessarily
marry her, and beget children for his brother. The first born of such
a union is to bear the name of the deceased. A brother who refused to
do this would fall into disgrace. Ruth 3-4 presupposes this custom. In
the case propounded by the Sadducees, seven brothers in succession
lived intimately with one woman, but not one child was born. With
their question in vs. 33: In the resurrection, therefore, whose wife
will the woman be? the Sadducees hope not only to gain a trick on the
Pharisees but at the same time deflate Jesus' image as a teacher. The
problem is indeed most cleverly put. If there is to be a resurrection,
then the seven brothers must also rise. But then, to whom does the
woman belong? Thus, despite their own denials of the resurrection, they
assume it for the sake of argument and put Jesus on the spot.

34-35. Luke omits the rebuke administered by Jesus in Mark's
account (Mark 12:24), perhaps on the ground that the Old Testament does
not in fact say anything about social relations after the resurrection.
The basic error in their thinking, suggests Jesus, is a confusion between conditions pertaining on earth and those that will pertain in the
age to come. In this age people marry and are given in marriage. Such
is not the case in the period after the resurrection. Moreover, the
Sadducees imply in their trick question that *all* people are expected to
rise. Jesus limits the participants in the resurrection to those who

are accounted worthy (cf.14:14). Thus is demonstrated a basic relationship between God's final judgment and man's responsibility to God's
expectations as defined by Moses. The Sadducees through their denial
of the resurrection invalidate such a serious view of moral responsibility.

36. As for the problem of raising up descendants for a brother,
it is ridiculous to cite Deuteronomy. Moses was concerned about sur-
mounting the reality of death by ensuring the survival of a family
name. The fundamental purpose of marriage, according to Moses, is to
establish a posterity. But, says Jesus, there is no need of this when
people cannot die any more. Not the fatherhood of a brother, but the
Fatherhood of God is the crucial factor, and those who are sons of the
resurrection (a Semitic expression meaning 'share in the resurrection')
are sons of God. Sadducees thought that the doctrine of the resurrection and specific laws of Moses were incompatible. Jesus's masterful
reply hammered out on their own playing field shows that this is not
at all a necessary conclusion.

Included in his argument is a further blow to Sadducean doctrine,
for Jesus subtly takes issue with their denial of the existence of
angels. But Luke does not permit the argument to be weakened here by
Mark's phrase that resurrected people 'are like angels in heaven' (12:
25). In place of the noun 'angel' Luke has an adjective 'angel-like'
(rendered equal to angels), used only here in the New Testament. In
contrast to Mark and Matthew, Luke includes the words 'and are sons of
God' par excellence. Its presence, therefore, in this text suggests
awareness of a point made in another source from which Luke may be
drawing. In the Old Testament "sons of God" is a term applied to
beings ordinarily understood as angels (Genesis 6:2; Job 1:6; 38:7;
Psalms 29:1; 89:6). In Luke's recital the expression is a double entente, suggesting heavenly beings, or angels, as well as children of God
(cf. 6:35, 'sons of the Highest'). Thus with his use of the adjective
'angel-like' Luke avoids the suggestion that those who are resurrected
will be angels, but at the same time focuses attention on the expression
"sons of God" as the category in which angels are to be understood. If
resurrected people qualify as "sons of God," then there is no reason
to deny the existence of the heavenly beings called "sons of God," or
angels. Again, it is not Jesus or the community that has chosen the
weapons of controversy, but when forced to the battle the representatives of the New Age are no amateurs in combat. We have here, then,
a sample of the high-powered discussion that enlivened also many a debate within and outside the church.

37. Jesus could have rested his case, but he moves deeper into
their own territory -- the Pentateuch. Moses speaks of the Lord as
the God of Abraham and the God of Isaac and the God of Jacob (Exodus 3:6).
Thus Moses showed, or suggested, that the dead are to be raised.

38. If God stands in a relation to these patriarchs who were long
dead when Exodus was written, then they must in some sense be alive,
for God is not a God of the dead, but of the living. (cf. Isaiah 26:19;

Daniel 12:2; Ezekiel 37). This last inference is supported by a further Lukan addition, for all live to him, perhaps related in some way to 4 Maccabees 16:25: 'knowing well that men dying for God live unto God, as live Abraham, and Isaac, and Jacob, and all the patriarchs' (cf. 4 Maccabees 7:19).

39. The Sadducees heard more than they bargained for, and the scribes are delighted at their discomfiture. Some years later a man named Paul would break up a meeting of the two parties by introducing the same topic defended here by Jesus (Acts 23:6-10). Teacher, you have spoken well, said the professionals. 40. Indeed, the 'amateur' from Nazareth had not done at all badly, for they no longer dared to ask him any question, a phrase taken over from Mark 12:34 (see Wisdom 8:12 on the wise man who confounds princes).

ABOUT DAVID'S SON - COUNTER PROBLEM   LUKE 20:41-44
                                        (Mark 12:35-37a; Matthew 22:41-46)

41. Once having taken the offensive, Jesus moves in further artillery. Since Luke had recorded a modified version of Mark 12: 28-31 at 10:25-28, he omits Mark 12:28-34, except for a portion of the last verse, and presents Jesus' query concerning Davidic sonship. Luke leaves the precise audience undetermined, but in order to include the scribes he deletes the Markan reference to the scribes (Mark 12:35, 'How can the scribes say') and writes in a more general vein, How can they say . . . ? "They" in this sense is colloquial. The question is not meant to deny the Davidic ancestry of Jesus. Luke is not in the habit of contradicting himself on themes to which he gives repeated expression (cf. 1:27, 32,69; 2:4,11; 6:3; 18:38-39; Acts 2:25-36; see also Romans 1:3). The point of the passage turns on the word how. Is the Messiah a purely national-political figure or does he transcend David in a way not anticipated by the popular interpretation?

42. Psalm 110 is introduced as evidence. The fact that David's authorship of the Psalm has been questioned does not invalidate the argumentation. Jesus is Messiah in his own right, but any counter-arguments from his contemporaries based on the Old Testament are legitimately met by sources generally accepted by them. To assume, however, that Jesus anticipated the results of modern scholarship and accommodated himself to the popular view of the authorship of the psalm is improbable. Twentieth century concerns are not to be projected into the biblical text in such a way as to distort the primary intention of the writer. In place of Mark's phrase, 'inspired by the Holy Spirit' (12:36), Luke refers to the general location of the passage, the Book of Psalms (see Acts 1:20; cf. Luke 3:4; Acts 7:42). Luke may have thought that the more specific reference would assist his readers to locate the passage more readily, but his twin-work suggests no consistent practice on this score. It is also quite possible, since the Sadducees are also presumed to be included in the audience, that Luke wished to avoid a phrase that might put the validity of Jesus' argument into question. More probably, however, Luke's theology of the Holy Spirit dictated the

change. Only Jesus and the disciples (and these only after Pentecost)
are described as having something done to them or acting 'in the Spirit'
(cf. Luke 2:27; 4:1, of Jesus; Acts 1:5; 11:16; 19:21, of disciples).
God or the Holy Spirit speaks 'through the mouth' of prophets or of
David (Luke 1:70; Acts 1:16; 3:18,21) but they are never described as
writing or speaking 'in the Spirit,' or as being 'full of the Spirit,'
a common phrase applied to a number of persons in Luke's works. For
Luke the New Age ushered in by the arrival of Jesus and endorsed by
Pentecost is the time of special endowment of the Spirit. Therefore,
the Holy Spirit can speak through the mouth of David and the prophets,
but only Jesus and those associated with him in the history of salvation are 'in the Spirit' or 'full of the Spirit.'

In Jewish thought prior to Luke's writing Psalm 110 was acknowledged
to be Messianic (cf. Acts 2:34; 1 Corinthians 15:25; Hebrews 1:13; on
the theme, cf. Psalm 89:3-4; Isaiah 9:7; 11:1-2; Psalm of Solomon 17).
Later anti-Christian polemic may have prompted rabbinic circles to refer the Psalm to Abraham (on the entire subject, see Strack-Billerbeck
IV, 452-65). In its original historical setting, the Psalm expresses
prophetic concern of an Israelite for his king (my Lord), who is
addressed by God, the Lord.

43-44. The promise of victory, once Israel lost its national prestige, naturally led to expression of the messianic interpretation of
Psalm 110. But this messianic interpretation lay along strict nationalistic lines. Luke, who emphasizes the outreach of the gospel to the
Gentiles, uses this citation from the Psalm to stress the superiority
of Jesus over any direct human descendant from David. The enemies
are not the Gentiles (as in Luke 1:71), but all who oppose God's elect-
ed Messiah. These would include the 'citizens' mentioned in 19:14,
whose downfall is described in 19:27; cf. 19:41-44). Zechariah never
dreamed that the 'enemies' (Luke 1:71) might have their headquarters in
Jerusalem. Israel does not know how the Messiah is David's son, for
they have not pondered the fact that he is described as David's Lord.
Hence they discredit Jesus, whom they measure in terms of criteria
narrowly established by their own traditional thinking. Gabriel in
his announcement to Mary had declared that Jesus would receive 'the
throne of his father David' (1:33). But he also identified Jesus as
the 'Son of the Most High' (1:32) and as 'the Son of God' (1:35). The
passion account will reveal the larger perspective from which the Davidic
sonship is to be understood (cf. 23:46). The Sadducees, who deny a
resurrection, will find it even more difficult to believe that Jesus
is truly the Messiah (see on 16:31). Thus their narrow theological
position and manner of interpreting the Scriptures invalidates even
their own messianic hope. That Luke associates the question of Davidic
sonship and resurrection is clear from Acts 2:24-36.

A Study in Contrasts   LUKE 20:45-21:4

BEWARE OF THE SCRIBES   LUKE 20:45-47
                                           (Mark 12:37b-40; Matthew 23:1,6)

This final sample of Jesus' public teaching climaxes the development of thought initiated by the recital of the entry into Jerusalem. The lines of kingship have been clearly defined. All that remains is to recite the death of the King and then present him as the resurrected Lord. But the question of Messianic credentials requires one last appraisal of Jesus' relationship to the destruction of Jerusalem and the events of the end-time. There will be no city left for a son of David to rule. How then is Jesus David's son? And what is the disciples' role in the new Kingdom? The answer to such questions is the burden of 20:45-21:36.

45. Luke's doctrine of the hazards of wealth prompts him to retain Mark's recital of Jesus' indictment of the scribes and the story of the generous donation by the widow (Mark 12:38-44). Closely related to crass messianism is ostentatious display and materialism. They are an invitation to the disaster about to be described in the apocalyptic discourse. Despite all the premonitions Jesus has of his death, he does not play it safe. In the hearing of all the people he makes his indictment of the scribes. It will be the seal on his death warrant. The words, however, are an address to the disciples. Association with Jesus as Lord should not encourage them to jockey for position (cf. 9;46). But their memories would be short (see 22:24).

46. The picture of the scribes is not overdrawn. In similar vein Epictetus described philosophers of his time who demand a 'thousand benches' for their audience and put on 'a fancy cloak, or dainty mantle, and mount the pulpit.' (*Discourses* III, 23,35) After delivering his sermon the orator says, 'Today I had a much larger audience.' His friend replies, 'Yes, indeed, there were great numbers.' Replies the orator, 'And they are clever at getting the point.' To which the friend answers, 'Beauty, sir, can move a stone!' (*Discourses* III, 23, 19) Only within recent memory did a Pope disclaim some of the pomp and circumstance that obscured the gospel, and it has not been long since bishops discouraged the use of the title, 'Your grace!' Catering to mediocrity, and diplomatic speech that lacks prophetic clarity - this is the way to ecclesiastical success, declaims Erasmus in *The Praise of Folly* (32-33), and all of it under a facade of liturgical piety that bores God with long prayers.

47. A prophetic tone is further apparent in the statement that they devour widows' houses, taken in pledge for debts that cannot be paid. For these and similar injustices, all committed in the name of a Law in which the scribes were experts, the prophets once called down fussilades of divine wrath (cf. Isaiah 1:23-24; 10:2-3; 22:3-5; Ezekiel 22: 29-31; Zechariah 7:10-14; Malachi 3:5; cf. Deuteronomy 10:18; 24:17; 27:19; Psalm 68:5). Those who, like the scribes, are in positions of

leadership will <u>receive the greater condemnation</u>, on the principle
that to whom much is given of him will much be required (cf. 8:18).
The apocalyptic discourse in chapter 21 will relate how finely God's
mill can grind.

A POOR WIDOW   LUKE 21:1-4
                                                   (Mark 12:41-44)

   1-2. The story of the poor widow is introduced to demonstrate the
contrast between ostentatious religion and true devotion. However, the
RSV obscures an important point in the text. In vs. 2 Luke describes
the woman as 'needy' (in a departure of wording from Mark 12:42), not
merely <u>poor</u>. In vs. 3 RSV correctly renders <u>poor</u>, for this account
rounds out what Luke has to say about the priority of the Good News.
It is sent to the 'poor' (see 7:22; cf. 6:20). The Kingdom belongs to
a woman like this, and the scribes will learn it, but too late. Of
faith that transcends material security Jesus has frequently spoken.
This widow, not the ruler spoken of in 18:22, parts with her last resources and commits herself totally to her God. Luke has two other sayings
introduced by <u>truly</u> (9:27; 12:44). The third is reserved for this
woman. Further commentary would blur the matchless artistry of this
introduction to the apocalyptic discourse.

NEWS ABOUT THE END-TIME   LUKE 21:5-36
                          (Mark 13:1-36; Matthew 24:1-22, 29-35)

   Luke has given no indication that Jesus left the temple at any
time between the observation made in 20:1 and the recital beginning
at 21:5. The second chapter of Luke's gospel displayed Jesus speaking
with wisdom in the temple (2:46-47), and there his last days before
the arrest are to be spent. Therefore Luke omits Mark's note that
Jesus went out of the temple (13:1) and alters Mark's wording about
the listeners' view of that splendid edifice. What the disciples had
seen outside the temple is now referred to in their discussion within
the temple. Since the instruction is public (see 20:45; cf. 21:37-38)
and not, as in Mark, directed in private to a narrow circle (Mark 13:3),
Luke omits the names of specific disciples mentioned by Mark.

   The discourse falls into five main sections:

   a. Verses <u>6</u>, <u>8-11</u>. Warning about false messiahs and
       prediction of great disasters.
   b. Verses <u>12-19</u>. Persecution of the disciples, and
       their witness.
   c. Verses <u>20-24</u>. Judgment on Jerusalem.
   d. Verses <u>25-27</u>. Cosmic disturbances and the coming of
       the Son of man.
   e. Verses <u>28-36</u>. Warning about preparedness.

In keeping with his doctrine that the credentials of Jesus are not determined by observation of signs (cf. 17:20-21), Luke makes a number of significant alterations relative to the Markan account. This assessment is valid even if it could be demonstrated that Luke relied on other sources, or even wrote without dependence on Mark. Chiefly Luke is interested in eliminating too intimate an association of end-time signs with the destruction of Jerusalem. Also he aims to clarify the role of the mission to the Gentiles in the context of apocalyptic hope.

Introductory Dialogue

LUKE 21:6-7
(Mark 13:2-4; Matthew 24:2-3)

In response to Jesus' prediction of the destruction of Jerusalem (see also 13:1-8; 19:27; 41-44), the disciples ask when will this be? They do not merely mean, 'Tell us the time,' but as their next question reveals, 'What extraordinary demonstration (sign) will take place about the time this is to happen?' Such an event, if it must occur, could mean only one thing -- the Messiah would arrive! (This interpretation is clearly indicated by the subsequent information concerning false messiahs.) Luke shows that Jesus rejects such a sign (note the singular), and in the rest of the discourse uses the plural form (vss. 11,25).

False Messiahs and Great Disasters

LUKE 21:8-11
(Mark 13:5-8; see also vss. 21-23;
Matthew 24:4-8; see also vss. 23-25)

Jesus avoids a direct answer to the disciples' question and issues a broad warning about false messiahs and political disturbances (cf. Revelation 2:20; 12:9; 13:14; 18:23; 19:20; 20:8). Thus vss. 8-9 form a general introduction to the more specific description that follows in vss. 10-11. Four major differences relative to Mark are apparent. a. Addition of the phrase The time is at hand! (vs. 8) as part of the false expectation. b. The insertion of first (vs. 9). c. The alteration of 'not yet' (Mark 13:7) to "not be at once" (Luke 21:9). d. The omission of 'this is but the beginning of the sufferings' (Mark 13: 8). With these changes Luke succeeds in lengthening the interval between what the disciples might consider a sign and the actual arrival of the Parousia. It is best, says Jesus, not to draw hasty conclusions.

8. The many who come in his name (vs. 8) are not people who claim to be Jesus making his return, but false claimants to the messianic office. They come making claims that belong properly only to Jesus, for he alone is entitled to be called Messiah. Some of them will say, I am he! This expression is applied to God in the Old Testament: Exodus 3:14; Isaiah 43:10-11; 48:12; 52:6. It is applied frequently to Jesus in the Fourth Gospel: 4:26; 8:24, 28,58; 13:19; 18:5,6,8. In Luke 22:70 the phrase appears in a crucial context dealing with the question of Jesus' identity. Mark uses the phrase three times (6:50; 13:6; 14: 62). The first of these is in a story omitted by Luke, who prefers the

apocalyptic restraint of the account of the Transfiguration to misunderstandings Mark 6:45-51 might innocently encourage at the time Luke was
writing. The phrase clearly connotes claims that transcend normal
human experience and is therefore appropriate in an apocalyptic context.
Other false messiahs will say, The time is at hand! This phrase is not
equivalent to 'The Messiah is here!' It means that some will under the
guise of messianic authority assert that the wind-up of history, as
described in popular apocalyptic, is about to take place. In other
words, the identity of the Messiah is to be dependent on spectacular
cosmic events. Luke inserts the saying into Markan material in order
to emphasize the falseness of such a view, for throughout his gospel
he has demonstrated that Jesus' credentials are independent of the
end-time fireworks.

9. The word and at the beginning of vs. 9 is too strong. Luke's
use of the conjunction here is more like the colloquial 'so.' Prediction of wars and international unrest was standard in Old Testament apocalyptic (Isaiah 19:2; Jeremiah 4:20; Joel 3:9-14), and some of the
language in Luke 21:10 reflects 2 Chronicles 15:6. Such things come
first, but it is erroneous to conclude that the end of the end-time
follows immediately.

Verses 10-11 do not form a separate paragraph, as suggested by RSV.
They complete the thought of vs. 9 and form a pivot for transition
to the second portion of the discourse. The disasters are described
in most dire tones for maximum effect. One would think that great
earthquakes and great signs from heaven would be sufficient indication
that the end was imminent. In the Old Testament, war, famine, and pes-
tilence are frequently linked as divine judgments (1 Kings 8:37; Jeremiah 14:12; 21:7; Ezekiel 14:21). Earthquakes are mentioned in connection with the great Day of the Lord (Isaiah 13:13-16, echoed at Luke
19:44; Haggai 2:6; Zechariah 14:4; Revelation 6:12). There was thus
good reason for the popular imagination to seize on such events, especially in connection with the judgment on Jerusalem, as a sign that
the end was in the offing. Luke therefore heightens appreciably the
Markan description in order to negate the false conclusion that the
end-time follows a discernible time-table. The Kingdom, it will be
asserted in vs. 31, is near, but nevertheless indeterminate.

Persecution of the Disciples   LUKE 21:12-19
                                       (Mark 13:9,11-13; Matthew 24:9;
                                                    10:17-21; 24:13)

12. At the end of Mark 13:8 the cosmic disturbances are viewed as
the 'beginning of the sufferings.' This phrase may have been taken by
Mark's readers as a reference to the 'birth-pangs of the Messiah' (cf.
Revelation 12; Deuteronomy 2:25; Jeremiah 6:24-26; Micah 4:9). In order
to avoid any ill-conceived conclusions Luke eliminates the phrase and
instead says, before all this, and then introduces the persecutions the
disciples must undergo. The phrase "before all this" also replaces the
word 'first' in Mark 13:10, the thought of which is transferred to Luke

21:24, thereby giving greater coherence to the Markan sequence. The persecutions mentioned in vs. 12 echo those of 12:11, and the Book of Acts is the continuing commentary (see also 2 Corinthians 6:5; 11:24-29).

13. As Philippians 1:12-14 testifies of the Apostle Paul, the disciples will find in their persecutions an opportunity 'to bear witness' (testimony). (In Mark 13:9 the thought is that their testimony will spell judgment on the opposition; cf. Micah 1:2).

14-15. At Luke 12:11-12 the Lord had promised the disciples that the Holy Spirit would give them the proper words in a crisis. The thought echoes Exodus 4:15 and anticipates the experience of Stephen (Acts 6:10). See also Acts 3:12-26 and 4:8-13 on the eloquent boldness of Peter. He whose life had begun under the power of the Spirit (1:35) will continue his ministry through Spirit-endowed disciples, and the hostility he encountered will be theirs. 16. Since much of this hostility would come from their own relatives, Jesus had issued the stern requirement in 14:26-27 (cf. 18:19-20; Ezekiel 38:21-22).

17. They would be hated by all. This does not mean that everyone would hate them (see Acts 2:47), but that they could expect hostility from any direction (cf. Acts 28:22). 18. Yet, in spite of all this, they receive assurance that not a hair of their head would perish (cf. Acts 27:34). These words echo the thought of 12:7 and are a promise of ultimate security.

19. Their bodies they may and will lose, but not their real selves (cf. Revelation 20:11-15, and see on Luke 12:5), rendered here by RSV as lives (cf. 9:24; 12:4-5; 14:26; 17:33). In their endurance (cf. 8:15; 1 Peter 2:20) they will gain them. With this reassertion of a favorite theme Luke replaces Mark's phrase: 'But he who endures to the end will be saved.' The end does not come within the lifetime of all the disciples.

Judgment on Jerusalem   LUKE 21:20-24

(Mark 13:14-17,19,10; Matthew 24:15-19,21)

This section is almost completely rewritten by Luke, principally to eliminate the suggestion that the end of the end-time is to be associated with the destruction of Jerusalem.

20-22. Mark refers to a horrible desecration of the temple, 'desolating sacrilege' (13:14), which is to precede its actual destruction. His phrase is borrowed from Daniel 9:27, where reference is made to Antiochus Epiphanes, who erected a heathen altar in the Jewish temple (1 Maccabees 1:54-59). Antiochus became a symbol of Antichrist (see 2 Thessalonians 2:1-12), a figure closely associated with events of the end-time. Since the destruction of Jerusalem had already taken place by the time Luke was writing his gospel, Luke records Jesus' prediction in more explicit terms, specifying that Jerusalem is to be surrounded by armies (cf. 19:43; Revelation 20:9). Thereby he makes unnecessary Mark's call for special wisdom: 'let the reader understand' (Mark 13: 14). Also, by eliminating Mark's apocalyptic note he is able to re- assure his own readers that the credentials of Jesus were not invali- dated by the non-appearance of the end of the end-time in association with the destruction of the city. If anything, the destruction of the city endorses his credentials, for none but his enemies would deny that Jesus was, like Elijah, a man of God. But the fire that rained down from heaven fell not on Samaria, but on Jerusalem (see 9:34; cf. 2 Kings 1:12).

In Mark the mission to the Gentiles takes place between the resurrection and the destruction of Jerusalem. In Luke the apostolic mission continues beyond the destruction of the city. Thus Luke opens the way for fresh interpretation and application of Jesus' apocalyptic discourse. Not the end would be near, but the desolation has come near. More pointedly than in Mark's account, this desolation is viewed as judgment. The phrasing echoes Deuteronomy 32:35 and Ezekiel 9:1, and Luke adds the further note (Luke 21:22) that all is in fulfillment of the Scriptures (cf. Hosea 9:7; Jeremiah 5:29). Details in Mark 13:15-16 are omitted at this point, since they were used in Luke 17:31.

23. The woe pronounced on pregnant mothers repeats the thought of 19:44. Luke is at pains to emphasize that Jesus' earlier prediction in his lament over the city found horrible literal fulfillment in days that are but recent memory. The phrase wrath upon this people (vs. 23) is a 'tag' from 2 Kings 3:27 and replaces Mark's direction to pray that the flight may not 'happen in winter' (Mark 13:18). The detail is unnecessary since the destruction, from Luke's perspective, is a thing of the past. At the same time he emphasizes more strongly than does Mark that the "wrath" applies to the particular nation of Israel, not the entire Church. Those who rested their case in the Law find the curses of the Law pronounced to the letter. Deuteronomy 28:64 warns that Israel will be taken captive because of its transgression and scattered among all the nations (cf. Daniel 9:13). Luke 21:24 is the commentary on that oracle of the Lord.

24. The phrase trodden down by the Gentiles (cf. Revelation 11:2) is borrowed from Zechariah 12:3 (LXX). Since the Markan reference to the sparing of the elect (13:20; cf. Isaiah 54:7) might suggest a hasten- ing of the end, Luke deletes it and at this point introduces Mark's earlier reference to the Gentiles (13:10), but with modified phrase, until the times of the Gentiles are fulfilled. Between the fate of Jerusalem and the actual arrival of the end lies the accumulation of responsibility for the Gentiles. In Daniel the various nations are assigned a 'time' by God (Daniel 11; cf. 1QS 4:18) and then undergo judgment. Luke's readers, however, would also be aware of the vast missionary out-reach to the Gentiles during the interval (cf. Romans 11:25).

Finally, it should be noted that in his rewriting of Mark 13:19-20 Luke modifies Mark's use of Daniel 12:1. Mark 13:19 reads: 'In those

days there will be such tribulation as has not been from the beginning
of the creation which God created until now, and never will be.' Since
Jerusalem's destruction is not the climax of history, Luke preserves
his stronger rhetoric for the end described in the succeeding paragraph
(vss. 25-26). Moreover, in Daniel a resurrection of the righteous from
their graves is discussed in association with the passage reproduced in
Mark 13:19. Again Mark's presentation might give rise to misunderstanding and encourage the type of computation expressed in Daniel 12:
11-13. Luke therefore discusses the anticipated deliverance in a
subsequent consolatory passage (vss. 28-33), thus removing the end
of the end-time from any connection with any one particular historical
event.

Cosmic Disturbances and the
    Coming of the Son of Man   LUKE 21:25-2
                                     (Mark 13:24-26; Matthew 24:29-30

25-26. Luke omits Mark 13:21-23, since false Messiahs have already
come under discussion (see on 21:8). He also omits Mark's specific
reference: 'But in those days, after that tribulation' (13:24), again
to dissociate the signs of the end from the destruction of Jerusalem.
As noted earlier, the distress of mankind is sketched in darker tones
than in the earlier description of the fate of Jerusalem (vs. 19). In
place of Mark's citation (13:24) of Isaiah 13:10, Luke paraphrases
the thought concerning cosmic disturbance (cf. Isaiah 24:18-20; 34:4)
and picks up Isaiah's description of the terror that overcomes mankind
(Isaiah 13:7). The roaring of the sea and the waves appears to reproduce the thought of Isaiah 17:12 (see also Wisdom 5:22).

This revision prompts the transfer of Mark's mention of stars to
the beginning of the verse: "And there will be signs in sun and moon
and stars." The Markan description of falling stars is omitted, for
Satan is the one who falls from heaven (Luke 10:18), and this was already taking place in the course of Jesus' earlier ministry.

27. Then, and only then, will they see the Son of man coming. This
is the climax of the expectation expressed in Daniel 7:13. Luke always
uses cloud in the singular (9:34,35; 12:54; Acts 1:9), and his alteration of Mark's plural form (Mark 13:26) is of a piece with his other
references (9:34,35; Acts 1:9) to the Shekinah, that is, the display
of God's visible presence (cf. Exodus 34:5). Jesus, as the returning
Son of man, does not simply come on clouds as a visitor from outer
space. He arrives as one endowed with full divine credentials. What
chosen disciples experienced at the Transfiguration (9:34-35) all mankind will observe at the end of the end-time. Jesus entered into his
glory through his resurrection (24:26), thus realizing his enthronement
expressed before the high priest (22:69), and with power and great glory
he makes his climactic appearance. Thus Luke affirms the present realit
of Jesus' Kingship apart from the promised consummation, but rejects
any attempt to infer the time of the consummation through speculation
based on signs. The disciples had asked, 'What will be the sign when

this is about to take place?' (21:7). Jesus gives no one sign, only
signs (vs. 25); and these of such a nature that no prediction can
be based on them, for they are common to the experience of mankind
throughout his history. All this does not mean that Luke denies an
early arrival of the consummation. His primary interest is to discourage deduction about apocalyptic conclusions from particular historical
events. Once this has been impressed he is prepared to submit the
Lord's reassuring consolation in vss. 28-34.

Warning about Preparedness
LUKE 21:28-33
(Mark 13:28-31; Matthew 24:32-35)

This section forms a unit and vs. 28 should be paragraphed with
vss. 29-34. What the Lord announced to his own generation can now be
pronounced to the Church of Luke's time, for the signs have been dissociated from the destruction of Jerusalem. In the midst of international and cosmic disturbance the disciple need not lose heart. The
Lord *will* return, and soon!

28. Your redemption is drawing near. The word for 'draw near'
has been frequently used by Luke of the Kingdom and of Jesus' approach
to the city of Jerusalem (10:9-11; 18:35; 19:29,37,41; cf. 24:15).
The term is appropriate here in contrast to the claims of the false
messiahs recorded in vs. 8. The Greek term underlying the word redemption appears only here in Luke's twin-work. A shorter form of this
noun is used at 1:68; 2:38. In 2:38 it is applied to Jerusalem. Perhaps Luke preferred the longer form, expressive of full and final deliverance, in order to preserve the distinction he has made between the
fortunes of Jerusalem and the Church. Redemption, as used here, does
not connote pardon for sin, but rescue from tribulation and realization
of the benefits that accompany God's defeat of all hostile forces (Luke
1:68-72; Romans 8:23; cf. Ephesians 4:30). Thus it is the climax of
redemption understood as forgiveness of sins (cf. 1:77; 3:3; 24:47).
According to Lukan doctrine God reaches out to gather the lost that they
may share his company (see chapter 15). This final deliverance is the
realization of the promise expressed in 13:29-30.

29. Luke adds to "the fig tree" (Mark 13:28) all the trees, in
order to avoid a limited association with Israel, whose judgment in
prophetic writing is on occasion associated with the fig tree (cf. Jeremiah 8:13; Micah 7:1). 30. Just as the fresh foliage in spring signals the coming of summer, so the disasters and cosmic disturbances
signal the nearness of the end. You see for yourselves is a Lukan
addition. The disciple will need no one to inform him, as the false
claimants attempt to do (vs. 8). 31. These things, like the phrase
in 1:20, does not refer to *all* details in 21:25-27. In Mark 13:29
the subject of the verb in the concluding phrase is unexpressed, and
RSV attempts to supply it: '*he* is near.' Luke 21:31 supplies the subject: the Kingdom of God is near. Far from being a sign of the absence
of God's reign in connection with Jesus, the disasters observed are
indications that the final phase of the Kingdom is about to make its

appearance. The redemption is spelled out as the Kingdom of God in
order to reinforce beyond the realm of contradiction that the Son
of man does not return as a nationalistic deliverer.

32. Now Luke is able to bring into focus the most difficult
saying of all: Truly, I say to you, this generation will not pass away
till all has taken place. Luke knows well enough that Jesus' contemporaries had passed away at the time his gospel was published. Was
Jesus, then, mistaken? No, says Luke, his solemn statement was misunderstood. What Jesus said was that *this kind* of generation with
whom he had to deal would not pass out of existence till everything
took place. What was it that prompted Jesus to make such an indictment
of "this generation"? It sought after signs (cf. 11:29-32). Very
well, they shall have all the signs, but not the kind they seek, and
in the meantime the Gospel will go to the Gentiles (cf. Acts 28:25-28).
It has been suggested that Luke identifies "this generation" with mankind in general, but this is improbable, for mankind obviously could
not disappear before the end. However, that Israel should reject the
witness of its own Messiah and his accredited apostolic messengers,
this is a unique phenomenon requiring explanation, for it seems to
call into question the credentials of Jesus. Luke therefore exploits
the very problem as a proof of Jesus' ultimate success. In place of
the Markan phrase 'all these things' (Mark 13:30), Luke has simply
all. This broadens the disciples' outlook to things beyond the signs
already specified and is the climax of his doctrine that the Kingdom
comes 'without observation' (17:20). The Kingdom is among them in
its first phase, and it will suddenly be among them in its final phase.

Verse 33 forms a conclusion to the apocalyptic portion of the discourse
and introduces the final admonition. The words of Jesus are said to
have permanence in order to reinforce the point that the disciples'
ultimate success in standing before the Son of man (vs. 36) is determined by obedience to the word of Jesus (cf. 8:14-15; 13:22-30), and
blessed are those who 'hear the word of God and do it' (8:21).

The Markan statement on the limitations of the knowledge of the
Son (13:32) is completely eliminated, for everything has been delivered
by the Father to the Son (Luke 10:22). Acts 1:7 is not in contradiction with this conclusion.

Concluding Admonition to Preparedness   LUKE 21:34-36

The admonition in this section is similar to the instruction given
in 17:26-37 (cf. 12:41-48).

34. The disciples are to be prepared at all times, for there is
no single sign of the return of their Lord. That day, the day of the
return of the Son of man, comes suddenly (cf. 17:24) and like a snare,
that is like a trap springing shut on its victim (Isaiah 24:17-18).

35. The judgment attending Jesus' return is not only for Jerusalem, but for all men. Once more Luke reiterates his doctrine that the Parousia is to be dissociated from the destruction of Jerusalem. The phrase all who dwell is also used in Revelation 14:6.

36. Verse 8 introduced false messiahs who say, 'The time is at hand.' Jesus, the true Messiah, says: Watch at all times. Watchfulness means to be on the alert against falling into temptation (cf. 8:13; 22:40,46). To escape all these things means to survive the temptations, especially by making bold confession (12:9; 21:12-19). Then the Son of man will confess them before the angels of God (12:8) or, as the discourse concludes: They will stand before the Son of man.

TEACHING IN THE TEMPLE   LUKE 21:37-38

Against the charge that Jesus had spoken traitorously against the temple (Acts 6:14; cf. Mark 14:58), Luke sets the pattern of Jesus' continuing instruction in the temple. Only obedience to the word of Jesus could save that edifice from the fate that awaits it. Israel's leadership must accept the major responsibility, for all the people were eager to hear him, as was evidenced by their early arrival. Jesus the reservoir of wisdom spells true security for those who love instruction (see Proverbs 1). Note: At this point a few manuscripts include the story of the adulterous woman, traditionally associated with the Fourth Gospel (John 7:53-8:11; see in RSV the marginal note at John 7:52).

THE PLOT OF JUDAS AND DISCOURSE
IN THE UPPER ROOM   LUKE 22:1-38
(Mark 14:1-2, 10-25; 10:42-45; 14:27-31;
Matthew 26:1-5; 14-29; 20:24-28; 26:31-35)

The most obvious departure from Mark in this section is the omission
of Mark 14:3-9, the anointing in the house of Simon the leper. Luke
recorded a version of this account in 7:36-50. Its inclusion at this
point would have interrupted the close connection he wishes to establish
between the resolution of the leadership (22:1-2) and the Satanic dimension in which that resolution is to be viewed (22:3). Moreover, the
story includes instruction about the poor, a topic to which Luke has
previously devoted considerable space.

Satanic Plot   LUKE 22:1-6
(Mark 14:1-2, 10-11; Matthew 26:1-5, 14-16)

<u>1-2.</u> Luke does not make a strict distinction between the <u>Passover</u>
and <u>the feast of Unleavened Bread</u>. The former marked the sacrificial
rite, performed on the afternoon of the 14th day of the month Nisan (see
Exodus 12). The period following this sacrifice and the eating of the
Passover (which took place in the evening hours of the beginning of the
15th of Nisan) was designated the Feast of Unleavened Bread (Leviticus
23:5-6). This feast continued for seven days (Exodus 23:15; Leviticus
23:6). In popular parlance the entire period, including the sacrificial
rite, was <u>called the Passover</u> (cf. vs. 7). Ironically the religious
leadership seeks to kill Jesus about the time preparations were made
for the killing of the sacrificial lamb. Their plot was complicated by
the popularity Jesus enjoyed among the populace. Quiet efficiency, they
hoped, would keep dirty linen from hanging out to public view. Ironicall
they all made the front page.

<u>3.</u> In their quandary <u>Satan</u> introduces himself as an ally. He had
departed from Jesus 'until an opportune time' (4:13). The word for 'time
in 4:13 is the same word used in 8:13 and 21:36. Jesus had warned his
disciples to watch in time of temptation. Now Satan seizes his opportunity for the final showdown with Jesus and uses Judas, one of the twelve,
as his instrument to discredit Jesus once and for all. Thus the events
that follow are seen in a cosmic dimension as a contest between demonic
forces and God (cf. John 13:2; 1 Corinthians 2:8). A related example of

Satan's participation in the death of a righteous man is recorded in
an apocryphal work, *The Ascension of Isaiah*, chapter 5.

<u>4</u>. For the first time Luke mentions the <u>captains,</u> or temple guard,
assigned to the Sanhedrin. It is an ominous note. Judas means business, and his quandary (<u>how</u> he might deliver Jesus into their hands)
is the answer to their own (vs. 2).

<u>5</u>. Jesus had also repeatedly warned his disciples about the pro-
per use of wealth. Mammon now changes hands in the slimiest transaction
history shall ever record. More culpable than Judas, however, were the
religious leaders. Instead of seeking to save this wretched man <u>they</u>
<u>were glad</u> to hear his proposal.

<u>6</u>. And he who had been warned to watch 'at all times' (21:36)
now sought <u>opportunity</u> (literally, an appropriate time) to <u>betray</u> him.
The only stipulation was: in the absence of the multitude (cf. vs. 2).
This did not leave much choice. Night would see the doing of the deed
(22:53).

Preparation for the Passover   LUKE 22:7-13
(Mark 14:12-16; Matthew 26:17-19)

<u>7</u>. The fourteenth day of Nisan has now arrived. The lamb was to be
<u>sacrificed</u> in the afternoon. Satan has marked his victim, but Jesus is
in full control and heads with full knowledge toward that death which will
set up a Kingdom far outweighing all the kingdoms once offered him by
Satan (Luke 4:5-6).

<u>8</u>. As one dispatching royal emissaries, he <u>sent</u> Peter and John. Two
only are mentioned, for this is a solemn apostolic mission (cf. 10:1).
Since 9:51 the face of Jesus had been fixed on Jerusalem, and the messengers
had been sent 'ahead of him' (9:52). Now the final turn of that journey is
to be taken and messengers are for the last time sent on ahead. The selection of <u>Peter</u> and <u>John</u> in the narrative is perhaps prompted by their presence together in 8:51 and 9:28 (cf. Acts 3:1-2; 8:14). Once they were witnesses of his extraordinary resurrection power (Luke 8:49-56) and then of
his Transfiguration (9:28-36). Moses and Elijah had spoken of the 'exodus'
(9:31) Jesus was to accomplish in Jerusalem. Now Peter and John are to make
the initial preparations for that climactic event. At the same time Luke
points out that Jesus knows better than to entrust Judas with the final plans.

<u>9</u>. In keeping with his stress on the mastery of Jesus, Luke alters
Mark's account which shows the disciples taking the initiative (14:12).
Their question (<u>Where will you have us prepare it?</u>) comes *after* Jesus'
command. The word for <u>prepare</u> (alternate rendering, "make ready," vs.
12) appears four times in this account (vss. 8,9,12,13) and it is difficult to escape the conclusion that Luke sees in the events that follow
the fulfillment of the announcement in 3:4-6, introduced by the cry:
'Prepare the way of the Lord' (see also 1:17, 76; 2:31; 9:52).

10-13. This recital has some of the formal character of 19:29-33, and the stress on Jesus' detailed knowledge of apparently trivial circumstances heightens the picture of one in full command of the situation. A woman with a pitcher would have been the normal expectation, hence the word Behold (verse 10). ·Once there had been no room in the guest room (vs. 11; see on 2:7). Now Jesus himself secures one for a farewell banquet. The concluding sentence (vs. 13) parallels 19:32.

The Last Supper   LUKE 22:14-22
                                    (Mark 14:17-25; Matthew 26:20-29)

14. At 20:19 the opposition was unable to take advantage of the "hour" to arrest Jesus. ·Now the hour has arrived (cf. 22:53), but in Jesus' own chosen time. This interpretation is signalled by Luke's alteration of Mark 14:17. Jesus did not sit at table, as RSV renders, but reclined. This is a banquet scene (cf. 11:37), and it is a feature of the Passover feast that Israel displays its deliverance from bondage by assuming the posture of freemen. Slaves wait on those who recline (cf. 17:7-8; John 13:4). In place of 'The Twelve' (Mark 14:17), Luke says that the apostles were with him (cf. 17:5), anticipating the special instruction to be given to the apostles as leaders in the new community. Luke revises the Markan order of events by presenting first the ritual of the Passover meal and then the announcement of the traitor. This rearrangement makes it possible for Luke to illuminate the meaning of the Last Supper in the light of the reaction of the disciples and Jesus' instruction on the themes of Kingdom, service and faith. (For other banquet scenes, see 5:27-39; 7:36-50; 11:37-54; 14:1-24).

15. Repeatedly Jesus had warned his disciples about his approaching fate (cf. 9:22; 9:44; 12:50; 13:32-33; 17:25; 18:32-33). Now in this solemn hour he tells them for the second last time (for the final reminder, see 22:37). Since he will celebrate no more Passovers with them, he desires earnestly to eat this one with them. Let them note it well -- death will make this one his last! Verse 16 explains his words. The Kingdom of God is about to reach a climactic phase. The Passover is the commemoration of Israel's Exodus. From the perspective of Luke 9:31, Jesus has come to Jerusalem to 'accomplish' (literally, fulfill) his exodus. Thus the Passover comes to full meaning in the events about to take place on a hill outside Jerusalem.

17. In place of Mark's order, bread followed by wine, Luke presents first the words spoken about the wine (cup for the contents), in order to reinforce the thought expressed in vs. 16. Jesus enters into the glory of his Kingdom only after his suffering (cf. vs. 69 and 24:26). Like a Nazirite (see Numbers 6:1-4) he separates himself from the ordinary joys of mankind to devote himself totally to his task, the suffering that is before him. That will be his cup! (cf. vs. 42). Therefore he gives the disciples the cup out of which he would ordinarily have drunk and tells them to share its contents among themselves. Since each had his own cup, this procedure should have made a profound impression.

<u>18</u>. He accompanies this action with a solemn oath: <u>From now on I</u>
<u>shall not drink of the fruit of the vine until the kingdom of God comes</u>.
Thus this celebration is a foretaste of the messianic Banquet (see on
Luke 13:22-29) and anticipates Acts 1:4; 10:41.

<u>19</u>. Then he took a loaf of bread and, as he had done at the taking
of the cup, gave <u>thanks</u>. The Greek word for giving of thanks is the
source of the term 'Eucharist' (cf. Acts 27:35). His words accompanying
the distribution are the climax of his exposition of the meaning of the
celebration: <u>This is my body</u>. With these words he explains that the
Passover comes to full meaning in his person. As the loaf was broken
into pieces before their eyes, so he will shortly be destroyed. (Most
versions include a marginal notation on the omission of vss. 19b-20.)

<u>21</u>. Jesus had said that he would be 'handed over' (the word
rendered <u>betrayed</u>) into the hands of men (9:44; cf. 18:32; 22:4,6). The
deed has already been set in motion. And the hand of the traitor shares
the Master's wine and bread (cf. Psalm 41:9). In brief, the suffering
so often predicted is as close as the traitor himself.

<u>22</u>. But there is more to Jesus' word concerning the traitor. It
is part of his final appeal and instruction to the apostolic circle.
Jesus goes to his death <u>as it has been determined</u>. The word "determined"
appears only here in the gospel, but several times in Acts (2:23; 10:42;
17:31; cf. Romans 1:4) to define God's over-arching providence and purpose in connection with Jesus Christ. Jesus goes to his death because
he must accept the full consequences of being identified with God's purposes (cf. Luke 13:32-33; 22:42). Judas is not compelled to betray Jesus. Jesus had warned his disciples (and Judas was certainly not excluded) about hypocrisy (12:1). Now through this solemn pronouncement
of woe (cf. 6:24) Jesus makes one last appeal to this man who violated
not only the most sacred code of hospitality but rent the very fabric of
his own soul. The betrayal has not yet taken place. Judas could still
refuse to carry out his end of the bargain.

Final Instruction and Admonition   LUKE 22:23-38
                                          (Mark 10:41-45; 14:27-31;
                                          Matthew 20:24-28; 26:31-35)

After the pronouncement on the traitor there follow two disputes
among the disciples. Their contrasting nature suggests the appalling
lack of understanding Jesus encounters in his chosen circle. From an
artistic viewpoint, the first question on the identity of the traitor
permits an easy transition to the content of the second dispute, which
provides Luke with the opportunity to present Jesus' own interpretation
of his action and a correction of any misunderstanding respecting the
political attitudes of the community. This intention of the evangelist
is supported by the fact that he omitted Mark 10:41-45 at 18:34 but
here presents a revised version of that account.

LUKE 22:25-28

25. The contrast between the kings of the Gentiles and the prescription of service given to the disciples should set at rest forever, Luke
suggests, the ghost of subversiveness. The charge brought in 23:2 was
patently false. Benefactors renders a Greek word that served as a title
for rulers in Syria and Egypt -- *Euergetes* (see, for example, the prologue
to Sirach). In many cases the title would conceal tyranny under extravagant expenditure.

26. Disciples are not to follow that pattern. The long history of
tyrannical oppression and search for office in the church is a testimony to Luke's profound grasp of the relation between gorged egos of
pompous men and the crucifixion of him who renounced all titles and kingdoms. In keeping with his earlier reminder that even the most faithful
slave is still an 'unworthy' slave (17:10), Jesus explains to his disciples that they are not to use their positions as avenues for self-
aggrandizement (cf. 1 Peter 5:3). If seniority is to be determined by
age, then let the older be as the youngest. Since the younger men would
recognize their obligation of obedience to the older members of the community (cf. 1 Peter 5:5), this is a striking invitation to humility.
The leader is to be open to the possibilities of service and not be
anxious about his own prestige as an authority-figure.

27. Jesus himself is in their midst as one who serves (cf. John
13). The word "serves" is related in its Greek form to the term
'diaconate.' In Mark (10:44) the road to greatness lies through service. In Luke's account Jesus says that he who is the greatest (vs.
26) should imitate Jesus through dedicated service. The reason for this
change appears to have its origin in the disputes about leadership in
the early Christian community. Peter was acknowledged as preeminent in
the Jewish community, second only to James. His credentials, however,
were apparently viewed with some suspicion in the hellenistic community,
and the problem of his denial had to be faced. Luke's record of Jesus'
words suggests that the Church is to make service to the fellowship the
primary criterion of greatness. Jesus' willingness to accept the Father'
assignment, at great cost to himself, sets the pattern for their ministry. Since all their service pales into insignificance before his own,
he alone is entitled to the term *Euergetes*, or Benefactor (cf. Acts 10:38
'he went about doing good').

The entire discourse is in harmony with the Lord's instruction in
Matthew 23:8-10, where the disciples are admonished not to delight in
the title 'Rabbi' or 'Father' or 'Master.' Jesus would have considered
ridiculous the fuss made in books of etiquette on proper address of
either ecclesiastical or civic dignitaries. When all are servants under
one Father and Lord there is no place for status-seeking. Servanthood
is the only legitimate status in the Kingdom.

28. Much of Jesus' ministry was spent in encounter with those who
sought signs of his credentials (cf. 11:16). At 20:2 he was asked by
what authority (the word is related to the term 'those in authority,'
22:25) he acted. His entire life had been a renunciation of Satan's
earlier attempt to direct him along the path of normal status-seeking

222

(4:6). Thus Luke does not violate his pattern of presenting Jesus' public ministry as free from Satanic temptation (cf. 4:13 and 22:3), but nevertheless recognizes his conflict with the hostile establishment (cf. Acts 20:19). His disciples have continued with him during that entire period and they will share in the Kingdom about to be established.

29. The Messianic Banquet described in 13:22-30 and anticipated in 22:16, 18 is to become reality. The Father has appointed, or 'covenanted,' a Kingdom for Jesus. These words are in harmony with Luke's earlier correction of popular hopes for the restoration of David's dynasty (1:32-33) and reflect the language of 2 Samuel 5:3, which states that the elders of Israel covenanted with David. Luke alters the thought of the Old Testament passage and emphasizes that *God*, not Israel, makes the royal covenant with Jesus. The latter, in turn, appoints (a verb that corresponds to the noun 'covenant') the disciples as chiefs of state at the royal table. In brief, Israel's royal hope can be fulfilled only in Jesus, and on God's terms. Once more the reversals expressed in the Magnificat come to the fore (1:52-53). Judas reclined at a table (22:21) that was only a foretaste of the Messianic Banquet, and he did not remain with Jesus in his trials. The greatness he sought would be forever denied him, for another would be chosen in his place to assume responsibility for one of the thrones (cf. Acts 1:16-26).

30. The language of Psalm 122:4-5, with its stress on the house of David, appears to underlie the promise in vs. 30. The twelve tribes of Israel are the community of believers gathered after Pentecost. The Church is in continuity with Israel (cf. 2:32; 3:6; Acts 3:25), linked by the Spirit under one Lord, the Messiah of Israel (cf. Acts 10). Judging is the official function of those who sit on the thrones. In this respect they are like the Judges of ancient Israel, who were sent from time to time to rescue God's people from their enemies. Thus the apostolic task is one of compassionate concern for people. At the same time the text sounds a wisdom motif: the suffering righteous are ultimately triumphant (cf. Wisdom 3:8).

31. The thought is expanded in the personal address to Simon, significantly minus 'Peter,' a term meaning 'Rock.' The repetition of his name expresses the solemnity of the address (cf. 10:41). Satan had in fact demanded all of the disciples (the pronoun you is plural) for sifting, and he has been successful in one case (22:3). Mark records a stern warning to Peter in connection with his confession at Caesarea Philippi: 'Get behind me, Satan!' (Mark 8:33). Luke had omitted the saying in his parallel recital (9:18-20), perhaps in order to give prominence at this point to Simon's misunderstanding of Jesus' role as the Messiah.

32. To learn the route of service is not easy, and Simon evidently revels in the privileges he has enjoyed as participant in special revelations (cf. 9:28). In any event, he did become a recognized leader in the early Christian community and his credentials must be reaffirmed, for he had denied his Lord. How was he different from Judas? Answer: His

faith did not give out completely, for Jesus had prayed for him. He who stands, stands by the grace of the Master (cf. 1 Corinthians 10:12). Although Jesus had to pray especially for Peter, all the disciples must realize they are no match for Satan without reliance on him who renounced all the kingdoms they find so difficult to renounce.

But one might still ask, did Jesus fail to pray for Judas? This is a Western approach to problems that are of no interest to Luke. The evangelist is primarily concerned with the point that Simon's restoration to the community depends on Jesus, and his prayer in behalf of Simon is a sign or symbol of the larger service he renders in behalf of all through his willing acceptance of the fate he endured at Calvary. Thus the warning addressed to all the disciples, and then especially to Simon, is a reminder to the total community. And Simon is to understand that judging the tribes means to <u>strengthen</u> the <u>brethren</u>. In this way Simon will be rehabilitated for service to the Church (cf. John 21:15-19).

<u>33-34</u>. Jesus' word of assurance is all the more vital since he had said that anyone who denied him before men would be denied before the angels of God (12:9). Shortly <u>Peter</u> (now the 'Rock-man,' spoken ironically) would be guilty of that crime. Cockcrow would be the third watch preceding the final early morning hours. In such brief space of time his fervent protestations would reach their melting point (vs. 34; cf. vss. 54-62). Undoubtedly there were others like Simon who failed in a crisis, but strengthened by their brethren they would find fresh hope. Luke is among those who do not apply the Lord's words to a given case with inexorable and judgmental logic. He had recorded memorable words on the subject of forgiveness (6:36-38). Even Judas could with tears of repentance have halted his headlong career toward destruction. Peter did shed them (22:62) and later became a fearless witness to his Master (cf. Acts 4:8-12,19; 5:18; 12:3-11). He did make good on his promise to follow his Lord to <u>prison and to death</u>. But there *was* that cockcrow! And he too made the front page.

<u>35</u>. Luke is ordinarily careful about observing correspondence between various parts of his writing. All the more remarkable, therefore, is the wording in vs. 35: <u>When I sent you out with no purse or bag or sandals . . .</u>, a clear echo of 10:4, which is part of the account of the sending of the Seventy (two). The Twelve, however, were sent out earlier and with different specifications (9:3). The question, <u>Did you lack anything?</u> focuses attention on the disciples' peaceful and law-abiding intentions. They did not go out with purse or bag, for they did not intend to enrich themselves, as bandits would do, at the expense of others. And yet they lacked <u>nothing</u>.

<u>36</u>. <u>But now</u> the situation is different. Jesus and his band are to be classed as outlaws. If that is the case, they must act like outlaws. Let them take purse and bag and sell, if necessary, their mantles in order to purchase swords. The language is, of course, quasi-satirical. Jesus is not really encouraging the disciples to buy swords. But the leadership will presently identify him with brigands and revolution-

aries (cf. 23:2,5), and his own band will be subject to police control (cf. Acts 4:1-3; 9:1-2). The directive may also suggest awareness of demonic powers (cf. Strack-Billerbeck IV, 1, 519).

37. Thus Isaiah 53:12, And he was reckoned with transgressors, finds ironic fulfillment. The transgressors are the disciples. Jesus identifies with their situation (cf. 5:8-11; 27-32) and invites certain death. The two-fold stress on fulfillment echoes 13:32 and 18:31, and the phrase in me is emphatic. By claiming the suffering as his proper goal, Jesus also claims the messianic function.

38. The disciples misunderstand the irony in Jesus' remarks and think that he actually intends them to secure swords. Unaware of the tremendous scope of the hour of truth that is about to dawn they think in terms of a slight scuffle. The Master need not worry, they would handle it; and two swords should be enough! So impressed are they with their own prowess and preparedness for combat that they preface their display of arms with the word Look. Jesus answers, It is enough, that is, two swords should make us look sufficiently like brigands. With such grim humor Jesus further shows his mastery over the dark hours that now confront him, and Theophilus could not miss the point -- this man and his arsenal pose no political threat!

AGONY ON THE MOUNT OF OLIVES
LUKE 22:39-46
(Mark 14:26,32-42; Matthew 26:30,36-46)

In the preceding recital (vss. 14-38) the Lord tried to impress on his disciples the nearness of the struggle in which he was about to engage. Mark presents dialogue between Jesus and the disciples on their way to the Mount of Olives (14:26-31). Luke introduced part of it in connection with his presentation of events in the upper room, and omits the rest (Mark 14:27-28, 31). This makes it possible for him to submit the present section as a unit, in which the engagement of Jesus is probed to its depth.

39. As was his custom echoes 21:37 and suggests to the reader that despite his knowledge of the plot against him Jesus does not hesitate to meet his assigned responsibility. That this is Luke's intention is clear from his slight alteration of Mark 14:26. Instead of the comprehensive pronoun 'they,' Luke shows that Jesus takes the initiative and the disciples followed him.

40. Since Luke avoids the name Gethsemane, perhaps because some of his readers might be puzzled by the additional place-name, he simply states when he came to the place. Earlier Jesus had taught his disciples to include in their prayers the petition: 'lead us not into temptation' (11:4). Luke considers the subject so important that he inserts the directive at this point (cf. Mark 14:32). In the present context the word temptation bears special import, for Jesus has spoken of the nearness of the Kingdom (22:16,18), and fiery trials were anticipated in the end-time (cf. Zechariah 13:9; Malachi 3:1-3; 4:1). The time of

suffering endured by Jesus is a kind of Apocalypse. The disciples, who were called to watch in every time (21:36), must now pray that they do not fall into the hands of Satan. The Son of man comes precisely in an hour like this -- when they least expect it.

41. Having stressed the fact that all the disciples are directed to pray, Luke omits reference to Peter, James and John (Mark 14:33), and in place of the phrase 'going a little farther' (14:35) he indicates that there was at least a stone's throw between Jesus and the disciples. Thus his withdrawal from the disciples at this crucial moment is the second reminder in a very brief space of time that he will not long remain with them (cf. Luke 22:35-38). Ordinarily prayers were offered in a standing position (cf. 18:11,13). The posture of Jesus is therefore an expression of profound humility and an indication of the depth of his inward struggle.

42. Jesus does not go to his death with bravado. He plays no hero's role. Nor is his death to be construed simply as a tragic miscarriage of justice. If he dies, Luke wants his readers to know, it was the Father's purpose. No other credentials are necessary. But without that purpose his death would be as the death of other men. He had renounced an earlier cup (cf. 22:17-18) in order shortly to drink his cup of death (cf. Mark 10:38-39), but its contents are bitter. To the Father, his constant port of call (Luke 2:49; 10:21-22; 22:29) he now turns. If thou art willing, remove this cup from me. The very agony that prompts him to request his Father to explore a different way dramatically puts in sharp relief the spirit of complete obedience expressed in the concluding clause: nevertheless not my will, but thine, be done. He has passed an initial test. Once Satan had suggested that the criterion of Divine Sonship was Divine protection (4:3-13). Jesus renounces the traditional criterion. One can appear to be repudiated even by God, and yet be the instrument of God's purpose.

43. Luke had omitted Mark's earlier reference to ministration of angels at the temptation (Mark 1:13). Now, in this 'apocalyptic' hour, an angel strengthens him for his remaining task (cf. Daniel 10:18-19). The words from heaven accent the fact that God directs him on the present path (cf. 9:31).

44. The crucial responsibility that is his finds expression in the term agony, which is a transliteration for a Greek term suggesting anxiety over the issue of a great contest. The intensity of the struggle is emphasized by the observation that he prayed more earnestly, and that he sweated profusely. The simile like great drops of blood calls attention to the fact that he is shaken to the depths of his being. The entire scene is reminiscent of 2 Maccabees 3:14-36 and describes a martyr dedicated wholly to his Lord.

As the margin in RSV states, vss. 43-44 are omitted in some manuscripts, but the language is Lukan, and the thought is in harmony with other themes in the gospel. Perhaps copyists thought that the description in these verses detracted from the divinity of our Lord. If such

226

is the case, they not only missed Luke's point, but also came close to misunderstanding the Gospel.

45. In a sense Jesus has already died a death. The word rose is therefore most appropriate in the context. He is now ready for the supreme confrontation. But he who had endured the profoundest agony imaginable finds his own companions sleeping. Once before in the presence of extraordinary revelation they had fallen asleep (9:32). It is clear that Jesus will receive no help from that source. Misunderstanding from his closest friends is not the least of his burdens. Yet Luke protects the apostolic circle from other embarrassment. He omits Mark's reference to the rebuke directed at Simon Peter (Mark 14:37), and relates only one period of slumbering, instead of three as in Mark (14:37,40,41-42). Finally, he gives them an excuse. They slept for sorrow. It could not have been more than superficial, for sleep and grief are not bosom companions (cf. Psalm 6:6; Lamentations 1:2). The total result is a scene of remarkable artistic, as well as theological, effect. Jesus is not the product of the Church. The Church is the product of Jesus. Yet Jesus is a model for the Church. As he successfully overcame his temptation, so the community must be watchful if it is to be prepared for the coming of the Son of man (cf. 21:34-36).

THE ARREST
LUKE 22:47-53
(Mark 14:43-49; Matthew 26:47-56)

47. Luke stresses that the arrival of Judas and his cohorts takes place while Jesus issues his warning about temptation (vs. 46). Now in an hour when all seems lost, the disciples will be faced with the choice of deciding for or against Jesus, and Simon will in a short while illustrate the meaning of Jesus' words. Judas had his instructions to betray Jesus without the presence of a crowd (22:6). Now Luke writes, 'Behold, a crowd . . .' The RSV omits the interjection, with some loss of meaning. Judas has his crowd, but it consists of chief priests, temple-guard and elders (vs. 52). To betray him now with a fraternal kiss was the quenching of the last flicker of light in his soul.

48. Every syllable in the reply of Jesus carries its own freight: 'Judas, with a *kiss* are you betraying the Son of man?' Surely not this way, not after all that I have said to you about hypocrisy! Judas had heard his words about the Son of man who was to be betrayed (9:44) and then to return in glory (21:27). Does Judas dare to trifle in this way with his own destiny? The curtain of silence rings down on this what seems to be a last invitation to a wretched soul who demonstrates the truth that the One we ought to love the most is at the mercy of the things we ought to love the least.

49-51. The companions of Jesus now unveil their arsenal. It was wise of Jesus not to count on them. The best one of their swordsmen could do was hack an ear off the high priest's slave. 'Stop! No more of this!' says Jesus, reinforcing his command with a repair of the damage. Thus Luke emphasizes that Jesus is guiltless of political intrigue.

52-53. Should there be any doubt in the matter, it is dispelled
by the succeeding words of Jesus addressed to the leadership. Do they
actually think that he is a robber, or revolutionary brigand whom they
must capture with the help of swords and clubs? He had not hidden
from them: He was within their reach daily in the temple (cf. 21:
37-38). Why did they not take him there? The fact is, they themselves
have been taken into Satan's plot. Jesus had rejected Satan's offer of
'authority' (4:6, the same word rendered power in 22:53). The religious establishment now takes it. This hour is appropriate for demonic
designs (cf. John 13:20; Colossians 1:13; Ephesians 6:12). But any
power they may have is of the Father's permissive providence (cf. John
19:11). They are the real brigands (cf. 19:27), who cloak evil behind
a facade of religion. John the Baptist had spoken of the day that
would 'give light to those who sit in darkness' (1:79). They voted
for the night.

IN THE CUSTODY OF THE HIERARCHY   LUKE 22:54-71
              (Mark 14:53-54, 66-72, 65; 15:1; 14:55-64;
              Matthew 26:57-58, 69-75, 67-68; 27:1-2,59-65)

Luke, in keeping with his frequent presentation of contrasting
scenes modifies the Markan order of events in order to depict the solemn
confession of Jesus against the background of Peter's denial. Also he
apparently considers it more probable that the judicial examination by
the Sanhedrin took place not at night but during the day. On the other
hand, he does not deny that the leaders held an informal meeting, for
vs. 54 clearly states that Jesus was led off to the "high priest's house."
Attempts to charge the evangelists with total distortion of Jewish legal
procedure ignore elementary facts of life. An establishment, when
pressed to protect its own security, manages to circumvent technicalities. The history of the church is itself filled with depressing evidence of that fact. A political scientist commented in reaction to an
ecclesiastical committee's maneuverings to give the ax to an office-
holder who had fallen into disfavor with higher powers: 'In political
circles I know what the ground rules are. Here I can't lay my finger
on the tactics.'

Charges of anti-Semitism that have been made against Luke are palpa-
ble distortions, for Luke is very fond of Jews. Especially Luke is concerned to point out that it was not the Jewish people but their leaders
who brought ruin to Jerusalem. If the evangelists are to be charged
with anti-Semitism, then the prophets of ancient Israel were anti-Semitic,
for the evangelists merely update the pattern of judgment pronounced in
the Old Testament. However, anti-Semitism does display its ugly head
when especially the Christian reader of the gospel thinks that 'the Jews,'
not he, are under the evangelist's scrutiny. Seven million Jews have
known the pain of such evil application of the text.

Denial by Peter
(Mark 14:53-54, 66-72; Matthew 26:57-58, 69-75)

<u>54-57</u>. Peter is still a follower, but now <u>at a distance</u> (cf. 23:
49). Mark has the first remark of the <u>maid</u> addressed directly to Peter.
Luke sketches the downward descent of Peter more dramatically. First
he hears his exposure as an associate of Jesus before the group gathered
around the fire. There the skin-saving disciple makes his first denial,
exactly in the terms predicted by his Lord (vs. 34).

<u>58</u>. The pressure intensifies. This time it is a man from the
group (not the same maid as in Mark 14:69), and he addresses Peter
directly. The maid had said, 'This man also was with him' (vs. 56).
This man says, <u>You also are one of them</u>. Now it is not a matter only
of being associated with Jesus, but of being implicated with a band of
suspected men. His memory going worse by the minute, and having disclaimed any relation with Jesus, he now renounces his own larger fellowship as he heads toward his own self-isolation. Denial of the fellowship is tantamount to denial of Jesus. In time of persecution this
would be the real temptation.

<u>59</u>. Mark presents the third denial as taking place 'after a little
while' (14:70). Luke brings Peter closer to the hour of cockcrow with
the phrase <u>after an interval of about an hour</u>. Again it is a man who
speaks, this time identifying him, as the maid had done, to the assembled
group. This identification of Peter as a <u>Galilean</u> introduces the incriminating suggestion that Peter is a dangerous revolutionary (cf. 13:
1-2).

<u>60</u>. Peter, acting more like a jellyfish than a 'Rock-man,' takes
the customary dodge, 'Man, I don't know what you're talking about.' Luke
mercifully spares him from the terrible oath assigned him by Mark (14:
71). But Peter, who had come to warm himself at the fire (Mark 14:67),
has now passed through the hotter fire of temptation and hears the cockcrow. (In Mark the cock expressly crows twice, see Mark 14:30,72, thus
heightening the callousness of Peter).

<u>61</u>. Somehow Jesus was able from the house to see Peter who was in
the courtyard. Only one look, and Peter remembers the <u>word of the Lord</u>.

<u>62</u>. Jesus had predicted Peter's denial, but he had also predicted
his own suffering and death. With sensitive economy and consummate
literary art Luke suggests that now it is all too clear to this disciple.
<u>And he went out and wept bitterly</u>. His Lord, even in this disastrous
hour, did not forget Peter, and now the sea must dry up to contain his
sorrow. But, as the sequel shows, this was the beginning of Peter's
rehabilitation (cf. vs. 32). And Peter would see a living definition of
loyalty and constancy (see 24:34).

Mockery   LUKE 22:63-65
                                        (Mark 14:65; Matthew 26:67-68)

With his usual fine literary tact Luke presents the scene of mockery, which incorporates ingredients in an earlier prediction made by Jesus (18: 32). From Peter's experience it is clear that Jesus had prophetic powers. The demand for Jesus to prophesy stands therefore in sharp contrast to the previous demonstration and points to Jesus' willing acceptance of the humiliating path assigned him. Prophecy, however, is more than ability to sort out future events. In its primary form prophecy is the ability to discern God's hand at work in the events of history. Jerusalem will know that there was a prophet in her midst. They will not play blindman's buff in A.D. 70!

Trial Before the Sanhedrin   LUKE 22:66-71
                              (Mark 15:1; 14:61-64; Matthew 27:1; 26:63-65)

66-68. The assembly of the elders is the Sanhedrin, the high court of the Jews. To their first question, whether he is the Christ, that is, the Anointed One or Messiah, he declines an answer. They have made up their minds about him, and their conclusions about the function of the Messiah would not square with his own understanding of messiahship. Therefore they would not believe him if he answered in the affirmative, and they would permit no cross-examination of the type expressed in 20:21-44. Instead he speaks to them of the triumph of the Son of man. In this way he is able to affirm that the very road to Messiahship lies along the unorthodox path of rejection and death.

69. Luke does not say that they will 'see' (Mark 14:62) the Son of man, for Jesus takes his seat at the right hand of God from now on, and this is hidden from the eyes of hostile men (Stephen 'sees,' Acts 7: 56). His death is the way to enthronement. And the power is that of God, not of the kingdoms of this world, nor of messiahship construed in nationalistic-political terms. Most carefully Luke refrains from saying the Son of man is coming. That would have been the normal apocalyptic view. Not end-time demonstration, but divine vindication, is Luke's main point. Thus the affirmation is in harmony with Jesus' earlier predictions of suffering in association with the title, Son of man. (9:22,44; 18:31). In 24:26 and 46 there is no possibility of misunderstanding, and suffering is therefore explicitly affirmed of the Christ, the normal title accorded Jesus in the community.

70. The Sanhedrin sees its opportunity and asks, Are you the Son of God, then? The term is also Messianic (cf. Luke 2:7; 3:22), and in Luke's account carries the main weight of Jesus' identity. He is the one obedient to his Father's assignment, and Luke wants the full weight of the judgment to fall at this point. Jesus was crucified, not because he was a political revolutionary or just another Galilean agitator of messianic hopes, but because he carried out God's will. There is no pleading of the fifth amendment possible. Yet the answer must be

guarded, for the interrogators do not share with Jesus the same concept of Sonship. As is usually the case in theological controversy, they were 'talking past each other.' Therefore he answers: You say that I am. The word you is emphatic. They must accept full responsibility for whatever assumptions they put into the question. On the other hand, he will not deny it. I am. Many false Christs would come and say, "I am" (cf. 21:8; 'I am he!'). Only Jesus has the right to that solemn affirmation, and with this self-identification as the Messiah he tacitly affirms that one of the days of the Son of man has arrived! (cf. 17:22).

71. As far as the Court is concerned, the trial is over. Jesus has incriminated himself. But the reader is invited to a different verdict. Jesus could have chosen Peter's road, but he took this path in order to find Peter. Significant is Luke's omission of the introduction of false witnesses who in Mark allege that Jesus would destroy the temple (Mark 14:58). Luke has an answer ready for what is tantamount to a charge of sedition, but preserves it for the Book of Acts, where he enters into the question at some length through Stephen's speech (cf. Acts 6:14 and see especially 7:44-50).

JESUS BEFORE PILATE AND HEROD   LUKE 23:1-25
            (Mark 15:1b-2, 11-15; Matthew 27:2,11, 20-23,26)

In this section Luke is apparently indebted to Mark, but is also dependent on a source that linked Herod and Pilate. Of special interest is his stress on the threefold declaration of innocence (vss. 4, 14, 22). This is in accord with Luke's repeated effort to clear Jesus in the eyes of Roman officials of any charge of revolutionary activity.

Accusation Before Pilate   LUKE 23:1-5
                    (Mark 15:1b-2; Matthew 27:2,11)

1. The whole company is the Sanhedrin (cf. Acts 23:7). In order to introduce first the charges made by the hierarchy, Luke alters 'delivered' (Mark 15:1) to brought.

2. At 6:7 the scribes and Pharisees were looking for grounds of accusation. Now they vocalize with distortions of statements made by Jesus. 20:21-25 revealed the lie in their accusation respecting tribute to Caesar. And, as was implied in 22:67-68, the hierarchy read their own anti-Roman political hopes (cf. 23:19,25) into the term Christ (Messiah). Their addition of the word king, a 'loaded' word, was designed incrimination, amply refuted by the material presented in 19:28-21:38. But this is the way in which truth is twisted through appeals to fear and insecurity.

3-4. The brief dialogue between Pilate and Jesus is in its Lukan form a brilliant literary gambit. Through his omission of Mark's reference to many accusations made by the chief priests (Mark 15:3), Luke also gives sharper prominence to Pilate's direct question and Jesus' equally direct answer. With the secular authorities dialogue was possible! However, the form of the reply, You have said so, shifts to Pilate responsibility for the import of the question (cf. 22:70). Thus Luke lays before his readers a bald affirmation of Jesus' kingship made in the presence of the Roman prefect and in vs. 4 climaxes what could have been a most incriminating admission with Pilate's verdict: 'Not guilty!' The word "no" in the phrase I find no crime in this man is emphatic. A high Roman official had affirmed that recognition of Jesus as a king was not incompatible with loyalty to Caesar! The 'crowds' (multitudes) are mentioned in order to show that the fears of the hierarchy (22:6) were groundless (cf. 22:47). Jesus knew the fickleness of the crowd (cf. 8:4-15; 9:41; 11:24-30; 12:13-15, 54-59). Rabblerousing was not his forte (cf. 9:57-62).

5. The accusations recited in this verse build a bridge to the introduction of Herod into the narrative. Emphasis is placed on the teaching done by Jesus. Luke had well documented the nature of that instruction. Jesus was no threat to Roman security. And Pilate knew that this was dust in the eyes of the jury. The hierarchy was in fact losing its grip on the people (cf. Acts 4:17; 5:28; 17:6; Mark 15:10), and charges of 'confusing the people' reveal not so much concern for people as for vested interests now threatened by exposure to the truth. History records that preservation of religious tyranny through appeal to public order and social stability is not a rare phenomenon. Judea means the land of Palestine. Mention of Galilee is part of the inflammatory propaganda, for Galilee was the hot-bed of revolutionary uprisings. Mark refers to the accusations only in a general way (15:3-4) and does not explain why Pilate was prompted to inquire about Jesus' kingship. Lu not only shifts the accusations but spells out two of them explicitly, thereby offering suitable motivation for Pilate's question. Luke will correct the geographical perspective. Not from Galilee to Jerusalem, but from Jerusalem the proclamation will go forth (24:47; cf. Acts 1:8), for church is in continuity with the center of Jewish religious thought and l

Trial Before Herod   LUKE 23:6-12

6-7. The fact that Pilate asks whether Jesus is a Galilean suggests that the governor has received no previous complaint concerning his prisoner. His question also provides an easy transition to Herod's role in the trial of Jesus. Psalm 2:1-2 is cited in Acts 4:25-26, and Herod and Pilate are equated with the kings and rulers mentioned in the Psalm. Luke anticipates the later apostolic proclamation through his inclusion of Herod at this point and at the same time secures the witnesses required by Jewish law. According to Deuteronomy 19:15, a charge is to be sustained before two witnesses. Simeon and Hannah attested that Jesus is the Messiah (Luke 2:25-38), Moses and Elijah spoke of his exodus (9:30-31). Now two officials of state are to affirm his innocence in the face of false accusation. Paul experienced a parallel type of arraignment before Roman and Jewish officials (Acts 25:13-26:32).

8. Herod is typical of those whose wish to see Jesus but are prompte

in that direction by misunderstanding of his person. Unlike Zacchaeus, who wished to see who Jesus was (19:2) and then repented, Herod sought to see Jesus (9:9) but in the moment of truth repeated the mistake of his nation and demanded a sign (cf. 11:16,29). Within the passion account this reference to a sign is especially noteworthy. Jesus is in his very humiliation himself the sign (cf. 2:34). But some lessons are never learned!

<u>9</u>. Despite repeated prodding, Herod receives no <u>answer</u>. Jesus once again resists the temptation to secure his own safety (cf. 4:3-12). Some of Luke's readers would also note a suggestion of divinity in the silence of Jesus, while others would hear a tolling of judgment (cf. Revelation 8:1). Luke himself may have intended to express a wisdom motif. According to Wisdom 8:12, even the powerful will wait on the wise man in his silence. Sirach 20:1 states that the wise man remains silent in the face of reproof that is uncalled for. The fool, on the other hand, 'multiplies words' (Sirach 20:8). Martial, the Roman Epigrammatist, put it bluntly: 'There is no glory in out-stripping donkeys.'

<u>10</u>. The vehement accusations of the <u>chief priests and scribes</u> lend sharpness to the verdict of innocence tacitly pronounced by Herod. <u>11</u>. But first this royal clown vents his frustration by joining with his soldiers in a round of buffoonery (cf. 18:32), climaxed by a mock en-thronement. Jesus in the hour of this mockery is nevertheless God's own messenger (cf. Acts 10:30, the only other instance in Luke of the phrase <u>gorgeous apparel</u>). Pilate had sent Jesus to Herod (vs. 7); now Herod returns him to Pilate. Thus he excuses himself from jurisdiction over Jesus. Besides, Jesus was popular in Galilee!

<u>12</u>. In any event, Herod and Pilate resolve a standing feud, and some readers would infer that Psalm 2:2 had found contemporary express-ion (cf. Acts 4:25-27). The incident is one of many that display Luke's keen perception of the opportunism that infects much political activity in both secular and religious spheres. Hitler's temporary pact with Stalin is but one modern illustration of the fact that contrived political solu-tions make bedfellows of otherwise incompatible parties when egos are at stake. Rational and scholarly temperament may be seen teamed up with the most erratic invention of scurrilous political tactics, (see, for example, prefaces to German books published during the Nazi terror).

Pilate Strives for Acquittal   LUKE 23:13-16

<u>13</u>. Pilate now summons the <u>chief priests</u>, who had also appeared before Herod, together with the <u>rulers</u> and the <u>people</u>. This last group appears to be identical with the 'crowds' (vs. 4), but the term "people" in Luke-Acts takes in a larger scope, referring ordinarily to Israel as an entity. Acts 4:27 mentions the "peoples of Israel" in association with Herod and Pilate. The "people" are included at this point in the passion narrative in order to emphasize that Israel must assume a large share of responsibility for the death of Jesus Christ, while at the same

time hearing the verdict of innocence pronounced on him. On the other hand, Luke does not mean to imply that all the people were hostile to Jesus. Throughout his narrative he displayed their good-will toward Jesus, and a 'great multitude of the people' laments him on his way to the cross (vs. 27).

14. Also, from Pilate's remarks "You brought me this man as one who was perverting the people," it is clear that not all the individual people within the larger group known as the people of Israel were responsible for handing Jesus over to Pilate. In his choice of the term, Luke is partly stimulated by the demands of the apostolic mission. Can Israel, understood as a totality, be forgiven for rejecting her Messiah? Or has God rejected Israel and turned His eyes only to Gentiles? Luke affirms availability of divine pardon for anyone in Israel who reverses the verdict pronounced before Pilate (Acts 2:21-40, see especially vss. 38-39). Thus theological compassion, not anti-Semitic sentiment, directs the wording of his narrative. Pilate announces before the leaders and the people of Israel that Jesus is clear of all charges made in his presence.

15. He also interprets Herod's return of the prisoner as a verdict of acquittal. In view of Herod's earlier alleged efforts to kill Jesus (13:31), this attitude on the part of the Jewish ruler would impress Luke's public. At this point Pilate attempts another tack. Between the lines the reader is to infer that Pilate is aware of the rising thirst for blood. 'Look!' says Pilate, 'this man has done nothing to deserve the death penalty.' In other words, Jesus may be disturbing the people, but it is not a capital offence.

16. Therefore, he says, I will chastise him and release him. The chastisement to which he refers is equivalent to 'teach him a lesson.' This was a light beating or whipping of the type administered to juvenile gangs, and was accompanied with a severe warning (cf. Acts 16:22-24; 22:24). In short, Jesus was to receive a suspended sentence. Verse 17 is correctly relegated to the margin as a later copyist's attempt to explain the outcry for Barabbas. In keeping with his intention to show that Israel as a totality is responsible for the crucifixion, Luke omits Mark's recital of the proceedings leading up to the request for Barabbas. Thus he achieves a starker contrast between the innocence of Jesus and the suppressed anti-Roman stance of the hostile assembly.

The Sentence   LUKE 23:18-25
(Mark 15:11-15; Matthew 27:20-23,26)

In Mark the crowds make their outcry at the suggestion of the chief priests. Luke includes the chief priests in the phrase they all cried out together. Away with this man echoes Isaiah 53:8. The expression this man is uttered with contempt. The name Barabbas means 'Son (Bar) of the father (Abba)' and is not really a name but a description of relationship between himself and his father. The latter may have enjoyed special status as a leader in his community, with the honorific title

'Abba!' At Matthew 27:16 (see the marginal reading) the original text may have included his real name, *Jesus*. If Luke knew of this tradition, he omits the name, perhaps out of reverence for the Lord.

<u>19</u>. Luke sketches the specific crimes of Barabbas in order to contrast the verdict pronounced by Pilate and the evil choice of the people. Jesus was not anti-Roman. If there was any misled revolutionary sentiment, it lay on the side of his enemies. Luke stresses that the activity of Barabbas took place <u>in the city</u>. Not Galilee (cf. vs. 6) but Jerusalem is the locale of guilt.

<u>20</u>. Once more Luke indicates that Pilate was convinced of Jesus' innocence (cf. Acts 3:13). <u>21</u>. And now the blood-thirst rises with the demand for crucifixion, the extreme penalty for revolutionaries. <u>22</u>. Pilate repeats his earlier verdict and proposal (vs. 15).

<u>23-24</u>. Mass protest reaches a crescendo and not even Luke can spare Pilate from the dreadful ignominy he must share in history's most lamentable travesty of justice. The mantle of greatness had been handed to the prefect of mighty Rome, but he would have been better off never to have tried it on for size. Attempting to go down quietly in history as a clever administrator he ended up embalmed in the Apostle's Creed. Luke softens Mark's indictment of political cowardice by omitting the words, 'wishing to satisfy the crowd' (Mark 15:15), thereby relieving Pilate of express decision respecting the fate of Jesus. Well aware of political realities, Luke emphasizes that citizens must ultimately bear responsibility. It would be difficult to find any indictment of civic pressure expressed with profounder economy of language.

<u>25</u>. Luke recalls the dramatic possibility expressed at vs. 19; but now highlights for the last time the contrast between Jesus and Barabbas, and with a tone of incredulity concludes the trial with these words: <u>but Jesus he delivered up to their will</u>. Barabbas is given to them in answer to their demand. Pilate makes no decision in the case of Jesus, who is simply handed over to them to do with as they wish. This is in contrast to Mark who attributes to Pilate the order for crucifixion (15:15). From Luke's account it might be inferred that the Jews were responsible for carrying out the execution they had demanded. But the impression is a result of Luke's theological interpretation. Pilate would, of course, be in charge of the actual execution.

THE CRUCIFIXION   LUKE 23:26-49

Warning to the Women of Jerusalem   LUKE 23:26-31
(Mark 15:21; Matthew 27:32)

<u>26</u>. At this point in the narrative Luke omits the mockery by the soldiers (Mark 15:16-20), perhaps for one or more of the following reasons. In the first place, having described the mockery in Herod's

court (Luke 23:11), he is able to spare Rome this embarrassment. Secondly, he wants his readers to understand that especially the Jewish leadership was responsible for leading Jesus off to the scene of crucifixion.
This would account for the indefinite subject in the phrase as they led
him away. Thirdly, the mockery revolves around Jesus' royal claims, a
subject to be treated more extensively in vss. 33-43. Mark's identification of Simon as the father of Alexander and Rufus (Mark 15:21) was
apparently helpful to the readers of that gospel, but in Luke's time
the sons may not have been prominent. The scene, however, is important
to Luke, who emphasizes discipleship as willingness to identify with
Jesus (cf. Luke 9:23; 14:27). Thus this Simon is a model for those of
Luke's readers who may be subject to persecution from religious quarters.

Verses 27-31 are peculiar to Luke. Luke's readers would expect some
lamentation over such an illustrious personage as Jesus. But Roman
law forbade wailing at the death of a criminal, especially one convicted
of treason. Luke therefore uses this occasion to incorporate a lament
but with some revision of the conventional pattern of lamentation. In
his eyes the death of Jesus is no tragedy. The tragedy lies on the
side of Israel. Hence he carries out in this recital his theme of
judgment (cf. 13:1-9; 19:42-44) and contrasts the innocent Jesus with
guilty Jerusalem. At the same time he is able to show that all the
inhabitants of Jerusalem shared the verdict.

27. Yet the people, that is, Israel, must hear the divine verdict
on *their* verdict. Women were the principal participants in ancient
funeral rites, and the dirge of these women, accompanied by beating of
the breast, is a lament for one consigned to the dead. Some impetus
for the inclusion of the description may have been provided by the prophet Zechariah:

> And I will pour out on the house of David and the
> inhabitants of Jerusalem a spirit of compassion and
> supplication, so that, when they look on him whom
> they have pierced, they shall mourn for him, as one
> mourns for an only child, and weep bitterly over him,
> as one weeps over a first-born.   (Zechariah 12:10)

But all the tears of Jerusalem could not wash out this stain of infamy.

28-29. Jesus' stern prophetic warning is not a pronouncement of
vengeance for the injustice being perpetrated. Rather, through their
choice of Barabbas, Israel has chosen a road that will lead to certain
ruin and has rejected him who was their real source of security (cf. 19:
42). The words in vs. 29 reproduce the content of 21:23. Verse 30 includes a quotation from Hosea 10:8. In the context preceding Hosea 10:
8 the prophet speaks of Israel's predicament in being without a king
(vs. 3). Luke seems to sense the horrible parallel between that anarchy
and Israel's crucifixion of their own last royal hope (cf. Luke 23:38).
They had cut off their nose to spite their face. And they will cry to
the mountains and hills to cover them. This is an expression of total
disaster; death itself would be more merciful (cf. Revelation 6:16; 9:6).

Verse 31 explains the prophecy in theological terms. <u>Green</u>
trees are difficult to burn. <u>Dry</u> trees burn quickly. In the phrase
<u>if they do this</u>, the word <u>they</u> is best referred to God (cf. 12:20).
The meaning of the sentence is: 'If God permits this to happen to
one who is innocent, what will be the fate of the guilty?' (cf. vs.
41). Thus the entire address by Jesus is a call to repentance. It
is a reminder that the passion history is not designed to evoke sentiment or resentment against those responsible for the death of Jesus.
'Weep not for me, but weep for yourselves . . .' (vs. 28). It was
with deep insight that Luke had portrayed Jesus as weeping over Jerusalem (19:41). Now as the lamented one he expresses his last lament.

Crucifixion and Mockery   LUKE 23:32-38
                          (Mark 15:27,22-24,29,31-32,36,30,26;
                          Matthew 27:38,33-35,39,41-42,48,40,37)

32. Peter had assured Jesus that he was prepared to go to death
with him (22:33). Instead two men who had been sitting in death-row
join Jesus in a common fate. The skin-savers stand off at a safe distance (vs. 49). Luke does not appear conscious of any association with
Isaiah 53:12. His interest in the two criminals will shortly be apparent.

33. In place of the name Golgotha, which even Mark felt in need
of interpretation (15:22), Luke uses a Greek rendering meaning <u>The Skull</u>.
The expression <u>one on the right and one on the left</u> would suggest a
picture of a king with two cabinet members (cf. Mark 10:37). Kingship
is the theme of vss. 33-43, and the crucifixion between two criminals
is the first of three examples of public mockery of the King of the
Jews (vs. 38).

The prayer in vs. 34 is in such harmony with the spirit of Luke's
gospel and his picture of Jesus that it is difficult to question its authenticity. Yet it is even more difficult to account for its omission
in a number of manuscripts. It has indeed been argued that the prayer
was omitted because of a conviction that the destruction of Jerusalem
was God's judgment for the crucifixion, but a similar omission does not
appear at Acts 2:38-39, where forgiveness is proclaimed to Israel. It
is more probable that the prayer uttered by Stephen (Acts 7:60) suggested
a parallel utterance for the passion account. Also, in its present position it interrupts Luke's sketch of the mockery and destroys the
dramatic impact of the word addressed to the repentant outlaw (vs. 43).
In short, loss of the prayer as an authentic Lukan statement does not
diminish his picture of Jesus. Companionship with sinners was Jesus'
method of actualizing forgiveness, and that is the climactic assertion
in vs. 43. If the words were originally included by Luke, they inform
the reader that Jesus did not threaten his executioners, as the condemned
were accustomed to do, but rather accepted his death as a faithful witness
should. Thus in the *Martyrdom of Isaiah* (5:14) the prophet is praised
for neither crying aloud nor weeping when he was sawn apart. By contrast,
the psalmist cries for vengeance (Psalm 69:22-28; see on Luke 23:46).

34b. The mockery described in vs. 35 is here filled out with words drawn from Psalm 22:18. Gambling for the prisoner's garments would be especially humiliating to the helpless sufferer. In Jesus' case the implication would be especially clear: His career as Messiah is at an end.

35. Although Israel is implicated in the crucifixion, Luke preserves the people from direct participation in the mockery. The people were watching (cf. Psalm 22:7), from curiosity, but perhaps with some respect (cf. Luke 23:48). The rulers, that is, the hierarchy, engage in the mockery (cf. Psalm 22:7; Psalm 80:6). A reader to whom the dramas of Aeschylus were familiar would recall the words of Strength addressed to Prometheus, bound fast to a rock:

> Now revel there in insolence!
> Rob from the gods for mortals of a day?
> Then let these earthling darlings ease
>   your pain!
> False is the name the gods have given you:
> INGENIOUS CONTRIVER. Ha!
> These bonds will test your skill.
>   (*Prometheus Bound*, 82-87)

Unwittingly the mockers reproduce aspects of the temptations recorded at Luke 4:1-13, 23. Typical of the misunderstanding Jesus encounters throughout his trial and suffering is the suggestion that he save himself if he is indeed the Christ of God. They are ignorant of the fact that he who cautioned his own disciples about losing their life while attempting to preserve it (9:24) could not violate his own instruction, for he was among them as one who rendered service, the only route to greatness (22:27). Their further description, Chosen One, recalls the identification made by the voice from heaven at 9:35 (cf. Isaiah 42:1). Readers might have been quick to note that the term had been applied to the Son of man in Enoch 39:6, and that the declaration made at Luke 22:69 was coming to fulfillment in these hours.

36. Soldiers now enter the act. Mark had introduced them earlier into his narrative (15:16-20). Luke reserves the recital of their mockery for this moment, since their horseplay related to Jesus as a royal figure. Also, divorced from the praetorium (Mark 15:16), their mockery would not reflect so strongly on the Roman military. In a situation like this one could expect something of the sort. Luke, as the construction of his sentence reveals, interprets their offer of very poor wine (vinegar) as a jest (cf. Psalm 69:21).

37. Satan had offered Jesus the kingdoms of the world (4:5-7). The soldiers now challenge Jesus to demonstrate his kingship by saving himself. They are stimulated by a description of the crime affixed above the victim's head. The wording itself is meant to be a jest: 'The King of the Jews is This One,' with the word This written contemptuously. For Luke, of course, this is a high point in his narrative. Jesus *is* the King of the Jews. His only crime was to be what he truly is, and the

cross is the place of his enthronement, for greatness is won through renunciation of self.

Long Live the King

39. Luke is now prepared for his climactic definition of the Kingdom. One of the outlaws utters the third temptation. Jesus ought to save himself and the two criminals. Again it is a misunderstanding. Jesus cannot do both. If the Messiah (Christ) is to seek and save the lost (19:10), he cannot save himself, for it was his association with publicans and sinners that brought him into disrepute.

40. One of the outlaws expresses Luke's theology. Fear of God ought to prompt the other to ponder more deeply his fate. 41. As a 'hanged' (vs. 39) criminal, he ought to know that a curse rests on him (cf. Galatians 3:13, a quotation of Deuteronomy 21:23). Yet he shares the same fate with Jesus. However, Jesus is innocent, while the other two are guilty (cf. 2 Maccabees 7:18). Jesus has not left his assigned path (done nothing wrong). The outlaw's word This man corrects the jest in the title. If Jesus suffers in this way, how fearful a thing it must be for a guilty man to fall into the hands of the living God! (cf. 1 Peter 4:17-18). The words are, of course, a reminder to the Israel of Luke's time to re-evaluate her rejection of the King. Coming from a criminal, they are an exceptionally forceful declaration of Jesus' innocence.

42. He now addresses the King, beginning with the name assigned by the angel (1:31; cf. 2:21). According to the angel's word, he was to be called Jesus, and he would 'reign over the house of Jacob forever.' The criminal endorses this association and introduces one of the most dramatic moments in this gospel. Remember me when you come into your kingly power. The kingdom does not come with 'signs to be observed,' said Jesus (17:20). And some would not taste death until they see the Kingdom of God (9:27). This man affirms the truth in an astounding demonstration of faith. Luke brings his doctrine of the Kingdom to full expression in this dialogue.

43. In answer to the indeterminate "when", Jesus answers with a solemn oath-like Amen saying: Truly, I say to you, today you will be with me in Paradise. The word today carries most of the weight. Not in some apocalyptic future, but in this hour the Son of man assumes his reign, and one criminal is 'taken and the other left' (cf. 17:35). This "today" is the climax of many "todays" (cf. 2:11; 3:22; 4:21; 5:26; 13:32, 33; 22:34, 61), and especially of the encounter with Zacchaeus (19:5,9). The outlaw will be with Jesus (cf. Philippians 1:23). This is the characteristic mark of Jesus' kingly activity -- association with the lost. To the end Jesus affirms his mission to publicans and sinners. Of such is the Kingdom of God (cf. 7:28). The unknown outlaw will enjoy the most intimate association, for he will be with Jesus in Paradise.

"Paradise" (cf. 2 Corinthians 12:3; Revelation 2:7) is a singularly appropriate word in the context. Its ordinary meaning is 'garden' or 'park' such as a king would have at his disposal (cf. 2 Chronicles 33:20 LXX). The word appears frequently in Xenophon's descriptions of the royal properties located in Persia. To be with the king in his private gardens was an indication of singular status. In the inter-testamental period the term was used of the realm reserved after death for the righteous (Testament of Levi 18:10). Thus the choice of this word climaxes Luke's interpretation of the Kingdom and explains the promise made at 22:29-30. Since the mention of paradise would remind readers of Adam's original home (see Genesis 2:8), recollection of Luke's association of Jesus with Adam in the genealogy (see Luke 3:38) would easily be made.

Return to the Father   LUKE 23:44-49
                    (Mark 15:33,37-41; Matthew 27:45,50-51,54-56)

<u>44-45</u>. The final coming of the Son of man was earlier associated with cosmic disturbances (21:27). But repeatedly it had been affirmed that the Son of man must suffer and die (9:22,44; 17:25). Luke's record of the darkness and the rending of the curtain therefore alerts the reader to the fact that in the moment of his deepest humiliation Jesus is indeed the Son of man. In his present enthronement, affirmed by the dialogue between Jesus and the criminal, the statement made before the Sanhedrin concerning the session of the Son of man at the right hand of God comes to fulfillment (22:29). Yet Luke does not follow the pattern of contemporary apocalyptic thinking and does not deviate from his protest against the demand for signs. In keeping with his approach to the question of Elijah's role in events of the end-time, Luke omits reference to Elijah (see, on the other hand, Mark 15:36).

The chief priests might have been impressed had Jesus made a spectacular descent from the cross as the darkness engulfed them. Luke rather follows the pattern set by ancient historians, who call attention to the magnitude of a critical event by describing spectacular portents. Thus Lucan depicts the encounter of Pompey and Caesar at Pharsalia as an object of cosmic interest, when the 'sorrowing deity in heaven gave notice of the battle by the dimness and obscurity of the sun' (*The Civil War*, VII, 199-200). Despite the fact that an eclipse is impossible at the time of the full moon, Luke employs the normal language used to describe an eclipse. This extraordinary moment of history is accompanied by an extraordinary celestial phenomenon. The second portent is the rending of the <u>curtain</u> of the temple. This is the first sign of the destruction to overtake Jerusalem (cf. 21:20; 23:28-31). Israel had asked for a sign. Herod had demanded signs. They get more than they bargained for.

<u>46</u>. In contrast to the customary maledictions hurled at their tormenters by crucified criminals, and in contrast to the curses expressed, for example, in Psalm 69, Jesus closes his ministry to mankind with a peaceful prayer from Psalm 31:5. Psalm 31 speaks of scorn heaped on the

sufferer, but also of confident trust in the Lord who delivers the faithful out of the hands of their enemies. At twelve years of age Jesus had affirmed his loyalty to his Father (2:44). Faithful to the end, Jesus entrusts his <u>spirit</u> to the Father for safe-keeping. Significant is Luke's elimination of the Markan cry of dereliction (15:34). In Mark the cry accents the moment when Satan attempts to discredit Jesus through a cry that suggests God's rejection of one who is viewed by the mockers as a lawless person. Jesus, says Mark, expels the demon and overcomes him with his last breath. Luke, who emphasizes Jesus' return to the Father, records instead the prayer of peace. Jesus has ridden triumphantly the crest of Satan's last temptation, exemplified in the mockeries (see on 4:9-13), and is the son of God as declared before the Sanhedrin (22:70). The word for <u>breathed his last</u> is carefully chosen. Literally it means, 'he gave out <u>his spirit.</u>' None of the evangelists use the expression, 'He died.' To the end Jesus is in full command. He terminates his life under orders (cf. 4:29-30; 13:31-33). No one ever grasped more clearly the fate of the innovator face to face with political realities. A Florentine bureaucrat only succeeded in expressing it tediously:

> The reformer has enemies in all those who
> profit by the old order, and only lukewarm
> defenders in all those who would profit by
> the new order, . . . Thus it arises that on
> every opportunity for attacking the reformer,
> his opponents do so with the zeal of partisans,
> the others only defend him half-heartedly, so
> that between them he runs great danger. . . .
> Thus it comes about that all armed prophets
> have conquered and unarmed ones failed; for . . .
> the character of people varies, and it is easy
> to persuade them of a thing, but difficult to
> keep them in that persuasion.
>
> Niccolo Machiavelli, The Prince, in "The
Modern Library," New York: Random House,
1950, pages 21-22.

Jesus, who renounced the way of armed might (Luke 4:5-8), had carefully counted the cost. He did not make the mistake of that ill-fated tower-builder and miscalculating general (14:28-32) described in one of his sermons, but steered straight for that bastion which was impervious to all other force except the power of the New Age. Satan who had boasted that the religious and political establishments were in his pocket (see Luke 4: 5-7) would discover that the obedience expressed this day was to generate a force no power on earth or in hell could stop.

47. Lucan said of the day of Pharsalia: 'How great these men, of whom the world took note; all heaven was attentive to their fate' (*The Civil War*, VII, 205-206). A similar emotion finds expression in the description of the centurion who <u>saw what had taken place</u>. The birth of Jesus elicited the praise of shepherds (2:20); a hardened worldly centurion is driven to similar response by his death. The chief priests could argue

that Jesus was under the wrath of God. This centurion reads the proceedings differently. He is another of a long series of witnesses who on that day pronounced a verdict of 'Not guilty!'

Certainly this man was innocent! In street language: 'He was framed.' The word for innocent is often rendered 'righteous.' To be righteous means to be in harmony with God's law. Jerusalem, with all her vaunted boast in the Law, was clearly in the wrong. This man was in the right. Only one other centurion is mentioned in this gospel (7:2,6). Of the latter Jesus had said, 'I tell you, not even in Israel have I found such faith' (vs. 9). The centurion at the cross was of that breed. Mark records a more explicit identification of Jesus as the Son of God (15:39). Luke attaches more importance to the Roman's declaration of acquittal and takes care of the divine association in his record of Jesus' last prayer (vs. 46).

Thus in the moment of ultimate conflict the insults, lies, innuendos, pretexts and evasions of Jesus' enemies proved useless. His unique individuality differentiated him from all that had ever lived on the face of the earth and demanded fresh definitions for what mankind had hitherto understood by defeat and victory. 'Nice guys finish last,' wrote a Hebrew poet (see Ecclesiastes 8:14); it was another cliche for which Jesus again would find a refutation.

48. The crowds came to gawk and went home to pray. Luke's juxtaposition of the centurion's verdict and this response of the crowd reinforces his theme of repentance in the face of coming judgment. Like the publican in the temple (18:13), they beat their breasts in a confrontation with the ghastly wrong done that day. Had the law permitted, they would have been wailing. The description, stimulated perhaps by Zechariah 12:10-14, is part of Luke's pronouncement of hope for Israel (cf. 23:27-31). A criminal had secured executive pardon (vs. 43). Israel will soon hear the apostolic absolution (Acts 2:36-39).

49. In contrast to the centurion and the crowds who now display some understanding, all of the male acquaintances of Jesus stood at a distance (cf. Psalm 38:11; 88:8; Luke 22:54). They treat him as a pariah one to be shunned, and a man who is not even a relative must attend to his burial (vs. 50). The women are mentioned almost as a separate group. They had been previously identified at 8:2-3, and Luke emphasizes that they saw these things. (RSV obscures this point by making all his acquaintances part of the subject of the verb "saw.") As the primary witnesses from Galilee, they are to play a leading role in the narrative of the resurrected Lord (see 23:55-56; 24:1-11). Only after his resurrection will the disciples and the women be able to endorse the verdict of the centurion and thus be witnesses to the world (24:47-48).

THE BURIAL OF JESUS   LUKE 23:50-56
                        (Mark 15:42-43, 46-47; 16:1; Matthew 27:57-61)

<u>50</u>. The story of the burial is of such significance to Luke that he introduces it with the word 'Behold' (omitted by RSV). No relatives or disciples came forward to do the last honors, but Joseph of Arimathea had the nerve to do so. Joseph was a member of the Sanhedrin (<u>council</u>). Like Zechariah (Luke 1:6) and Simeon (Luke 2:25), he was a <u>righteous</u> man, a term describing his religious standing. But one can appear religious and yet fail to act justly toward a fellowman. Luke therefore emphasizes the integrity of his character with the word <u>good</u>, and supports his description with the parenthetical observation that he had not given his vote to the decision against Jesus. Thus Joseph, a member of the Sanhedrin, is the last witness in the passion account to the innocence of Jesus. Since "Joseph" was such a common name, Luke cannot avoid mentioning his hometown <u>Arimathea</u>, but as a courtesy to his readers notes that it was a <u>Jewish town</u>.

<u>51</u>. Simeon anticipated the consolation of Israel (2:25), and Hannah had spoken to those who were awaiting the redemption of Jerusalem (2:38). Joseph <u>was looking for the kingdom of God</u>.

<u>52</u>. Yet he does not hesitate to ask for the body of Jesus. Release of a criminal's body could be secured only by special administrative action. Had Jesus been the anti-Roman revolutionary claimed by the hierarchy, Joseph would never have dared to make his request. Most carefully Luke informs his own jury that Pilate never changed his mind about the innocence of Jesus. At the same time he notes that the kingdom is intimately associated with the fate of this body (cf. 22:18-19; 24:21-26). Whether Joseph himself considered Jesus to be the Messiah is not stated.

<u>53</u>. The reverence with which Joseph handles the body of Jesus contrasts against the earlier background of cruelty and mockery. Limited by time, for the sabbath is approaching, Joseph does the best he can. The ritual uncleanness incurred by his contact with the dead could be removed in the evening (cf. Leviticus 22:4-7). Perhaps to avoid unnecessary objections from his colleagues, Joseph lays the body in a tomb <u>where no one had ever yet been laid</u> (cf. 19:30). Burial chambers would be considered contaminated by the body of a criminal. But the fact is we have no data on Joseph's motive. As far as Luke is concerned the precaution was fortuitous, for great weight is to be attached in the community to the fact that Jesus died and was buried (1 Corinthians 15: 3-4). There is to be no doubt as to the identity of the one who comes out of that grave, and Luke underlines his description with three firm negatives. Nor is negligible the observation that the tomb was <u>rock-hewn</u>. Thereby the reader is informed that the body is in a secure place and in the same breath is prepared for the information that a stone had been rolled in place at the entrance (24:2).

<u>54</u>. In order to allow more time for the preparations made by Joseph, Luke transfers Mark's note concerning the lateness of the hour (15:42) to the end of his story of the burial. His readers would know that purchases would be forbidden on the <u>sabbath</u>, which was about to begin, namely on the evening of Friday, the day of Preparation for the sabbath.

(In John 19:14 the day of Preparation is the day on which the passover lamb was slain; cf. John 19: 31,42).

55-56. Luke's arrangement of the narrative also allows a little time for the women to prepare spices, and he is at pains to note that they rested on the sabbath, according to the commandment. Jesus did not teach his disciples disrespect of Jewish law. In Mark the women make their purchases on the morning following the sabbath (16:1). Luke emphasizes the careful observation of the women in order to establish the veracity of their later identification of the resurrected Lord. They saw the tomb, and how his body was laid. Thus they are witnesses of his death, burial, and shortly of the resurrected Lord, the triple ingredient of much apostolic proclamation (cf. Acts 2:22-36; 1 Corinthians 15:3-4). After a long series of episodes displaying many varieties of cowardice on the part of men, Luke must have found refreshing the courageous bearing of what has been called the 'weaker sex.'

PART SEVEN: THE RESURRECTED LORD
LUKE 24

EXPERIENCE OF THE WOMEN   LUKE 24:1-11
                                    (Mark 16:1-2, 4-8; Matthew 28:1, 5-8)

1. Strictly speaking the recital in chapter 24 is not an account
of the resurrection of Jesus but of the resurrected Lord and his appearances. The women (23:55) having scrupulously observed the sabbath period, proceed as early as the law permitted to carry out their intention
of anointing the body.

2-3. Luke contrasts the discovery they made (the stone rolled away)
against the discovery they failed to make (the body). The marginal addition *of the Lord Jesus* is not Lukan. The evangelist makes his point.
There was one body in the tomb, and that body was not there!

4. In this time of their distress, behold, two men stood by them.
The language is strikingly similar to that of 9:30. Luke had prefaced
his account of the Transfiguration with statements about the Son of man.
He was to come in the glory of his Father and the holy angels. And
there would be some who would not die before they had seen the Kingdom
of God. The Transfiguration was not the inauguration of the Kingdom, but
a preparation for the understanding of the suffering of Jesus. Now,
after his suffering, the glory with which he is to return has begun
(cf. 24:26), and the women are among those who see the Kingdom of God.
As in the earlier account the two men (perhaps some thought of Moses and
Elijah) make a glorious appearance (cf. Acts 1:10). However, there is a
difference. In the account of the Transfiguration Jesus has dazzling
raiment, and Moses and Elijah appear with him 'in glory' (9:31). Here
the two men wear dazzling apparel. Thus the glory of Jesus receives only
an indirect confirmation.

Throughout the account of the appearances recorded in chapter 24
Luke adheres to his eschatological doctrine. Jesus never appears in
glorious form. That is to be reserved for his final coming (21:27).
Most carefully, however, Luke associated the resurrection with the Transfiguration in order to emphasize that the Kingdom is present reality even
though the popular apocalyptic expectation is not satisfied. The word
for stood by is used, among other passages, in 2:9 and 21:34 (cf. Acts
12:7; 23:11). In 2:9 it is rendered 'appeared,' in a context describing
the glory of the Lord. The announcement to the shepherds affirmed that
God's glory could be apparent in association with even so unapocalyptic
an event as the birth of the Messiah and his placement in a manger.

Similarly the glory of God transforms a tomb into a throneroom. In the second passage, 21:34, the word is used of the Parousia (cf. 1 Thessalonians 5:3).

5. The reaction of the women is typical of Daniel's responses to special revelations (Daniel 7:28; 10:9, 15). Through his careful use of apocalyptic-type language in this and the preceding verse Luke prepares his readers for the pronouncement at vs. 7 on the destiny of the Son of man. The question is a word of rebuke. If the women had listened to the words of Jesus they would know that the tomb is not the place to look for him. The margin reading, *He is not here, but has risen*, was borrowed by copyists from Matthew 28:6 (cf. Mark 16:6).

6. Mark 16:7 records that the women were to announce to the disciples and Peter that Jesus had gone on ahead of them to Galilee. Since Jerusalem is the center of activity at the beginning and the end of his gospel, and since the good news is to proceed from Jerusalem (Luke 24:47; Acts 1:8), Luke concentrates appearances of the risen Lord in Jerusalem. Therefore, instead of giving them a message the two men remind the women of what Jesus had told them while he was with them in Galilee.

Verse 7 reproduces the content of words recited at 9:22, 44; 17:25; 18:32-33. The last of these passages was addressed only to the Twelve and includes specific information not found in the earlier prophecies, namely that Jesus was to be handed over to the Gentiles. Luke incorporates this thought in the term sinful men. Moreover, the word crucified is a clearer description of the type of death Jesus was to undergo. The sentence is therefore of interest also as an example of the modification a saying by Jesus might undergo in the course of transmission of the Gospel.

Modern readers may be struck by the fact that Luke submits no proof of the resurrection based on the emptiness of the tomb, on remarkable signs following the resurrection (cf. Matthew 28:2-4), or even on appearances of the Lord. We ask whether a dead man can actually come alive out of a grave. Luke is more concerned about the identity of the one who came out of the grave. He must demonstrate that the resurrected Lord is Jesus! Hence the two men say explicitly that Jesus, while he was in Galilee, spoke to them of the fate of the Son of man. Neither Matthew nor Mark include a word about the Son of man in their accounts of the resurrected Lord. Luke considers the subject of prime importance. Jesus said that the Son of man must suffer and die and then rise on the third day. The women had observed the death and burial. Now they are confronted with the decision of faith. It is one thing to believe that Jesus rose from the dead, but this would not necessarily imply a decision concerning his meaning for faith. It is another matter to accept the fact that the Son of man is Jesus. If the women are willing to believe this, the resurrection will be no problem, for it would be inconceivable to them that the Son of man could fail to make his appearance. The new item for faith, then, is that the Son of man instead of first appearing in glory at the end of the age should be identified with Jesus of Nazareth, and that he makes his appearance on the third day. Luke here climaxes his rejection of popular apocalyptic and says no more about the Son of man. With the exception of Acts 7:56, the focus henceforth is on the identity of Jesus as the Christ (cf. Luke 24:26, 46 and often in Acts).

8-9. The women remembered his words, that is, they respond in faith, and rush to share the news with the eleven (Judas has decreased the number of the Twelve, cf. Acts 1:16-26), and the rest of the disciples.

10. With labored syntax Luke distinguishes two groups of women in order to bring the apostles to the fore and emphasize that they were guilty of unbelief. The women who made the announcement to the larger circle were Mary Magdalene, Joanna (cf. 8:2-3), and Mary the mother of James (perhaps the son of Alphaeus, cf. 6:15). The rest of the women who were with these three announced the news to the apostles. This specific term is carefully chosen in order to stress the purpose for which the news is given -- proclamation to the world (cf. vss. 47-49).

11. The apostles consider the report an idle tale and refuse to believe the women. Considering their own previous record of comprehension of Jesus' mission, this response was not only ungallant but foolish.

PETER'S UNBELIEF

Verse 12 is relegated to the margin by RSV, but the content is important in view of the sequel, and need not be considered an interpolation from John 20:3-10. Verse 24 says that other men had gone to the tomb, and vs. 34 raises the question whether the Lord had appeared to Simon. Textual evidence for the inclusion of vs. 12 is overwhelming. Of the women it was stated that they had observed only the absence of the body. Peter sees the *linen cloths* in which Jesus had been wrapped. Yet he goes off *wondering at what had happened*. Wonderment here is not faith but its opposite. Like the rest who come under indictment at vs. 41, Peter is guilty of unbelief. Clearly, evidence of the senses is not sufficient to help one grasp the reality of the resurrection of Jesus. Thus Luke prepares his readers for the understanding that Jesus himself, through his exposition of the Scriptures, must be the teacher of the community (cf. vss. 32, 45). Well had Jesus said that unless Moses and the prophets were heeded, men would not believe (cf. 16:31), and that when the Son of man comes he will scarcely find faith on the earth (18:8).

TWO WITNESSES ON THE ROAD TO EMMAUS

13. Luke prefaces his most distinctive contribution to the Easter story with the words 'And behold' (omitted by RSV). The pronoun in the phrase two of them refers not to the apostles, but to the larger circle

of disciples. That very day underlines the fact that the events about
to be recited took place on the third day specified at vs. 7 (cf. vs. 21).
Once again Jerusalem is mentioned so that the reader might not conclude
that the first appearance of Jesus took place in Galilee. Emmaus, modern
Kulonieh, lies in the direction of Joppa.

14-15.   The two disciples were not merely discussing what had happened
but were 'debating' with one another (cf. 22:23; Acts 6:9; 9:29). They
need an umpire to resolve a disagreement that has been instigated by
post-mortem inquiry, which in any case has never been known to bring a
corpse back to life. At this moment Jesus himself drew near. The name
is important, establishing the continuity between the Christ of faith
and Jesus of Nazareth. The words drew near recall the term used of the
Kingdom of God (10:9, 11), of Jesus' earlier approach to Jerusalem (18:
35; 19:29, 37, 41), and the apocalyptic redemption (21:28). The fact
that he went with them suggests further the continuity between the activity of the resurrected Lord and his earthly ministry. He who was deserted by most of his acquaintances (23:49) does not abandon those whom he
has chosen.

16.   Despite the fact that it is Jesus himself, they do not recognize
him. Luke's use of the passive verb, were kept, points to God as the
agent. Similarly the disciples were kept from understanding Jesus' prophecy of his death (9:45), and the fate of Jerusalem was hidden from the
eyes of her inhabitants (19:42). See also 2 Kings 6:15-20. Seeing Jesus
after his resurrection is therefore more than a matter of ocular recognition. What the mind does not anticipate it does not believe, and in the
absence of faith the eye is blind. Only Jesus was empowered in the opposite direction, being filled with wisdom (2:40), and he will enlighten
the disciple.

17-18.   In response to Jesus' question, the two men appear sullen.
RSV renders sad, but misses the point of this adjective, used only one
other time in the New Testament (Matthew 6:16). It is the reaction of
one who frowns indignantly, and the sarcasm in Cleopas' counter-question
explains the choice of the term: 'You're putting us on. Every other
visitor to Jerusalem knows what happened there, but you don't?' Little
did they realize how right they were about his being a stranger in Jerusalem.

19.   He leads them on and asks, What things? Their reference to
Jesus of Nazareth recalls 4:17-30. Well did they have cause, in view
of the promises made at Nazareth, to anticipate the redemption of Israel
(24:21). Writing for his Greek public, Luke phrases the first part of
the description: 'Who was a man, a prophet . . . ' Jesus belongs to
a class of men who deserve the highest respect and adulation. Men of word
and action were admired by the Greeks (cf. Thucydides, *The Peloponnesian
War*, I, 139,4). At Acts 7:22 Moses is described as mighty in his words
and deeds. Here the order is deed (cf. Luke 9:43; Acts 2:22) followed
by word (cf. Luke 4:22, 36; 7:7). Jesus is a prophet greater than Moses.
Before God and all the people (cf. 2:52) is a further testimony to the
integrity of Jesus.

20. "All the people" of the previous verse contrasts with the chief priests and rulers, who are made to bear the guilt of the crucifixion.

21. The men do not deny the validity of their preceding description but complain that a further expectation is apparently not to be carried out, namely the redemption of Israel. In chapters 1 and 2 this traditional nationalistic viewpoint finds expression (1:68, 74; 2:38; cf. 23:51; Acts 1:6). The complaint made by the two disciples offers Luke opportunity to correct the traditional hope. Redemption indeed came for Israel, but the things that pertained to her peace were hidden from her eyes (Luke 19:42). Jesus, however, will reign as successor to David through a world-wide mission (cf. 24:47; Acts 1:6-8 and see Isaiah 11:10; Romans 15:12). The men refer to the third day with a kind of expression of last hope fast fading away.

22-23. Yet, as their succeeding remarks show, they do not deny the possibility that Jesus may be alive. Their words about the women suggest how 'two men' (24:4) easily become transformed into angels in the course of tradition. They do not say that the women saw angels, but that they had seen a vision of angels. And these angels asserted that Jesus was alive. 24. Some of the men from the circle of disciples also went to the tomb (cf. vs. 12) and confirmed the report of the women, but -- and this is the primary complaint -- him they did not see.

Very skillfully Luke uses the dialogue and skepticism of these two men to sharpen the contrast between false expectations and apostolic instruction. Their comments also indicate that the disciples were not gullible and that the women did not make wild reports. Finally, the empty grave did not awaken faith in the resurrection, but faith in the resurrection led to affirmation of the emptiness. But the chief purpose of the dialogue is to prepare the reader for the understanding that Jesus himself is the key to proper comprehension of the Scriptures.

25. Jesus criticizes the two men for not being quick enough to believe all that the prophets have spoken. The word all is important. They concentrated on the parts that promised deliverance for Israel (vs. 21) and the prosperity of the golden Davidic age (cf. 1:32-33; 68-71) but overlooked the parts that spoke of the suffering experienced by God's chosen emissaries.

26. The phrase was it not necessary repeats a dominant theme in the gospel (cf. 2:49; 4:43; 9:22; 17:25; 19:5; 22:37). Not fate, but a Father's purpose watches over the destiny of the Christ. The latter term describes the Anointed One or the Messiah. Jesus says that he who would qualify for the office of Messiah must suffer and through that route enter into his glory. They should not expect to be able to see him, but they ought to believe in his victory over the opposition. Of special note, however, is the fact that glory is here not associated with apocalyptic splendor, but with one who seems to be an ignorant tourist. His glorification began at the time of his suffering (22:69; 23:42-43). Acts 7 contains a resume of the kind of treatment to which

a Messiah might be exposed and is also a sample of the kind of exposition used in the church to demonstrate the continuity between Jesus
and the Old Testament (see also Luke 22:37; cf. Deuteronomy 18:15; Psalm
22; Isaiah 53).

27. With the phrase concerning himself Luke does not mean to say
that Jesus called the attention of the two men to himself, but showed
how the prophecies applied to the Jesus they had known.

28. The rendering he appeared to be going further is not quite
accurate. Jesus 'pretended to go on further' (cf. Mark 6:48; Job 9:11).
Far from suggesting dishonesty on the part of Jesus, Luke indicates that
Jesus longs to continue communication with these two disciples (cf. Revelation 3:20). But only those who desire his company will come to
further realization of his identity.

29. As Lot did with the two angels (Genesis 19:1-3), they urge
their companion to accept the hospitality of their quarters. The day
is now far spent (see on 9:12), and the reader would sense the tension.
For the two men had said that it was now the third day (vs. 21). They
were not to be disappointed. Jesus went in to stay with them (cf. 19:5)

30. The Messianic banquet now takes place in their residence. However, the recital in vs. 30 does not reproduce the celebration of the
Lord's Supper (note the absence of wine), but the banquet scene in chapter 9. In chapter 9 Luke had associated the feeding of the 5,000 (vss.
12-17) with the question of Jesus' messianic credentials and the prophec
concerning the Son of man and his death and resurrection on the third
day (9:18-22). As at the occasion of the feeding of the 5,000 the day
is at its close, and the guests recline (9:14-15 'sit'; 24:30, at table)
As on the earlier occasion, he took the bread, blessed and broke it, and
gave it to the disciples (cf. 9:16).

31. Peter, after the feeding, had grasped something of the nature
of Jesus' person and declared him to be the Christ (9:20). Here the
eyes of the men are opened (cf. 24:16), and they recognized their guest,
who had now become their host (cf. 5:27-32). Thus Luke affirms that the
resurrection of Jesus is to be understood in terms of the fellowship he
extends to the community, a fellowship that is in continuity with all
his previous association with publicans and sinners, climaxing at the
cross (cf. 23:43). It is not important that he is seen physically by
the community. Therefore he vanishes out of their sight, but remains
visible to those whose eyes are opened. The language would be especiall
meaningful to hellenistic readers who would associate the terminology
with the return of gods or angels to the heavenly realms. (Jakob Wett-
stein cites Virgil Aeneid IX, 656-658; see also 2 Maccabees 3:34). He
has indeed entered into his glory (vs. 26). If this is the case, the
community need not be surprised that they do not see him. This is Luke'
contribution to the problem of the resurrection.

32. After the disappearance of Jesus the two men describe the great
agitation (cf. Psalm 39:3) they had experienced while Jesus was interpre

the Scriptures. It is the first example of the fire that was to be
cast down (12:49; cf. 3:16; Acts 2:3).

WITH THE ELEVEN AND OTHERS   LUKE 24:33-43

33. The men lose no time in returning to Jerusalem. This news
must be shared. They found the eleven and others who were associated
with them (cf. vs. 9) conversing about the events of the day. 34.
Some were saying, 'Has the Lord really risen?' Others asked, 'Did he
appear to Simon?' The latter perhaps in allusion to the fact that Peter
had only seen the grave cloths, not Jesus himself. RSV, together with
other versions and commentators makes of the verse a declarative statement, but then the subsequent verses (especially vs. 41) are incoherent,
and vss. 11-12 are left suspended.

35. In response to the perplexity of the group the two men recite
their experiences. Their report falls into two parts. Events on the
road and recognition at the breaking of the bread. Thus the community
is not dependent only on the personal witness of the two men, but primarily on the testimony of the Scriptures. However, reference to the
breaking of bread is not incidental. The disciples are not to look for
an extraordinary manifestation. Such anticipation can blind eyes to
present reality. Not 'Lo, there!' or 'Lo, here!' for 'the kingdom of
God is in the midst of you,' said Jesus (17:21). Through his continued
reception of the poor and the outcast and those despised by an establishment that had forfeited its authority will Jesus show his continuing
presence in the community (cf. Acts 4:23-31). This is in harmony with
God's promise spoken through the prophet Ezekiel: 'My dwelling place
shall be with them; and I will be their God, and they shall be my people' (Ezekiel 37:27). Especially significant is that prophet's prior
statement: 'My servant David shall be king over them' (37:24). God
dwells with Israel through King David. Luke affirms that the kingdom
is reality in him who was crucified as the King of the Jews, and the
resurrected Lord is this same Jesus who called sinners to his banquets.

36. Jesus himself now ratifies the words spoken by the two disciples.
Before his death he had said: 'I am among you as one who serves' (22:27).
Now again he stands among them, the same one they had known before.

37. The language, like that of vs. 5, contains apocalyptic overtones.
38. Why are you troubled? asks Jesus. Only once before was this description used in the gospel, namely of Zechariah at the appearance of the
angel (1:12). Thus Luke again affirms that Jesus is indeed 'in glory'
but that this glory is possible without standard apocalyptic fireworks.
Moreover, his presence ought to be a consolation, not a source of fear
(cf. 2:10). He comes to share his fellowship, not to destroy them in
judgment. Their questionings, left unexpressed, are known to the Lord.
They had experienced his penetrating understanding on an earlier occasion
shortly after his second prediction of his suffering and death. At that
time also they were ignorant of his meaning and displayed fear (9:45),
and climaxed their misunderstanding with questions about greatness (vs. 46).

In their present stance they are like the opposition (cf. 5:22; 6:8). Jesus is himself the sign who was to be spoken against 'in order that the questionings out of many hearts might be revealed' (2:35). But the disciples ought to be the last to require such exposure, especially since they, like the women, have received the testimony of two witnesses (cf. Deuteronomy 19:15).

39. Whether in the case of Jesus both his hands and feet were nailed to the cross cannot be affirmed with certainty, for procedures at executions varied. Nor is the point an issue in Luke's account. Attention is called to the hands and feet in order to establish the fact that the person they see before them is a genuine human being. Against false teachers who denied that Christ was really a human being, Luke affirms his corporeality. But recognition of corporeality does not necessarily spell faith. The disciples might have seen a genuine human being, but why did they not conclude that it was John the Baptist, to cite but one possibility? (see Luke 9:19) A further identification is therefore added: It is I myself. Imbedded in this phrase are the words 'I am.' Jesus had warned that many would come and say 'I am' (21: 8), but only Jesus, who before the Sanhedrin himself affirmed 'I am' (22:70), is the legitimate Messiah. Thus this reply by Jesus is a strong christological affirmation and is accompanied by the directive to handle him. The resurrected Lord is not a spirit, for he has all the components of a genuine body. Verse 40 is correctly relegated to the margin. Evidently a copyist rephrased John 20:20.

41. Despite these words and demonstrations the disciples still lack the faith to grasp what has happened. However, Luke excuses them somewhat with the qualification that they disbelieved for joy (cf. Acts 12:14). If what they hoped for turned out to be a dream, they would indeed have been most miserable of men (cf. 1 Corinthians 15:19).

42-43. Their unbelief helps motivate the final demonstration. In the presence of the company he eats a piece of broiled fish.

A comparison of the foregoing recital (vss. 36-43) with Mark 6:45-52 suggests that Luke omitted the Markan story at 9:17 in order to give force to its main features at the end of his gospel. Mark locates the event at *evening*; Jesus appears as one who intends to *go past* the crew in the boat; the disciples think they see a *ghost*; and are greatly *troubled*; Jesus identifies himself with the words *I am*; and the disciples respond with further *astonishment*. All these italicized items appear in Luke 24:28-29, 37-41. In the account of the resurrected Lord the christological and apocalyptic issues raised in the Markan account are pertinent. Earlier Luke had concentrated these themes in the recital of the Transfiguration (9:28-36). The Markan episode would therefore have been at that point superfluous.

PARTING WORDS AND ASCENSION

44. Having established his physical presence among them, Jesus now proceeds to affirm the continuity between his former words and subsequent

experience. He identifies himself as the person to whom Moses, the prophets, and the psalms apply.

45. The two disciples found their eyes opened at the breaking of bread. Now the rest of the company have their minds opened to understand the Scriptures.

46. Once again Jesus speaks of the Christ in the third person (cf. vs. 26). The form is similar to that used in sayings about the Son of man, and in neither case does the objective type of statement mean that the speaker is to be dissociated from the person described. Since this is the third recital in this chapter concerning the necessity of suffering and resurrection (cf. vss. 7 and 26), it is apparent that Luke attaches great weight to its content. Especially important is the phrase the third day. The story of the two men on the road to Emmaus confirmed that this was indeed the third day since the suffering had taken place. The Church, therefore, does not await a revelation of the Lord at some future time in order to validate the credentials of Jesus. He is validated on the third day and now assumes direction of his new community.

47. Repentance and forgiveness of sins should be preached in his name to all nations. This is all part of the *inference* to which one ought to be led by a proper study of the Scriptures, for no passage in the Old Testament states this in so many words. However, Jesus says, thus it is written. That is, this is what the Scriptures have in mind, or this was their tenor. And the disciples are to begin from Jerusalem. Jerusalem was to hear the consolation of the Servant of the Lord (Isaiah 61). To begin with Jerusalem means that the prophetic priority is recognized and that Jerusalem has opportunity to find forgiveness for crucifying the Messiah (Acts 2:22-40; 3:12-26). The Gentiles are included in the prophetic scope (cf. Isaiah 42:6; 49:6; Luke 2:32). The disciples are not initiators of a new program. They are not developers of propaganda.

48. Rather, they are witnesses (cf. Acts 1:8, 22; 2:32; 3:15; 5:32; 10:37-43) to God's own intentions including the beginning from Jerusalem, expressed in the Scriptures. A witness is one who attests to the truth. Hence these disciples, who have observed Jesus' life and death and now his resurrected presence, are singularly equipped to testify to the truth of the Scriptures, for these have come to fulfillment (vs. 44) in the person of Jesus. All is to be done "in his name" (vs. 47). An angel had proclaimed Jesus as the Christ (2:11). Jesus warned that many would come 'in my name' saying 'I am he!' and 'The time is at hand!' (21:8). But there is only one name by which the Christ is to be identified -- Jesus (1:31; 2:21), the sign that was spoken against (2:34). And in connection with his name repentance and forgiveness, not apocalyptic speculation or nationalistic hope, is to be preached.

49. With a final behold Jesus says that he will send the promise of his Father upon them. 'He who receives me receives him who sent me,' said Jesus (9:48). The sender is the Father, expressly called my Father.

Gabriel had announced that Jesus would be not only son of David (1:32) but 'Son of God' (1:35). The latter sonship dominates the final scene and is the answer to the question raised by the two men on the road to Emmaus: 'We had hoped that he was the one to redeem Israel ' (24:21). As the Son of God, Jesus comes to rescue 'all nations' (vs. 47). The thought anticipates a speech in Acts: All humanity is God's offspring (Acts 17:28), and he chooses one man to judge all mankind in righteousness. Of this he has given assurance to all men by raising him from the dead (Acts 17:31). Thus Luke synthesizes the national and the universal outlook of the prophets, for Israel is taken up into the single goal of repentance and forgiveness for all men, 'beginning from Jerusalem.' To expedite the disciples' mission Jesus will send the promise of the Father. From Acts 2:33 it is clear that the Holy Spirit is meant (cf. Acts 1:4; Luke 3:16). Thus their ministry will extend his own (cf. 4:18-19), and they will not be left to their own resources. Their mission is not a worldly political movement, but God's own operation, for they are to wait in Jerusalem until they are clothed with power from on high. Theirs will be the politics of the New Age.

50. Without any suggestion of a long interval of time Luke pictures Jesus leading his disciples out to Bethany. There the events of passion week had begun, and there he lifts his hands in blessing. Sirach 50 seems to have been in Luke's mind as he wrote vss. 50-52. Jesus resembles the high priest Simon, the son of Onias. When this priest came out of the temple he was resplendent with glory (vs. 5). Of Zechariah it was said that the people perceived he had 'seen a vision in the temple,' but he could only sign the blessing (Luke 1:22). But after his dumbness had disappeared he blessed the Lord God of Israel (1:68-79) in words similar to the blessing recited by Simon (Sirach 50:22-24). Most appropriately Luke concludes his story with the Great High Priest of Israel blessing his congregation. Through Jesus' word and deed all other blessings, including the *Benedictus* of Zechariah, receive a revised and fresh interpretation.

51. To bless means to assure one of God's favor and support. Thus the disciples, who had stood afar off (23:49), now are brought near to God by the One who departs from them in order always to be near them. Some copyists added the words *and was carried up to heaven*, reinforcing the suggestion of Luke's narrative that the ascension took place on the third day. In that event, the ascension recorded at Acts 1:9 would simply mean the end of a further series of appearances.

52. The blessing binds the disciples to their Lord in obedience, for they return to Jerusalem. Like those who were blessed by Simon, son of Onias (Sirach 50:22-23), like the shepherds in the fields of Bethlehem (Luke 2:10), they experience great joy (see also 1:44, 47; Acts 2:46; 8:8; 13:52).

53. In grateful response they spend their time in the temple blessing God. To bless God means that one gives thanks for benefits received. Luke began his gospel with a series of events that took place in the temple. There Zechariah received the promise of the birth of

John the Baptist. There Simeon had seen the light of the Gentiles
and the glory of God's people, Israel. There Anna had spent all her
time and spoke to all who were awaiting the redemption of Israel.
There Jesus had asked: 'Did you not know that I must be in my Father's
house?'

     According to apocalyptic hope, the righteous would arise in the
end-time. The centurion's verdict and the resurrection of Jesus together affirm that the end-time is now reality. He had thought the
unthinkable, dared the unbearable and achieved the impossible. We
only await the end of the end-time, for with Jesus came the New Age.

+++++++++++++++

THE HISTORIAN'S SUMMARY
Acts 10:34-43

     Peter began to preach: I am now convinced that God has no favor-
ites. His heart is open to any one -- any where -- who stands in awe
of him and lives accordingly. You know the story he dispatched to
Israel. It told the Good News of peace through Jesus Christ. He is
Master of all. That story went from one end of Palestine to the other,
beginning from Galilee after the baptism that John proclaimed. That
story told how God anointed Jesus of Nazareth with the Holy Spirit
and with power; how he spent all his time helping mankind and healing
all whom the devil was tyrannizing, for God was with him. We can testify to all that he did throughout the land and also in Jerusalem.
They hung him on a tree. But God restored his life on the third day
and let him be seen -- not by the entire nation, but by us whom God
previously chose as witnesses. We ate and drank with him after his
resurrection. And he ordered us to proclaim to the nation and to testify that God appointed him to be judge of the living and the dead.
All the prophets testify and declare that by his authority anyone who
believes in him is entitled to forgiveness of sins.